NORTE
NORTE 4 AL NORDEST
NOR NORDESTE
NORDESTE 4 ALNORTE
NORDESTE
NORDESTE 4 ALESTE
LES NORDESTE
LESTE 4 AL NORDEST
LESTE
LESTE 4 ALSVESTE
LE SVESTE
SVESTE 4 ALESTE
SVESTE
SVESTE 4 ALSVR
SVSVESTE
SVR 4 ALSVESTE
SVR
SVR 4 ALSVDVESTE
SVSVDVESTE
SVD VESTE 4 ALSVR
SVDVESTE
SVDVESTE 4 ALOESTE
OESSVDVESTE
OESTE 4 ALSVDVEST
OESTE
OESTE 4 AL NORVESTE
OESNORVESTE
NORVESTE 4 ALOESTE
NORVESTE
NORVESTE 4 ALNORTE
NORNORVESTE
NORTE 4 AL NORVEST

MINISTRY OF CULTURAL AND ENVIRONMENTAL ASSETS
NATIONAL COMMISSION FOR THE CELEBRATION OF THE QUINCENTENNIAL
OF THE DISCOVERY OF AMERICA

NUOVA RACCOLTA COLOMBIANA

ENGLISH EDITION

ISTITUTO POLIGRAFICO E ZECCA DELLO STATO
LIBRERIA DELLO STATO
ROMA

MINISTRY OF CULTURAL AND ENVIRONMENTAL ASSETS
NATIONAL COMMISSION FOR THE CELEBRATION OF THE QUINCENTENNIAL
OF THE DISCOVERY OF AMERICA

NUOVA RACCOLTA COLOMBIANA

FRANCO GAY - CESARE CIANO

THE SHIPS OF CHRISTOPHER COLUMBUS

WITH CONTRIBUTIONS IN APPENDICES BY:

FRANCESCO QUIETO - ALDO ZIGGIOTTO

Translated into English by

LUCIO BERTOLAZZI

and

LUCIANO F. FARINA - Ohio State University

ISTITUTO POLIGRAFICO E ZECCA DELLO STATO
LIBRERIA DELLO STATO
ROMA

Originally published as *Le navi di Cristoforo Colombo*
Translation © 1996 by Lucio Bertolazzi and Luciano F. Farina

NATIONAL COMMISSION FOR THE CELEBRATION OF THE QUINCENTENNIAL OF THE DISCOVERY OF AMERICA

ENGLISH EDITION OF THE «NUOVA RACCOLTA COLOMBIANA»

Published and printed by Istituto Poligrafico e Zecca dello Stato - Libreria dello Stato

Edited and translated by The Ohio State University

Revised Translation:

L.F. FARINA

Volume Editors:

L.F. FARINA and P.L. MIRAGLIA

The Nuova Raccolta Scientific Commission had assigned the volume devoted to *The Ships of Cristopher Columbus* to Professor Cesare Ciano and Admiral Franco Gay.

As, sadly, Professor Ciano passed away when he had already compiled a substantial amount of notes and gathered a considerable number of sketches and drawings, Admiral Gay rigorously and respectfully incorporated them into the final draft compilation. It is with affectionate regret for the unforgettable friend and valiant scholar — Professor Cesare Ciano — that his contribution is hereby acknowledged.

PAOLO EMILIO TAVIANI

INTRODUCTION

Curiosity about the distinctive nature and features of the vessels which Christopher Columbus sailed from Palos on August 3, 1492, with the aim of discovering a new way to the Indies, is rather recent. Up till last century the interest of historians did not go beyond the fact that the Genoese sailor used three little ships whose picture could be vaguely found in ancient naval representations, without specification of years and generally classified as from the late Medieval period. Without much attention to details, what was often suggested was a type of sailing vessel implausibly similar to modern ones, commonly seen portrayed in numerous paintings, prints and various other artistic productions intended to celebrate this enterprise.

During the last century, on the eve of the fourth centenary of Columbus's voyage and the ensuing international celebrations, the first studies on this subject began and, as a result, numerous acceptable reconstructions of the Santa Maria *and of the two other caravels appeared, culminating with the life-size replicas commissioned by the Spanish Committee for the 1892 celebrations led by Columbian scholar and Captain Cesareo Fernandez Duro.*

Reconstructive naval archaeology, a branch of naval studies interested in reconstructing shapes, riggings, armaments, manouver mechanisms, living conditions aboard the vessels through a critical evaluation of ancient documents and all kinds of iconographical representations, is a recent science established less than a hundred years ago thanks to a few dedicated scholars, especially Auguste Jal, author of the Mémoires d'archeologie navale *and of a monumental* Glossaire Nautique. *Its applied principles could only rely on very few authentic wreckage findings (modern submarine archeology did not exist yet) and had to draw conclusions based solely on surface evidence and the interpretation of written sources-original documents as well as extant traditions. More often than not, this led to the risk of accepting chains of inferences that produced erroneous theories.*

Because of the general fascination for his extraordinary enterprise, even Columbus's vessels fell under the scrutiny of naval archaeology experts who often were not just scholars, but seamen as well and, therefore, equipped with greater competence than their scholarly predecessors, and ended their reductive tendency which pretentiously limited their engagement with ships to a mere humanistic approach or literary knowledge. Ever since, up until the eve of the fifth centennial, a great deal of published disputes over Columbus's vessels has appeared, reflecting the ever-increasing research tools and growth of documentary knowledge. The numerous reconstructions that have been proposed and are under close evaluation, indeed document the progress in approximating the actual models, albeit fully cognizant that certainty in this area will hardly ever be possible. In fact, the unending wealth of theories, assumptions and ongoing attempts offers no definite model — much less a graphic depiction, clearly inconceivable at the time — on account of the fact that we do not possess even an approximate description of these vessels, whose dimensions escape us and for which it can barely be claimed we know much beyond their names.

This should not be too surprising because Columbus's enterprise, commonly regarded as an extraordinary event, was in his time only one of many exploratory journeys that turned out to be successful; a success, furthermore, whose scope seemed to be pretty narrow by the time Columbus returned to Spain. Its obvious limitations were reflected in its meager results, namely, that the way to the Indies had not yet been found and the discovered lands had none of the mythical riches the Orient was expected to yield. Maybe this is the reason no one thought of preserving, for the sake of posterity, all that was related to that event, or at least its more appealing features for future consideration. We need only recall that there is no surviving portrait of the sailor; that his original board diary — regarded as a secret document because it contained clues that might have aided unauthorized people to retrace the Atlantic exploration — disappeared from the archives that were to preserve it; that no court painter was charged with making a commemorative portrait, as customary at the time; and that very few documents by the hand of Columbus are extant. Consequently, one cannot be surprised at all if that which concerns the technical aspects of the sailing were equally subject to neglect. Moreover, the nao *and caravels had no special feature over the many ships usually found in Spanish harbors; they had no distinctive characteristics to make them worthy of special mention, much less anything deserving to be enshrined.*

The very flags used by Columbus's fleet, in spite of their traditionally symbolic meaning conveying special honor to the bearers, not only were not saved, but were not even described, which makes our "uncertainty" for what they were like an understatement. Quite understandable, after all, is the little attention reserved for the technical aspects of an enterprise which overwhelmingly involved many human aspects of higher consideration. Indeed it helps to explain why so often numberless happenings of significance in world history are recorded without recognizing in the least the technologies that made them possible. There is, then, sufficient justification for the not so caring Spaniards who, at the end of the fifteenth century, listened to the stories of those who crossed the ocean only to go back to their daily chores, unconcerned for the vessels that made that crossing a reality. And even if the Spaniards, in an outburst of pride and enthusiasm, had wished to save the surviving caravels — or one, at least — as monuments for posterity sake, the ships would certainly not have survived to the present, because wooden constructions were exposed to too many hazards, especially in the past. Only in 1580, i.e., almost a hundred years after the voyage of discovery, Queen Elizabeth of England ordered the preservation of the Golden Hind, *the vessel used by Sir Francis Drake in the first world circumnavigation by an Englishman, the second actually after Magellan's (who did not really complete it, as he was killed by the natives of the island of Matan in the Philippines). This ship, which had been drydocked, was made accessible to the public for more than a century, till the day when this precious relic was destroyed by fire.*

Even today, however, in spite of the greater technical interest for enterprises, ships are almost never destined for preservation, even when connected occasionally to glorious moments of history or special scientific events, because their cumbersome size makes for difficult location and expensive maintenance. Still there are some exceptions (which we shall not list), especially in countries with long and established maritime traditions. Deplorably, and more often than not, it happens that with the suppression of the ship the full technical documentation relating to it gets lost as well: construction blueprints, reports and calculations are thus wasted, depriving scholars of the necessary elements to study their aspect and characteristics, as well as the degree of technical evolution they embodied.

FRANCO GAY

PART I

Chapter I

SHIPBUILDING AT THE END OF THE FIFTEENTH CENTURY

As late as the seventeenth century, all construction of marine ships was performed without actual project drawings. With nothing on paper, the plan was all in the builder's head, where it developed gradually from the time of his apprenticeship, thanks to his everyday experience. Further, during the lifetime of the superintendent or of the master carpenters who actually executed the work, such "project" underwent but minimal changes, reflecting only minor deviations from tradition, introducing, as a rule, only those changes the validity of which had been demonstrated either by his own previous experience or by that of others.

Over a period of time, variations introduced in various shipyards would slowly and gradually determine change from accepted standards to a new one of improved characteristics and performance. Consequently, it is futile to try and find ancient documentation, even a rough draft, of a construction plan; furthermore, shipbuilders totally lacked training in modern technical drawing, which did not exist then. An architect of Columbus's time could prepare building plans with layout and elevation, but would not be able to project on a plane the complex and variable tridimensional shapes of the keel of a ship. On the other hand, there really was no need for it.

The construction of a ship at the end of the fourteenth or early fifteenth century took place on sites that it would be an exaggeration to call shipyards. Generally speaking, we are talking of seaside lots where all the needed materials were stored and where, on stocks summarily prepared, seasonal assembly of the hull could be started, weather conditions permitting. The building process and the sequential operations of workers of various trades — carpenters, caulkers, sawyers, blacksmiths, ropemakers, etc. — filled the jobsite with scattered, miscellaneous items and materials, around which a small community of workmen moved laboriously, in the midst of scents of freshly cut lumber, of pitch and resins, while stepping on layers of sawdust and leftover wood and iron scraps.

With the passing of time, the site of a shipyard nearly resembled a mine, as reported by a letter of Buontalenti to the Purveyor of Leghorn, Alessandro Puccini, in charge of the execution of the works in the harbor: "In the arsenal on the square, there is so much iron scrap that, were it to be sent to the ironworks, could possibly make for plenty of hardware for the project."

Thanks to the knowledgeable and diligent activity of the workforce, a ship's construction advanced speedily, so that building and outfitting it could be done in two or three months. Obviously, everything was handmade with a limited number of tools, including a number of two-handed saws used to cut logs and shape beams and boards. These were later dressed to fit diverse purposes by means of adzes and hatchets, which the master carpenters skillfully employed to give timber the desired final form. Raw wood had to be curved into futtocks and the ends of beams dressed to fit the mortise joints, the dovetail joints and the gardboard strakes making the various pieces blend together; all was done by masterful use of adzes and hatchets. Augers were employed to bore holes for spikes or wooden dowels [1] with a cross-section larger than the hole; other implements were: hammers, finish chisels and caulking irons, forges to heat the iron necessary to manufacture nails and fittings; anvils, vices to hold the planking to the frame futtocks before the final fastening with nails or wooden pegs; and hot vats to melt the pitch for caulking operations.

The timber — oak or male oak for the keel, futtocks, stempost, sternpost, the outer planking; occasionally larchwood or pine, two types of wood normally destined for the inner planking, decks, and deadwork frames; perfect logs of sprucewood or pine for masts and yards; flexible and resistant beech for oars; light elm and poplar for all decorative and embellishment works; boxwood, walnut and chestnut for multipurpose blocks of several types — all this timber came quite frequently from woods located at a remarkable distance from construction sites. Spanish yards received the best white male oak from the Galician sierras, the Pyrenees or even the Gargano [Southern Italy]; spruce from Andalusia and Corsica, and pine from Flanders. Timber was acquired on growth locations and trees chosen depending on their natural configuration with select bifurcations suited for futtocks or other curved parts and then transported on carts or, whenever possible, floated through waterways to

[1] Pegs of extremely hard wood, used up to the mid-16th century, but ever less frequently afterwards. The fastening by sledgehammer forced square pegs into holes set on an iron slab, in order to always ensure the same diameter. These pegs, once forced into auger-made holes held the planking to the main frames with extraordinary strength.

the place closest to the shipyard. All trees had to be cut during the right season: oaks either at the beginning of winter, when the "blood [sap] of the tree is asleep" and at waning moon (because a trunk felled with a new moon is subject to woodworms and to faster alteration of the alburnum) or, better, during a December or March full moon, with a dry wind, provided the lymph had not frozen in harsh cold. Pine and spruce trees, instead, required harvesting at the end of the winter season, before the flowing of new lymph, they too, of course, during the correct moon phase. The twofold concern of the owner of the forest was to moderately satisfy his customers by felling trees at the right growth age when the yield was at its best, while making sure, as well, to avoid despoliation of wooded areas by excessive or inconsiderate harvesting. Because tree-growth is measured in decades, intensive harvesting would, in the best of circumstances, leave behind unproductive woods throughout the remainder of the owner's life (be it a private citizen, a community, or the State itself), when it actually would not destroy it and leave a soil barely capable of producing deciduous wood.

Next the logs, stripped of their bark and reduced to pre-established sizes, had to be left to season at the yard — where they would be eventually used — for a minimum of three years in open air or soaked in seawater for two years. Such long curing time could hardly be reconciled with the haste to build and, had the shipyard not set aside a sufficient supply of timber to season — something quite unlikely, given the modest size of the businesses, which were mostly family-run — it would produce a ship that could hardly endure the wear and tear of time. Thus, often a ship had structural deficiencies that were further aggravated by the fact that the submerged hull is subject to thrusts different from and in fact opposite to those exercised by gravity when it is under construction on drydocks. In addition, the cargo volume and distribution on board, which varied with every voyage, contributed remarkably to this tendency of the hull to deform with the passing of time, up to the point of no longer being seaworthy.

The most striking deformity to which a wooden ship inevitably became subject to was the arching of the keel, caused by the upward thrust a hull receives in its mid-section, where the shape is fuller, in contrast to a downward gravitational push at its wedgelike ends, where the displaced water exerts a much smaller, tendentially negative thrust. This phenomenon was of course more pronounced for long hulls. In our case, a sail-propelled freight vessel built in compliance with the ancient *dos, tres y as* rule (ratios between width, length and height equal, or nearly so, to the numbers 2, 3 and 1) suffered less damage in comparison to that effected on a long, oar-propelled ship. This reality had to be confronted and, indeed, a few builders used to give the keel under construction a certain amount of preset arching with ends upwards, so as to compensate the reverse strain borne by the vessel in the water.

The shipbuilding process adopted practices still followed today in some small yards on the Italian coastline where wooden fishing boats are built, but for one basic difference though: modern-day tool automation makes the toil less taxing. As timber is no longer cut, bored and shaped exclusively by hand, the art of handling an adze — the pride of ancient master carpenters who exhibited excellence in dressing edges and surfaces — has consequently vastly diminished.

Thus, modern hulls are definitely more refined and regularly show clean cuts with small serrated grooves left by a beltsaw, rather than primitive-looking, rough hewing. This is a key telling difference that allows to clearly distinguish recent makings from ancient vessels while indeed explaining why modern reconstructions are so dissimilar from their old prototypes.

Just as a moderately knowledgeable person can tell the difference between authentic antique furniture and modern reproductions — mainly on the basis of imperfections or irregular beam cogging creating a rough, antique-looking finish of unexposed points, revealing lack of precision in execution — so too would a layman immediately notice the differences between a ship built four or five hundred years ago and present-day replicas.

Very few ships, either whole or in part, have come down to us from ancient time. Excepting Egyptian, Roman, Norman vessels and so on, of which we do have some relative intact specimens (such as the Viking ships), or other notable remains, we limit our considerations to ships built around the fifteenth century.

One of the most remarkable archeological finds of an era not so distant from the one that is of interest to us, is the rather well preserved hull of an Hanseatic cog [or cockboat] of 1380, discovered in 1962 during harbor excavations for a drydock on the Weser river at Bremen [Northern Germany]. It took a few years to recover this artifact. Its dating is almost exact, having been calculated dendrologically, i.e., the age of its wood determined by comparing the yearly-growth rings. Also, the rings' variations from year to year express constant characteristics for all trees grown on the same site during the same time. This makes it possible to produce diagrams covering long periods of time, which are applicable to all trees coming from the same area. Once the felling year of a log is established with certainty (as for instance, in the case of lumber used in making a building whose date of completion is documented), such dating can be

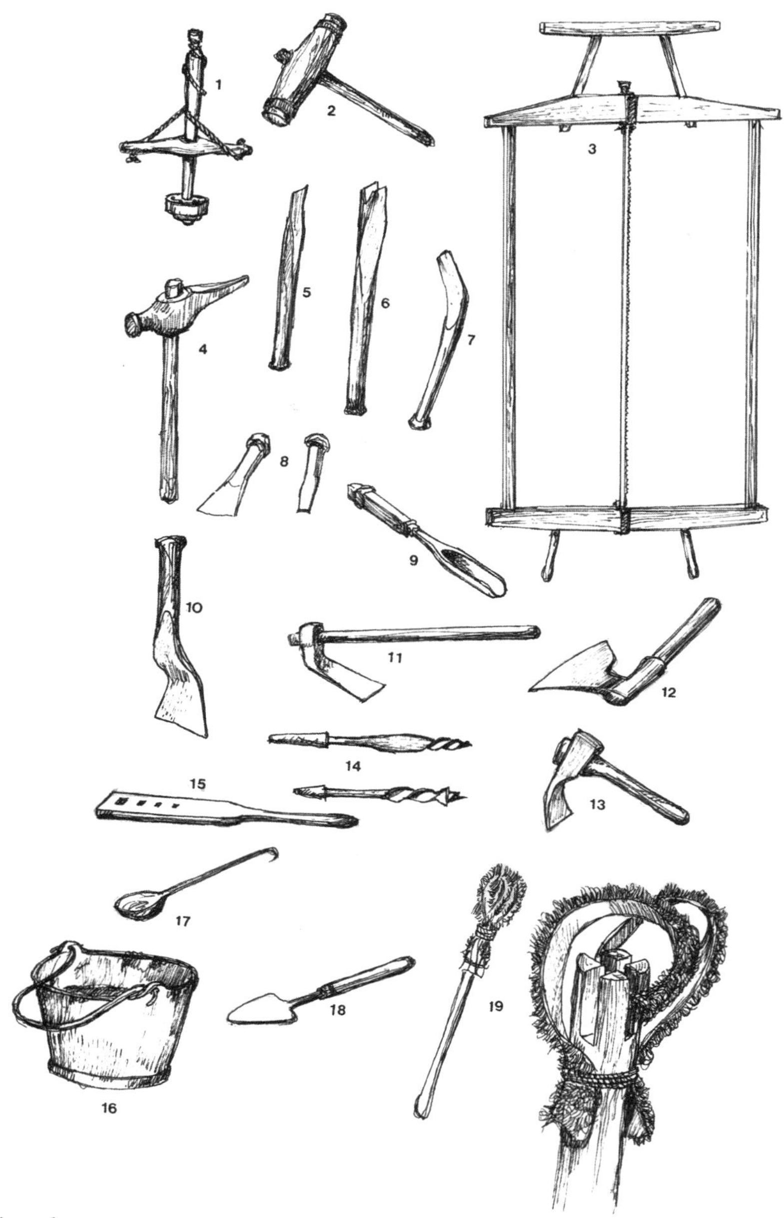

Shipyard tools.

1) rope drill - 2) mallet - 3) frame-saw - 4) caulking iron - 5) single tip chiesel - 6) double tip chiesel - 7) curved chiesel - 8) chisels - 9) gouge - 10) goose-neck caulking iron - 11) long carpenter adze - 12) axe - 3) agier adze - 14) screw augers - 15) nail setting bar - 16) pitch pot - 17) pitch ladle - 18) pitch-spreading brush made with sheepskin strips.

Depiction of tree limbs of suitable shapes for select purposes in shipbuilding. (From W. zu Mondfeld).

The same kind of tree may bear different shapes, depending on soil quality, climate and location in the forest. Oak, essential in the construction of ships, was better when it came from tree grown in moderately dry, iron-rich soil and in the temperate climate of Southern Europe.

Trees grown in the thick of woods, protected by other trees around, yield straight-grain timber, branching off only at the end of the trunk, but because of greater moisture and less sunshine such timber is softer. Isolated trees, on the contrary, freely develop long, curved branches quite valuable for construction needs, and yield a harder wood but, being unprotected from the weather, are often affcted by disease.

Construction timber can either be of a lean nature, with thickly serrated growth rings, of high density, but susceptible to moisture and prone to splitting, or else — just the opposite — be of a fatty nature, less affected by hygrometric variations, of lawer density and good for planking.

In terms of growth rate, a thicket wood oak generally takes twenty-five years to reach a height of twenty-five feet, thirty to get to thirty feet. Further growth was modest but a forest-grown tree of over one-hundred years could rise to a height of eighty to ninety feet.

related to the specific diagrams and cross-checked backward or forward in time, and then compared to other timber of similarly undisputed dating, thus obtaining a comparative scale as reliable as a calendar. In this particular case, it was possible to establish that the latest rings, the one closests to the bark, in some parts of the cockboat dated back to 1378 with their provenance being the region around Kassel [Hesse-Nassau, West Central Germany].

Factoring in the time required for transportation (by flotation from the mountainous area crossed by the Weser) and the fact that the wood had been axe-hewn when still fresh — microscopic analysis did ascertain the absence of fungi or insects of the kind that feast on seasoned wood — it was soon possible to estimate that in all likelihood no more than two years had elapsed between the cutting of the tree and its utilization in shipbuilding. Another salvaged wreck of interest in documenting the construction techniques of the time is the right side of the English carack [galleon] *Mary Rose*, which sank in 1545, was recovered in 1982 and is now preserved in a drydock section specifically built at Portsmouth. And finally, although of a much later period, we have the prodigiously intact hull of the Swedish vessel *Vasa*, launched in 1627, sunk in 1628 and salvaged in 1961.

For all these three hulls, whose dating spans over three hundred and fifty years, it was noticed that the shipbuilding techniques, despite a remarkable series of design improvements introduced throughout that long a period of time, were substantially identical, as were the materials and the tools employed to shape them. We should also underscore the obvious presence of imperfections and work inaccuracies, as previously mentioned. Imperfect workmanship is to blame for the main defect of all medieval hulls, namely, their frequent coming apart under the action of the waves and, consequently, the need for constant repairs to prevent water infiltration and leaks between planking seams. A major defect, considering that a vessel was itself structurally robust being made of reinforced parts of remarkable thickness and, as it shall be seen later, had strong binding ties, both inside and outside the planking.

Obviously, the study of these rare archeological findings does not reveal all we would like to know about ancient shipbuilding techniques, yet many lacunae or uncertainties can be filled by looking at the common practice of artisans in the field of traditional shipbuilding, because this field has shown no substantial changes indeed for the last 600 years except for some technological improvements due to work-tools automation, as earlier pointed out.

On land lots strong enough to support the weight of the construction [2], short pieces of beams, referred to as "blocks," were laid out at a short distance from one another setting on top of them the long and sturdy beam that constituted the keel, a rectangularly shaped backbone of the entire construction. Whenever the length of the ship made it impossible to lay a single-piece keel, two or more beams were mortised, i.e., connected together with a scarf joint, either in a slit and tongue [double] or dovetail type, depending on the carpenter's preference and skill, but done in all instances with the utmost care, to ensure that such an assembly would in the end prove to be of strength equivalent to that of a single beam. Although not particularly large, the ships used by Columbus for his voyage had a keel no less than 35 feet long, probably longer, and almost certainly made by at least two jointed beams.

When building his vessel, an experienced shipbuilder would take care to give his slip a north-to-south orientation, so that the sun would strike equally both the right and the left sides of the ship under construction ensuring that the fitted wood would be uniformly heated on both sides and not subject to uneven deformations that might jeopardize in the end the symmetry of the craft.

Early on in the work, the carpenter had to bear in mind as well the launching operation of the completed ship, and therefore give the construction platform a gentle four-to-five degrees slope that would facilitate her sliding into the water. Whenever the ground did not have a natural incline — which, indeed, was not uncommon on shores generally dotted with small shipyards — he had to ensure the setting of higher docking blocks from bow to stern or viceversa. In any case, such blocks had to reach five or so feet in height, to allow working underneath the hull.

The launching could be indifferently made bow first or stern first. The latter is generally preferred because of the fuller shape of that part of the vessel, which provides a higher flotation thrust as it plunges into the water, improving its lifting and detachment from the slipway. This must not have been a major concern of shipbuilders in Columbus's age, since the vessels' broad shape made for equal heaviness at stern and bow.

Let us now go back to the description of a typical yard, where no more than ten workmen — including the apprentices — helped to hoist, under a foreman's direction, the vertical beams that would stand erect at

[2] In case the shipyard's ground did not meet these requirements--a likely occurrence, considering that such yards were of necessity located either on beaches or on a river bank--a stronger foundation was arranged by excavating the ground and filling it up with crossed layers of timber and stones.

Erection of the first stern frame of a caravel. The element is lifted with a hoist consisting of two beams connected at the top and equipped with proper tackles. Temporary props keep it place.

The first star-shaped futtocks at the prow end inserted into the stemhead and supported by props.

called because of its rounded shape), fastened to the keel by means of special joints and stiffening brackets. The connection between keel and stempost consisted of a curved element, the stemhead, jointed at one end to the keel and at the other to the stempost, with the entire curved section reinforced with brackets. Stern- and stempost were large, heavy pieces of a composite nature, i.e., assembled units which had to be lifted by a hoisting mechanism — albeit a primitive one — constituted by two posts of sufficient height, connected at the top by a strong binding and fixed in at ground level in a divaricated position. Branched at a wide angle this device afforded enough forward flexible motion, bending as much as the stays would allow while operated through tackles. Known as the hoists, these devices had tackles secured at their top ends: for centuries, along with the windlass and capstan, they constituted for shipbuilders the most powerful machines available, capable of lifting heavy loads, up to several tons.

Once stempost and stemhead stood erected into place and properly secured, work on ground level shifted to the largest main futtock that occupied the ship's middle line. Here the master carpenter demonstrated all his skill and ability in developing a plan that was merely stored in his mind, not on paper. Shipbuilders at that time, and still as late as the entire seventeenth century, were used to "eye-only working," i.e., approximation (some actually never stopped doing so in small shipyards), banking on the experience of former master artisans who in turn had learned it from their seniors. These masters were, generally, extremely jealous of their trade and reluctant to pass it onto newcomers. As part of a habit that has survived until recent times, masters used to work in complete silence, surrounded by young apprentices, volunteering very little in the way of explanation, frequently hiding their secrets, however minor; yet, the more alert young men were able to learn thanks to their sharp spirit of observation. As if by magic, a foreman would outline on the sandy yard's dirt the profile of the main futtock, which his own experience told him should be of certain dimensions, proportional to the ship's length and of a shape dependent upon the vessel type being built. If the ships previously built had proven good, there was really no need for innovation, and therefore their shape was reproduced without variations, but for the larger or smaller size specified by the commissioning owner, while preserving constant characteristics. This clarifies why all the scholars who have attempted a reconstruction of Columbus's ships, have done nothing else but reproduce — based on available information — basically identical, Columbian-age vessels. All possible uncertainties notwithstanding, one can in fact reasonably assume that such a resulting ship, conscientiously analyzed and reconstructed, may constitute a good approximation of the vessels the Genoese mariner used, although not truly identical. Based on the described outline drawn on dirt, templates of the futtock frame were prepared and actual assembly begun right on the ground, following the selection of the *stortame*, i.e. the twisted timbers made to fit the curved portion of the futtock, using adzes and other worktools. Actually, the U-shaped frame required shaping and preparing a good number of timbers to be subsequently placed and secured on it side by side.

Up to not long ago, the technique for building wooden ships of medium or large dimensions involved joining the frame-forming timbers to each rib very tightly side by side in a staggered way, with the semiribs somewhat farther above and below and butted against similarly disposed pieces in pairs of broken joints (pairs called either floors, futtocks, or top timbers, depending upon their framing location: floors next to the keel, first futtocks around the bend or upward curve and second futtocks or top timbers those high up). The planks formed the garboard or connecting plane which is part of the garboard-strake.

This remarkably sturdy structural construction method was perfected, however, at a much later date than the Columbian age under consideration here. Even the Swedish *Vasa* of 1637 — one of three successfully salvaged hulls cited earlier, affording us the opportunity of a hands-on investigation, so to speak — exhibits a rib frame built in a much simpler way with her many timbers merely held together by juxtaposition and overlapping sideways. Indeed, such a noticeably simpler system made for a less robust structure, yet the fact that so many ships so built have sailed, and endured turbulent waters, is clear evidence it served its purpose.

Upon completion, the main frame would then be lifted from the ground by means of hoists, set onto the keel and secured to it with strong pegs. The next frames to be positioned near the stern and poop, were manufactured in a row and likewise put in place and tightened to the keel with three kinds of elements that ran parallel to the keel itself over the floor timbers, known respectively as the keelson or inner keel (the major one), the side members or timber strakes and the contra or top members. The gradual width reduction of the ship, running from stem to stern, was again determined by the foreman who followed simple geometrical rules, irrelevant here but for the fact of noticing that they too were the product of every master carpenter's accumulated experience.

To be sure, against our statement that no design plan existed, it should be admitted that some actually concise manuals and a few written rules did exist. They concerned measurements that illustrated the sketches of rakes and their oblique projection, that is, instructions on how to ensure the proper slope assigned to the stem- and sternposts; the width of the

Futtock frames secured to the keel. Visible at the bow end, are the V shaped ribs, sharply contrasting with the wide-angled ones of the midship section.

View of the bow's harmonious arrangement of V — and U — shaped frames.

The hull framing of a caravel is completely in place. The next step is to dress it up with planking.

Edge-to-edge planking being fastened to the frames by means of carpenter's clamps.

main beam, which, by rule of thumb was made progressively narrower, to accommodate the called-for setting of the hull; and the list of points near both the stern and bow, where the futtock frames had to open up in a starlike shape and "go for the branches," as they used to say in Venice, namely, at which point floor timbers should no longer be used, but replaced with crutches and Y-shaped bifurcations of big branches, because near the ship's ends the rib-to-frame angle resembles a V rather than a wide-angled U.

Technically and materially, the futtock frames at the stern and bow ends were the most difficult to manufacture given the conditions ship-builders had to contend with at the time. The shape of the hull, at either end, was not as regular as at midship, since in order to come together at both ends it must follow curving lines. Furthermore, the framings had to be consistently perpendicular to the planking fixed onto them, which therefore had to narrow down in a fan-like fashion, especially near the bow, to the point that its last "apostles", i.e. knightheads, should be nearly parallel to the stempost to which they are firmly fastened. The frames then are, in these places, much closer together with spacing between them no greater than the width of each frame, and reinforced with timbers to further strengthen the structure.

The shape of the stern of medieval ships was round and structurally similar to the bow. In the fifteenth century square sterns made their first appearance and, indeed, the caravels were forerunners of this new line. A square or transom stern did not make construction any easier, on the contrary, it made it more complex, yet it signaled that something was beginning to change in the shipbuilding trade and that from a structural point of view it was altogether possible to experiment with harder-to-make, but better fitting shapes. Consequently, in Columbus's time, there were both square stern ships, including the caravels, and more traditional round stern *naos*, such as the *Santa Maria*.

As its construction progressed, the backbone structure as a whole was held together in different ways, either through temporary, that is provisional, ties commonly known as reference points, but destined to be removed once their function was exausted; or through structurally supporting elements, such as long beams running lengthwise over the futtocks and parallel to the keel. Their purpose was to interconnect the frames, thereby making the whole system sturdier, namely, the kelsons, the limber strakes on each side of the kelsons, the top boards, the strake of inside planking, the beam shelves and the undershelves on which rested the structural beams [3] bent

[3] On the ships of Columbus's time the convexity value or deck beam curvature (*bolzone*) was quite pronounced to help the discharge flow of the water off the deck.

to a different degree and connecting horizontally the two side arms of the main frames while supporting the decks. These structurally important elements, needed to tie transversally the whole framework, did not rest yet — as it will be done in later ages — on the stringers, i.e., the longitudinal runners (or beam shelves) connecting and strenghtening the main frames, but were placed between ribs and fastened to their inner surfaces. The earlier method did not guarantee as much sturdiness as the one introduced later featuring deck beams resting on shelves and butting against a rib to which they were bracketed. Yet, such a relatively unreliable method still marked a progress over the previous technique, abandoned less than a century earlier, when the deck beam rested on top of planking boards protruding a bit from the hull. (The Bremen cockboat built with this technique made it possible to verify the exact positioning of all four large deck-holding beams). Beside supporting the decks, the function of these transverse beams in this case was also to hold the framework together preventing potential outward splitting. The innovative technique focuses instead on decreasing the inward thrust against the hull, which is a more logical approach considering that, although the weigth of the cargo has a tendency to push open the hull, such force is sufficiently countered by the pressure of the water from the outside, amounting to an inward push. The deck beam end protruding outside the planking has challenged many highly distinguished experts who could never explain the nature of those strange markings that, in very old drawings, seemed to point to a decorative purpose on the ship's sides in correspondence of the decks. A mistery clarified only thanks to progressing naval archeology and to studies of the Matarò model, a precious "ex voto" possibly from around 1450, discovered in St. Simon's sanctuary at Matarò and presently preserved at the Prince Hendrick Maritime Museum in Rotterdam. This model shall be discussed at greater length in chapter four, the one dedicated to Columbus's ships.

Extremely important was the responsibility of making sure that all these elements be set in their proper place in full respect of all right angles and simmetries. This task befell to the master carpenter who fulfilled it with the mere help of a square, compasses, a plummet or plumb bob and some chalk. The positioning, as close to perfection as humanly feasible, of the main futtock frame, made checking that all other elements did fit properly much easier. The rigor with which all these operations were to be carried out naturally implied ensuring the hull's perfect simmetry and consequent performance at sea.

This full skeleton of transversal and longitudinal ties connected by means of mortise joints, pins and nails, stood onto its slipway, supported by numerous props and flanked by scaffolding, as needed to reach its higher parts. The "felled forest" was once more rising toward the sky or, as they used to say in Venice, with a more poetic expression, "the hull is back in its woods."

At this point, the entire framework had to be dressed all over and as needed with solid oak planking boards of variable thickness, sawed off at the yard from logs placed on top of special tresles that allowed two sawyers to operate lengthwise a double-handed saw, by pulling alternately while standing respectively on top and below the log. The resulting sawing action was rather irregular, owing to the sawyers' shifting position, an irregularity easily noticeable on archeological findings.

The inner planking was worked on first, applying the bottom boards or strakes below the shelf, leaving some undone to ensure airflow through the woodwork. Next came the covering of the decks, which completed the stiffening of the structure as a whole thus readying it to receive the outer, much thicker planking without affecting the frame with deforming pressures. In order to force fit the oak boards, up to four inch thick in our case, against the curvilinear hull shape, they were customarily heated on a reed-fueled fire which softened their inner structure and made them more pliable to bending. Each planking run, generally not too long owing to the higher cost of taller and older trees, was fastened to the frames at one end and clamped with vices all along the hull's curvature; this procedure called for constant moistening of the boards as well as heating them with reed torches. As work progressed, the carpenter checked for smoothness with the utmost care, between the planking and the main frames, using adzes to thin down excess wood or intervening to add, as the case demanded, pieces of wood so as to bring it to its correct quarter round[4]; however, adding had to be avoided as much as possible, because it adversely affected structural firmness. It should not at all be assumed that each planking stave run featured perfectly regular boards all of the same width, as it is the case with modern wooden boats. Their desire to utilize the available wood to a maximum degree and reduce costs (bearing in mind that actually less than one half of a one hundred year old tree could be used) compelled builders to utilize as well some pieces that would have normally been considered undersized. This explains the patched-up look of planking on the recovered ships, which probably did not affect the vessels' sturdiness.

[4] In shipbuilding, the quarter round or correct right-angle refers to the vertical section formed by the hull and a rib, specifically to their dihedral angle enclosed by the planes of the main frame and the structure's outer surface. It expresses the more or less curvilinear run of the hull and varies both all along each rib as well as from rib to rib. Only with fully correct angles does the planking adhere smoothly to the rib frames at all points.

Once the planking was fastened to the main frames with ductile iron pins and nails, male oak plugs were used to fill in the auger-made nail holes, before the caulkers could start their job (in smaller yards, however, the same workers took care of everything) of sealing any seam opening between planks, using long, tar-impregnated oakum strips, forced into fissures with chisel and mallet before pouring a coat of hot pitch over it.

Shipbuilders in the Middle Ages were rightfully concerned that all the timber pieces would hold together as long as possible. Sea fortunes shift frequently, as is well known, and no matter how much caution is exercised in sailing, all ships would certainly have to face in a lifetime the difficult moments of a tempestuous sea shaking her and her cargo, subjecting the hull to abnormal stresses. Indeed, even during normal navigation, on calm or moderately agitated seas, the waves's pressure exerts constantly diverse stress patterns, which subject the hull structure, regardless of its natural flexibility, to an ongoing wear and tear that ceases only in the tranquil waters of a harbor.

Classical-age historians repeatedly narrate of entire fleets composed of hundreds of vessels, destroyed during frightful storms. These storms were undoubtedly powerful, yet could they have caused such stunning disasters and been equally damaging, had the ships not been so fragile and improperly built? Furthermore, the vessels of these unlucky fleets were, almost without exception, military crafts (thus their special mention by contemporary historians), in other words long, light ships with oars that consequently, given these very characteristics, were less sturdy than their shorter, more compact freight vessels. Improved costruction techniques made fifteenth-century ships less subject to the vicissitudes of the ocean and produced stronger models. Yet, not uncommon among the possible causes of serious distress that could lead to the loss of a ship was the disjoining of the planking through active seepage, ranging from simple leaks to visible cracks. Seeping and leakage has affected vessels even in more recent times, as in the case of the *Guipuzcoa*, the sole survivor from Admiral Don Juan Pizarro's fleet. After five years of trying navigation and little chance for serious maintenance, this vessel returned to Spain in 1746 in such disarray that it had become necessary to wrap a cable several times around the keel to hold her planking boards and framing together, with bilge pumping kept up day and night.

To strengthen a hull it was customary at the time to double the outside planking by means of furring strips or girdering (generally in correspondence to the shelter and lower decks) tied against vertical buttresses and thick beams which ran from the top edge of the ship's inner wall flush down to the load waterline. These stiffeners served the double

Weather [main] deck's structural view, showing its beams before the laying of the plankings.

Use of a double-handed» frame-saw, oriented vertically. (From a fifteenth century print owned by the Sawyers' Artful Trade in Venice).

Use of augers in boring holes for water-discharging "trumpets".

purpose of strengthening the hull while further protecting it against pier-bumping in the harbor; in other words, they also had a side fender-like function. The resistance to sailing that these hull protrusions — particularly when the ship under full sails was tacking on one side — must have been remarkable, yet the shipbuilders' faith in these structures was such that they endured through the entire sixteenth century.

The sealing and color mixtures used at the time were based on resins, oils and bitumen and therefore hulls generally exhibited a somber brown hue, off and on brightened by a few colored touches, on external projections and on the ornamental parts of the superstructures. The most commonly used colors, occasionally seen on paintings reproducing ships, were red, white, ocher and black, obtained with inexpensive mixes of oxides and dyes blended with oils: they did not last long but coats of paint were easily reapplied at intervals.

Such paintings, however, were not always realistic, subject as they were to an artist's inspiration or mood of the moment and conditioned by the amount of colors on the palette. Also, artists who decorated prestigious vessels were in the habit of using much more chromatic hues than on ordinary ships, where ornamental elements were scarce indeed.

The color white was obtained from lead or zinc oxides or from gypsum; yellow, from terras that reflected in their particular hues iron oxides to a varying degree, introducing a vast range of shades (pigment-prepared yellows were too expensive); but the choice of reds was very ample, either from varieties of red terras (Venetian red), whether natural or burnt, or from properly treated iron minerals (hematite).

The quickwork, the immersed part of a ship, required utmost attention because from its good maintenance depended the hull's preservation and from its cleanliness a top performance at sea. Since water-resistant paints were virtually unknown, it was customary to smear on a ship's bottom a putty of white tallow blended with soap or fish oil, sulphur and cerussite and lead white. Sometimes, a small quantity of human urine was added as well in formulas that varied on the basis of selected substances. Such a concoction devised by suppliers of this infamous mixture, had a potency, that is, a degree of compound toxicity intended to ward off the proliferation of mollusks and submarine vegetation, as well as to ensure lasting effectiveness of their compound in water.

The smeared coating had a short life and, whenever possible, it had to be removed at least once a year, to avoid irreparable damage to a ship's bottom. A fuller description of this operation of cleaning a vessel lying on its side, known as careening, is at p. **221** and following.

The major portion of the internal outfitting and setting of the masts was generally done on the construction stocks since, especially when the ships were of small dimensions, it was more convenient to perform these operations with the craft still on land.

Next came the moment, finally, to "marry" a vessel to the sea. The methods for launching a ship were several and owners of small yards most likely chose the least laborious one, as well as one that would shave costs as much as possible. In any case, it was necessary to set up ahead of the building stocks, all the way to the water edge and a few yards under water into the sea, a strong path of ties — the wedgeblocks — at a short distance one from the other, and onto which "driving" boards were fastened to act as tracks. Small-size crafts merely required a single U-shaped, well greased track, along which the keel would be made to slid. Solid planks, firmly implanted on each side of the slipway, almost forming two supporting walls, would prevent the ship from unevenly leaning to one side during her short travel, which was slowly accomplished with the aid of pulling tackles as well as of stays that ensured against too fast or abrupt movements. The lively ceremonies of modern, obstentatious launchings were entirely unknown to small yards, concerned mainly with bringing the ship to the sea without too much haste and in full safety.

When the vessel were of large dimensions, however, the pulling out to sea involved a more complex system. The single track approach was no longer sufficient, given the heavy weight of the hull. On wedge ties predisposed under the hull had to be placed two parallel driving boards onto which rested two long beams transversally fastened, the slipways. Any remaining space on these bilgeways all the way to the keel was filled with vertically set props, chocks and shims. The whole ensemble constituted a launching cradle solidly braced to the hull by means of cables, i.e. lashings. Simultaneous removal of the building stocks onto which the keel had been leaning until then, and of the buttresses that had kept it upright, left the keel at this point supported exclusively by its launching cradle. At the right moment the last stays and the last sea-facing props were pulled away, letting the craft slide along generously greased driving boards, and made to advance toward the sea with the help of tackles and large levers when the motion was not spontaneous, making sure, however, that the speed be never excessive and always under control. Launching was then a delicate and complex operation, supervised by experienced specialists, and its successful completion was the supreme crowning point, encompassing as it did all their efforts poured into the making of the ship.

Chapter II

THE EVOLUTION OF SHIPS DURING THE MIDDLE AGES

Based on what is known, the previous chapter was an attempt to describe as much as possible how a ship was built in the time period under consideration. We chose as comparison small-size commercial crafts, similar to those used by Columbus for his voyages; however, proportionally speaking, the construction of large vessels — and some were really gigantic — followed the same principles. A separate description, of no interest here, should be reserved for vessels built specifically for warfare. Their basic type in the Mediterranean was the oar galley whereas in Northern Europe the preference was mostly square-rigged ships outfitted with artillery. The construction of nationally owned warships, as was the case for instance in Venice, took place in special workshops called arsenals, where the purchase of materials, their storage as well as the construction of the hulls and the manufacturing of riggings, sails, oars, artillery, ammunitions and specific weaponry followed fairly rigorous rules, dictated by the need to produce a war instrument as efficient as possible. The large arsenals of Venice and Costantinople were "industrial" sites of this type — besides, possibly, some smaller ones in Genoa, France and Spain — sufficient to satisfy the needs and the economic capabilities of the respective States. In Genoa, the municipal arsenal was actually a quite modest entity, that served both the government and the private sector (really contracting more with the latter than with the Republic), but its production was complemented by several other yards, located on small Ligurian beaches, which specialized in galleys and other crafts and operated more or less as described in the previous chapter.

Part of this introduction on Columbian ships is a general overview of the various vessels, revisiting history starting a couple of centuries back and looking at the slow evolution of wooden European shipbuilding in the Mediterranean and the Atlantic-before the development of ships that, as a result of the geographic discoveries and newly opened horizons for Europe, would be needed to ply ocean routes well beyond the modest Mediterranean- and North Sea-bound Atlantic sailing which, although more dangerous, still ran offshore along the coast.

Evolution of the Mediterranean ship

First to be considered in this overview are the Mediterranean vessels representing the outcome of an intense commercial activity that flourished in these waters during the Roman era: an activity which progressively diminished, but did not vanish, with the fall of the Western Roman Empire and the barbarianizing of such a large portion of Europe. Mediterranean naval traditions were extremely ancient and had produced, over centuries of slow evolution, efficient sailing crafts that suitably satisfied the needs of trade and of war. These ships were wide and potbellied, with a single central mast fitted with a large square sail, on a long sloping yard that leaned toward the prow, much like a bowsprit, which supported another light yard with square sail, a bit smaller and with two rudders on each side of the stern, resembling overall the large Roman freight ships, except for their smaller size, called for by a reduced volume of trading. Vessels of this type continued to service the Mediterranean throughout the entire High Middle Ages. Although next to nothing is known about them, these ships will be the starting point of our discussion. They can only be presumed to have been similar to the Roman freight vessels, but they do serve the purpose of filling the information gap of the so called dark centuries, and take us into an age much closer to ours when, following the Arab invasions and subsequently the Crusades, trade exchanges intensified and the documentation of sailing practices became more frequent and more accurate.

We shall not yield to the temptation of attempting a classification of ships mentioned in various documents, first because such references are usually so vague as to imply either that anything else was superfluous for the readers of the time or that they did not demand more detailed explanations; also because such a generalizing classification would mean very little, given the independent local trends which focussed on their specific needs. The denominations of these vessels are of little — if any — help, since from place to place they merely reflected either the different types of merchandise they moved or that which they were allegedly designed to transport, rather than their structural characteristics. Quite frequently, the names of ships reflected either a construction detail or a feature typical of their site of origin; that differentiated a ship from another only for the trained eye of a seaman.

In order to avoid getting lost in minute distinctions involving *acazie*, *cumbarie*, *ippogoghi*, *tarete*, *galandre*, *marciliane*, *buzi*, *orche*, *pandore* we shall stress the enduring essential distinction of classical times between freight ship and warships. Freight vessels were characterized by the prevalence of sails over oars as a means of propulsion — with oars seldom used, and then only as an auxiliary source — whereas warships normally employed sails only when favorable conditions allowed it.

This distinction, which originated in the classical age, had its own logic in the fact that an oar-propelled vessel ensured a warship its fundamental characteristics, namely, that of moving about autonomously during doldrums and freely maneuvering as needed. Conversely, an oar ship had serious limitations: her dimensions, and the large number of men that she carried onboard, allowed only a reduced cargo capacity; it was very expensive to keep her operational; it was unfit for rough seas and long sailing beyond tacking; and, finally, she had to rely on logistic support owing to the enormous quantities of food and water that her crew needed. Yet such limitations were bearable when the campaigns took place in the good season and, even better, when the fleet's role consisted in supporting the operations carried out by a land-based army.

The perilous Northern seas presented a different situation for such military crafts, because an oar vessel would experience greater difficulties while operating there even in good weather. Ultimately, round ships carrying armed men and, later, primitive artillery seemed to enjoy greater flexibility from an operational point of view.

On the other hand, sail vessels — the focus of our concern, because we do not plan to discuss the galley or the subfamily of oar ships related to it, although they would survive through the mid eighteenth century — were the best crafts available for transporting goods: a large cargo hold capacity; inexpensive operation, since it would take only few men to handle a ship; fit to navigate in all kinds of weather (bad season included) and on open sea routes. And when calm or contrary winds stopped the navigation, all it would take was patiently waiting out the unfavorable metereological conditions.

These ships travelled the Mediterranean much more frequently than one could imagine. Even very early on in the second millennium — before the great impulse to trade brought about by the Crusades — the merchant marine was the vehicle of a remarkable flow of goods centered, since the collapse of the Western Roman Empire, in Costantinople: there merchants convened from all over and dealt in all sorts of goods, from silk to wine, to cereals, oil, spices, and so on.

Whereas the commercial centers in the North and North-East could be reached from Costantinople on land or by waterway, the goods destined for the Western Mediterranean markets such as Venice, Marseille and Barcelona were transported by an uninterrupted flow of ships. From these port cities, the merchandise was then moved over land toward the continental market centers of Bavaria, the Rhein valley, Champagne and Flanders. From Flanders and other northern harbors ships carried it on to London as well as the towns on the Baltic Sea.

Typically, the earliest representations of medieval Mediterranean ships depict a single-mast vessel with square sails. Around the end of the ninth century two Greek manuscripts reproduced rather accurately — betraying an expert hand — two small ships of a type common at the time, but showing a triangular, lateen sail.

The "lateen" denomination given to this sail should not deceive. This sail's triangular shape has nothing to do with Latins, or classical antiquity for that matter. Yet the term's origin is uncertain and open to differing interpretations. According to some scholars the sail got its name from Northern Europeans who, when they saw it in the Mediterranean — the Latin sea — did not go to the trouble of finding out whether it had in fact originated on those shores. The most widely accepted explanation for this term makes it a corruption of the misunderstood expression *alla trina*, that really referred to its triangular shape. In January 1978 Pino Dell'Orco, a naval archeology scholar, published an interesting article in the *Rivista Marittima*, titled "Remote origins of the Lateen sail," in which he theorized that it truly was of Mediterranean origin owing to reefing, that particular technique of rolling up one side of a square sail, with the other side still extended, whereby the area exposed to the wind formed a triangle of sort — a procedure adopted because in this fashion it was possible to better hold the wind. This suggestive theory hypothesizing a Mediterranean origin for the lateen sail conflicts with another which identifies its origin in the Indian Ocean and ascribes its diffusion toward the West to the Arab invasions. Actually, we shall later point out that the Arab sail *a saettìa* [pointed] and *al terzo* [reefed (reduced to a third point; from *terzarolo*)] shares common features with the lateen sail. The latter could thus be an improved offshoot of the former, the use of which subsequently spread throughout the entire Mediterranean basin and on the Atlantic shores of the Hiberian peninsula, at least as far up as the Tagus delta — presumably because of its suitability to coastal navigation that constantly requires hauling close to the wind.

This "Arabic" sail was probably not entirely unknown even earlier, because some of its prototypes, documented as far back as the third and fourth century A.D., show some small boats with a triangular sail.

At any rate, further considerations about its origin aside, the triangular sail very soon came to be the predominant type throughout the Mediterranean and the Black Sea countries, owing to the distinctive advantage it enjoyed over the square sail, that is, its ability to catch the wind well; by

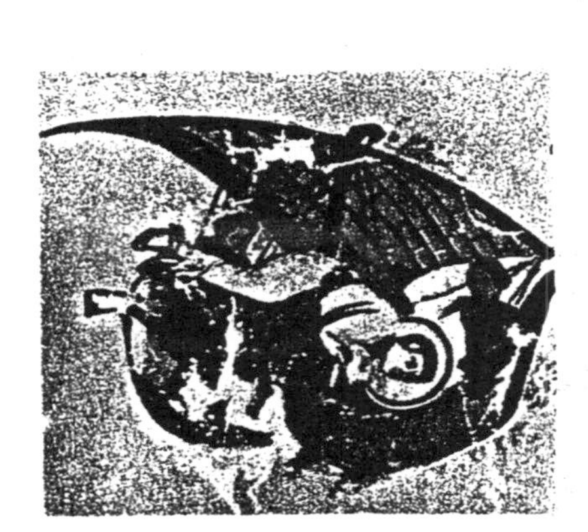

Medieval ships with lateen sail in ninth-century Greek miniatures.

Small lateen-rigged boat, from a 1359 mosaic in the Zen chapel of St. Mark's basilica, Venice.

Lateen-rigged *acazie*, from mosaics of the St. Mark basilica, Venice. More interesting than the crude representation of the hull is the fourteenth-century documentation of three-masted ships exhibiting both lateen rigging (the furling by sailors shows some of the sails already bound to the yards and lowered to the deck) and two lateral rudders.

trimming the sail in such a way as to leave the smallest possible angle between the direction of the blowing wind and its own plane surface-but still with a workable sail-a ship is able to advance even with the wind coming from her prow.

When navigating by wind propulsion, a vessel cannot in general sail straight to its destination but is forced to tack and follow what looks like a staggered course, proceeding first on one side and then on the other, thus advancing diagonally bit by bit toward its destination. In areas where the winds have a constant regimen, sailing becomes much easier. The adoption of the lateen sail represented a critical step forward for the art of navigation.

In all likelihood, it was the diffusion of the lateen sail that led shipbuilders to the adoption of a second mast, fitted either with lateen rigging or with a square sail, to navigate with aft wind or running free. This new possibility meant a definite progress from the single mast with one sail, for it allowed both a better balance of the sails' thrust centre and, with some experience, improved a ship's ability to hold a steady course by herself, without frequent rudder corrections.

However, handling a lateen sail was more complex and more difficult than maneuvering with a square one. All that the latter required was to trim the yard into the wind by means of two tackles, the clewlines, fixed laterally to the top of the yard frame. With a square sail on a single mast, tacking was possible only while running free, with aft wind. With a midship wind, on the other hand, the maneuver was impossible to execute and poop-turning was the only recourse, although it forced the ship to revolve by a half turn, wasting, quite obviously, some time and distance to the wind.

A lateen sail, on the contrary, made it feasible to tack close-hauled regardless of weather conditions and thus offered a clear advantage, because in addition it produced no loss of distance to the wind. To carry out this maneuver required lining up the ship with the wind, gathering the wind-slammed sails that flapped like flags, and raising the yards vertically and shifting them to the opposite side of the mast. It appears that at least up to the first half of the sixteenth century yards were positioned outside the shrouds of the masts and that, therefore, a yard had to be shifted to the front of the mast and the fully gathered sail had to be simultaneously moved to the opposite side while unhooking the sheet that kept the sail taut and hooking it up again on the opposite side, once the sail had been moved to the new position. This was quite a difficult maneuver, well illustrated by a drawing in a small notebook attributed to Raphael, which shows a frigate or brigantine with the crew taken up in this operation. We think that this demanding operation could not have been executed without having a sheet on the lee side ready to be hooked onto a clewline before letting go of the taut sail, while the shrouds at lee side were let loose during the passage of the sail. With the sail outside the shrouds it was not possible to close-haul more than so much, but this problem was relatively unimportant, considering that the main sails, the square ones, could be trimmed only very little. By the middle of the sixteenth century, the English and the Dutch mounted yard and sail inside the shrouds. This solution allowed the yard to be shifted behind the mast during the change of board. Sail, sheets and vangs were subject to less stress and remained steady, merely switching the side on which the sail caught the wind. The sail, given the encroaching shrouds, could not be fully opened up before the wind, but, on the other hand, it worked better in sailing on a bowline because a sheet could be hauled in to its maximum extent. The entire operation of changing the setting of a lateen sail was complicated and tiring, requiring the joint effort of the whole crew. The setting of oriented sails was controlled by two tackles hooked at the lower end of the yard and by two arms, the vangs, hooked about half-way up the yard's upper end.

While from the Mediterranean the lateen sail spread to the Atlantic and North Sea mercantile marines, from those regions came into the Mediterranean another invention critical to the progress of navigation: the central rudder braced onto the sternpost. It is not known when this invention was adopted; some people think that a central rudder can be seen in a manneristic small boat appearing in bas-relief on the baptismal font of Winchester cathedral, dated around 1180. Yet, the strange implement evident at stern end resembles anything but a helm. Undisputable, instead, is a graffito on an inside wall of the church in Fide, Gotland [Sweden], which shows a clearly depicted ship with one mast, a large square sail, and a perfectly delineated rudder with braced gudgeons hinging onto the pintles on the supporting sternpost. The tiller, instead of being hinged on top of the rudder, is laterally placed next to the sternpost in this graffito, the reliability of which is confirmed by the fact that the same detail appears on several maritime seals of the time. Undoubtedly this drawing is of the beginning of the thirteenth century, and its detailed accuracy bears witness to the fact that the author was scratching on the wall something he was familiar with, not a novelty. For once, the disfiguration of a monument turns out to be a valuable contribution to historical research.

In the Mediterranean the centrally mounted rudder, known as Navarrian in origin (i.e., original to the former kingdom in northwestern France and northern Spain), very gradually displaced the two laterally mounted rudders, no doubt more inconvenient and less reliable. However, these

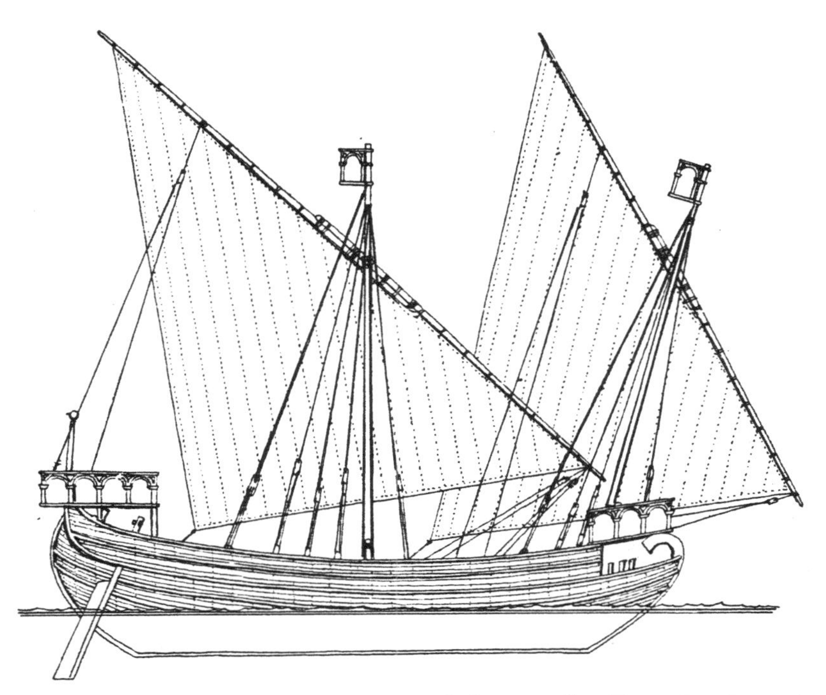

A thirteenth-century Venetian vessel with lateen sails. (From Landström.)

The complicated maneuver to change course, or heave, using a lateen sail is well represented in this drawing, taken from a small notebook attributed to Raphael. Visible at the base of the mast are the men who, after raising the car vertically, are transferring the yard from one side of the mast to the other. The sail is completely slack before being rolled to the opposite side, once the car is secured in its new position. The depicted ship could be either a frigate or a brigantine.

Tacking maneuver of a lateen sail external to the shrouds. (From "The Square Sail" by Sergio Bellabarba and Giorgio Osculati. *Enciclopedia di navi e modelli di navi*, 1979.)

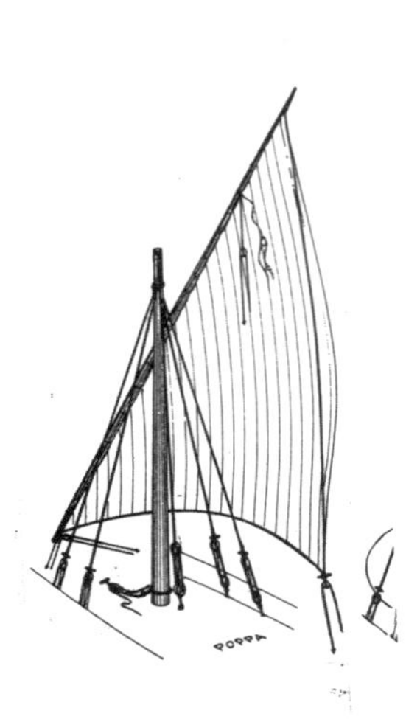

Fig. 1: Starting position with port tack (wind from the left side)

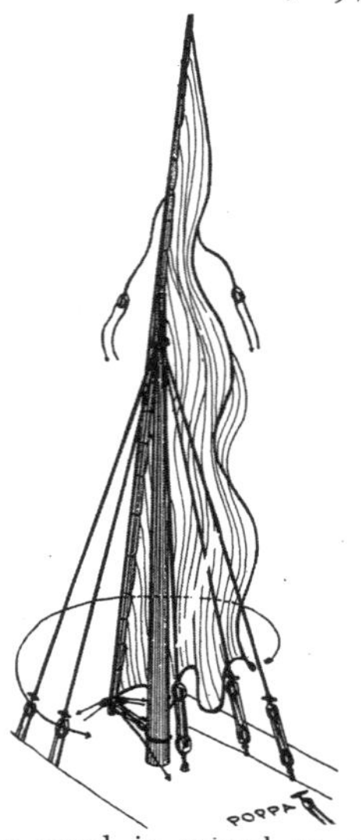

Fig. 2: The yard is raised to an almost vertical position, the mainsheet is loose. The sail begins to switch boards, shifting around, i.e. outside, the shrouds and in front of the mast.

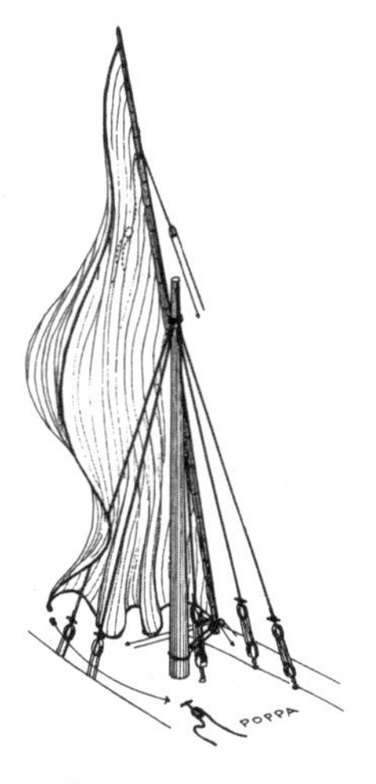

Fig. 3: The yardbeam has changed boards, and the sail is pulled back toward the left side of the stern.

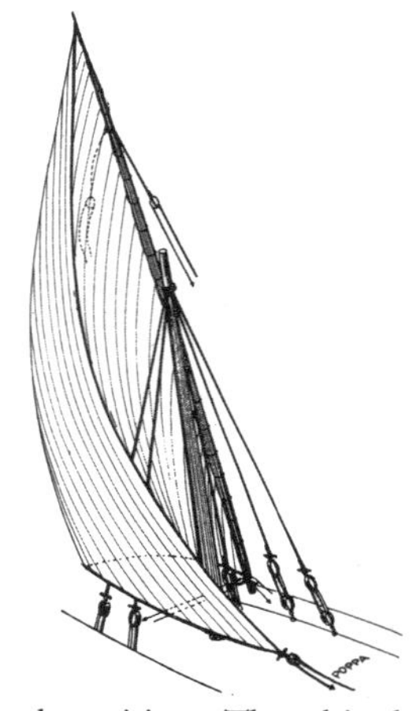

Fig. 4: Final position. The ship has heaved, with the wind coming from the right side (starboard tack), the mainsheet is again hauled close ("hardened," in sailor's language). Notice the vang, ringstrapped to the base of the mast (secured only in positions 1 and 4), needed to vertically lift the yardbeam.

Indispensable requirement to be able to shift the "primitive" (i.e., external to the shrouds) lateen sail during tacking:

1) The list (or tilt yard) is stretched behind the mast;

2) The shrouds are stretched taut by blocks and made movable by means of buntline toggles;

3) The middle stay is missing, or else it is stretched as described above for the shrouds.

shovel-shaped lateral helms were still used, long after the Navarrian type had been introduced and adopted in the Mediterranean, through the fourteenth century as ship iconography increasingly evidenced in frescoes, bas-reliefs, miniatures etc.

The mosaics of St. Mark's basilica in Venice, trustworthy being the product of people who lived by and on the sea and dating back to the time of the first Crusades, contain reproductions of two- and three-masted ships with lateen sails, a backwardly curved bow, a shape still found in use around one hundred years ago, and with two lateral rudders. Indeed, at the end of the fifteenth century, Venice's harbor was crowded also by vessels with lateral rudders.

Those improvements that war-related necessities swiftly brought about for military crafts are incorporated into merchant traders at a much slower pace. These still maintained, as Vingiano states, "their stout shape, heavy displacement and, hence, slow navigation," especially because for precious or small cargos that required little stowage capacity it was possible to employ galleys or some such vessels derived from them, including the large *taride*, as they were called in Venice.

The large Mediterranean medieval ships

Considering that up to this point we have used moderately reductive terms, readers might have gained the impression that all medieval fleets were made up of small-size ships. The greater part of the boats that plied the Mediterranean or the North Seas were quite surely cockleshells by today's standards, yet, just to give an idea of their size, they had burdens, i.e., approximate displacements varying from about fifty to one hundred tons.

Besides these small-sized ships built in great number on numerous small yards spread along the coasts, there also were much larger shipyards capable of building — it must be given due note — with the same "primitive" construction techniques, vessels of far larger dimensions.

Relevant information to this effect can be evinced from several contracts between Genoese suppliers and various monarchs such as, for instance, the one between Louis IX and Guglielmo of Varazze. Guglielmo, the chancellor of the municipality of Genoa, had agreed to provide to the French sovereign, for his last crusade against Tunis (1270), twelve two-masted vessels that measured almost 110 feet in length and 30 at the beam — each specifically suited for transporting as many as one hundred horses — with a carrying capacity or burden (tonnage) calculated to be around 600 tons. In another contract, a ship about 93 feet long and 24 feet wide is specified to require a 97 feet tall main mast with a circumference of 6 feet and 4 inches, and a second mast 90 feet tall and a circumference of 6 feet. In describing Medirerranean vessels employed by Louis IX in his crusades, Jal lists the *Roccaforte* (or *Rocheforte*), a Venetian ship having all-out length of 124 feet, and a beam of 43 feet, with three decks running from bow to stern. The horse stables were beneath the lower deck, in the holds, while the troops were lodged on the decks. Another unit, the *Santa Maria*, had a keel length of 78 feet, with all-out length of 122 feet and beam of 43 feet. This ship required a crew of 110 seamen.

According to Jal, as reported in Joinville's chronicle (*memoir n.* 6 about the principal round vessels of the Middle Age), king Louis the Saint returned from Egypt on a ship that carried 800 people, and the chronicler does not cite this event as an extraordinary thing. To impress the folks of the time, clearly accustomed to seeing vessels of considerable dimensions, it took a vessel like the *Mondo* [the World], so named because of her prodigious size. Finally, a generalizing statement confirms that in the thirteenth century there were builders who possessed the techniques needed for constructing large ships: Geoffray de Ville Hardouin reports at one point that "[t]here were, on five ships, seven thousand armed men." Thus, each such vessel must have carried on average one thousand and four hundred soldiers, who, to be so identified, likely carried with them their weapons and equipment as well.

The ratio between length and width of these ships tells us that the fineness coefficient was minimum, given such an accentuated roundness in the merchant traders's shape.

Early on in the fourteenth century, the naval traffic in the Mediterranean intensified, thanks to the Crusades which, although they did not fulfilled their proclaimed purpose, nevertheless caused the castles where medieval Europe had retreated in isolation to open to the rest of the world. Increasingly larger ships became necessary. Only large vessels could guarantee the transportation of larger quantities of merchandise and, for military undertakings, of soldiers and their cumbersome gear.

For the crusade that lead to the conquest of Costantinople (1203), Venice was able to deploy 110 large freight ships and several other smaller crafts which transported to the East an army of 40,000 men and 4,500 horses, supplies and war machines. According to Ramusio the ships that carried the army to Costantinople were about 230, but Sanudo mentions 300 vessels. Overall, these figures are always inaccurate, because they often included merchant ships and warships that transported a limited number of warriors.

Above: Church graffito in Fide, Gotland, representing a nordic ship of the beginning of the thirteenth century with a central rudder. The tiller is mounted laterally onto the rudder as done in earlier times.
Below: Large Mediterranean ship, single-masted and with central rudder: this graffito is on the third right-hand side column of the second archway to the left of the main portal of St. Mark's basilica in Venice. It is believed to date back to the end of the thirteenth century or the beginning of the fourteenth. Under the bow one can see a stylized anchor.

Mediterranean merchant trader of the end of the fourteenth century, from a reconstruction by Bjorn Landström.
On a sturdy, full-shaped hull rises an enormous mast, made of several beams held together by multiple bindings and steadied by shrouds tensed with stretch-screws and scored hearts fixed on the inside of the hull, and ratlines to climb into the crow's nest at the top on the masthead. The sail shows two transversally placed spars, bowlines and a central bolt-rope [reinforcement], not visible on the drawing, but clearly implied by the mainsheets passing around the mast. Notable as well is a winch in front of the quarter-deck.

For the next-to-the last crusade, in 1248, king Louis IX departed from Aigues-Mortes with only twenty-eight large vessels supplied by the Genoese, not counting those for transporting horses and provisions. Yet in Cyprus, where the crusaders spent the winter, was gathered a mass of 1,800 ships, large and small (mostly small), some specifically built for the undertaking. All of them, after some vicissitudes that it is superfluous to list, reached Damietta in Egypt, where they fought against a correspondingly numerous Muslim fleet. During his second crusade, Louis IX arranged to have transported overseas, this time to Tunis, approximately 60,000 men. These events confirm that the ships in the Mediterranean were quite numerous and that some of them were about as large as a third-rank vessel of the eighteenth century.

As for the large human cargo transported (the *Paradisus Magnus*, a Genoese ship that carried Louis IX to Cyprus, could board eight hundred men), it should be noticed that such large number of people was really crowded in extremely reduced spaces, in the lower decks or exposed to the weather on the main deck. Deck space was so limited that at night it forced people to lie down very close to each other, with one's head next to each other's feet, in a head-to-tail arrangement. Even on boarding ships for pilgrims where, after all, passengers paid their way and therefore could expect something better than just transportation and an infamous food diet, they did not enjoy a sheltered deck space measuring more than six feet by two that had to hold their belongings as well. Select noblemen or people of means received a bunk place on the stern quarter deck, where there was more room and better airflow.

Giovanni Villani's *Cronaca* reports that around 1304 "...certain people from Bajona in Gascony, with the ships that they call cockboats, passed through the Sibilia straight and came into this sea, coasting and pillaging; ever since Genoese and Venetians and Catalonians embraced cockboats, abandoning navigation on large ships, because of their greater safety and, furthermore, on account of their being less expensive, and this marked a big change in crafts for our merchant marines."

It is therefore from the beginning of the fourteenth century that Nordic vessels, which had gone through an evolutionary process different from that occurring in the Mediterranean, began to exert a remarkable influence upon the Mediterranean shipbuilding art. There had certainly been many contacts beforehand; we have seen, for instance, the lateen sail adopted by the Northern seamen and the single central rudder adopted into the Mediterranean tradition. The continuous exchange of information and experiences that sailors traded in the commercial harbors visited by ships from different countries, undoubtedly favored the spread of innovations to everybody's advantage. Similarly, with the advancement of technical knowledge progress also affected the art of sailing in general, with improved specifics for maneuvers, hydrography, coastlines, winds, currents and other various aspects of open-sea running. Improvements that together helped to avoid sailing disasters while increasing safety in navigation.

Nordic and Atlantic Ships

Coastal navigation in the Northern seas and the Atlantic ocean had contributed little to the progress in the art of sailing over the course of the first millennium. Those were rough seas, and what little trading was necessary could usually be carried out with less danger by land, with the exception of that directed toward the British isles.

But around the end of the seventh and the beginning of the eighth century something stirred, particularly in the Scandinavian peninsula. The long oar-propelled ships, with double planking, such as those found at the Nydam peat bog in Schleswig [Northwest Germany] in 1863 and at Kvalsund, Norway, in 1920 had evolved into real ships (with no deck yet) with a large square sail and a single lateral blade rudder, mounted on the right side of the hull by means of a strong binding made of pine roots. (The "steer board," i.e., the side where the rudder was mounted, called *styre board* in Swedish, is now called the *starboard* in English, denoting the right side of the vessel, in much the same way that the term *port*, i.e., the left side, was possibly derived from the fact that ships preferred leftside docking precisely on account of the absence of the rudder assembly.)
The celebrated Viking ships were developed along these lines. Some of these vessels have providentially survived through the centuries, so that we need not make up elaborate and, often, implausible conjectures about how they were built.

The hull of a large Viking warship was brought back to light at Gokstad in 1880. The ship was a *Drakkar* (dragon) or *Skeid*, used as a funerary monument. It was buried under a thick layer of blue clay that had preserved it perfectly, to the point that the oak wood making up the hull was "as sound as though the ship had been built the day before." Other such findings had taken place at Borre in 1850 and at Tune in 1867. A further discovery, made in 1904 at Oseberg near Sandfjord, was that of a ninth-century ship, called *Karv*, which appeared to have been built for recreation or fishing. Freight boats, probably the most numerous, were instead named *Knorr*; a specimen of these was found buried in mud in Ross Fjord in Denmark in 1962, where it had sunk. Much shorter than warships (between 15 and 20 meters all-out, and 4 to 6 meters at the beam), they had a broader round hull, better suited for cargo, were made of pine wood and had a half deck at the bow and the stern ends. The state of preservation of freight ship relics is not good, being the result of shipwrecks, whereas warships or pleasure boats, worthy of becoming the sepulchre of important people, were preserved virtually untouched with all their fittings intact.

All these vessels shared many construction features, whereas the decorative elements differed from type to type and were probably missing altogether in *Knorrs*.

The wheels, both curved, were set onto a robust single-piece oak keel.[5] The planking, consisting of overlapping strakes, was fastened to the slim framing with bindings made out of fir roots, whalebone stripes or also thin raffia filaments. Wool strands were used for caulking. Such a primitive construction system had the advantage of conferring to the ship a higher flexibility than she would have had if her framing had been rigidly connected with metal nails. Besides, these were very light hulls, probably not long-lasting, although easily repairable.

We have dwelt briefly on the main structural characteristics of these Nordic ships, because they have influenced all the following crafts sailing in those seas. The construction with overlapping strakes, instead of flush planking (long since the prevalent method in the South), would be commonly used by Northern shipbuilders through the fifteenth century.

Viking ships, though flimsy in appearance, certainly crossed the North Atlantic several centuries before Columbus's exploit, reaching the coast of Newfoundland and the American mainland. Chance or, perhaps, necessity had driven these adventurous seamen that far, but an echo of their achievements must have passed on in folk tales. The fact that distant overseas lands, be they Asia or something else, could be reached by crossing the ocean was well known to the mariners who put to sea at the end of the Middle Ages — though with quite different designs.

For an examination of ships of more recent construction, one needs no longer rely on fortuitous archeological discoveries. A relatively abundant documentation is available thanks to a great number of illustrations on manuscripts and on the seals of maritime cities reproducing pictures of ships with great attention to details, for their authors saw the actual ships every day and were thus very familiar with the models.

[5] It has been calculated that, to make the keel of the Gokstad ship a 75-foot tall oak had been used, When a replica of this ship was built in 1893 to cross the Atlantic and be shown at the Chicago International Exposition, a Canadian oak was imported for the keel, because it had been impossible to find a tree of such size in Norway.

These vessels had slender bow and stern, high fineness coefficient, moderate draft, overlapped planking (though nailed down, and no longer bound the Scandinavian way), deck support beams protruding outside the hull, lateral blade rudder, light embattled fake castles at bow and stern ends, of almost identical dimensions, which had exclusively defensive purposes. Oar propulsion had by this time been abandoned, and the large square sail was supported by a single central mast, surmounted by a small towery top, this too with a defensive function.

One of the problems faced by sailors was to reduce the sail's surface when the weather turned bad, and wind conditions deteriorated to the point of negatively affecting the ship's safety on account of the large quantity of exposed sail.

In ancient times, two entirely different systems were adopted to solve this problem. The first one, adopted in Northern Europe, perhaps of Viking heritage, was to lower the yard a little and trim the sail from below, rolling and tying up a portion of it like a sausage by means of sheets predisposed on the sail itself. The portion of the sail thus subtracted to the wind is called *terzarolo* [reef, in English], an antique term already documented at Dante's time. We find it, in fact, in some famous verses of the *Divine Comedy* (Inferno, XII, 7-16[**]), addressing this topic with referring to the Venice Arsenal: *altri fa i remi ed altri volge sartie, chi terzaruolo ed artimon rintoppa* [some at the oars and others furling sails, some reefing or mending sails]. The denomination quite likely reflected the fact that the reduced portion corresponded roughly to one third of the whole sail. The reef itself shows a reinforcing stripe (the reef band), sewn onto the sail itself which contains regularly spaced eyelets [reef points] through which hemp brails [the sennits] pass from side to side of the sail, held by line knots (the reef's earings) whereby the trimmed portion of the sail is tied up.

These terms and related techniques would still be extant, if we still plied the sea on sailships. With the difference that the ancient custom was later (in the seventeenth century) reversed, placing the portion of sail to be trimmed, delimited by the reef band, not below but above, thereby reducing the sail but avoiding the crudely described "sausage" operation as it could be tied down to the yard spar. Anyway, this sail-reducing technique, or reefing, was a very ancient practice, perhaps adopted by the Scandinavian themselves, certainly used in the thirteenth century by seafaring populations in the North Sea.

The second system, entirely different, was used in the Mediterranean, and is still documented on Columbus's *Santa Maria*, a Spanish ship. We describe this technique right away, thus clearing the field from this subject.

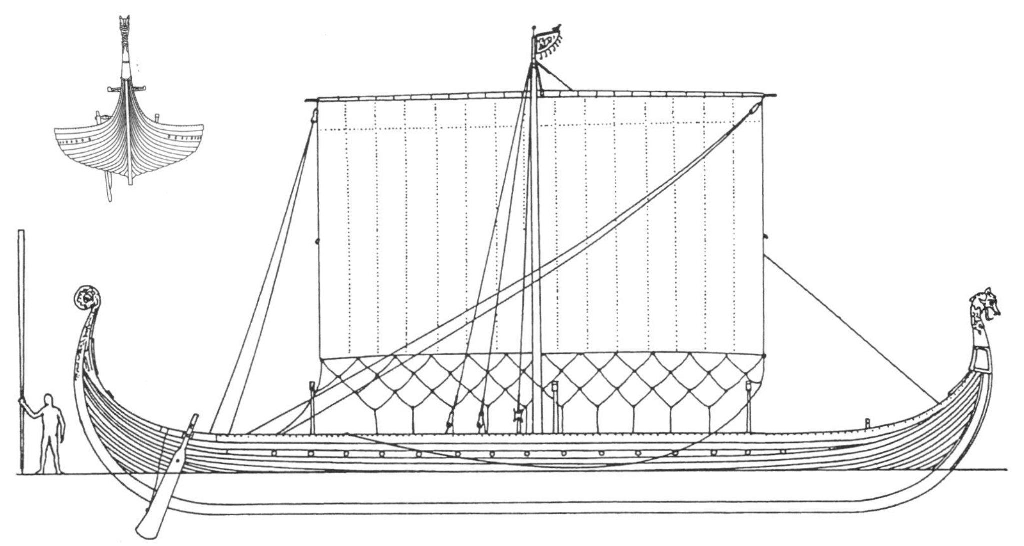

Viking Drakkar, a long warship (drawing by F. Gay).

Norwegian freight boat.

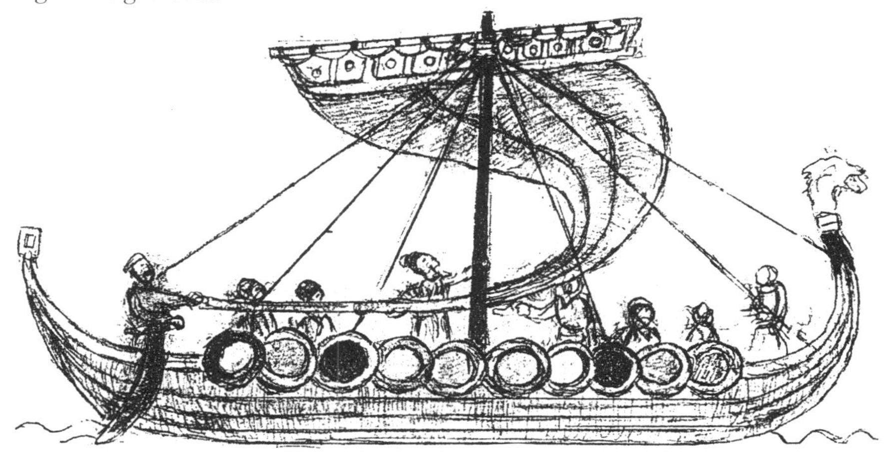

Norman warship of the same type as the Drakkar (from the Bayeux tapestry). Sketches by C. Ciano.

Norman ship on a Dunwich seal of about 1200. The derivation from Viking models is evident.

A thirteenth-century Winchelsea seal.

The procedure was quite radical: instead of reducing the sail's surface while keeping it whole, one would remove a part of it outright. The full sail in fact consisted of two or three independent sections, tied together with a binding rope (see depiction on p. 44). Performing this operation required lowering the yard as needed, with the added benefit that in bad weather this improved the ship's stability. The method had its advantages: the removal of canvas lightened the load on the masts, and the unremoved portion of sail, typically made of heavier fabric suitable for bad weather, was just the right amount. There were, however, drawbacks: the operation of removing the detachable sections, referred to as "bonnets," was laborious. It had to be done in a timely fashion and with not too stiff a wind, not to mention the fact that the lacing constituted a weak point for the entire surface: it created a gap through which the wind would force itself, and tended to tear up the sail. Furthermore the two or three sections, even when tensed together, ballooned under the wind's thrust in an uneven fashion that, while it could be tolerated when running free, was just about the worst occurrence when there was the need for tacking, catching the wind close-hauled.

To ensure that, when the full sail surface was restored, the bonnets could be properly fastened at the right place and prevent mistakes due to haste or confusion, sails and bonnets frequently bore corresponding marks, which traditionally carried a religious meaning. (Sailors, exposed to the dangers of their trade, were particularly devout.) For instance the letters *A V M G P* on the left front side of a sail, followed on the right side by the letters *P G M V A*, conveyed an invocation to the Virgin Mary, the object of the highest devotion: *Ave Virgo Maria Gratia Plena* and *Pande Gratia, Maria, Virgo Admirabilis* ["Hail Virgin Mary, full of grace," and: "Display your grace, admirable Virgin"]. Two other documented religious refrains were *DOMINUS TECUM BENEDICTA* ["The Lord be with you, blessed one"], couched on the line joining the first and the second bonnet, and *AVE MARIA GRATIA PLENA*, repeated on the second bonnet from the top and on the lower edge of the sail.

At the end of the thirteenth century Nordic ships had a single look, with almost no difference between the military or mercantile types. Certainly there was the capability to build larger, more capacious, perhaps more seaworthy vessels (although this cannot be ascertained from the extant seals and miniatures). Their ships exhibited an increasingly prominent bow and stern castles, projecting beyond the cutwater at bow and beyond the stern wheel (it would be improper to speak in terms of a post, in this case, because the prow and poop yards are rounded.) There still was a single central mast, with the large reef-rigged square sail: a sloping yard made its appearance at the bow end, not in order to rig a sail (like a bowsprit), but as a fastening post for the blocks through which the tacking cables ran.

Then a new sailing technique made its appearance. In order to navigate to a windward point, which is properly referred to as *tacking* or sailing on a bowline, a square sail must be hauled taut [close-hauled] so as be trimmed almost parallel to the keel, but not perfectly parallel, because in such case it would not work. Incidentally, this would not even be feasible for a square sail, since the yard, encumbered by the mast-supporting riggings, cannot be trimmed at an angle smaller than approximately 60 degrees,[6] and the sails would not carry, since they cannot efficiently exploit the wind at angles smaller than 45 degrees. To set or trim a square sail in this way, one must operate from above with one of the clewlines that help to turn the yard by hauling it taut sternward[7] and from below by pulling the master sheet on the corresponding side. The vertical part of the sail, which remains before the mast, would not carry efficiently if it did not have a tacking cable, precisely the *bowline*, which holds it taut by pulling toward the bow.

Overall, bowline rigging consists of different elements: several bull's-eye cringles, small rope handles or metal rings spliced onto a sail's edging cord known as a leechrope (i.e., onto the ropes or cables sewn to the sail to reinforce its vertical hems), several bridlelets (rope sections connecting two cringles like a bridge), and finally the bridle or head-framer that pulls together a number of bridlelets in a single point tensing them sternwards (see fig. p. 57).

We realize that for a person not too conversant with naval subjects this string of unfamiliar names (as well as others that will follow) may perhaps result unintelligible and tedious, notwithstanding some efforts to give plain explanations of the terms. Yet, whoever approaches so specific a subject as ships should figure in a needed special effort to get acquainted with a jargon borne with hardly any change throughout the centuries and without which it would be exceedingly difficult to describe a ship and her components.

[6] Braced or trimmed, i.e., oriented in one or the other direction, working on one of the arms or clewlines that start from a yard's top ends and run down the sides terminating at the ship's stern.

[7] The master sheets (ropes) are single or double cables, possibly equipped with a system of pulleys and tackles, which pull the clews, that is, the lower corners of a sail, either to stretch them out in the wind or hauling them close. A square sail has double cables for each of its lower-end clews. Similarly, triangular and trapezoid sails, the lateen sail included, have two master sheets, but both are fixed on the single lower clew; only the lee-side sheet is hauled in, keeping the other ready to be pulled when heaving, which obviously calls for re-orienting and thus trimming the sail.

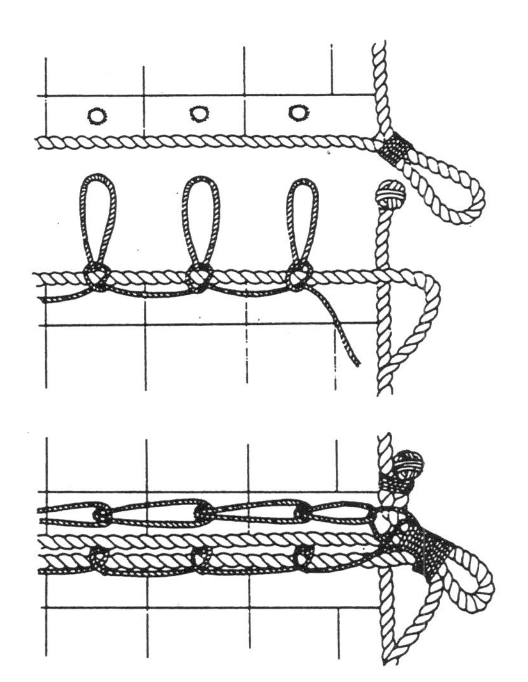

Tying a bonnet to the sail. Above: sail and bonnet separated; below, sail and bonnet tied together. (From *Die Shiffe des Cristoforo Colombo* by W. zu Mondfeld).

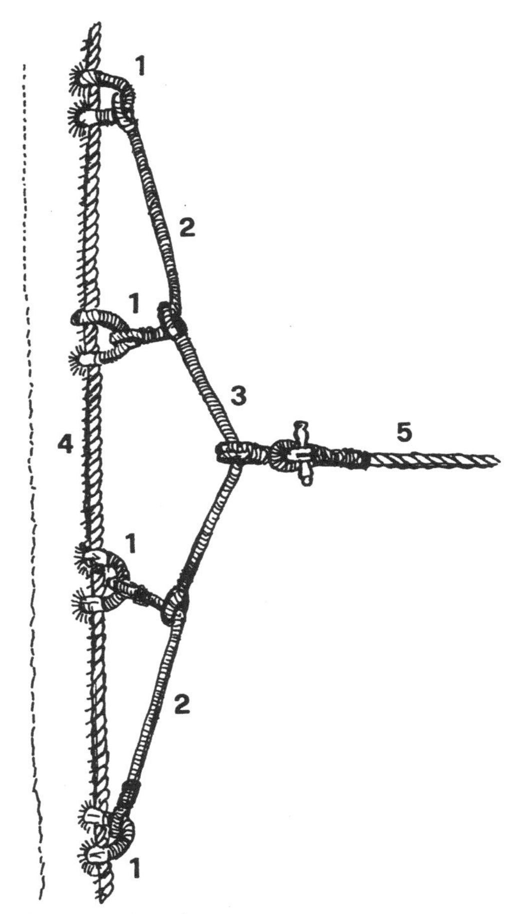

Tack rigging.
1) bose - 2) bridlelets - 3) bridle - 4) leechrope - 5) tackrope.

Hanseatic cog on a seal from Elbing of 1350.

Stralsund seal. Aside from a lack of proportions, on both seals the representation of the fourteenth-century Anseatic cockboat is very accurate.

Tackropes and bowlines became commonplace on Nordic vessels around this period [end of the thirteenth century]. In the Mediterranean, where the lateen sail was in use, there was no need for bowline sailing, because in a triangular sail the section exposed to the wind is almost entirely sternwards of the mast, while the part facing the bow remains hauled taut by the yard itself.

Similarly, the fact that Nordic vessels had their bow and poop both spear-shaped may have led to the introduction of the single rudder hingedonto the sternpost. Before adopting this solution, however, the rear of Nordic ships had to abandon the prevailing curved shape and actually become a post. That probably occurred in the thirteenth century when some merchant towns and outposts of northern Germany formed the Hanse or Hanseatic League.[8] At that time, a different, though not much more advanced craft began to prevail: the *Kogge*, or cog (cockboat).

Cogs and Caracks

The first known cogs, as they figure especially on the seals of trading seaboard cities, look so remarkably different from the crafts employed until then as to make one suppose that this kind of vessel had been conceived in an entirely novel way, forsaking what had been a tried and true tradition. (It is almost certain that those engraved on seals were the most popular types of ship, or vessels assumed to be emblems of wealth and security.) However, this had seldom happened in the naval field, where every innovation was the product of evolution and typically derived from enlarging previous models. Thus, putting aside the theory that cogs were born as an autonomous invention, one can conjecture that she was indeed derived from a locally used craft, already successfully experimented.

The cog originated in all likelihood on the Baltic sea, perhaps near the city of Lübeck, the seaboard center of the Hanseatic League. The Baltic is a land-locked sea with much different characteristics than those

[8] It is hard to describe the juridical status and equally difficult to establish with certainty when this trade confederation, or Hanse, came about. Born as merchant guilds, each member party was under the control of their hometowns before gradually becoming regional associations that would coalesce into the Hanseatic League [*Hansa* in OHG]. Probably, the guilds reflected verbal agreements among merchants involving charters, customs and precedents, progressively broadened and formalized in 1241 by the cooperation agreement between the free cities of Lübeck and Hamburg forming the League's central nucleus [based on Lübeck's unwritten law]. It was joined successively by up to 90 cities as full members and 74 more cities qualified as members at large.

found on the irascible North Sea. Merchant sailing in the Baltic did not require slender or particularly well-built ships such as the ones that plied the lanes to England, France and Spain. A simpler and rougher construction of the type Baltic shipbuilders could offer as the fruit of their regional experience satisfied their needs once it met the requirement of large holds warranting the safe transportation of bulk goods to Scandinavia and Eastern Europe. The cog of that time — the thirteenth and the fourteenth centuries — seems to have been a ship of remarkable size, larger than its contemporaries, yet with very simple design, with straight stempost and sternpost slanting respectively forward and backward, as well as an almost flat bottom at midship that tied in, somewhat abruptly, with the wide V-shape frames at bow and stern ends, and overlapping planking boards inserted into notches predisposed on the main frames. Prow and poop were alike, rather sharpened so as to avoid the laborious operations required to curve the planking strakes, which, unlike the Vikings' long, well-worked and regular boards, were shorter pieces adapted quite irregularly patched depending upon their size. The hull was decked with a large hatch-way at the center, had a large adventitious (that is, not integrated in the rest of the hull structure) bridge at stern end as well as a small bow castle, projecting onto the yard. One single mast at midship with the large square sail, and a central rudder hinged onto the sternpost with bracing pintles and gudgeons (the pintle being the male pivot fastened to the rudder, which engages the gudgeons, rings secured to the sternpost) completed this coarse, roughly-hewn hull, oddly reminiscent of a schoolchild's paper boat. Had the Bremen cog, which revealed the real features of this kind of ship, not been found, the details so carefully represented on the seals might have been misread as stylizations concocted by an artist not familiar with life at sea.

For almost two centuries the cog was the unchallenged protagonist of North Sea trade without undergoing any substantial modification, save perhaps for the tendency of giving greater prominence to the stern quarterdeck, achieved by building it as a single piece with the bulkhead. At the same time, however, merchant crafts of similar characteristic were also being developed elsewhere, but the cogs that were built in England, in Portugal, and later on in the Mediterranean, all had round bow and stern, even if the latter maintained a straight post, by now indispensable to support the Navarrian-style rudder.

Even in the Mediterranean, therefore, cogs became the typical merchant ship. However, by the end of the fourteenth century and throughout the next, the Mediterranean model was quite different from the prototype developed almost two centuries earlier in the Nordic seas. The Venetian unit, which Vittore Carpaccio painted with painstaking care (in the last

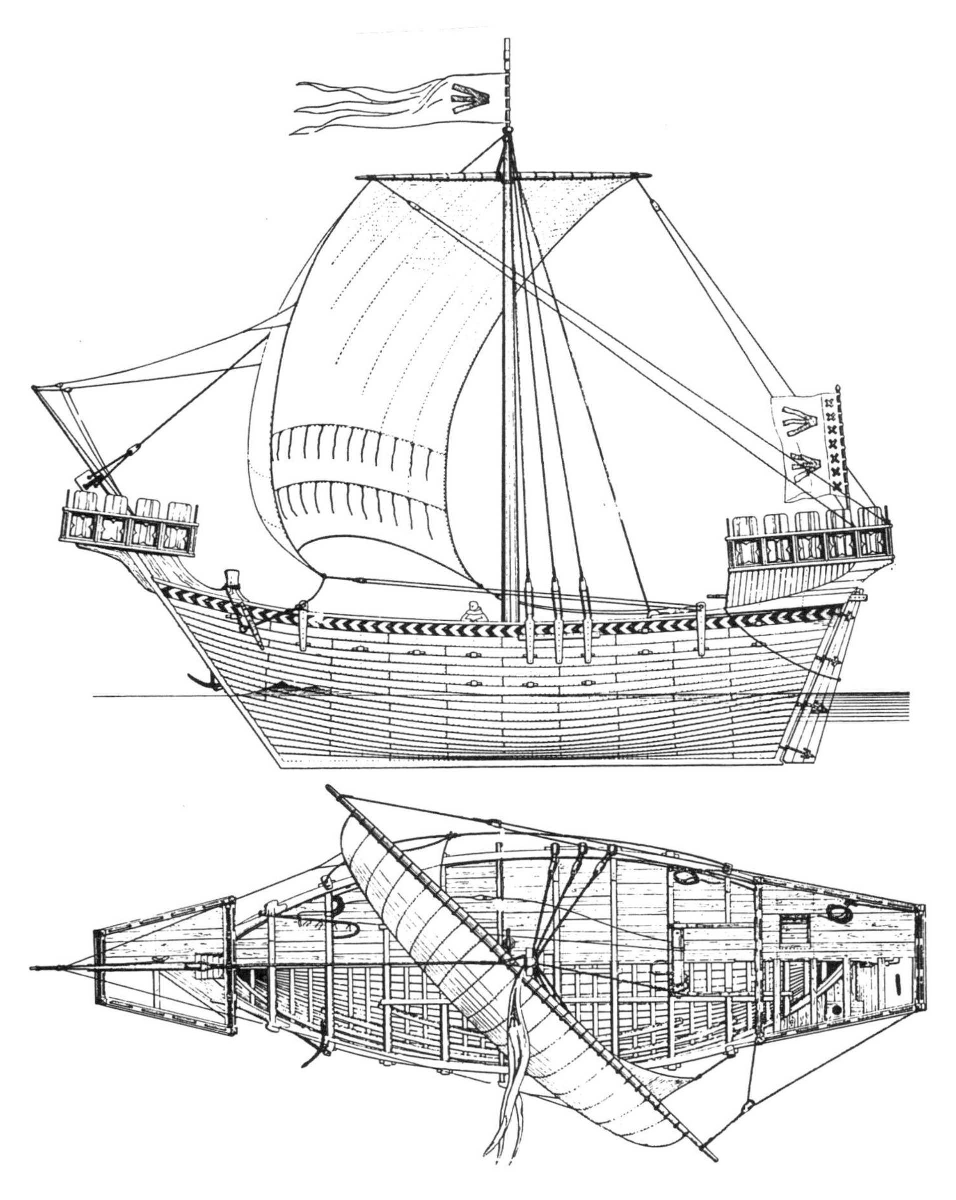

A fourteenth-century Hanseatic cog, designed by Giorgio Osculati, reproducing basic features of the cog found at Bremen and documented in city seals of that time. (From *Enciclopedia di Navi e Modelli di Navi*, 1978).

Venetian cogs in a detail of a canvas from the St. Ursula cycle by Vittore Carpaccio. One may notice that these fifteenth-century Mediterranean ships are quite different from the original Nordic cogs. Many details of these vessels are similar to those which appeared in the same age on the Iberian ships along the Catalan and Andalusian coasts, and which by then belonged to the same family of Mediterranean merchant marines.

years of the 1400s) had high rotund sides, round duckbreast bow and equally rotund stern, with the planking strakes rising toward the transom or transverse beams attached to the sternpost. The strakes, however, were butt-jointed (not overlapped) as typically done in the Mediterranean (where probably traditional shipbuilders could not construct a clinker-built vessel, that is one with overlapping planks, a working method alien to Venetian tradition). The hull was heavy and almost as wide as half its length, externally strengthened by conspicuous longitudinal furrings or runners and by sturdy vertical ribs which buttressed the structure further bolstering its solidity. The big central mast, surmounted by a striking round crow's nest and sporting a huge square sail as the main part of the rig, was complemented by a small foremast rising from the forecastle, also fitted with a square sail, and [on the stern] by another small mast, the mizzen mast, with a lateen sail. The prow's castle or forecastle was an important but patently light structure, higher than the quarterdeck, but not very prominent on these Venetian cogs.

Although the original Nordic cogs, quite likely kept on combing the Mediterranean, the much improved, latter-day Venetian cog had scored a major advancement. It now was a rather elaborate type of ship, not too far off from what will be the standard Mediterranean ship of the end of the 1400s (to which category belonged the *Santa Maria*).

By the fifteenth century the differences in shipbuilding between northern and southern Europe may be considered as by and large obsolete. Another huge vessel plowed European seas: the carack, seemingly of Portuguese origin, which spread through the Mediterranean during the fifteenth century. (Its name, however, already occurred in Dandolo's *Cronaca*, as early as the thirteenth century, to denote large freight galleys which could transport 300 men and 300 horses. The uncertainty surrounding ambiguous denominations of medieval ships is still a cause of perplexity.) These caracks, as beamy and massive as cogs, with carvel-built side plates with girdling planks fastened vertically with wales, could displace up to two or three thousand tons and had therefore considerable cargo capacity. On the bow there was a high forecastle like that on cogs, and similarly high platforms, but the stern was surmounted by a sizable battlement, too.

Square poops first appeared on sixteenth-century caracks: we shall fully discuss this novel element in describing the caravels, as this feature would characterize the galleys and all large sailships ever since. Masts were improved with respect to earlier versions: the prow boom, inclined a bit forward off the bow, anticipated the bowsprit, onto which the spritsail would make its first appearance, so called because the small square sail gathered under the bowsprit was diagonally extended by a sprit to keep the bow on course when broadsailing. Called *civadiera* in Italian, its name, of uncertain etymology, seems to have come from Spanish *cebadera*, the hay sack tied under a horse's muzzle, allowing the animal to feed without being pulled him off the cart. At bow end there was, as usual, the fore mast with square sail; at midship the imposing main mast with a large coursesail [storm sail popularly], known in Italian as *trevo*, *treo*, *trego*, *treguo*, *treso* or *trieggo* (the squaresail with rectangular rather than trapezoidal shape, like the lower sails of the major masts) and a small topsail above the round top, then a mizzenmast and a fourth minor mast [the jury mast] at the extreme aft nicknamed the "good venture" mast, both with lateen rigs. For the first time ratlines appear on the shrouds, and this, too, is an innovation coming from the North: before their introduction, to go from the deck to the crow's nest or the main yard there was a mast-supported ladder-step with bars forked at each end, placed horizontally between adjoining shrouds, the forks fitting upon each, so as to keep them apart as they approached the mast-head. During the sixteenth century the large-tonnage carack, equipped to carry numerous artillery pieces, acquired increasingly elaborate masting and riggings (topsails and auxiliary top gallant sails on the two main masts, lateen topsails above the tops of the mizzen and 'good venture' masts) and became the most powerful vessel in Atlantic fleets.

Counting the crew, soldiers and passengers (when the ship was on a commercial voyage), more than a thousand people could be on board of one of these mastodons. Daniele Bartoli wrote: "...she can hold a veritable population of men in addition to a world of merchandise, so that including officers and sailors, soldiers... merchants accompanied sometimes by their entire families, slaves and all other service crews, the number amounts to eight hundred and occasionally even one thousand heads, each one with his assigned station, more or less comfortable depending on his office and rank."

Arab ships

In order to be able to contextually describe the ships that carried Columbus and his men to the other side of the Atlantic, we have so far backtracked in time, and attempted to summarize the major stages of development. We have deemed useful to begin by giving a rough idea about how a generic small-size ship — comparable to the Columbian vessels — was built and then, proceeded by way of introduction to the coming discussion on the shapes and features of the ships used by the

Two drawings from the treatise on shipbuilding by Timbotte of Modone, *circa* 1445, displayed at the British Museum, London. They represent, schematically, a cog and a large ship, perhaps a carack, of the second half of the fifteenth century. The carack, described as having a capacity of 700 casks, is 36 feet high at the bow, 14 and-a-half steps long at the keel, 21 feet high at the stern. Prominently visible are the external girdles and vertical ties that reinforce the hull.

Two fine woodcuts by the unknown master W.A. represent Flemish cogs of the second half of the fifteenth century. Perspective distortion aside, these drawings accurately depict many details of the hull and fittings of ships that were quite similar to contemporary Spanish vessels such as the *Santa Maria*. Clearly shown are the quarterdeck and the castle, though they look as if they were leaning onto the hull proper, and exhibiting some openings that might have been no longer present on the Columbian flagship. Note also that topsail and jury mast are missing, while the spritsail yard, apparently missing too, is probably stored on the castle deck together with the bowsprit. One should as well notice (top figure) the central leechrope, though the sheet holding it downward is missing. The strange arching of the rigging that make the sails resemble curved canopies, albeit extremely inefficient, served the double purpose of reinforcing the sail itself while avoiding, as it ballooned, the wear and tear against the strong mainstay on the bowside.

A detail from another woodcut by W.A. From bow to stern, one may notice the small spritsail yard, with its sail gathered and the clewlines and masterlines seemingly needled through holes in the castle parapet; the bow arch with lateral steps to ascend to the castle; the ratlines on the mainmast's shrouds; the main yard with the furled sail; and, in great evidence, the small wooden balls of the parrel-truck holding the sail arrangement of the upper yard. On the hull, the scupper holes or limbers, a conspicuous channel bar or shroud fender [to spread the shrouds and keep them clear from the bullwork] and possibly other permanent fenders, of unclear function, hardly discernible under the main girdle. The stretching screws or shroud tensors appear to be wrapped, as it was common habit, to keep the dead-eye blocks and relative cursors (short ropes or lanyards) dry.

Large carack, from a woodcut by W. A. (*circa* 1470), with ample forecastle and quarterdeck, a sizable mizzen sail, two armored crow's nests accessible by rope ladders hanging along the masts, since there are yet no ratlines on the shrouds. Quite detailed is the running rig: runners and tackles of the yards and spars, brace ropes and trails [clew-, bunt-, and leechlines].

Perspective views of the hull of a fifteenth-century Hanseatic cog. This type of vessel, too, evolved so much as to resemble, by this time, most other large ships of the late Middle Ages. (Drawing by E. Lusci)

Schematic representation of a late fifteenth-century carack. By then, the difference between cogs and caracks was probably just in their dimensions — with the caracks being larger and showing more extensive development of the sail rigging, which ensured greater balance. The sixteenth-century galleon would derive from a further evolution the carack and from the acquisition of more modern hull shapes, developed on the basis of accumulated experience in long oceanic navigations on caravels. (Drawing by F. Gay)

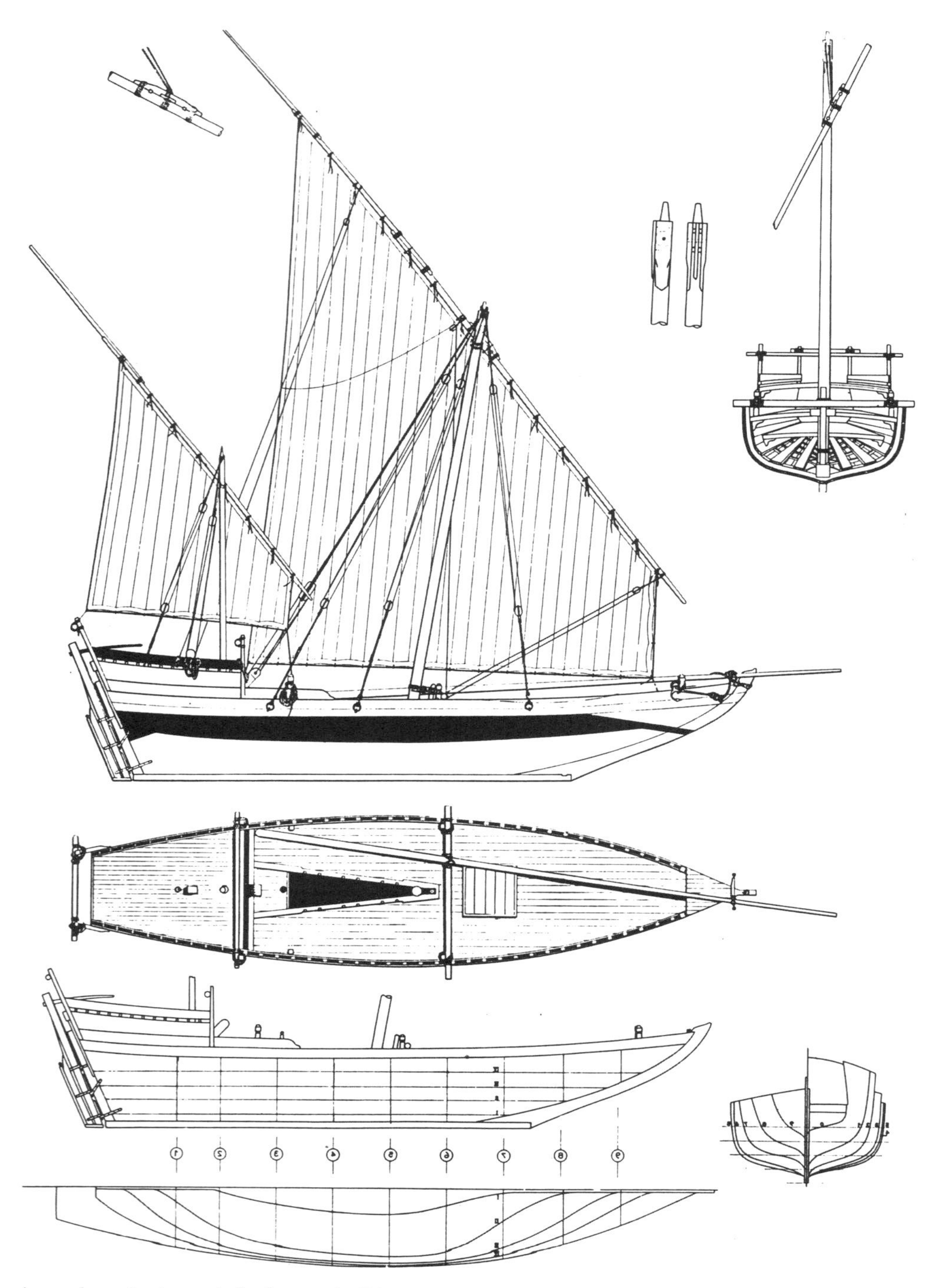

A modern Arab *sambuk*, from a building plan by Enzo Lusci. The characteristic sail shape used on Arab vessels is well illustrated.

Genoese navigator, to offer a review on ships' evolution in the Middle Ages. Thus, we tried to illustrate the conceptual development of vessels that preceded the *Santa Maria*, in particular up to the end of the fifteenth century. We shall now elaborate on which other influences played in the rise of the caravel, whose origin remains a bit mistifying on account of its remarkable differences in respect to the types of crafts considered up to this point.

Our panoramic overview would not be complete without mention of another very important area of maritime trade, although probably not as fervently active as the European: the Indian Ocean and the seas around the Arabian peninsula. There are many noticeable similarities between an Arab ship such as the *sambuk* and the fifteenth-century Portuguese and Spanish caravels. The *sambuk* was a small decked craft of about thirty tons or little more, one or two forward-raked masts and sails not exactly rectangular as lateen sails, actually almost quadrangular, with their fore side so short as to deceptively appear triangular. Referred to by the Europeans as the cutter-sail or lugsail, from the name of a small, fast Saracen boat, it was the type of sail exclusively employed on Arab vessels. As indicated earlier its shape might well explain the theory of a scholar, Pino dell'Orco, about the origin of the lateen sail, interpreted as the outcome of a modified square sail for tacking close-hauled, i.e., in bowline sailing. Until recently *sambuks* navigated along the coasts of the Red Sea, Somalia and the Indian Ocean reaching as far as the northwest coast of India. Yet, owing to the increasingly widespread adoption of motors, sail-fitted *sambuks*, too, have now all but disappeared.

A *sambuk's* hull, like that of similar crafts, had sleek lines, though a bit fuller at midship, forward-pitched bow, deep keel, and a mirror-like square stern. Thanks to their large sails, supported by two forward raking or sloping masts, these vessels excelled in catching the wind, to the point of sailing at 60 to 65-degree angles against it. Still, this may not be much if compared to gaff-sails mounted, for instance, on modern sailboats, but more than acceptable for tacking.

The somewhat crude construction of these small crafts was not of detriment to their seaworthiness, so much so that large ones engaged in difficult sailings with small crews along the western shores of the Indian Ocean and open-sea crossings to reach the islands.

The actual resemblance between *sambuk* and caravels might suggest that the latter served as a model to Arab shipwrights. From the coasts of Africa to the Persian Gulf, one could have seen until recently several crafts with lugsails, two or three masts, sleek shapes like the caravels': Europeans identified all such vessels as *dhows*, a name that actually did not designate one specific type. Generically speaking, the various *bagla*, *boom*, and *ghania* were vessels with similar characteristic and could also be regarded as direct offsprings of Portuguese ships and, more particularly, of the caravels that plied those routes from the fifteenth century onward.

Certain, however, is also the news that during the voyage that took him to Calicut in 1498 Vasco da Gama met two *sambuks* on the eastern African coasts, north of the Mozambique channel, after leaving Mombasa, Kenya. This reliable report would defeat the hypothesis that these Arab boats might have derived from the caravels. On the contrary, when the Arabs saw European ships for the first time, they admired their sturdy construction, but judged them slow and difficult to handle. If we are not ready to concede that caravels, *sambuks*, and similar vessels originated independently, thus attributing the striking resemblance of these ship types to similar circumstances and needs, we could suggest the opposite theory, that is, that caravels may have emerged as the product of an influential and long-standing Arab presence in the Mediterranean, especially in Spain, which affected the evolution of European crafts.

Dividing the ancient world into separate compartments — with Europe on one side and, on the other, the Arab, or Chinese, or other nationalities — is a mistake. The reciprocal exchange of knowledge must have been, if not intense, certainly commonplace, aided as it was by trades that brought in contact different peoples, even geographically far from one another, thus making possible the transfer of ideas. Proof of this in the seafaring field is the recollection that, when Vasco da Gama reached Malindi, north of Mombasa, where he received a generous welcome, he obtained an Indian pilot, Malamo Canaca or Cano, to continue his voyage to Calicut. When this man saw the nautical instruments used by the Europeans, he showed no hesitation, proving that he was well acquainted with them. Since no other European ship, as far as we know, had ever ventured in those waters, one must conclude either that those instruments were devised simultaneously in two different parts of the globe, by intrinsic necessity; or — more plausibly — that knowledge of them had spread everywhere thanks to contacts between seamen.

The caravels

In his *Memoire n. 6* August Jal, in discussing the caravels, claims that this type of ships would not be remembered any longer than the *palandra* [a Dutch river craft] or the *orca* [or whale, a Dutch transport ship] — two medieval ship types, amongst many others of which very little is known

Studies of Arab *sambuks*, by Enzo Lusci. The evident similarity of this ship type with Portuguese caravels has prompted some to conjecture that the Arabs imitated the design of the caravels. The shape of these *sambuks*, however, is much more slender than the caravels'.

Single-mast lateen caravels with the respective fishermen/owners' signatures. (Sketched in the *Memorial de los hombres de mar del Puerto de Santa Maria*).

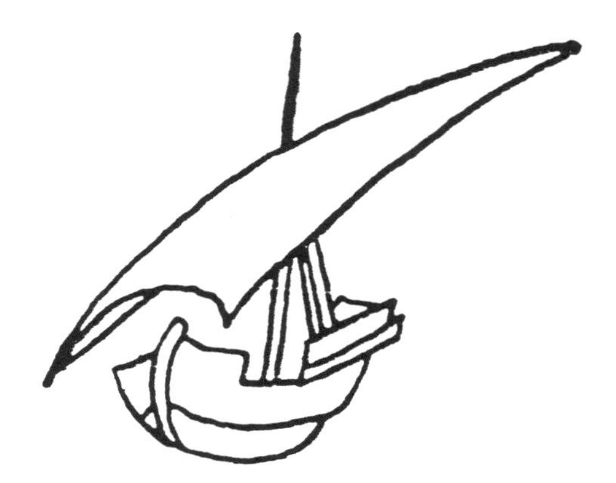

Single-mast lateen caravel from the *Arte de navegar* of 1545 by Pedro de Medina. Assuming the drawing is not just a decorative reproduction, it demonstrates that small single-mast caravels were still used for fishing along the Iberian coasts in the middle of the sixteenth century.

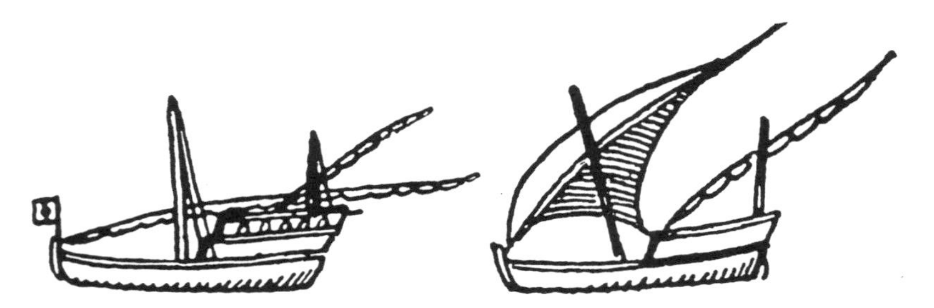

Double-mast lateen caravels in Lisbon harbor, from the *Theatrum Orbis Terrarum* by Abraham Ortelius (1570).

— had such vessels not crossed the Atlantic Ocean with Christopher Columbus. This seems utterly untrue, for among the many naval types which deserved to have their namesake preserved well past the time of their active existence — such as, for instance, the trireme, the galley, the galleon etc. — the caravel excelled above all others. This was so not merely because of Columbus's feat, but rather owing to the immense contribution that this modest vessel gave to the geographical discoveries that opened the old world to the new and made humankind aware that, as John H. Perry says, "all the world's seas are but a single sea... Any reasonably strong ship, manned by a competent crew, stocked with enough supplies and endowed with the means of finding and holding a route, may reach any country in the world that has a coastline and hence return, wherefrom she sailed."
The word "caravel" has gained such a widespread popularity that even those generally ignorant of seas and ships resort to it to designate (mistakenly) any small fragile- and flimsy-looking ship. Similarly, the term "galleon" evokes, by contrast, a world of sea battles, pirates, treasures and storms with which real galleons had little to do. And this is so not only among our contemporaries, as it held true in the past as well, to the point that the Spaniard themselves, long after the galleon had ceased to exist, continued to call the vessels connecting Spain and her American colonies with this designation.

The term 'caravel' had been used in Portugal since the second half of the thirteenth century. In the *Foral de Vila Nova de Gaia* it is written: "...Quod piscatores dent maiordomo de unaquaque caravela unum piscem" and also "*...caravela* extranea qui entrauerit per focem de Porti...." They were fishing boats, then; the term perhaps included ships with similar but not identical characteristics, depending upon the place where they had been built.

In the *Memorial de los Hombres de Mar del Puerto de Santa Maria* appear some rough sketches of caravels next to names, probably of their owners. They look like small boats with a tiny quarterdeck and a single lateen-rigged mast. After a long process, a new style of craft was evolving that would bear features decidedly superior to those of any previous ship. It was a propitious synthesis of what the tepid and sunny Mediterranean and the cold and dark Northern seas had inspired in shipbuilders (forgetting for a moment any Arab contribution), a new beginning for the evolution of ships and the art of sailing.

Of the Mediterranean ship the caravel retained the basic construction on a strong skeleton, with butted, non-overlapping strakes, that is, a rigid and solid framework. She was fitted with lateen sails, which offered the advantage of easy tacking. From Nordic vessels, the caravel inherited a slimmer shape (with the fineness coefficient even further increased, in part abandoning the *dos, tres y as* rule), a marked deck saddle, the high and slender bow to face the long Atlantic waves, the single rudder (which by now had become a common acquisition even if, as we have already pointed out, lateral-helm vessels still existed in the Mediterranean) and, finally, an absolute novelty, the flat stern, an element that made the ship easier to build and to maneuver, but adopted at a later time, during the fifteenth century. By the time of Columbus, anyhow, it represented a consolidated feature. This stern type was specific to the caravel, but successfully spread to all later-model ships, until the eighteenth century. It allowed finer profiles in the quick work making the hull more apt for speed. Furthermore, and this too was a novelty, the hull was privileged compared to the superstructures, since the caravel had no castle at the bow — an actual impediment, otherwise, for the lateen sail's long spar — and only a low stern quarterdeck, well connected to the hull of which it was a part, which extended almost to midship, protecting helmsman and crew from bad weather.

This kind of ship never had large dimensions, and many caravels were definitely small boats. The largest hardly exceeded one hundred tons and had a low draft, two characteristics that amounted exactly to what was needed in discovery voyages, during the course of which it might be necessary to tack along unknown coastlines and their untested bottoms, or to approach beaches with insidious cliffs, or to penetrate rivers' estuaries. They had usually two, seldom three, masts with lateen sails (the advantages of which we have repeatedly extolled).

The combination of these elements made the caravels much preferable to other slow and cumbersome medieval ships for exploration voyages; in such travels, moreover, it would not be economically expedient to risk large and expensive vessels with multitudinous crews. Even less suitable for such enterprises would have been, obviously, oar-propelled ships, averse to rough seas and overloaded with oarsmen, for whom one would have to guarantee food and drink at unknown places and among likely hostile peoples, had there been any. Although we do not know for certain, only one exploration voyage may have been attempted with galleys: the one organized by the Vivaldi brothers, whose fate and that of their companions remains a mystery.

Strangely, the caravel was born (or adopted) on the Iberian coasts by Portuguese and Andalusian mariners, who up to that time had given a rather modest contribution to sailing. One may justly regard that western edge of Europe as the meeting point of the Nordic and Mediterranean seafaring people; a location equal to a melting pot wherein even an Arab component

Lateen caravels and *naos* in Valença do Minho's harbor at the beginning of the sixteenth century; from the *Livro de Fortalezas de el Rey Don Manuel* by Duarte Darmas. The three-mast caravel, whose fore mast is lower than the main mast, is probably a square caravel (square sails on the fore mast and possibly also on the main mast, although the yards are not visible).

Portuguese caravels drawn on a 1520 nautical chart by Lopo Homen.

Two round caravels reproduced on the *Theatrum Orbis Terrarum* by Abraham Ortelius (1570). These caravels, following by about one century the discovery period, were fitted with four masts: three with progressively smaller lateen sails and one, the foremast, with a trysail and a topsail. A similar rigging was on the *carabelas de Armada* that Bartolomeo Crescenzio mentions in 1607, in his *Nautica Mediterranea*, as the ships used by the King of Portugal to run escort to the Indian fleet against the danger of pirates. Thus outfitted these vessels, according to Crescenzio, "proceed into the wind, the way the tartans do in our seas [the Mediterranean]." The name 'caravel' was later attributed also to ships that had only a remote derivation from the original, such as the heavy Turkish caravels, the bulky Algerian and Tunisian corsair caravels (displacing up to three hundred tons and armed with about forty artillery pieces), the small Normandy fishing caravels with two masts and square sails and jibs.
The history of Spanish caravels comes to a conclusion at the beginning of the seventeenth century; the last mention of such ships is found in a document of 1639. In Portugal, some still existed as late as the mid 1700s.

could be theorized to have blended in — for it had been the Arabs, lest we forget, that had for a long time given their contribution of knowledge and experience to those countries.

The Arabs had employed ships that they called *caravos*, which the *Cronica del Rey d'Alfonso el Onceno (XI) de Castilla* mentions with regard to the *rendez-vous* of the Granada, Tunis and Bougie armies at Albahcen in 1339, as well as to the siege of Algesiras of 1342.[9] The terminological affinity is suggestive, but D'Albertis, in his classic study on the Columbian ships, notes that the likeness is all and only in the name, or rather in the diminutive (*carabos-carabella*), since the *caravos* were fairly large vessels that could transport from 50 to 60 horses, a capability hardly consistent with ships of modest displacement such as the caravels. It should also be considered, however, that fifty is not a very large number of horses, if one takes into account how the poor animals would be stowed onboard, side by side in a barely sufficient space, kept suspended with a canvas belt under their bellies to prevent their falling down and lashed from time to time so they would kick and thus exercise a little. In any case, the generic comparative classification of crafts, rated and qualified by the various authors with a simple adjective — large, small, average size-is but an unreliable clue. The relativity of such a classification, for example, may be aptly illustrated if we recall that Pantero Pantera, writing in 1614, after describing big freight ships defines the caravels of his time as *piccioli* [tiny], when in reality they were considerably larger than those used by Columbus, to the point that a Fernan Mendes Pinto, citing them in 1538 in his *Peregrinationes*, labeled them instead as "high-side ships."

Resorting to such literary sources takes us down an insidious road, where the boundaries between truth, invention and exaggeration are hardly discernible. Nor do the etymology scholars, on the other hand, provide us with a better service; on the contrary, they drown us in a sea of peremptory definitions, where the effort to furnish an explanation by any means whatsoever yields to most imaginative inventions. Lope de Mendonça concocts an unlikely fusion of *cara* (face) and *bella* (fine), allegedly because the ship, when looked at from the stern, impressed one with her beauty and slenderness (in opposition to the expression *nao a cara de caranca*, "dog-faced ship," from which the name 'carack' would have come!). The well-known Jal resumes this odd etymologizing and then, following in his *Glossaire Nautique* the etymology offered in the 1700s by Du Cange, advances the hypothesis that the name would derive from the Latin *carabus*, a rela

[9] "...*[D]e los que facen los Moros que dicen caravos....*" "*...sesenta galeros et muchos caravos que traia cada uno cinquenta o sesenta caballos....*"

tively small ship, thence the diminutive form *carabellus* — caravel. Moreover, common people offer explanations ad libitum reflective of their own perception of a caravel, when in actual fact, as for all the naval types, there was a score of vessels classified as caravels.

At the beginning, they certainly were small fishing boats, without a deck, and with a single sail. Crafts, in other words, that gradually became bigger, fitted with a flush deck and more complex rigging and sails to finally become, as we shall see, entirely different ships from their prototypes. One should never put too much stock on names, which are naturally predicated of very different things. Just to give an example, a person who wished, a few hundreds years from now, to understand what the name 'frigate' meant could trace it to a small Mediterranean oar-propelled ship, a large seventeenth-century sail warship (though there were merchant ones, too), a small-size escort of about fifty years ago, a major contemporary missile-launching unit displacing three or four thousand tons, a typical small Portuguese boat of the Tagus area similar — interestingly enough — to an early caravel, and finally (why not?) a large tropical sea bird [known also as a man-of-war bird]. According to modern dictionaries, in current Italian language 'caravel' is also the name of a carpenter's hard glue [formerly used to join a caravel's boards], a hydrozoan, the *physalia* (a sort of jellyfish [nicknamed as well Portuguese man-of-war]), and finally a variety of pears and apples.

The typical Portuguese and Andalusian fifteenth-century caravels, the ones of interest to us, displaced approximately fifty tons [10] (in today's terms) or slightly more. They were twenty or twenty-five meters long, and were fitted with two or three lateen-sail masts, the first one set just prow side of midship, with a large sail inserted in a yard, measuring in length a little more than the ship herself. When the big yard was lowered, it rested on forks, one at stern and one at bowside close to the posthead, or perhaps on the posthead itself, if shaped to receive it, as suggested by some sketchy illustrations in which the posthead appears to be forked.

The second mast, a little less than a half as tall as the first, rose from the low quarter deck and carried a sail half as large as the main one. A third little mast, when it was present, was set at the extreme stern in an unstable fashion, but given its dimensions it did not have to bear much load and carried an even smaller sail.

The increasingly longer and more adventurous voyages by the Portogueses offshore the African continent, shrouded in the most jealous

[10] References are always to dead weight values [i.e., cargo excluded], the only meaningful ones at the time.

secrecy to avoid foreign competition, contributed to refining the art of building larger had spread the rumor that only their ships could sail along the African continent in full safety, whereas other types of crafts, such as cogs, [Dutch] hulks and other big freight ships, would have certainly wrecked, had they ventured in those waters. In order to prove their statement and instill a deeper fear into unwelcome foreigners, they went sometimes to great lengths to carry out expensive, if wily, deceits. It happened, for instance, that two artillery-carrying hulks, following a ninety-caravel fleet that had sailed from Lisbon on December 10, 1481 under Diego de Arambuja and headed for Guinea, were disassembled after unloading the materials, merely in order to lend credit to the legend that only caravels could return safely from such a perilous voyage.

Yet, apart from these cunning ways devised to protect their own monopoly--tricks that were evidently of little use to protect a secret by then well-known to Andalusian seamen--the Portuguese sailors were quite aware, by their direct experience, of the fact that their own light caravels were far superior in open seas to the heavy round vessels that had, as their major propulsion element, the large square mainsail.

We have already pointed out that the caravel had different proportions from those prescribed by the Catalonian rule *dos, tres y as*. Proportionally speaking, her length had increased to an index equal to 3.3, 3.5. Thinner, with sleek lines, sides flared upwards to gain positive thrust when heaved sideways to gain against the wind and a square stern clear of heavy superstructures made her a lighter, stronger and faster craft than any other merchant ship, while her lateen rig allowed her to tack well and drift less. Indeed, owing to the presence of a lateen sail and the necessity to maneuver the "car" or fore peak of the yard [i.e., the lower and thicker of the two spars], her builders had eliminated the forecastle, useful only when the ship was fitted with a bowsprit and its related sail. The lateen sails, trimmed in the butterfly fashion,[11] allowed her also to sail before the wind; anyway, in case of necessity, all caravels could hoist a trysail in place of the lateen sail on the foremost mast. Since with this type of navigation the square sail proved more useful, once a ship was sailing farther offshore and finding steadier wind from the aft quarters, some caravels were equipped with mixed (i.e., both types of) riggings. Fitted with a fore mast lower than the central one and set close to the

[11] This expression refers to the arrangement given to the yards of lateen or trapezoidal sails when running before the wind (on a vessel having no square sails). One of the lateen sails (or one of the trysails) is hauled in at leeside and the other at portside, so that the aft sail does not hide the wind from the foresails.

bow, the lateen caravels became *carabelas redondas* (square caravels). The latter were frequently larger than the unmodified ones and were at times fitted with four masts, of which the fore one carried, besides the trysail, also the topsail, while the bowsprit held a spritsail. Illustrations of large or "evolved" caravels of this type, which could transport up to 200 tons of cargo, are still found in documents of the latter half of the 1500s and the beginning of the following century.

The big caravels, subsequent to the glorious discovery age, were occasionally called *carabelas de Armada*; these were certainly ships of the royal fleet, destined to escort the convoys in their long voyages to India, or themselves deployed as military transport ships.
Bartolomeo Crescenzio in his *Nautica Mediterranea* of 1607 and Pantero Pantera in his *Armata Navale* of 1624 also mention these vessels. In 1618 the brothers Bartolomé and Gonzalo Garcia del Nodal went with two caravels of this kind on a reconnaissance mission of the straits of Magellan, and their ships performed so well that, according to their captains, were sail-planing. In the memoirs of the Palermitan scholar Francesco Maria Gaetani, marquis of Villabianca, written toward the end of the 1700s, we notice that the word 'caravel' was still in vogue at his time. Yet it designated smaller four-mast vessels: "...all corsair wood, brought by the Algerians, Tunisians and Tripolinians from Africa."

The first *carabelas redondas* probably originated in the Atlantic harbors of Spain; they were in fact labeled Andalusian-style caravels, but searching for primacy in their usage is of little value. What is certain is that the transformation of a lateen-rigged caravel into a square one was indeed possible and something that was performed without difficulty as the need arose, so much so that Columbus, as we shall see, before sailing off on his first voyage retrofitted the *Pinta* from lateen to square, and likewise he did for the *Niña* at the Canary Islands. (According to the biography by Ferdinand Columbus, Christopher's son, however, it was the *Niña*, not the *Pinta*, to be so converted in Spain.) [12]

Thus, throughout a two-hundred-year span several versions of these vessels were created, with changes usually involving the sail plane, because the hull in all likelihood did not undergo substantial modifications. Actually, in Columbus's time there were still *caravelloni* [13] and *caravellotti*, terms that

[12] It was probably a transcription mistake or a memory slip, for, to be sure, it was the *Pinta* and not the *Niña*.

[13] In his *Disquisiciones* (I, 130), the cited Scholar Duro maintains that the word *carabelon* is a diminutive rather than an accrescitive form, just as *galeaza* is to *galea*, and *carracon* to *caraca*.

are found frequently in the works of ancient Spanish writers and are also mentioned in Ferdinand Columbus's *Historie*, along with the lateen caravels, the square caravels, the Portuguese, Biscaian and Galician caravels.
Mired in a sea of conjectures, one can understand the bewilderment of a scholar of caravels like Fernández Duro who sums up all the arguments into the broad statement that, in the end, the term 'carabela' did not refer with this assertion, because, as one could verify, when writers of the time — unlike those of later ages, when the caravel became an almost mythical concept, and therefore less and less understood — intended to address a specific type of vessel, they consistently resorted to using its specific designations, as it is the case, or their descriptions of the first Portuguese voyages along the western coasts of Africa, done with *barchas*, that is, small and probably undecked ships that could have been the caravel's forerunners but certainly were not caravels; when vessels of different type accompanied the *barchas*, they were identified by specific designations.
Concluding the first part of our discussion, it should be reiterated that in regard to the caravels of Columbus's time factual certainties abound, with some confusion lingering due, more than anything else, to the long time span over which this type of ship was in use. Generally, every craft type undergoes a constant evolution, steadily growing from smaller to larger or from simpler to more complex. Chroniclers and historians alike do not seem to volunteer pertinent information when the subject matter falls outside their competence — shipbuilding in this instance — and frequently represented past achievements in terms of the instruments available in their own time. This fact complicates research a little, but recent studies, both deeper and more selective, have finally cleared the field from many inaccuracies and fantasies. Consequently, the generic characteristics of a caravel at the end of the 1400s can be established with sufficient approximation, regardless of whether this "ideal" caravel may or may not reflect accurately specific models such as the *Pinta* or the *Niña* — which is, to repeat once more, an entirely different matter.

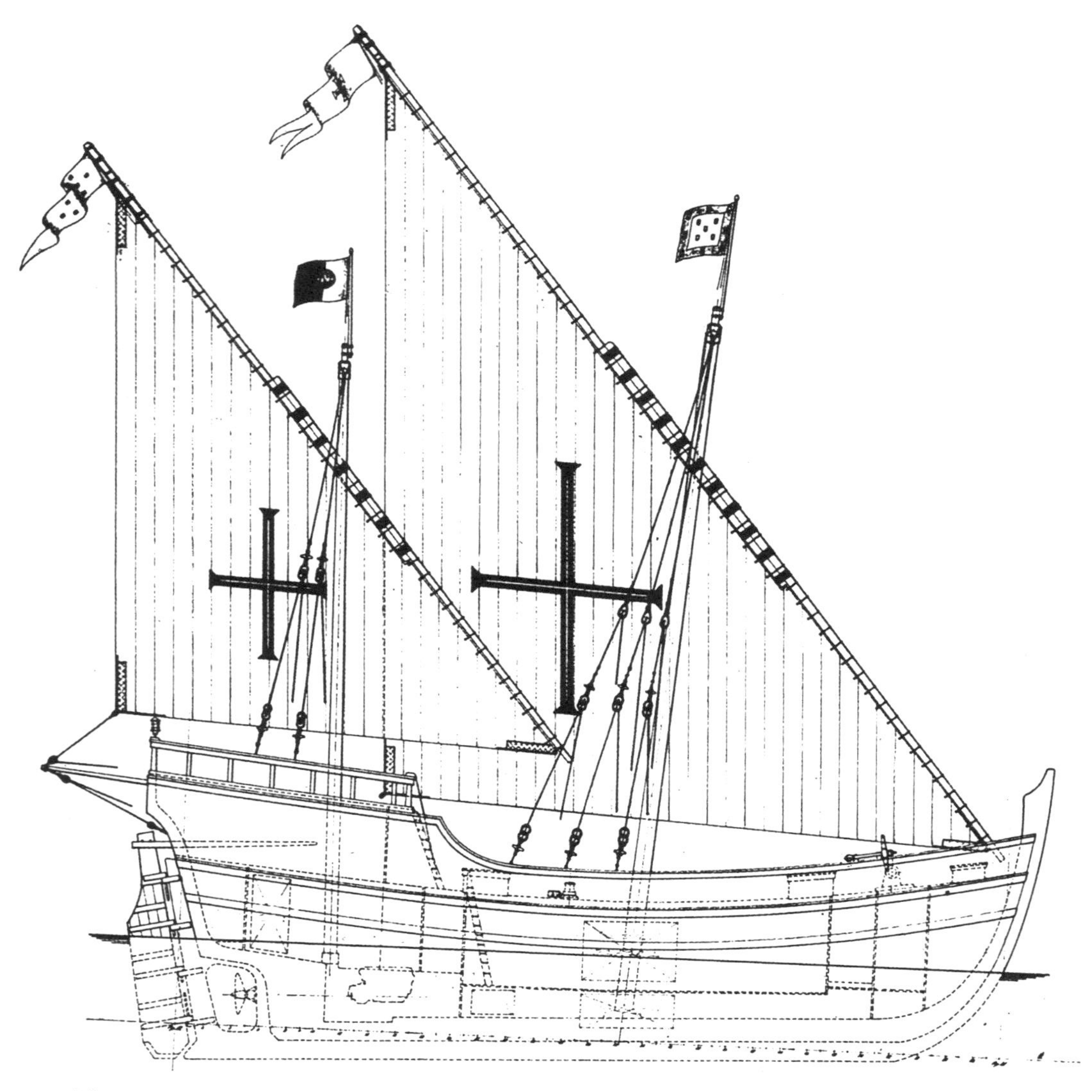

The caravel *Boa Esperança* that, together with the *Bartolomeu Dias*, was rebuilt in Portugal between 1987 and 1990 to commemorate the fifth centennial of the great Portuguese navigations and discoveries in Africa, culminated in the passage of the Cape of Good Hope. The two-mast caravel, with a hull profile very similar to the Spanish caravels of Columbus's time, has an internal space distribution suited to the demands of modern sailing, including an engine that loudly proclaims its anachronistic design. One should understand, however, that safety reasons (the ship retraced Bartolomeu Dias's route) have imposed such a compromise.

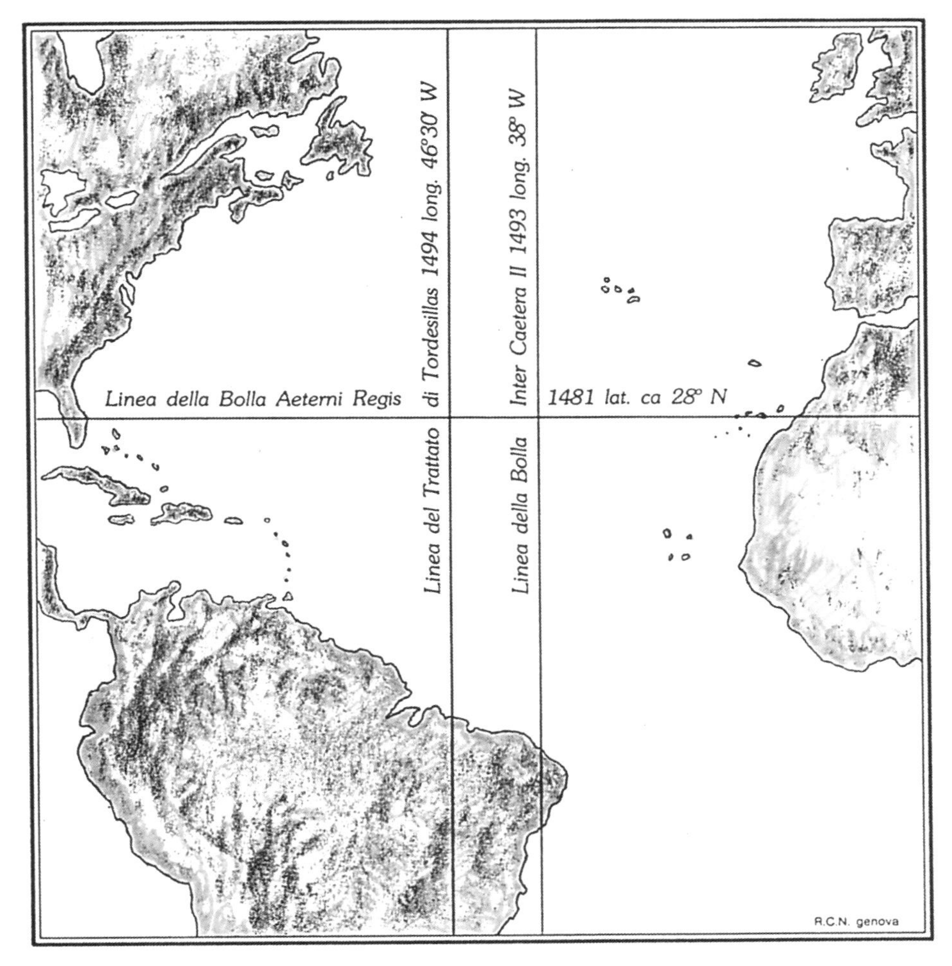

With the intent to protect their rights to the [West] Indies route (in case they found it), the Portuguese turned to the only authority that, at that time, could provide such an assurance: the Pope. In order to obtain a Papal bull that would sanction those rights they needed to establish a connection between their true interests and the propagation of the faith, along with the fight against the infidels. The Portuguese plan was to make contact with the mythical kingdom of Prester John, though it was not known where it was, and with the Indians, whom some believed to be Christian, too, or at least well-disposed toward Christians, and thus join their forces to those of European nations and expel the infidels from the Holy places. The bulls issued by the Popes on this subject were several: The *Romanus Pontifex*, of 1455, conceded to Portugal exclusive rights to the conquest of Saracen lands along the African coast. The bull *Aeterni Regis*, of 1481, divided the unknown world horizontally into two regions, reserving to the Portuguese rights to the lower region. There followed four bulls by Alexander VI, who had been solicited by the Spaniards: the most important of those, the *Inter Coetera* (1493), drew an imaginary boundary from north to south between Spanish and Portuguese interests, passing 100 miles west of the Azores and the Cape Verde islands, a somewhat vague definition because the Azores and Cape Verde islands are not on the same longitude. The objections raised by the Portuguese against this division threatened to cause a war until the Portuguese proposed to the Spaniard to move the line by 270 miles westward-a proposal that the Spanish sovereigns, attracted by the illusory mirage of having within their grasp the riches of the Orient, gladly accepted. The treaty, sealed at Tordesillas on June 7, 1494, allowed the Portuguese to conquer Brazil, the existence of which was not suspected at the time. (From *Istituto Idrografico della Marina. Agenda Nautica* 1992).

CHAPTER III

THE PORTUGUESE NAVIGATORS

D'Albertis reckoned that the Portuguese sent at least fifty caravels — "the best vessels sailing the seas" as Alvise Ca' da Mosto proclaimed in 1445 — two at a time, along the African coasts, before Bartolomeu Diaz could double the Cape Torment in 1487 and discover the passage to the Indian Ocean.

It is precisely to the Portuguese that we owe the impulse given to the search for new maritime routes in the fifteenth century. The ultimate success of this great enterprise, though slow and painful, was certainly due to the fact that new ships suited to those navigations were now available. With cogs, Dutch hulks, *marseillaises* [a kind of sloop], etc., it would not have been possible to travel so far and in relative safety. But other favorable elements must also be considered, because every event, whatever its significance, is usually the result of a live combination of several factors. At that time — after the end of the struggle against the Moors and the ensuing temporary settlement of the disputes with the kingdom of Castile — several elements worked in favor of a small Portugal: her possession of most of the Atlantic coastline on the Iberian peninsula; sustained economic development; a better judicial system, gradually emerging from the primitive common law of the Visigoths; and last, but not least, the determination of learned and provident rulers who knew how to funnel the nation's energies toward promising objectives.

King Don Dinis (1279-1325) devoted special care to the development of a merchant marine. While trade relations with Northern Europe (especially the Flanders) and the fishing industry were growing, he took the initiative to plant extensive state-owned pine forests, in order to supply the shipyards with timber, occasionally free of charge. The fame of Portuguese builders was such that in 1438 Bruges, at the time one of the most important cities in northern Europe (thanks to its manufacturing and the commercial ties it had established between the North and the South of the continent) allowed them the privilege to build caravels on its territory.

In order to reorganize his navy, Don Dinis summoned to Portugal even many Genoese seamen and among them Emanuele Pessagno, who was appointed fleet admiral and shipbuilding superintendent (1317).

The great adventure that had started to unfold in the first half of the fourteenth century, when Portuguese navigators (and Italians in their service) reached the Canaries and Madeira, continued thanks to the sons of don João, the first king of the house of Aviz: Duarte, future king, philosopher and man of letters; Pedro and Henrique, open and enterprising minds, capable of understanding that, beyond the African territorial conquests (the conquest of Ceuta in 1415 and the unlucky exploit in Tangier of 1437), the fortunes of Portugal could be realized on the sea by searching for trade routes with the Orient. The occupation of Ceuta was a very significant event, for it signaled the era of the great discoveries (some believe that 1415 should be the year marking the boundary between the Middle Ages and modern times). The siege, undertaken by 200 ships and 20,000 soldiers, was not, however, a difficult one: in actual fact, the city put up virtually no resistance, with only eight Christians dying for the enterprise. The twenty-three years old prince Henrique was the hero of the day.

The results of conquering that city, an outpost for the markets of gold and other African products, were disappointing, because the caravans traveling from the continent's interior and crossing "a sea of sand that stretched out for thirty-seven days of travel,"[14] changed itineraries once their end-station had fallen in Christian hands, jeopardizing the fate of their trades. This early disappointment, though, marked a push to search for other ways, i.e., different sea lanes, to reach beyond the desert. Thanks to the reports of Arab merchants and the few Europeans who had sojourned and gathered information for some time in northern Africa, it had been learned that the continent was not an enormous, sun-scorched sea of sand, but that beyond the desert there were fertile and inhabited lands--contrary to what had been claimed by Ptolemy, whose authority by then was declining. After all, the existence of Ethiopia had been known to the ancient world, and equally common was the belief that this mythical kingdom was Christian.

In this context began the work of prince Henrique, who would be remembered in history as "the Navigator," without actually having been

[14] Certainly the duration of the voyage could not be so exactly determined, as time was conditioned by unexpected difficulties encountered along the way. It lasted, anyway, five or six weeks.

one. The impulse he gave to the exploration of western Africa, although motivated for the most part by purposes entirely removed from scientific concerns or an adventurous spirit, bears nonetheless great significance for Portugal, as well as for European civilization, for which the boundaries of the old world expanded along those maritime routes, and was a prologue to Columbus's enterprise and all westward voyages that followed. Until then almost all sea travel had followed coastal routes between pre-established points (with the exception perhaps of the Scandinavians, who attempted long sailings in high seas). Now the Portoguese pilots became familiar with winds and currents, in order to plan a good voyage and ensure a safe return. They became acquainted with the regions of equatorial doldrums, the regimen of constant winds and currents, and thanks solely to the assistance of the few instruments that the age afforded navigation — the magnetic needle, the hourglass, the sounding line, and the firmament — they established ever more far-reaching routes toward unknown lands. To the first voyages there followed the compilation of charts, which helped pilots on later journeys. Thus, a new type of "oceanic" navigation developed, far out of the sight of coasts, heading north- or southward with the help of compasses until reaching the desired latitude, which could be calculated with sufficient approximation by measuring the North Star's height with the sea quadrant. Describing his voyage to Guinea, Diego Gomes wrote in 1462: *...ego habebam quadrantem, quando ivi ad partes istas; et scripsi in tabula quadrantis altitudinem polo artici, et ipsum meliorem inveni quam cartam* [I had a quadrant, when I went to those lands; and I wrote the altitude of the North Star on the quadrant table and I found this to be better than on the chart]. Only then one heaved toward shore and, once it was sighted, known conspicuous points were identified for a correct landing.

The return trip to Portugal required open-sea sailing, northwest bound, to avoid the area of contrary winds, the same that had helped in the incoming leg. As ships reached farther and farther to the south, the detour toward the open sea on the return leg became wider as well, to avoid the strong current coming from the Canaries and the winds blowing from the Moroccan coasts. However, sailors noticed that if they drifted too far from the beaches of Guinea they were in danger of exiting the stream of the Atlantic tradewinds and the counter-equatorial current, as well as the Guinea current coming from the east. Those navigators noted the values of magnetic declination, which had to be taken into account to caclulate the correct route, and discovered the south-westerly winds that prevailed in the gulf of Guinea. These forced the less suitable ships to follow the so-called *volta di Mina* [the turn of Mina] to return home, sailing due south first (to leave the Guinea current), then entering the south-equatorial current at latitudes between 3 and 10 degrees south, and finally reaching the south-easterly tradewinds before reaching again the North Atlantic.

The experiential knowledge thus gradually acquired was transmitted back home to other navigators and to the cartographers who updated their charts, as well as passed on to those who tried to infer general rules from astronomy, a science that until then had been used to compile horoscopes, rather than sailing rules. The history of the school of astronomy, cartography and navigation at Sagres was later widely extolled: it probably amounted to a center where data were collected and astronomers, geographers and cartographers could elaborate on the reports received from returning pilots. Most likely, scholars would learn more from these reports than they themselves already knew. These "schools" represented the foundation for subsequent voyages and explorations.

Cartography and nautical studies advanced everywhere, and the search for instruments, such as the astrolabe, which could be of help to mariners was a common aspiration. In all events, the Portuguese experiences of that age opened new horizons to the art of navigation, making sailors understand that the oceans were navigable, that the real hazards of sea-going were those they already knew--that at the Equator the sea did not boil and white men were not transformed into black ones by the sun, as it was previously feared. All the exploits that would be performed afterwards, including Columbus's navigation, are indebted to such early events.

In 1434 Gil Eanes had opened the southern ways by doubling Cape Bojador (27° North latitude). For his voyage, he had used *barchas* — smaller than caravels, as we described earlier, or perhaps their forerunners, equally swift, safe and useful to explore islets and river inlets along the coast. In order to venture farther one needed larger and safer crafts, but still small enough to be easily maneuverable, and with enough sail surface to tack deeply toward the open sea, the horizon or *volta do mar*, which was necessary to overcome the obstacle of the southbound currents near the coast on the trip back home.

The first reference to caravels sailing far off the African coastline is found in a 1441 chronicle of Nuño Tristao's voyage to the Rio de Ouro [Golden River], already discovered by Conçalves Balbaia in 1436.

In 1442-43 Nuño Tristao and others reached Cape Branco and the following year the Senegal delta. The large mass of fresh water that advanced a remarkable distance into the open sea led geographers (who studied at home the navigators's accounts) into thinking that it was a western branch of the Nile. In 1446 the mouth of the Gambia river was reached. Tristao and many of his companions were killed by Gambian natives. Seven survivors (including two seriously wounded), who in spite of their being sailors had no experience in the art of governing a ship, were led by a cabin boy who had learned by observing the pilot and managed to take the caravels back home, after two months of blind navigation, without sighting any land. This kind of feats actually confirmed the virtues of the caravels.

In 1455 and in 1456 Alvise Ca' da Mosto and Antoniotto Usodimare made two voyages in western Africa with commercial purposes, to be sure with the consent of the Portuguese. From the detailed travel report written by Ca' da Mosto, one learns how easily those routes were then plied: the long, open-seas crossing, following a course estimated by crude readings on the North Star (without instrumentation), no longer frightened anyone. Along the coast, instead, one would sail only in daylight and "with the sounding lead at hand," because navigation hazards abounded more below the surface, in the form of sand banks or submersed rocks, than on the open surface of the ocean.

Prince Henrique died in 1460, but the impetus he delivered to trade and maritime activities far outlasted his lifetime. By then, commercial interests in gold, ivory, spices, the slave trade — occasionally even encouraged by native rulers — had become so predominant that their advancement could not have been stopped by any single event. Meantime, Pedro de Sintra reached Cape Mensurado and Cape Palmas, where the African coast turns south-east toward the Gulf of Guinea. At that latitude the North Star was barely visible above the horizon; proceeding farther south, it would vanish altogether, leaving seafarers without their celestial reference. Yet in 1459 Fernao Gomes, an enterprising manager and dealer, obtained a trading license and won the bidding for a systematic commercial exploitation venturing as far as the Mina de Ouro, a coastal area still known as the Gold Coast, even though there were no mines of that metal but only a considerable trade in gold powder.

In 1471 captains sent by Gomes went beyond the delta of the Niger and found out that the coastline was again following the north-south direction. The end of the continental mass was still far away! Methodically, year after year, the Portuguese captains — Fernando Po, Lapo Gonçalves, Rui de Sequeira, in 1473-74 — pushed all the way to Cape St. Catherine, below the equator. Although most of Portugal's resources were absorbed by the exploitation of Guinea and by commercial enterprises, the southward progress continued by cautious stages, and without particular difficulties.

It was only under the reign of João II that the Portuguese began to think seriously about India and the fabulous economical opportunities that the products of the Orient could offer. Once more the mirage of wealth pushed men to seek a passage to India by sea, an objective that required exploratory, rather than commercial, expeditions. In 1482 Diogo Cao sailed from Lisbon, coasted along western Africa, cut throughout the Gulf of Guinea, discovered the Congo delta and pushed onward to Cape Lobo, announcing upon his return to have come very close to the southernmost tip of Africa. In 1485 he put again to sea, reaching Cape Cross, above present-day Walvis Bay in Namibia. The endpoint of Africa was by now relatively near, about 800 additional miles was all that remained unexplored.

Finally in the summer of 1487 Bartolomeu Diaz sailed from Portugal with two caravels and one freight ship loaded with the necessary means of sustenance to complement the limited cargo capacity of the caravels. Along southern Africa, while retracing Cao's route, the navigation was hindered by the contrary south-north currents and by the winds, also blowing from the south. At Angra des Aldeiras, Diaz left behind the freight ship that accompanied him and moved on with just the caravels. Still hampered by winds and currents, further south, Diaz took the courageous decision, probably offshore Cape Voltas, to abandon the coastal course and head toward the open sea, where he found that the adverse current had subsided and a gentle southerly wind, amenable to close tacking, was blowing. Diaz's caravels therefore continued their southbound course until they met westerly Atlantic winds that pushed them eastward. They kept sailing on that route until Diaz reckoned that the longitude of Cape Voltas had been surpassed by a good length. That meant that there was no more African land to the east — in other words, they had gone beyond the extreme tip of the continent. So Diaz decided to head north, landing two hundred and fifty miles east of Cape Agulhas, in present-day Mossel Bay, on the Indian Ocean.

His earlier decision to drift away from the coastline led Diaz to discover the circumnavigational route needed to reach the Indian Ocean by rounding the Cape well offshore. The famous Cape Tempest, the *Cabo Tormentoso* [Cape Torment] as he first called it, later renamed by king João Cape of Good Hope — Diaz saw it only on his return leg and in all likelihood was denied landfall there, on account of constantly rough seas. Local tradition has it, however, that Diaz landed on a rocky beach a bit west of the Cape that bears nowadays the name of Neptune's Dairy, reminiscent of a stirred-up foamy white sea, indeed, on one of the least welcoming places of that wonderful promontory.

Several years elapsed before the Portuguese would reap the fruits of the great discovery. Only five years after the first Columbian expedition and the discovery of the West Indies on the part of the Spaniards, Vasco da Gama set out from the Tagus with four ships: two, the *St. Gabriel* and the *St. Raphael*, were veritable warships, robust *naos*, or caracks, armed with twenty cannons each; the third one, the *Berrio*, was a small caravel from Lagos; and a nameless fourth ship, as far as we know, was a freight carack, a sort of supply carrier of the fleet. It was a well-prepared expedition with the requisite elements to face any occurrence: two ships to fight, if necessary, an exploration vessel and a support craft. The established destination this time was Calicut in India. The goal of the expedition was to affirm, before other European nations, the rights of Portugal to ply those routes to her exclusive advantage. The departure was preceded by solemn religious ceremonies, as customary at the time: a dedication to the Virgin Mary, the collective confession of the crews, with plenary absolution and commissioning of a blessed standard. A large crowd witnessed the ceremonial send-off paramount to an inaugural voyage, rather than an expedition toward the unknown.

Ever since, the maritime routes to the East and the West became distinct. Common, however, remains the inheritance of knowledge and expectations that allowed fifteenth-century seafarers to abandon the traditional coastal routes and venture confidently into the ocean, no longer as terrifying as it had at first appeared.

But at this juncture it seems proper to stop talking about the Portuguese, who have by now attained their goal, in order for us to resume consideration of the western course, the specific subject of this book.

A few years before Diaz's exploit, in 1484, Christopher Columbus, a stranger then, had introduced himself to the counselors of the king of Portugal, claiming to know the best and shortest way to reach the Indies by a westward route. The commission of experts--according to what ascertained by Taviani--was chaired by Diego Ortiz de Vilhegas, known as doctor Calçadilha, bishop of Ceuta, Viseu and Tangier, theologian, mathematician, cartographer, and the Court's appointed great Almoner. Other members of the commission were the renowned Jewish astronomer and cosmographer Josepho Virinho and the Court physician, master Rodrigo, also an expert in cosmography and astronomy.

These people did not share Columbus's optimism with regard to the dimensions of the ocean and, consequently, the relative facility of the proposed enterprise, nor did they have sufficient knowledge to disprove his theories. Anything seemed possible, owing to the lack of information on that part of the globe, limited to the vague and debatable statements by Marco Polo on the existence of "Cipango"--the Japanese islands.

What Columbus demanded to bring to fruition such an uncertain undertaking, probably looked excessive; especially after Diogo Cao, upon returning from his first voyage, had claimed to have come so near the end of the African continent, making a "western" enterprise seemed in itself a waste of resources. The passage to India had not been opened yet, but it seemed within reach; why try an unknown way in a different direction and end up not even at the desired point, but in civilized *Cipango* and *Cathai*, which were mighty and rich kingdoms indeed, but did not yield the spices and other goods so avidly sought in Europe?

Columbus's idea, though questionable, was not altogether without merit. The following year, the king granted to Fernão Dulmo from Terçeira a license to explore lands west of the Azores, including searching for a large isle to be possibly identified with the mythical Island of the Seven Cities. Dulmo sailed off in 1487, but, whether hindered by adverse winds blowing at the Azores' latitude or due to a lack of determination, found nothing and came back. So, the expedition decided by the king of Portugal apparently for the purpose of verifying Columbus's claim did not clear up the mistery. Don Ferdinand Columbus mentions a single caravel secretly sent by Portugal, under the pretense of shipping provisions to the Cape Verde Islands, whose crew "came back making light of the undertaking, and stating it was impossible to find a land in those seas." In spite of the confidential nature of the expedition — its secrecy is responsible for our dearth of information — a word of it leaked out to Columbus, who, indignant for such a royal subterfuge, left Portugal also "as secretly as possible." Columbus's wrath, mentioned by Don Ferdinand and Las Casas, must not have been too intense, however, because the relationship between João II and the navigator remained cordial. In a friendly letter of March 20, 1488, the king actually invited Columbus to come back.

The hypothetical theories concerning these events are many: conspiracies that involved Columbus's protectors; secrets known to him but that could not be revealed; the delivery of Toscanelli's letter with data that rekindled Columbus's belief in the veridicality of his thesis. Taviani also considers as plausible the thesis, put forth by others, that the Genoese had economical difficulties for which he had contracted debts that he could not honor.

When finally, in 1488, Columbus was again invited to the Portuguese court, he arrived there at the same time as Bartolomeu Diaz, who was just back from having rounded the Cape of Good Hope, making virtually irrelevant any consideration or need for a western route.

PART II

Chapter IV

THE COLUMBIAN SHIPS

After obtaining the Sovereigns' consent to the capitulations (stipulated in Santa Fe on the 17th of April, 1492) establishing his rights over the discovered lands and his share of the profits deriving from the enterprise, as well as the titles due him, and having finally received on April 30th the royal credentials for outfitting the ships assigned to him, Columbus went to Palos, a small harbor town on the Tinto river, where he arrived on the 22nd of May to take possession of the two vessels that the town had been ordered to supply to him. As punishment for past civil non-compliance, Palos had in fact been condemned to furnish to the Crown two manned caravels ready to sail for the period of one year.

Martin Fernández de Navarrete reports a passage of the Spanish Sovereigns' instructions to the citizens of Palos: "Fully aware of things you did and carried out against our interest, you were condemned by our decree to furnish in our service two armored caravels for twelve months at your expense and cost, when the time comes or whenever it would be so ordered by us." The financial value of this imposition has been calculated to have amounted to 350,000 *maravedis* versus the total cost of the expedition of approximately 2,000,000 *maravedis*. The remainder was covered for 1,140,000 *maravedis* by the Crown and for 500,000 by Columbus himself, who had obtained loans from Genoese and Florentine merchants.

In the Portuguese expeditions, as we pointed out, the caravels sailed in pairs but, uncertain (despite his own unlimited confidence) about the duration of the voyage, Columbus probably deemed it advisable to add a third vessel. He rented then a *nao*, the *Santa Maria*, owned by Juan de la Cosa, a Cantabrian [N. Spain] seaman living in Puerto Santa Maria, a small hamlet not far from Palos, and an acquaintance of Columbus for some time.

The reasons for the choice of a third unit for the flotilla are not known, but a few hypotheses can be advanced in this regard. The first reason is that a *nao*, having a larger cargo capacity than a caravel, could have carried a bigger quantity of provisions for the voyage, thus providing for his own as well as the other crews for a reasonable span of time. The second is that, still owing to her capacity, the ship could have transported back to Spain a larger quantity of the precious goods that would be found at the sites reached, which Columbus believed to be rich and highly civilized, and at the same time to be able to take onboard in a more convenient way than on the frugal caravels the foreign potentates that those countries might want to send as ambassadors to the Catholic Sovereigns. A third assumption was to figure that it was only due to Columbus's ambition to travel on a larger vessel than the other two, and enjoy living quarters more becoming to his upcoming title (from the moment he reached new lands, he would be addressed as Admiral of the Ocean Sea with the rank of Viceroy and Governor of the new territories, whether islands or mainland, unless subject to other jurisdiction) that determined his preference for a heavy, slow *nao* over a third caravel (limited as well, in terms of provisions, to fulfilling the needs of her own crew). In hindsight, however, throughout the voyage the larger *nao* would be to him just a source of complaints.

In the following pages we endeavor to gather everything that is known or presumed about the Columbian ships, keeping well in mind what was written on the subject by Samuel E. Morrison, that is, that the caravel fleet we see reproduced on ancient nautical maps or in books illustrations is only approximate, fictitious and at least fifty percent simply false.

The Santa Maria

We can begin by clearing away any doubt on the fact that the *Santa Maria* was a *nao*, while the other two ships, the *Pinta* and the *Niña* were caravels. This point, much debated in the past, is by now settled: it has been ascertained that the *Santa Maria* was a *nao*, on the basis of her size, her construction characteristics, her sails and rigging and, if nothing else, her poor marine qualities, which a caravel certainly would not have shown. As previously illustrated, the Iberic *nao* was a craft of not particularly large size; elsewhere she would perhaps have been called a cog because she shared many characteristics of the fifteenth-century cogs that sailed the Mediterranean, evolved by this time into more graceful shapes than its prototypes.

At any rate, in the *Journal* Columbus always refers to the *Santa Maria* as a *nao*, ditinguishing her from the *carabelas*[15] (example: he sent "las barcas de la nao y de la carabela") and only twice, in abridged passages when it is the author of the *Journal*'s transcription — rather than Columbus — to speak, the "three caravels" reference is used. Moreover, when Columbus speaks of the units of his flotilla collectively, he uses the word *navios* [ships] and not *naos*, taking care then of using terms more appropriately reflecting a seaman's knowledge.

The ambiguity originated, for some authors, from the instructions given to Columbus by the King and Queen on the 30th of April 1492, to employ *tres carabelas de armada*, a generic phrase written, in any case, before Columbus traveled to Palos to make arrangements about the ships assigned to him. In other places the expression *tres carabelas* is down right replaced by *tres fustas* — oar boats — an evident mistake of a clerk in charge of composing the document, but not well-versed in sailing terminology.

In any case, the question has been definitely put to rest by all knowledgeable historians, who no longer question the difference between *naos* and *carabelas* even if in everyday speech the mysterious charm of the term 'caravel' regularly manages to overcome the more generic designation 'ship' in utter violation of any technical disclaimer.[16]

Peter Martyr of Anghiera, who was Columbus's friend, wrote in his *Decades de Orbe Novo*, first printed in Seville in 1511, when referring to the ships of the voyage: *Tria nauigia unum operarium caueatum alia dua mercatoria leuia sine cauies quae ab Hispanis carauelae vocatur* [three vessels, one *caveatum*, and two lighter ones not caveata which Spaniards call 'caravels'].

[15] José Martinez Hidalgo has listed 81 citations of the *Santa Maria* as *nao* and 97 of the other two ships as *carabelas*.

[16] Among the authors who have sided with the three-caravels thesis we must include, unfortunately, Guglielmotti and Jal, besides Dionisio Alcalá Galiano who in 1892 titled an article of his on the *Rivista General de Marina*, "The caravel *Gallega* or *Santa Maria* or *la nao capitana de Colón*," and another serious Columbus scholar, Julio F.Guillén Tato who, on the occasion of the Barcelona Fair of 1929, was charged with the life-size reconstruction of the *Santa Maria*, a replica preserved in the Barcelona harbor near the antique Arsenal, a major attraction for tourists, many of which are convinced to be on board of the authentic *Santa Maria*. True to his thesis, the ship he reconstructed had some elements typical of a square caravel. The reconstruction was later modified several times, especially in its bow section, to make it more similar to a *nao*. The thesis advanced by Guillén Tato and Alcalá Galiano was that Columbus made reference to the *Santa Maria* as *nao capitana*, rather than to a type defined as carack. After the *Santa Maria* wreckage, however, the *Niña* kept being called a caravel, in spite of her carrying the Admiral onboard.

The word *caveatum* also has been a harbinger of controversy for scholars at the end of the last century. Assuming that *cavea* means hold — the interior of a ship — 'with hold' would mean with a deck; and 'without hold', hence, without a deck. Or does *cavea* possibly stand for 'topsail' and hence 'with top' [crow's nest] and topsail, and 'without top' meaning then without crow's nest and topsail?

We may rule out unhesitatingly the possibility that the two caravels lacked a continuous deck from bow to stern, because undecked ships would not have been called caravels but *barchas* or some other term, and also because no sailor, though prepared to make do with little, would face a voyage toward the unknown in an open boat: for sure, no one would have followed him. As for the fact that the *Santa Maria* was a *nao da gavia*, this has been ascertained.

Beyond this, however, there really are few other certainties. Dimensions, tonnage, rigging details and feature can be easily and variously imagined, but all based on inferences that rely on a scant availability of firm data, extrapolated from Columbus's *Journal* or few other contemporary sources, all second-hand to boot.

Certain it is that the *Santa Maria* had a bow castle and a quarterdeck aft, typical of the *nao*, and this is told in the *Journal* when, on October 12, the night preceding the sighting of land, it is written: *...a las diez de la noche estando en el castillo de popa vido lumbre aunque fue cosa tan çerrada que no quiso affirmar que fuese tierra. ...rogò (el Almirante) que hiziesen buena guarda al castillo de prora....* We know moreover that the sail rig of the *Santa Maria* was as specified by Columbus in the *Journal* on October 24, when he wrote: *...y entonces tornò a ventar muy amoroso, y llevaba todas mis velas de la nao, maestra, dos bonetas y trinquete y cebadera y mezana y vela de gavia y el batel por popa.* Therefore the master sail with the two bonnets, the square sail at the foremast, the spritsail under the bowsprit, the lateen sail on the mizzen mast, the topsail above the mainmast (we shall come back to these sails) and the tenderboat at stern. Let us reflect on this last sentence to try and understand its meaning. It was customary at the time to tow a large boat, or *batel*, when sailing in areas where one could anticipate the use of such a boat for landing, exploring, etc., sparing oneself in this way the fatiguing work of putting her to sea every time. Towing absorbed a minimum amount of energy and could also be of some advantage for the balance of the ship, especially when a vessel such as the *Santa Maria*, round-shaped, thus somewhat unstable on course and unresponsive to the rudder, was subject to "halberd" blows (denoting with this term a sudden, unexpected lurch of the bow under the thrust of the wind, combined with the action of waves on the stern when she, running before the wind, is less responsive to the rudder). It could also happen that in prolonged periods of good weather during the open crossing the boat was towed, for use in ensuring contacts with the other ships. In the above cited passage the *Santa Maria* was sailing close to the islands with *viento muy amoroso*, which followed a calm morning. It would therefore be difficult to understand Columbus's reference: *y el batel por popa* after listing the sails unless he had the intention, with that sentence, to allude to the lateen sail of the boat. If the boat was being towed, to trim a sail on her would have made no sense since, as we said, the towing resistance was minimal and such a maneuver would have required to command a couple of men on the tender, but all of this would have brought no benefit to the course of the ship anyway. We can suppose then that the Admiral had ordered to hoist the yard of the boat and its sail — which would normally be onboard the ship — somewhere on the *Santa Maria*, probably at the extreme stern in place, for instance, of the flag staff, just to put "all the canvas waving," as the saying goes. If our hypothesis is correct, this must have been customary technique in fair weather, rather than a correction maneuver.

This original-source information about the ship is too little to venture a reconstruction, albeit hypothetical, of a vessel even just resembling the *Santa Maria*. When studies on the Columbian ships, including the fundamental one by D'Albertis, blossomed in 1892, on the occasion of fourth centennial of the discovery, and it was decided to build a facsimile of the three vessels for the Chicago World Fair, it was necessary to refer to historical works of a general character relative to shipbuilding and to illustrations of ancient texts and nautical charts, such as the Italian one by Benincasa of 1482, preserved at the library of the University of Bologna; a Spanish one, by Juan de la Cosa (who, if he was the same person as the Juan de la Cosa, the owner of the *Santa Maria*, was a man well cognizant with what he was drawing, although not of very good hand), currently in the Naval Museum of Madrid; and finally the one by Diego Ribeiro, of 1529, kept in the State Library of Weimar. In all these cases, however, these small ships were drawn on the charts with a purely decorative intent, as it was customary at one time, without any pretense of making a faithful reproduction of the vessel. Besides, since several of these charts are successive to the "discovery," they may have embodied innovations or changes subsequent to 1492.

Other known coeval representations of ships, from which some elements common also to the *naos* can be drawn, are, choosing from the most significant, those which appear in the *Livro des Fortalezas de el Rey D. Emanuel*, by Duarte Dalmas (see p. 77); those in the nautical atlas by Piri Re'îs of 1513, preserved in Istanbul; those in a Portuguese nautical chart of 1510 (in the Civic Library at Wolfenbüttel) and also bas-reliefs, small moulds and paintings — votive offerings — where the ships are represented in a naive but detail-rich fashion. Among the most important paintings for our purpose, we remember the vessel shown in the famous Miracle of Saint Nicholas from Bari, by Gentile da Fabriano; the beautiful fifteenth-century cog in Bonfigli's composition "Miracle of Saint Ludwig" (Art Gallery, Perugia) and the ships painted with such mastery by Vittore Carpaccio in his Saint Ursula cycle, a true mine for the scholar, because details are plentiful and rendered with exemplary precision.

Thus mentioned are but a few of the fifteenth- and sixteenth-century preserved items that are available in large number especially in the pictorial production. Of course many of these are manneristic subjects, with fictional details that can be misleading, but a discerning critic can separate the good from the bad, the veridical from the certainly false, and derive from them valuable, telling indications for his knowledge.

Several years ago, in the Sanctuary of Saint Simon from Mataró, near Barcelona, the precious votive model of a Catalonian ship was discovered, dating back to the years between 1440 and 1450. Presently this model, the oldest known of the medieval period, is preserved in the Prince Hendrik Maritime Museum in Rotterdam. Executed for a vow, perhaps by a sailor delivered from a wreckage, the model is of rough workmanship and centuries of precarious maintenance have certainly not contributed to its good preservation. Many parts are missing, in particular at least two masts, but it does keep something of the rigging of the only mast left. The hull is very rotund, probably out of proportions and with scarcely credible shapes. It is, however, an "authentic model" that comes to us after a five-centuries span as a source of reliable information, thus of extraordinary value for the reconstruction of a ship coeval to the *Santa Maria*. The figure (reproduced at p. 109) is the reconstruction by Pino dell'Orco of the Matarò ship; the accuracy of the drawing can exempt us from a description and the reader will be able to recognize, without further suggestions, the common features of this coeval model and the present reconstructions of the *Santa Maria*.

Through the scant information available about Columbus's flagship it can be established that she had been built several years prior to 1492 (some say about forty, which looks excessive to us for in such case, even though wooden ships had a rather long life, after so many years her

The small ships drawn on Juan de la Cosa's chart (1500), preserved in the Naval Museum of Madrid, illustrate some elements relative to the sail types of ships and caravels providing limited information as well on the flags hoisted, but not much more.

Small ships like these, decorating Martin Behain's globe (1492), presently in the National Museum of Nuremberg, are not particularly informative; just as indistinct are those reproduced below, from Pirigani's chart of 1367. With similar documents, although well-known and cited, naval archeology was able to make only modest advances.

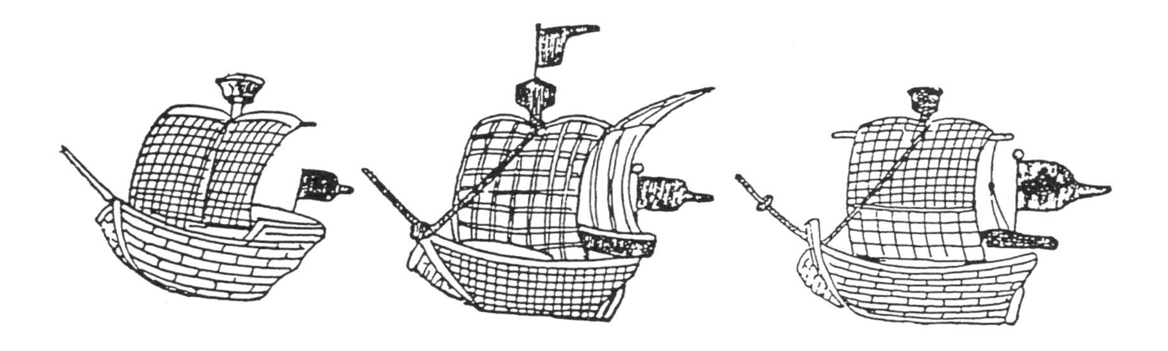

This ship, drawn by a skillful hand on a chart by Diego Ribero, has induced past scholars into many mistakes. The square stern and the topsails shape are typical of later ships, from after the fifteenth century. The chart, in fact, was drawn in 1526.

Vessels drawn on a *Hispaniola* [Haiti] chart of 1530 (erroneously attributed to Columbus himself). The ships are very similar to most old reconstructions of the *Santa Maria*, but obviously have features which are common to crafts later than the end of the fifteenth century, while preserving the distinctive bow shape of many medieval ships.

hull would have shown such flaws as to be considered unreliable for a demanding crossing) in Galicia (northern Spain), whence her original name *Gallega.*

This is a more plausible conjecture than the one according to which the ship was built in the town of Coindres (Santander) — a conjecture supported only by local tradition, but with no probative documentation. Just as tenuous is the hypothesis that when Columbus acquired her she had been a trading vessel commuting to the Netherlands, although in fact she had been built by commission of a group of Flemish traders.

When Columbus was looking for a third vessel to complete his flotilla, the ship was berthed in the harbor of Santa Maria near Palos, and was owned by Juan de la Cosa who offered her to the Genoese along with his service, as it is actually documented in the board roll of the *Santa Maria,* which lists Juan de la Cosa as "Master and owner."

The dimensions and cargo capacity of the Columbian ships, as already pointed out, cannot be accurately determined from any surviving document or note. D'Albertis tried to establish them through indirect information and a series of inferences. First of all, starting from the number of persons on board, he reached the conclusion that none of the Columbian vessels could be smaller than today's 100-ton displacement ships.[17] He then took into consideration the research effected in 1779 by Antonio de Capmany de Montpalau who, listing the arrivals of ships with load capacity greater than 50 tons in the Barcelona harbor between 1490 and 1533, found caravels of various origins (Portuguese, Italian, Andalusian, Catalonian, etc.)

[17] For those unfamiliar with the concept of tonnage, a word of clarification is in order: tonnage is a volume measurement used for all merchant ships to indicate their cargo capacity, while for warships, which do not have to load goods, the displacement ton is adopted as the unit of measure to specify their dimensions. The weight of the vessel is, in the latter case, equal to the weight of the displaced water, which can be easily calculated knowing the volume of the immersed hull (there are also several definitions of displacement, relative to particular conditions of the warship). The tonnage of merchant vessels — the measurement which is of interest in our case, since all the studies on the Colombian ships are based on that unit of measure, as appropriate for freight ships — derives from the old custom of measuring the vessels' cargo capacity in barrels, the type of containers most frequently adopted for maritime cargoes, and more easily accountable. From the concept of barrel — *tonel* or *pipa* in Spanish, *tonneau* in French — there derived the English *ton,* denoting a one-hundred cubic feet volume, i.e., 2.8317 cubic meters [corresponding to c. 2.8 metric *tons* of water]. From the English language the word *ton* in the shipping jargon arrived in Italy, becoming *tonnellata* »(that is, a capacity of tonnage, distinct from the usual metric *tonnellata,* a measure of weight).

with capacities, in quintals, variable between 1,200 and 7,250 (therefore very different among them) and ships (we omit crafts of other types that are of no interest here) with capacities between 5,000 and 17,000 quintals. These data, drawn from the *Libros de cuenta de los Recaudadores* where their capacity was listed next to the docked vessels and their respective dues for anchoring fees, could help only to determine a minimum and a maximum for the capacity of these ships. "To translate into a correct modern value "the 'quintal' mentioned by the ancient Barcelonian documents," so D'Albertis writes, "and to find the corresponding values of the *bota*, the *tonel*, or the *tonelada*, is not so simple, given that the value of *libras*, *arrobas*, *quintales* varied from one Spanish city to the next, just as different was in Italian ports the value of *libbre*, *rotoli*, *cantari*, *salme* and quintals. Yet, proceeding by comparison, though unaware of the exact value of old Spanish units, we should however be able to form a reasonably accurate idea of the capacities of the ships mentioned in the Barcelona document by relating them to modern values. In so doing, however, it is necessary to be cautious since, besides the variation existing between measures of the same name used in different cities, one is likely to run into erroneous interpretations of the same values given by more or less recent authors."

Relying on the data furnished by Giovanni di Antonio Uzzano in his treatise *Pratica della mercatura* [Practical Manual of Trading] written between 1425 and 1442, D'Albertis calculated — after several intermediate steps and on the basis of a few assumptions — that the antique Catalonian quintal "in round figures, approximated for onboard ship usage, can be estimated equal to 58 kilograms." Applying this value to the capacity of some medium-size ships that according to Capmany had called at the Barcelona harbor, D'Albertis was able to establish values between 70 and 200 actual tons, "cargo capacity, that is, not displacement tons since, as already pointed out, those ships paid anchoring duties on the basis of their cargo weight, approximately computed."

Assuming that Columbus's ships, owing to the voyage they had to make and the men and provisions they had to take on board, could not have a low cargo limit, D'Albertis grew convinced that they must have had an average capacity of 150 modern tons.

But, if in Barcelona it was customary to calculate a vessel's capacity in *quintals*, at Genoa in *cantari* and in Sicily in terms of *salme*, likewise, in other Spanish ports different weight units were used, such as the *tonel* and the *tonelada*. These different unit denominations are correlated to the nature of the goods handled in their place of origin consequently reflecting the unit most commonly adopted for a specific kind of traded commodity; thus in

Draft model of the Mataró ship, reconstructed by Pino Dell'Orco.

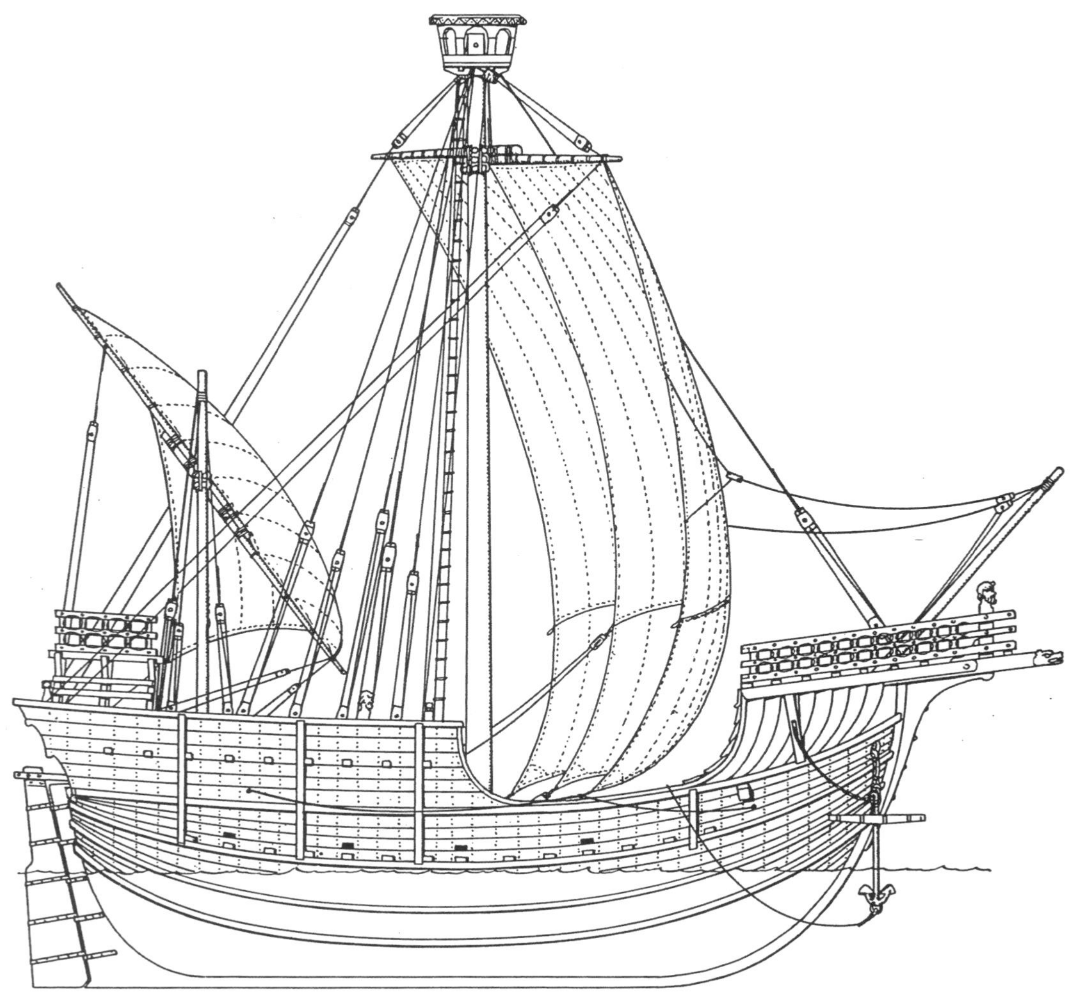

The Mataró ship according to Biörn Landström.

One may notice how, though working on the same available data, each author tends to interpret it in a different way. A clear example of this is readily seen as one compares Landström's reconstruction with that by Dell'Orco on the previous page. The proportions of the hull are also different. Landström has tried to give his Mataró ship an appearance more closely resembling that of a sea-worthy vessel (based on today's experience), whereas Dell'Orco adhered more strictly to the given dimension of the model, making for rather unlikely shapes, although there is no definite evidence available to rebut them.

Sicily it corresponded to a wheat measure were used, in the Flanders to wool bags, in the Biscayne region the traditional barrels weighed in *tonels* that were about 20% larger than the *toneladas* common for barrels in Seville. To complicate things even more, there were references to a *tonel macho* or *tonel grosso*, which only after the middle of the fifteenth century became equivalent, in D'Albertis's opinion, to the *tonelada*, giving rise to a new capacity unit.

Still following D'Albertis in his analytical study of these measurement units, one learns that

> with a decree issued by the King of Spain on September 10, 1495, a yearly stipend of 100,000 *maravedis* was granted to all those who would build and keep outfitted a 1,000-*toneles* vessel, of 80,000 for a 800-*toneles* vessel and 60,000 for a 600-*toneles* ship. The sizable amounts of money that the State was prepared to lavish on a yearly basis in order to facilitate the construction and maintenance of large vessels makes it more realistic to believe that a specific tonnage formula had by that time been adopted and that the *tonel* unit therein mentioned was well defined, for the purpose of establishing the capacity load of a vessel and, correspondingly, the sum that the Treasury had to pay to the shipowners.
> Another royal ordinance in 1511 fixed the price per *tonelada* that the Treasury had established to pay to the owners of ships rented on behalf of the government. Whereas the first decree mentions *toneles* and the second *toneladas* as the measurement unit to be used to calculate the capacity, or *arqueo*, of the vessels in question, one can deduce that a computation formula, sanctioned by practice and approved by the government, must have been in force, and applied by specialized appraisers in the estimation of a vessel's cargo capacity, which determined the yearly sum, or *acostamiento* as it was then called, that the government would disburse to the shipowners.

With the measurement units varying from region to region, it is naturally understandable that by the middle of the sixteenth century the Spanish government would attempt to reduce them to a single standard. The new unit of measure was determined to be *ochos codos cubicos*, i.e., eight cubic cubits. The matter, however, amidst the clash of centuries-old customs, must not have been settled easily if in 1580 the Marquis of Santa Cruz, general captain of the Spanish galleys, was still arguing for the need to regulate the measurement of cargo capacity. Only in 1590 a royal decree established a fixed formula for it, prescribing at the same time what should have been the uniform measure of the cubit, as it, too, differed from region to region thwarting every effort at regulation.

Diego García de Palacio, in 1585, in his *De la instructión nautica para el buen uso y regimento de las naos* (Mexico City, 1587), tells us that two feet and two thirds of a perch form a *codo*. In ancient times there was a six-span *codo*, each span being four fingers, and another of one and a half foot (equal to the length of the arm from the end of the middle finger to the elbow of a well proportioned man) — a measure used by pilots when sounding, i.e., counting how many times a retrieved length of sounding line could be wrapped between the elbow and the thumb. The French revolution had at least the merit of putting an end to this jumble of measurement units.

The new tonnage-rating system was studied by Cristobal Barrios. This system, D'Albertis maintains, probably unified and codified those already in use "considering that in all changes regarding seamanship custom always precedes law."

Although the value of the cubit was ill defined, D'Albertis believed that his own calculations approached with sufficient precision an average figure of m 0.56 [almost 2 feet], and that therefore the eight-cubic cubits parallelepiped of the Seville *tonelada* equalled 1.40492 cubic meters, an amount that he rounded to 1.405 cubic meters, while the value of the Biscayne *tonel* was equal to 1.685 cubic meters, rounding the third decimal digit.

The Seville *tonelada* finally prevailed in actual usage over the Byscaine *tonel*, also because Seville became the center of the trade with the Indies. Columbus himself, in the *Memorandum* for the Catholic Sovereigns delivered by Torres on January 30, 1494, recommended to rent vessels by *toneladas* as it was customary for the Flanders routes.

Escalante de Mendoza (*Itinerario de Navigacion de los mares y tierras occidentales*, 1575),[18] referring to Columbus's ships seventy years after the navigator's death, wrote that he "did not seek or have for such a great enterprise large vessels, indeed only small ones, not surpassing by much the 100 toneladas." Since there is no other mention about the tonnage of the ships of Columbus's first voyage (Don Ferdinand, however, lists the tonnage of the vessels of the fourth expedition: "three sailing vessels, seventy-barrel capacity the biggest and 50 the smallest," thus providing

[18] A manuscript whose publication was prohibited by the Council of the Indies, out of fear that the information contained in it, the result of twenty-eight years of sea-going experience, could benefit foreign competitors.

further indication), D'Albertis had to content himself with that posthumous, yet eminently credible, witness and so finally assigned a tonnage of 150 to 200 ancient *toneladas* to the *Santa Maria* (later settling on 179), corresponding to 210 or 280 modern tons; of 100 to 105 *toneladas* to the *Niña*, traditionally regarded as the smaller of the two caravels, corresponding to 140-150 modern tons; and of 105 to 115 *toneladas* for the *Pinta*.

The usage of *tonelada* must have been, anyway, rather widespread in the fifteenth century. In reference to it, Duro states that Columbus, Vasco da Gama and Magellan requested that their ships not exceed one hundred *toneladas*, because they needed low-draft, easily maneuverable vessels, requiring only a limited crew. On the other hand, considering the seas that they were going to face, the same crafts had to be quite sturdy, a prerequisite inversely proportional to their dimension. The larger the ship, the greater was the number of joints and reinforcements in the areas of higher stress, which furthermore were calculated without the slightest benefit of a scientific foundation, but in an empirical and approximate manner. Consequently, hull structures would often collapse, fatigued not only as a result of wave motions and cargo weight, but also by the excessive weight of masts, rigging and all other superstructures (indeed a further advantage of the caravels, consisted in their lack of superstructures except for a very limited quarterdeck, unlike other ships, which were loaded with castles and quarterdecks of considerable height). We quote from D'Albertis this interesting observation on the shrouds of fifteenth-century ships: "On ancient Spanish vessels the weight of the shrouds, of the fixed and running cordage as well as of the various cables was by no means insignificant: as a general rule, a ship had to have, for every ton of burden, two thirds of a quintal between shrouds and various cables. A 500-*toneladas* galleon had to have 332 *quintales de jarcia*, beside the current cordage, while a 100-*toneladas* ship would require 70 *quintales*."

On account of their weight and construction deficiencies, hulls had an excessive tendency to "weave"[19]; water infiltrations would start between the planking joints and these, and so, with the passing of time and the difficulty to execute repairs on distant shores, such deterioration put the survival of the ship in serious jeopardy.

Concentrating now our attention on the *Santa Maria*, it may be observed that the opinions of those who attempted a reconstruction of the

[19] In wooden crafts, because of either age or bad weather, it happens that the planking strakes or other parts begin to lose their perfect cohesion, so the various elements rub on one another. Thus the ship is said to *weave*, and her alterations can be measured with a "spy," that is, by the motions of a small wooden wedge inserted between the cracks.

ship, whether on paper or in actual size, are among them in disagreement. Auguste Jal and Fernández Duro (1892) claim her to be of 233 modern tons; D'Albertis, as we have seen, calculated a capacity varying between 210 and 280 tons which later, when designing the vessel with the dimensions that we shall see, resulted of 252 tons. Guillén Tato (1927) estimated her capacity at 202 tons, Martinez Hidalgo (1868) at 170. Others limit themselves to the main dimensions without venturing into complicated and perhaps useless calculations of the burden. All told, except for the exceedingly modest estimate by Martinez Hidalgo, the results are usually almost identical, with all calculations yielding a ship slightly larger than 200 tons. The latest reconstruction of the *Santa Maria*, executed under the auspices of the Spanish Committee for the Columbian celebrations, has resulted in a ship of 223.88 tons (of displacement).

It might be more interesting to know which hypotheses have been advanced for the dimensions of the *Santa Maria* — as well as for the two other ships — by the various scholars who have taken an interest to the problem.

The first reconstruction to be realized was the "Duro replica" authorized by the Spanish Commission chaired by Fernández Duro[20]. The starting point were the reported dimensions of the *Santa Maria* flagship, in Las Casas's *Historia* and in Don Ferdinand Columbus's *Historie* — identical in content but interpreted somewhat peculiarly by Jal: "...I found a river through the mouth of which a galley could easily enter... I entered ... as deeply as the length of the boat," too vague to estimate from a galley's beam the length of the flagship. The beam of a galley was about 17 feet, but one should also determine the type of galley implied by the reference; a merchant galley could have been 21 to 27 feet wide, and in her width ought to be included the oars as well, because a sailing galley would have kept her oars outboard, even under sail. If so, we could get to about sixty feet. The reference, as one can see, is too vague.

D'Albertis, on the other hand, worked his reasoning around the number of the people onboard, approximately forty men, and made room for them on a hypothetical *Santa Maria*, a bit larger perhaps than the real one, of 179 *toneladas* of capacity, probably without taking into account either Escalante de Mendoza's suggestion — a little more than 100 *toneladas*

[20] In reality Fernández Duro had collaborators such as Rafael Monleon, the naval engineer Casimiro Bona and the other members of the Commission, Emil Ruiz del Arbol, Aureliano Fernández Guerra and Juan de Dios de la Rada y Delgado, representing the Royal Academy of History. The plans were drafted by engineer Leopoldo Puente of the La Carraca Arsenal.

— or the fact that many of the people onboard did not belong to the crew proper (the Admiral, the master, the countermaster, the pilot, the physician and three valets), making for very tight quarters, consequently, for the participants to that lucky voyage.

D'Albertis made, however, still another valid consideration based on the heigth of the pillar, the supporting element located between the keel and the beams of each deck, which, by extension, is regarded as the measure of the internal heigth of the ship, that is, between keel and deck.

According to D'Albertis the *Santa Maria*, a vessel of modest dimensions, had only one deck, plus a horizontal partition inside, supported by the beams alone, and a single pillar, which must have been about 8 cubits long, i.e., about 14 feet. This estimate was made by D'Albertis on the basis of his own belief that the first internal longitudinal partition would have to be, from the hold bottom, 8 feet high in order to be able to receive three rows of barrels or "pipes" in what he defined as the hold or *cavea*. Furthermore, he figured that the second partition would have to rise above the beams of the first by three cubits, corresponding to about 5 and a half feet, for it to be able to hold two more rows of pipes. Still, the combined sum of these two elements did not reflect the actual height which could not be defined, because one should also take into account the thickness of the beam and the deck for about another cubit, or two more feet, for a total height of fifteen to sixteen feet.

At this point, making recourse to the *tres, dos y as* rule, D'Albertis was able to determine values of 25 feet for the main beam, of 79 feet for the length between perpendiculars, and of 56 feet for the keel length taken separately. Recalling, however, that the rule *tres, dos y as*, was not generally respected, the true values, presuming the height of the pillar as correct at over 14 feet, should translate into a vessel 29 feet wide at the beam and 86 feet long.

Martínez Hidalgo came to results slightly different from D'Albertis's. He started from Las Casas's inference that the cargo capacity of the *Santa Maria* was to have been around 100 *toneladas* and from what is written in the biography of Columbus attributed to his son Don Ferdinand, who confirms that figure. Having accepted this value, Hidalgo tried by successive approximations to compute a hull that had length, width and height capable of satisfying an approximate capacity of just 100 *toneladas*. A model corresponding to this capacity was thus built, in compliance with what could be regarded as realistic dimensions at the time; there resulted a ship 65 feet long between perpendiculars, 24 feet wide, with a pillar of almost 12 feet.

Other projects, models and authentic reconstructions were made in our century by various scholars, each one of them following his or her own reasoning to justify the dimensions attributed to the *Santa Maria*, though unable to go beyond pure conjectures.

As of this writing, it was not yet possible to know the criteria adopted by the Spanish engineers for their most recent reconstruction of the *Santa Maria* and the two caravels. Probably out of unjustified jealousy or, as Landström honestly admits, for fear of criticism, the plan's designers tend to be extremely stingy when it comes to giving information. The new *Santa Maria* has a maximum displacement of 223.88 tons, a figure hardly comparable with the tonnage of previous reconstructions. Such dimensions are in any case among the largest so far proposed.

With the information available to us, we have prepared the following metric table on which are listed the known data of all the most important reconstructions, whether realized in a model or actual size or even just planned, of the Columbian flagship, to allow for an easier comparison of the same.

As can be observed, the dimensions, although differing somewhat, never exceed the minimum and maximum parameters within which the *Santa Maria* can acceptably be placed. At the bottom of the table we have included, for comparison, the sizes of the vessel that would result from development of the model of Catalunian ship known as the "Mataró *nao*."

The hull and exterior shape of the Santa Maria according to various reconstructions.

We do not believe that any other ship has ever raised as much interest as the *Santa Maria* among the devotees of naval history, from the most serious scholars of the art of navigation to those modest hobbyists who endeavored to build, for their own satisfaction, a more or less exact model of the famous ship.

The recent celebrations of the "discovery" of the New World have also provided the necessary financial means to attempt full-size reconstructions once again of the flagship and its two companion vessels: such efforts have afforded the possibility of testing on life-size models the accuracy of the various scholarly theories.

The first reconstructions were realized a century ago, as already said, on the occasion of the fourth centennial of the voyages. In 1892 a Spanish Government commission, chaired by Navy captain Cesareo Fernández Duro, an expert on the Columbian ships, and whose committee members we have previously mentioned (see fn. 20), produced a full-size replica of the *Santa Maria* in La Carraca arsenal (Cadiz). The hull, built under the direction of naval engineer Leopoldo Puente, was launched on 26 June 1892, after sixty-three days of work. Once completely outfitted, the ship

DIMENSIONS OF MODELS AND RECONSTRUCTIONS OF THE S. MARIA

	length between castle and quarterdeck	length between perpendiculars	keel length	beam [widest point]	pillar [depth of hold]	draft	height from keel to mast head	total sail surface in sq. meters
1892 Replica by the Spanish government	28,60	22,60	18,50	8,10	3,80	3,00 max	27,25	435
Jal's studies	27,70			8,12				
1892 Duro-Monleón project	21,00	17,80	13,80	7,80	2,40		29,00	
1892 D'Albertis's studies	31,60	26,30	19,05	8,40	4,75	2,90	19,50 around	
1929 Guillén Tato reconstruction	25,70 in cover		18,70	7,50	3,30	2,20	28,00	415
1930 Anderson's model	24,70		16,50	8,20	4,10	3,30	24,70	
1961 Landström's studies	26,50 around	23,92	16,92	7,92	3,10 around	2,10 around	24,70 around	325
1964 Martínez Hidalgo reconstruction	23,60 in cover		15,80	7,92	3,85	2,10	26,60	
1966 Hinderer's studies	25,00	21,60	14,00	6,60	3,40	1,75	29,10	
1991 Studies and model by Monfeld and others	26,10	21,35	14,75	8,25	4,35	3,65	30,90	
1991 Reconstruction of the Spanish Commission	29,60		16,10	7,86	3,24			270
Mataró ship, mid-15th century (Dell'Orco drawing)	20,10	15,40	10,00	8,10	4,40		21,80	178

participated in the centennial celebrations at Huelva, and afterwards, under the command of frigate captain Victor M. Concas, set out to sail across the Atlantic, retracing Columbus's course. The ship left Santa Cruz de Tenerife on February 22, 1893, and met such rough seas that it found necessary to counter the violence of the waves around the hull by resorting to the ancient method of spilling oil on the sea surface. For those unfamiliar with this stratagem, suffice it to point out that the expedient — decreasing the force of the breakers in moments of great danger by easing off into the sea small canvas bags filled with oil-soaked hemp — is very ancient. The thin oily film which immediately spreads around the vessel creates a powerful diaphragm that prevents the waves from breaking against its sides. In older times, there was widespread fear that, once the expedient was enacted, the seas would become more furious than ever. Obviously, this derived from the fact that, once the oil was exhausted and the ship straggled off the oil-coated area by her own motion, she had to face waters as harsh as before.

Rough seas at the stern made the vessel lurch by as much as four points of the compass (90 degrees) — further irrefutable proof that the hull of a *nao* handled very poorly at sea. Regardless of this bad weather that held for a good part of the crossing, this "new" *Santa Maria* completed her voyage to San Juan de Puertorico in one day less than her original forebearer. The fastest tract, with a stiff N-NE breeze, covered 139 miles in 24 hours.

In sight of the island of Cuba, the *Santa Maria* was towed by the Spanish sloop *Jorge Juan*, which hauled her to Havana. Later, towed this time by the cruiser *Reina Regente*, the *Santa Maria* arrived to Hampton Road and New York, where she took part in a naval review. From New York, in tow of the American cruiser *Newark*, she visited Quebec, Montreal, Toronto, Detroit and Chicago, where the ship was donated to the Columbian World Exposition.

The general reconstruction plan was drawn on the basis of the documentation known at that time, albeit interpreted with a less critical mind than it would nowadays. Presently everyone agrees that the ship reconstructed by the 1892 Commission, although similar to a fifteenth-century vessel, incorporated many details dating to at least fifty years later. The main criticisms concerned: the shape of the bow castle, which was not triangular, as it was later verified, but more or less followed the curved lines of the underlying prow; the square poop, that was not to be found on cogs, caracks and ships of that time, since it had barely made its appearance as a feature of caravels; its abundance of ornamental elements, unlikely on an austere merchant vessel; a trapezoidal topsail instead of a square sail, as currently agreed by all scholars. Also several featured fittings are today regarded as too "modern" for a fifteenth-century ship, especially one as old as Columbus's *Santa Maria* was.

Practically around the same time, Rafael Monleón, an artist and the Commission's secretary, drew up a *Santa Maria* very similar to that by the Commission, with higher quarterdeck and castle, larger masts, square stern, and even fitted, quite implausibly, with auxiliary oars that, besides being of limited efficacy, could not have been used owing to the height of the freeboard. Overall, the entire Monleón project is generally even less credible than the Commission's plan [known as the Duro project, from the name of its chair].

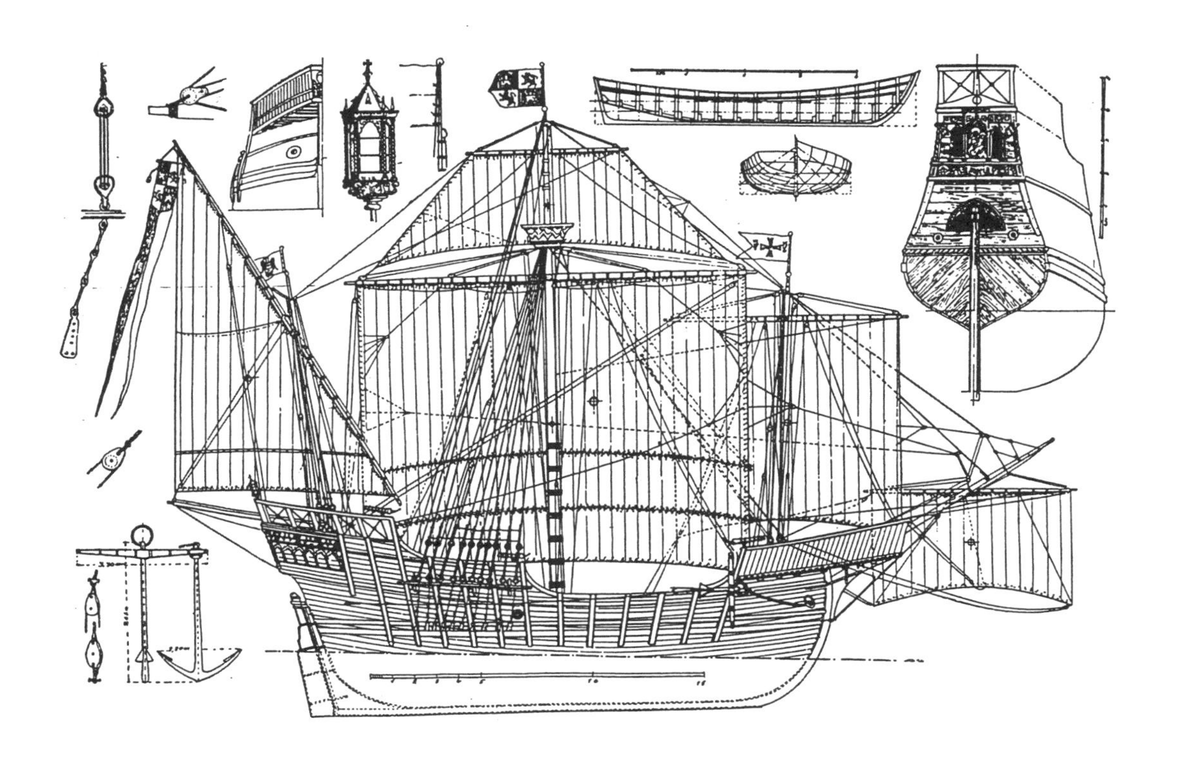

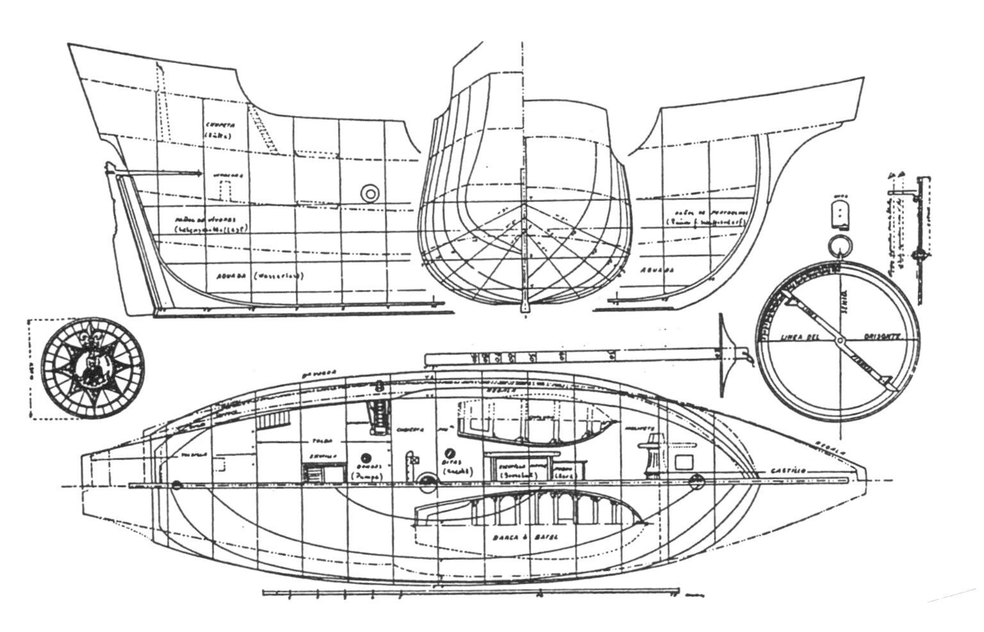

The 1892 reconstruction of the *Santa Maria* realized by the Spanish Commission for the celebrations of the fourth centennial of the discovery. It is known as the Fernández Duro project, from the Commission's chairman. Engineer Leopoldo Puente drafted the plans.

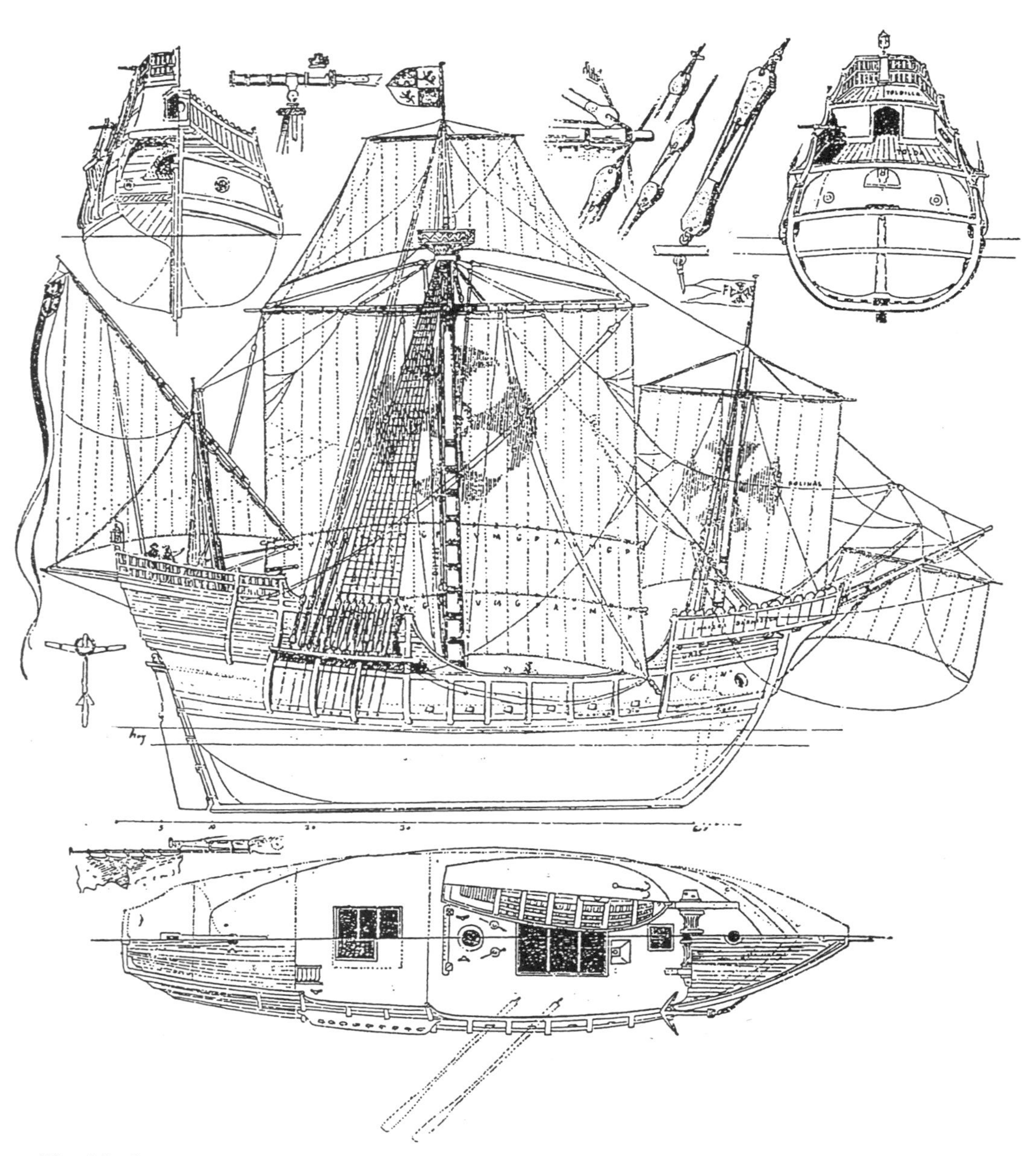

The Monleón project, also of 1892, similar to that of the Government Commission — of which he himself was a member — is less believable because of the excessive height of the masts and of the superstructures. The "skycam" view from above shows two oars, quite unrealistically.

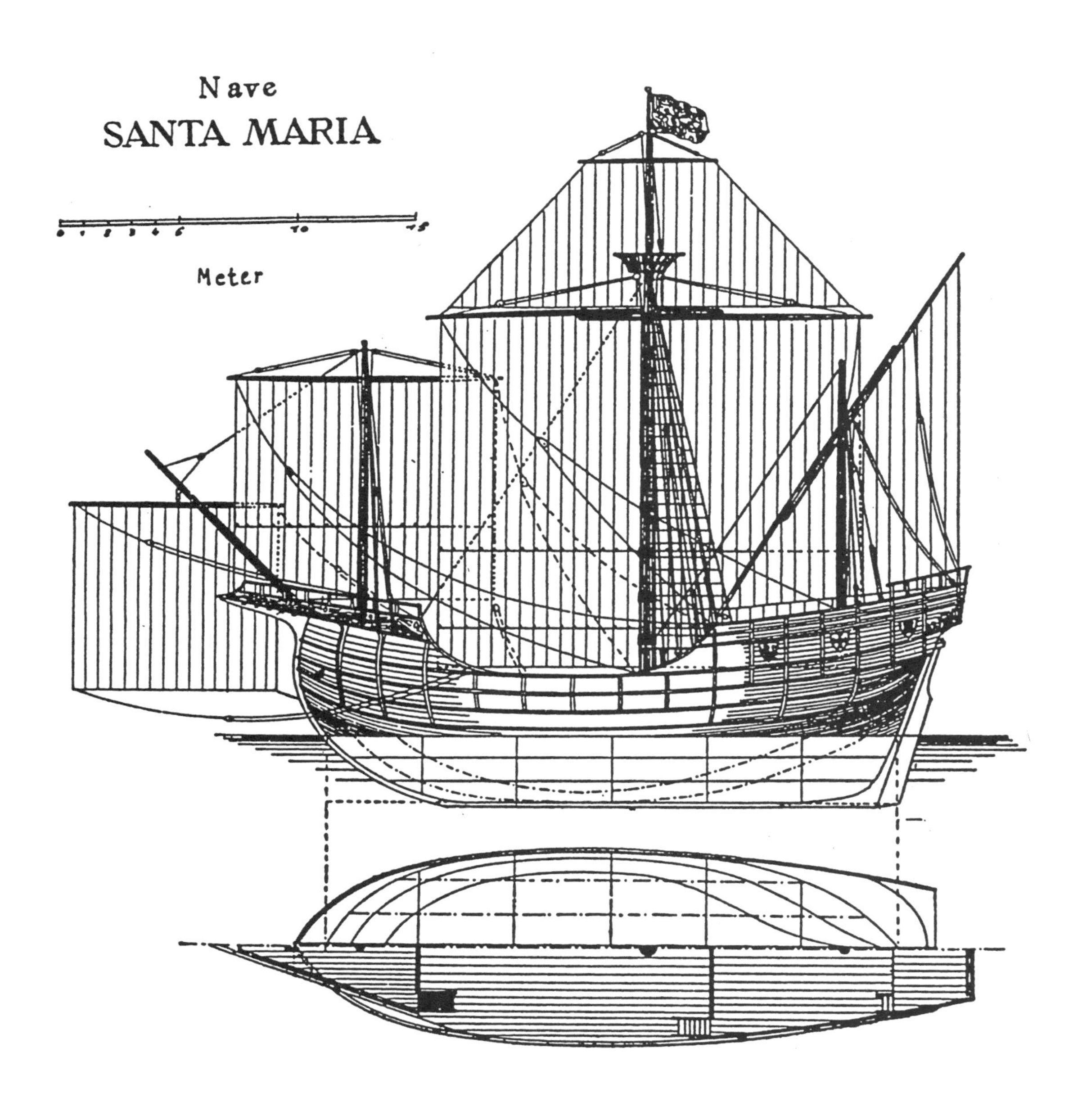

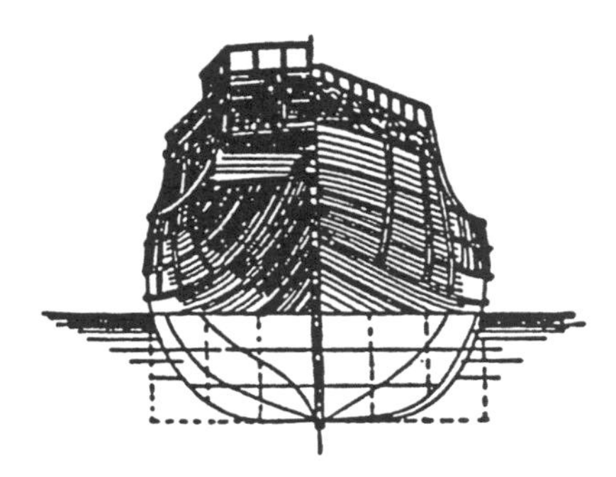

The *Santa Maria* as proposed by D'Albertis in 1892.

Full model of the *Santa Maria* according to D'Albertis, on exhibition at the Naval Museum of Pegli (Genoa).

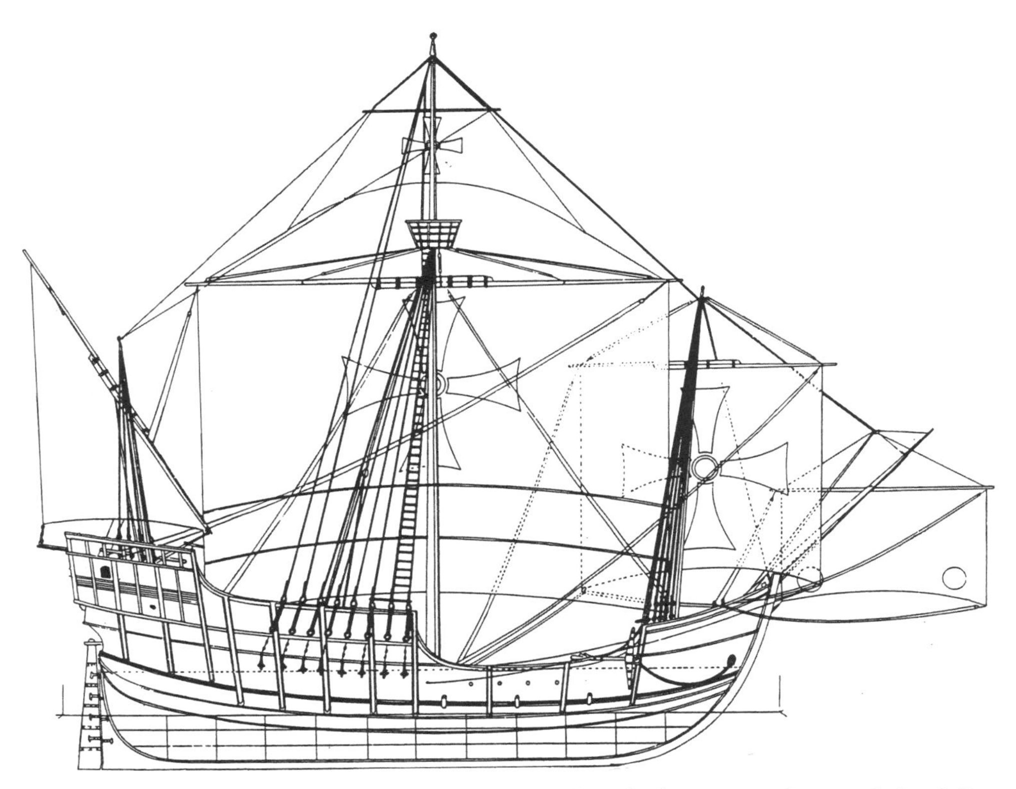

The 1929 *Santa Maria* reconstruction as a *carabela redonda,* or round caravel, by Julio Guillén Tato.

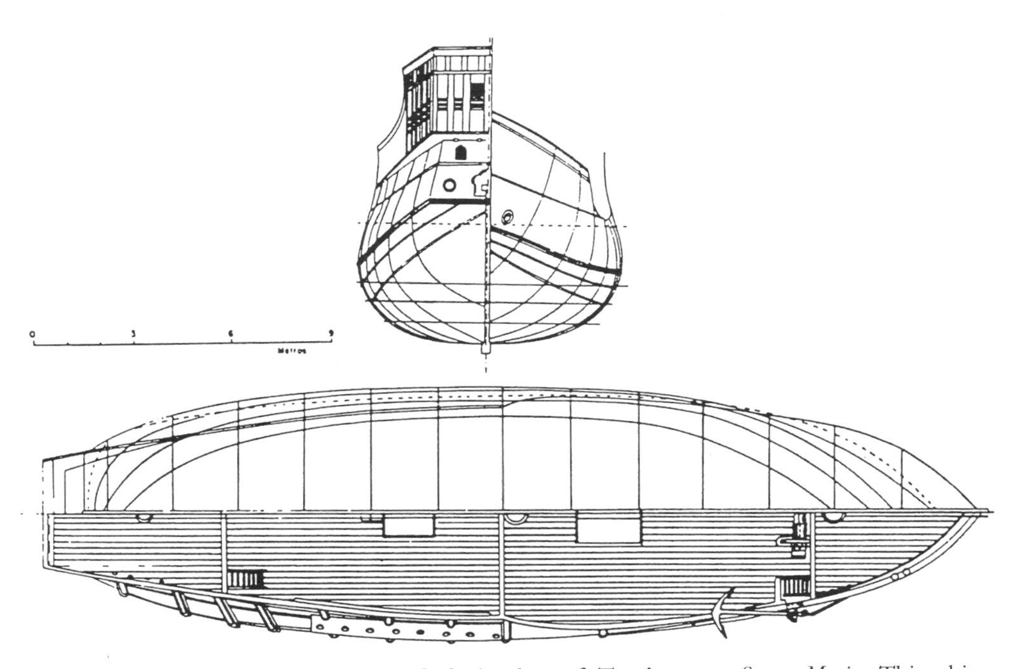

Fig. p. 123: Construction view and deck plan of Tato's 1927 *Santa Maria.* This ship, reconstructed full-size by the Echevarrieta shipyard in Cadiz for the Ibero-American exposition in Seville, sank in 1945 as it was towed from Valencia to Seville. A replica built in Valencia in 1951 for a film production was thereafter exhibited in Barcelona opposite the ancient Arsenal as an attraction of the local Naval Museum.

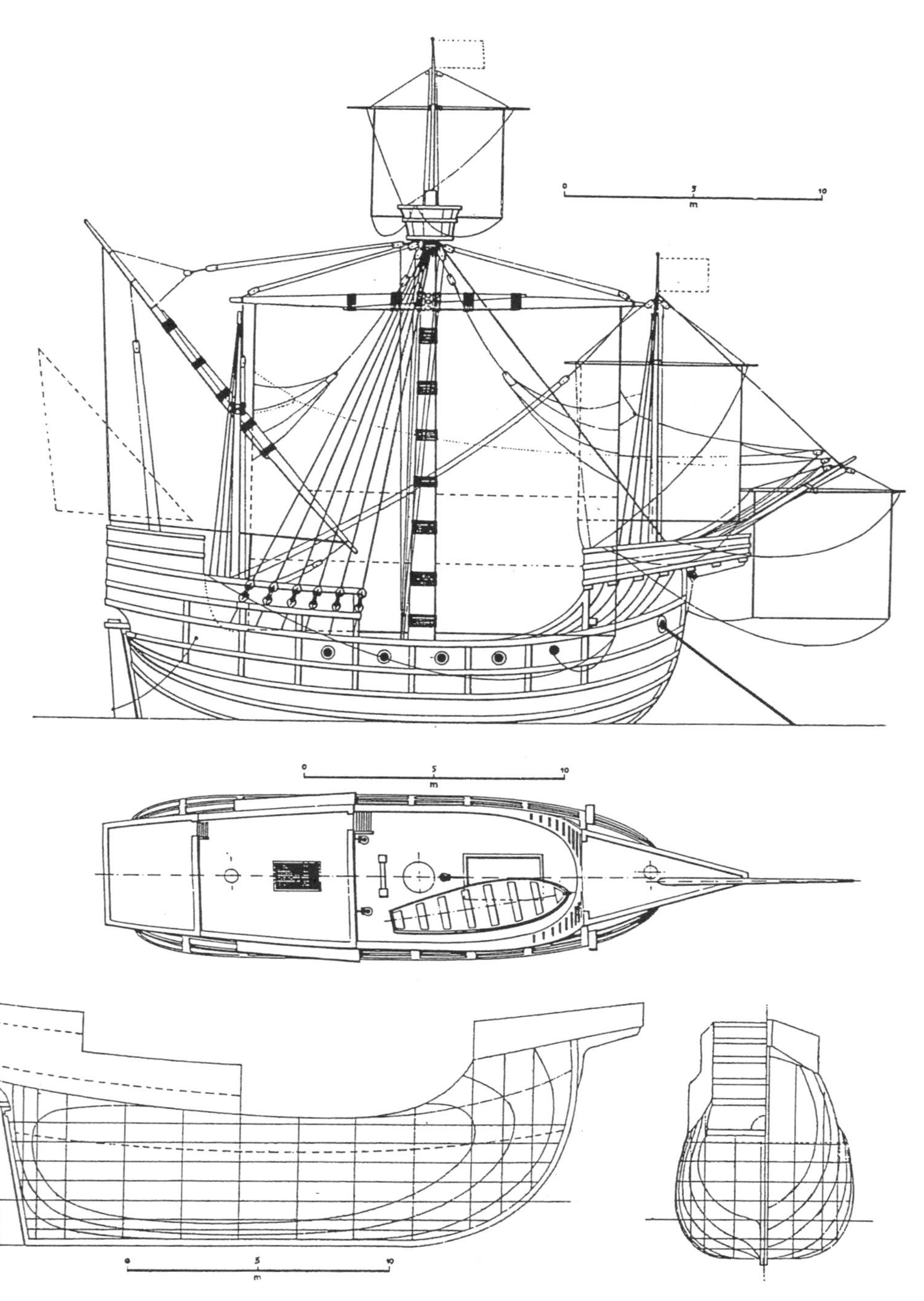

The *Santa Maria* according to a project by Wolfgang Hinderer, published by the magazine *Mechanicus*, in 1965.

Still around 1892, in Italy captain D'Albertis, one of the most perceptive scholars of Columbian problems, worked out an accurate study on the three expedition ships which appeared in Volume IV of the *Raccolta*, a collection of documents and studies published by Italy's Royal Columbian Commission.

We have previously summarized the reasoning through which D'Albertis came to determine the dimensions of the three ships and particularly those of the *Santa Maria*; his solution turned out to be the largest ship of those devised by the various authors. The drawings of the three vessels, barely mentioned in the *Raccolta*, were later re-elaborated and turned into large models by the Costaguta shipyards commissioned by the Genoa municipality. Presently, the three models are on exhibit in the Naval Museum at Pegli (Genoa).

D'Albertis's *Santa Maria* is even more credible as a reproduced model than in the sketchy drafts (reported on pp. 121-122), and appears to be more "of her time" than the Spanish reconstructions. She has a round stern, a well-proportioned set of sails with a trapezoidal topsail, and the hull ornaments — albeit limited to a series of shields on the flag rail — are indeed decorative elements that a merchant ship certainly would not need, being possibly a hindrance and in any case of no practical purpose.

In 1927-1929, on the occasion of the Ibero-American Exposition in Seville, the Echevarrieta shipyards (Cadiz) built a full-size *Santa Maria*, following the indications of then lieutenant Julio F. Guillén Tato and the plans of General engineer José Quintana. True to his erroneous conviction that the *Santa Maria* was a square caravel and not a *nao*, Guillén Tato gave to his creation many of the characteristics of this type of ship. In particular its bow, with the castle missing, was typical of a caravel, while the round-shaped stern with an important quarterdeck was closer to that of a *nao*'s. The topsail of Guillén Tato's "nao-caravel" was of very limited size, though preserving its acceptable trapezoidal shape (see page 123).

After serving out her role as an attraction at the Sevillan show, this ship remained docked opposite the La Rabida monastery for a long time. In 1945, while she was being towed from Valencia to Cartagena for much needed maintenance work, she sank on account of the poor conditions of the keel.

In 1951 the Lacomba shipyards in Valencia built a second replica of Guillén Tato's "caravel" that was to be used for the shooting of the movie "Alba de America." Brought subsequently to Barcelona (in 1952), she remained anchored in front of the Arsenal and of the Columbus monument, open to the public. In order to restore the vessel to the historically correct form of a *nao*, a hull-based castle was built at the bow end.

In 1930 R.C. Anderson designed and supervised the construction of the *Santa Maria* model for the Addison Gallery of American Art in Andover, Mass. He published some of the data for his project in the magazine *The Mariner's Mirror* (XVI, 2, April 1930). His well-proportioned and well-fitted *Santa Maria* exhibited, for the first time, a quarterdeck of reduced proportions, without excessive throw at the stern end and with a small and square topsail, whose master rope ran to blocks set halfway down the yard below.

In 1961, in his famous book *The ship*, Björn Landström drew a *Santa Maria* and left a short graphical sketch of it. His *nao* does not deviate from previous reconstructions; "...it is believed that overall this was her appearance, even though any single detail could have been different," he wrote, taking his precautions against a seasoned rank of critics ready to attack him. As to the actual criticisms levied against him, we shall mention only the one relative to the master ropes of the topsail featured now at the very top of the yard, which could even be a correct choice as it conveys a semblance of functionality of the sail itself.

In 1964 José Maria Martínez Hidalgo, at the time a Navy commander and the director of the Barcelona Maritime Museum, after a decade spent on studying the Columbian ships, had the satisfaction of seeing his project for a reconstruction of the *Santa Maria* become a reality at the Cardona shipyards in Barcelona, the one destined for exhibition at the World Fair in New York. The hull was carried to the United States on board the German vessel *Naidenfels*.

At about the same time, a second *Santa Maria* replica was commissioned by the Venezuelan government. Thus, these two *Santa Marias* by Martínez Hidalgo came to represent the epitome of all the evolution of the scholarship on Columbian ships up to that moment. As Howard I. Chapelle, the curator of the Smithsonian Institute in Washington and a renowned naval scholar, wrote: "Every new reconstruction of the Columbian ships has marked a steady progress over the previous projects."

Also to be remembered are the 1966 studies on the *Santa Maria* by Wolfgang Hinderer, published in the magazine *Mechanicus*. There the author surmises the possibility a fourth small mast with lateen sail at the extreme stern, which, we conjectured, could have been a way of using the boat's mast under favorable circumstances.

As the 1992 celebrations for the fifth centennial of Columbus's enterprise loomed on the horizon, the number of independent studies on his flotilla have multiplied. The Spanish Commission for the Columbian celebrations afforded the opportunity to reconstruct all three ships. The new

Santa Maria was rebuilt at Cadiz in 1991 and, after some calls in Mediterranean ports, sailed to the Americas to take part in the celebrations, together with the replicas of the two caravels. Unfortunately the Commission has been until now very stingy about sharing information on its projects, and so far all we have found is a side view.

Much more generous toward scholars and naval history enthusiasts have been Wolfram zu Mondfeld, Peter Holz and Johannes Soyener who, in addition to a detailed study on the Columbian ships, have published a series of minutely detailed reconstruction plans of the three vessels. The *Santa Maria* by Wolfram zu Mondfeld, which can also be admired in a beautiful model reproduced in his book (*Die Schiffe des Cristoforo Colombo*, Koeler-Herford 1982), conveys a rustic medieval aspect which, in all likelihood, is significantly close to that of the original.

Since it is impossible to dwell on every detail of each reconstruction, and being convinced that from their totality it is possible to draw a sense of what the original *Santa Maria* might have been like, we intend to outline her characteristics as an occasional interested visitor would do, curious to make the acquaintance of a ship ready to sail for her adventurous voyage.

The hull. – The discovery of the Mataró model has led contemporary scholars to the conviction that the *nao* was proportionally wider — in respect to the all-out length — than previously assumed.

It would be wise, hovever, not to embrace the Mataró model as fully reliable. It almost certainly is in fact a votive offering, which, though created by someone familiar with things of the sea, does not surely mirror reality. Had the author been a carpenter, he would have given the hull a more realistic shape. But its execution appears rough and approximate, with evident exaggerations, one of which could precisely be the excessively wide beam. As to the form of the keel, the model shows it as star-like and "V" shaped, with its maximum width not at the buoyancy line, but above it, on the deck's board line.

Aside from the proportions of its dimensions, this model has provided a number of indications concerning details of the hull, on its round and strong shape, fully strengthened by robust outside girdles running from prow to stern external to the planking, and extended also below the water-line level, thus producing a beneficial drift-abating effects. Some strong vertical ribs intersected the girdles from the buoyancy line, or just a little above it, as high as the bulwark. These vertically-placed elements, called *burlamacas*, besides strengthening the hull, had the additional purpose of protecting it when bumping against docks, acting indeed as veritable fenders.

These elements, commonly found in all the representations of coeval ships, were certainly featured on the hull of the *Santa Maria* as well, although no one can conclusively establish either their number or their position.

The castle. – The forecastle consisted of a straight-sided triangular platform, supported by the wheel fore and by a transverse beam aft, which was arc-shaped for aesthetical rather than structural reasons. On its sides, the castle floor was connected to the hull by a planking section that raised the bow protecting it from the surging waves. All around the castle platform was lined with distinctive boards [known as *pavesi*].

Impavesata was the technical and historical name given to a parapet rising from a deck or from another superstructure. On medieval ships, in fact, it was customary to raise and protect the battle side with some heavy wooden shield, or with the very shields of the armed men, which were also called *pavesi* [from Pavia, a northern Italian city]. When such a practice became obsolete, the term survived to designate the protected side.
The floor boarding connecting the ship's prow and the castle, which is believed to have been narrower at its top, exhibited either side-by-side boards, as evidenced by some reconstructions, or overlapped boards as shown in others including the Mataró model, in this instance certainly sensible. It should be noticed, however that the overlapping was not done in the bow-to-stern direction, i.e., with the fore board partially set over the aft board, as it would seem logical or natural, but ran the opposite way (as reasonably well-visible in the reconstruction of the Mataró ship by P. dell'Orco, p. 109). This arrangement caused the water of a wave, once it reached that height, to meet a series of small obstacle lines — the overlapping boards — and was thus channeled downward, away from midship. An expedient, this, certainly resulting from an ancient practice. On the other hand, the planking between castle and deck, which ended what we have described as an arc, had boards overlapped "correctly," in a roof-tile fashion one might say, because its function was only to handle the flow of rainwater.

The quarterdeck. – At stern the quarterdeck — a long platform superimposed to the deck — rested on beams spanning from side to side, in some places centrally supported by deck pillars. At the far end of the stern, the angular projection of the quartedeck, which had an almost rectangular structure, was supported by the main transom, a transversal beam set on top of the sternpost, flush with the upper surface of the poop and serving as support for the quarterdeck.

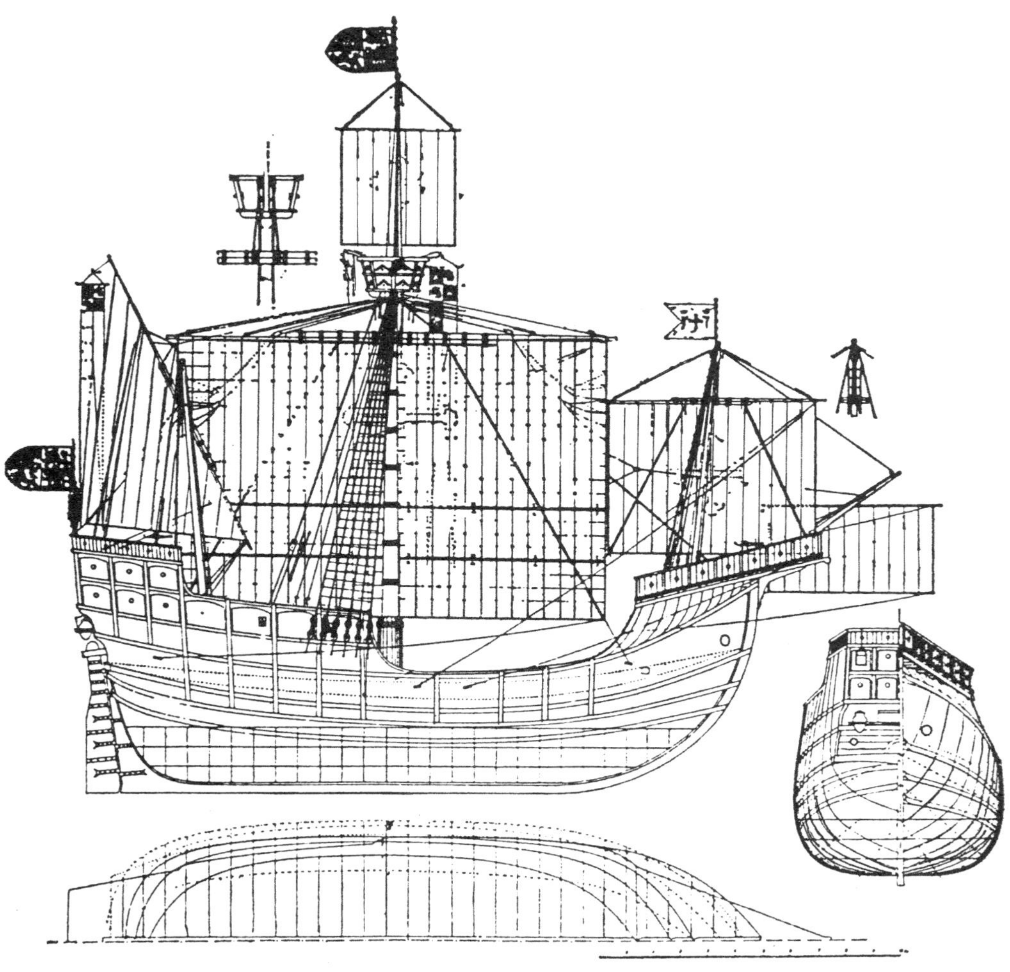

Sail rigging and construction plan.

Longitudinal and cross sections, and top deck.

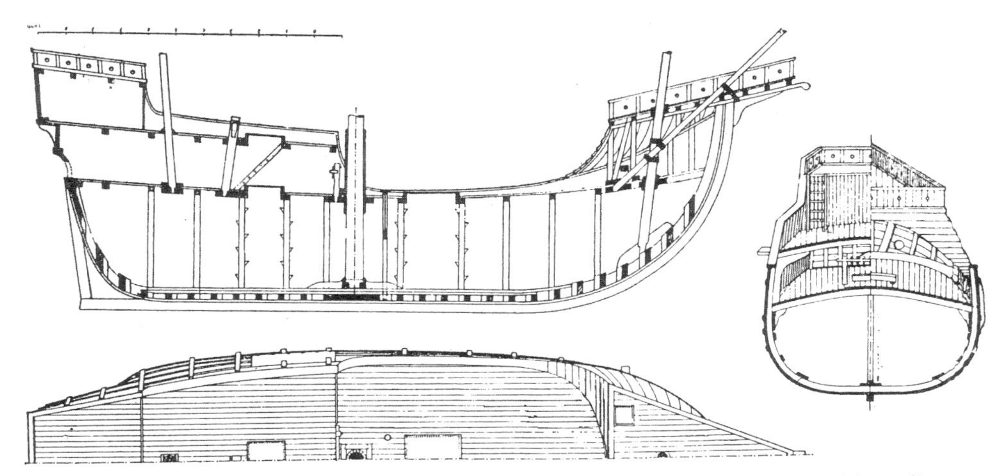

The *Santa Maria* according to the reconstruction by José Maria Martínez Hidalgo, director of the Barcelona Maritime Museum (1963). It may be pointed out that all the reconstructions that followed, in particular the one by the 1992 Spanish Commission, drew inspiration from this excellent work.

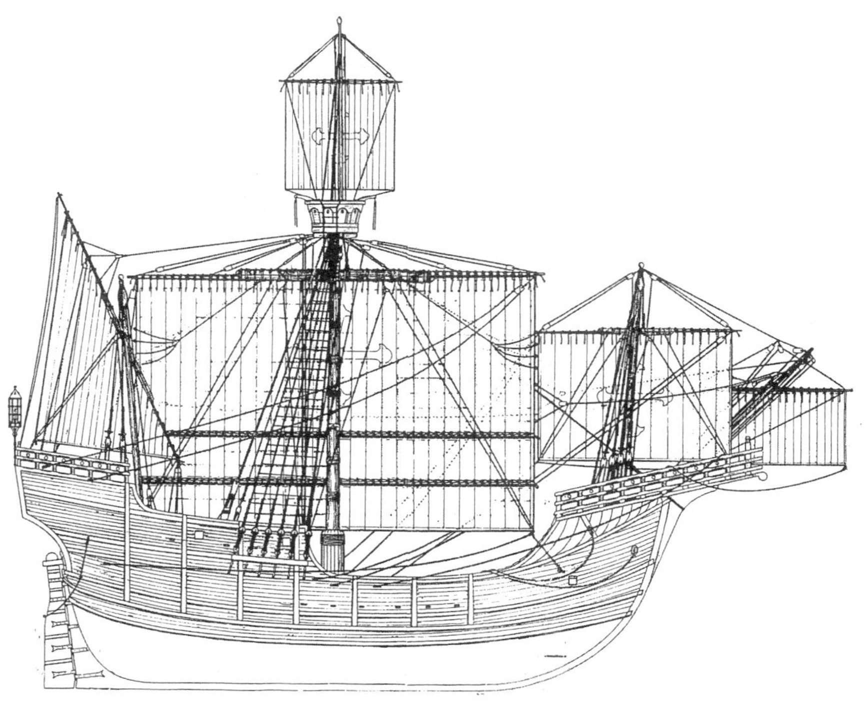

Reconstruction of the *Santa Maria*, executed in Barcelona on behalf of the Spanish Commission for the Fifth Centennial celebrations [1992].

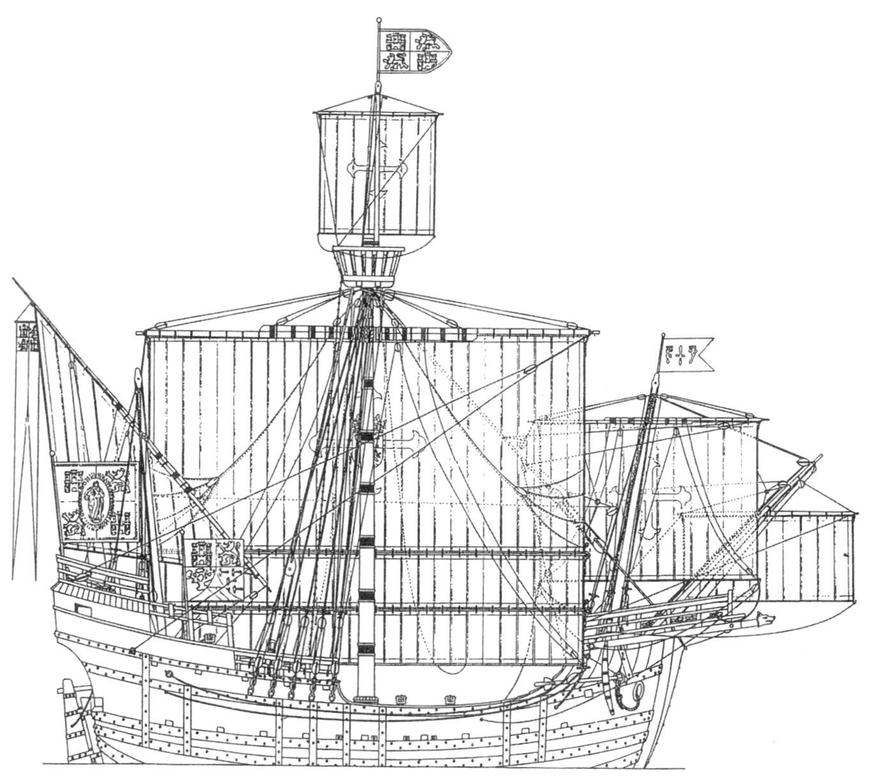

The *Santa Maria* in the 1991 project by Wolfram zu Mondfeld, Peter Holz and Johannes Soyener.

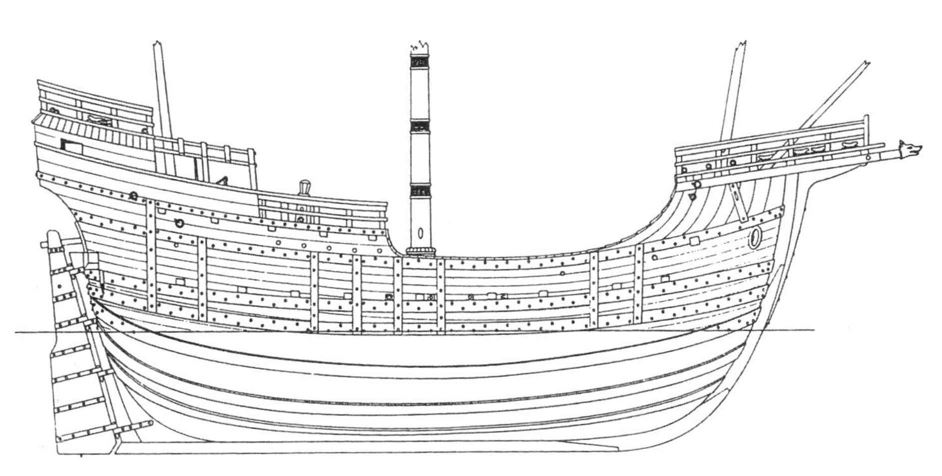

Side view of the *Santa Maria*, according to the project by Wolfram zu Mondfeld, Peter Holz and Johannes Soyener.

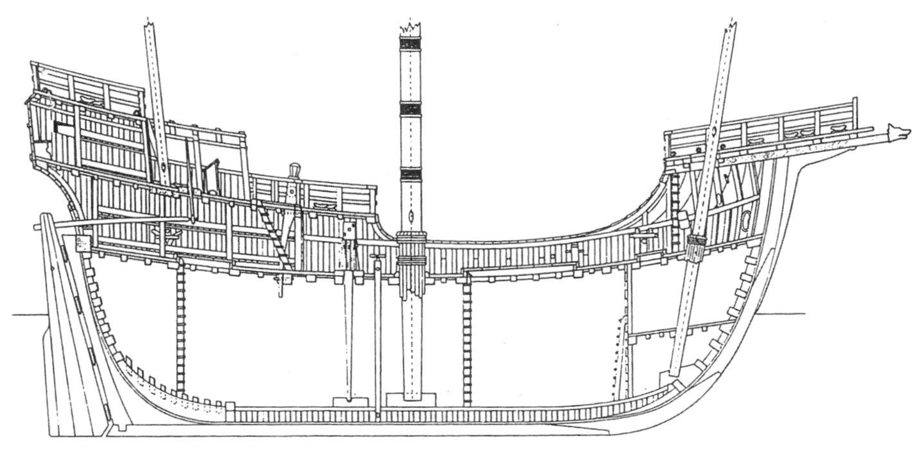

Longitudinal section of the same project by Wolfram zu Mondfeld and others. The large dimensions of the hull allow for a higher cargo capacity in the hold, perhaps larger than it was in reality.

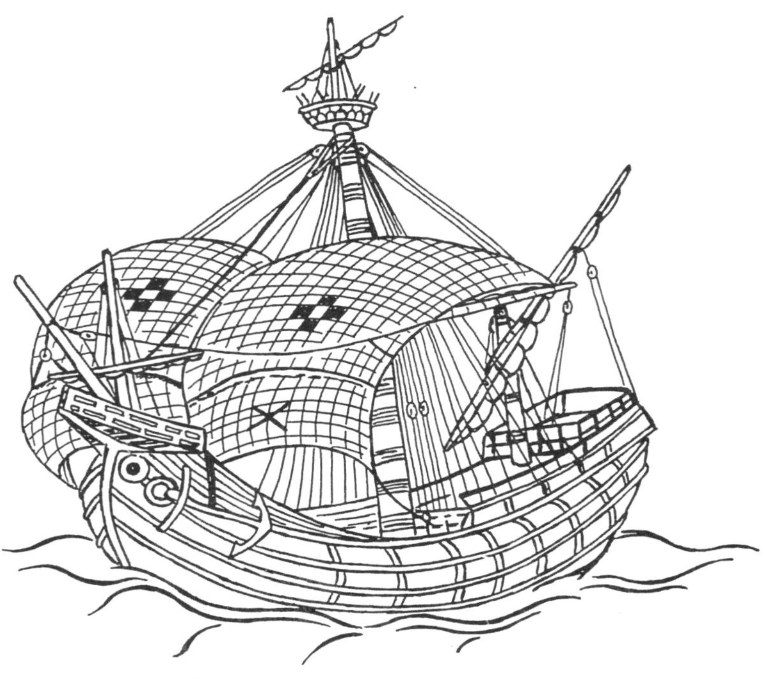

The most suggestive reproduction of a *nao* like the *Santa Maria* is found on a chart by Benincasa drawn up in 1482. Albeit roughly, all the elements that characterize a *nao* are represented. The vessel has all the sails gathered, except for the big master sail, which however is lowered to the mast's midsection, as if intending to gather up this sail as well in order to remove the bonnet (or do just the opposite operation).

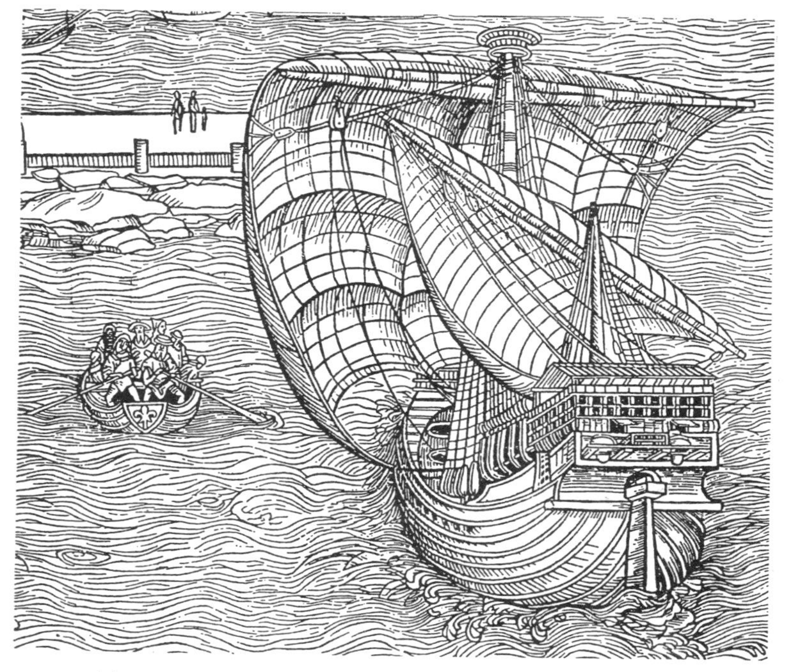

The ship engraved by E. Renwich to illustrate the book by Bernard von Brydenbach *Die heyligen Reissen gen Jherusalem* of 1486. The same vessel, turned in the contrary direction, was copied to illustrate an edition of the "Letter of Columbus" published in Basel in 1494. The shape of the poop and the position of the dredger are quite clear.

Landström and others argue that between the transverse beams resting on the ship's internal walls and the bottom of the superimposed quarterdeck above it, there was open space not covered by planking to let air circulate inside. This idea seems unconvincing, first because such an opening would cause water leaks in heavy seas, and furthermore because air and light could enter in abundance anyways, since the front of the quarterdeck was not closed.

Astern in the aft part of the quarterdeck there was a small cabin, closed in front, that everyone believes to have been Columbus's own quarters, where he securely kept the charts, the nautical instruments and the scanty remaining valuables of the ship. One could climb up to a *pavesi*-lined platform above the cabin, the highest point of the ship.

Their dimensions notwithstanding, quarterdeck and castle were rather light structures that did not weigh down the hull too much, as it would be the case in the sixteenth and seventeenth century when ships would feature, especially astern, huge quarterdecks and showy ornamentations as well as sculptures.

Shroud fenders. – Many reconstructions display shroud fenders or channels, if not for all the masts, at least for those of the main mast. Designed to secure the riggings and keep the ropes clear of the gunwales or bulwarks, they consisted of flat pieces of wood (or metal) projecting orthogonally off the shipsides and effectively contributed to rigidify the mast and shroud assembly. This "reconstructed" detail, too, raises doubts, because of its absence in a great many representations of ships of this period of time, wherein it appears that the shrouds are fastened directly to the shipside by means of iron plates or chain-plates, internally or externally to the hull [backstay plates and futtock plates]. In any case, the *Santa Maria* recently reconstructed by the Spanish Commission has shroud fenders for the main mast.

Bow and stern shapes. – One can derive information concerning the high and rounded bow shape even just by observing the ship drawn on the Benincasa chart, as well as from Vittore Carpaccio's large canvasses depicting the cycle of Saint Ursula (see p. 62). In 1495 Carpaccio painted his cog boats — clearly with a Venetian touch, but not too dissimilar from the ships that in his time were sailing along European coasts. He did so therefore at a time very close to Columbus's enterprise and, if it is true that the *Santa Maria* was by then already somewhat antiquated, one could also think that the cogs painted by Carpaccio were not brand new, but, more or less, coeval ships, comparable to the caracks engraved by the mysterious W.A. (see pp. 66, 67 and 68), dated around 1475, and the ship engraved by E. Renwich for Bernard von Brydenbach's book *Journey to Jerusalem* of 1486 (see p. 132). All such depictions confirm, incidentally, the chain-plates details discussed earlier.

As for the shape of the stern, on the other hand, by now everyone accepts with little hesitation that it must have been round, with planking strakes rising toward the main transom. The square or "mirroring" [right-angled] poop would appear on large ships early on in the sixteenth century, probably as a result of its success as a feature of caravels.

The square mirror stern, easier to build, made it possible to streamline the immersed part of the hull so as to improve the thinning of it underwater, making for a sleeker, more penetrating profile and rendering it more sensible to the rudder. All sixteenth-century galleons, recognized as direct offspring of caravels — albeit with greater dimensions — had a square stern and perpetuated this feature for all large vessels henceforth. Admittedly, the representation of square-poop ships is occasionally documented as well before the end of the fifteenth century, for example in the Globe of Martin Behaim, but it should not be forgotten that these charts were touched up in the following centuries and that, in any case, such artistic drawings were affected by artistic mannerisms.

Let us now pretend to be on board of our hypothetic *Santa Maria*, and observe the deck made of parallel boards, each approximately eight inches wide, caulked and protected with bitumen. This deck exhibited a strong arching toward the middle of the ship devised to aid the fast discharge of water that might collect on deck. We shall proceed from stern to prow to find out what is noticeable throughout those two hundred square meters or so of space where, for the entire voyage, sailors and the occasional passengers moved about.

The protected space of the quarterdeck was dark, plain and so low that a man just taller than the average could barely stand erect in it.

Rudder. – The most important item to be found in the space underneath the quarterdeck was the long helm tiller which protruded onto the deck from astern through a large hole, either round or semicircular, opened in the lower stern section of the quarterdeck. The tiller was handled with the help of two tackles, one on the left and the other on the right side, installed not so much to reduce the effort of the helmsman, who anyway received help from two "advisors," as rather to keep the tiller in the desired position as well as to prevent that sudden lurches in the boat's motion, acting on the rudder blade, transform the tiller into a deadly weapon.

The helmsman had a very limited view of the section of the ship in front of him. What was important for him to see, i.e., the binnacle with the compass in front of him, was always well-lit by a lantern suspended from the beams or by small lights inside the binnacle case itself. Besides this, all he could see was the remaining part of the deck as far as the bow and the lower part of the sails. He did not see the sky or the clouds, did not feel the wind's direction, and did not even have a view of the sea or of the obstacles existing in a tranquil harbor as the ship approached the dock. In order to guide the vessel correctly, he had only to follow the instructions conveyed by the pilot, on the deck above him, but transmitted through the advisors, and make sure that the compass needle kept on course. This may come as a surprise because the helmsman's role in itself has become larger than reality. Yet, even on modern vessels although the helmsman is in the deck-house and has the widest visual field, he does not act on his own initiative, as he is to promptly execute the orders he receives from the captain or the watch officer.

That things did not always go as described, however, especially in more relaxed moments, is illustrated by the wreck of the *Santa Maria*, which took place when everyone was asleep, except for an inexperienced cabin boy left at the helm, notwithstanding the fact that "the breaking and retracting of the waves could be heard from a good league's distance."

Yet the helmsman was not a blind automaton either, belonging rather to the most qualified crew members. He had to be endowed with a keen perception and feel for the motion of a ship, rooted in his long experience, the same experience that would instantly alert the pilot and the captain, even while dozing in their hammocks (at sea, sleep is light), when something was not right and their presence required.

Some reconstructions have envisioned the helmsman's place in open air, on the quarterdeck, with a complete view of the ship, the masts and the sky, maneuvering the tiller underneath by means of a vertical lever fastened on its tip and running through a hole made in the deck. We have reservations on whether this arrangement, later widely adopted, was already in usage at the end of the fifteenth century.

The rudder was a broad wooden piece of the same thickness as the sternpost, made of flush-pressed boards to attain the needed blade width and held together by a number of strong forged-iron strips. Some of these strips had at their inner end a pintle or rudderpin, that is, a sturdy pivot that engaged the gudgeon or socket, a hollow cylinder welded to an iron plate fixed onto the sternpost. Three or four of these pintles sufficed to join the rudder to the hull; its own weight, in fact, prevented it from slipping off loose except for when, in exceptional circumstances, it might be subject to abnormal stresses. Although remotely possible, to offset any chance that the rudder would slip off or break pintles and gudgeons from the stern, an event that would have caused the loss of this essential part of the ship, the rudder was secured to the hull by means of two chains loose enough not to interfere with its free and normal motion.

During the voyage to the Canaries, the *Pinta* had some trouble with her rudder. These vicissitudes are recorded in three distinct passages of Columbus's *Journal*: On Monday, August 6: "The rudder of the caravel *Pinta*, on board of which travelled Martin Alonso Pinzón, slipped off or came loose, which arose the suspicions on the account of Gomez Rascon and Cristoval Quintero, owner of the caravel, because he didn't like that voyage." The rudder was repaired but the day after "The rudder of the *Pinta* broke off again." Finally on August 9, at the Grand Canary, "they repaired the *Pinta* very well working hard under the watchful eye of the Admiral."

The aspect of sabotage in the break-off of the rudder of the *Pinta* has been examined by P. E. Taviani (*The Journal of Christopher Columbus*, Nuova Raccolta Colombiana, vol. I, tome II, Rome 1992) who holds it scarcely credible for the simple reason that a sailor would never so seriously damage the ship on which he must sail, especially in largely uncharted waters. But even if Gomez Rascon actually did attempt to discourage Columbus and cause him to renounce his project — indeed an impossible task with a person as obstinate as the Admiral — after failing he was well-behaved throughout the duration of the voyage.

Just before the tiller bar there was a narrow manhole that allowed access into the hatch underneath, a section that D'Albertis figured was divided in two levels with transverse beams, better fitted for storing the casks. A little farther on, a fairly wide wooden stairway led up to the quarterdeck through a hatch-way. Still below deck, just under the quarterdeck was usually located a capstan for hauling-in and all other related loading operations required on a ship, such as hoisting the heavy yard of the lower square sails, or for lowering and retrieving a lifeboat, as well as general loading and unloading of goods. In other instances this indispensable implement was located fore, in such cases it was featured near the castle.

The the space between deck and counterdeck could host a pair or more of those artillery pieces that a vessel would carry as a cautionary measure, rather than to face the serious threat of a pirate or enemy ship with foul intentions. But this topic will be addressed later.

The mainmast rose from the deck before the quarterdeck, and sank down into the hatch to rest onto a stanchion well-fastened onto the keelson.

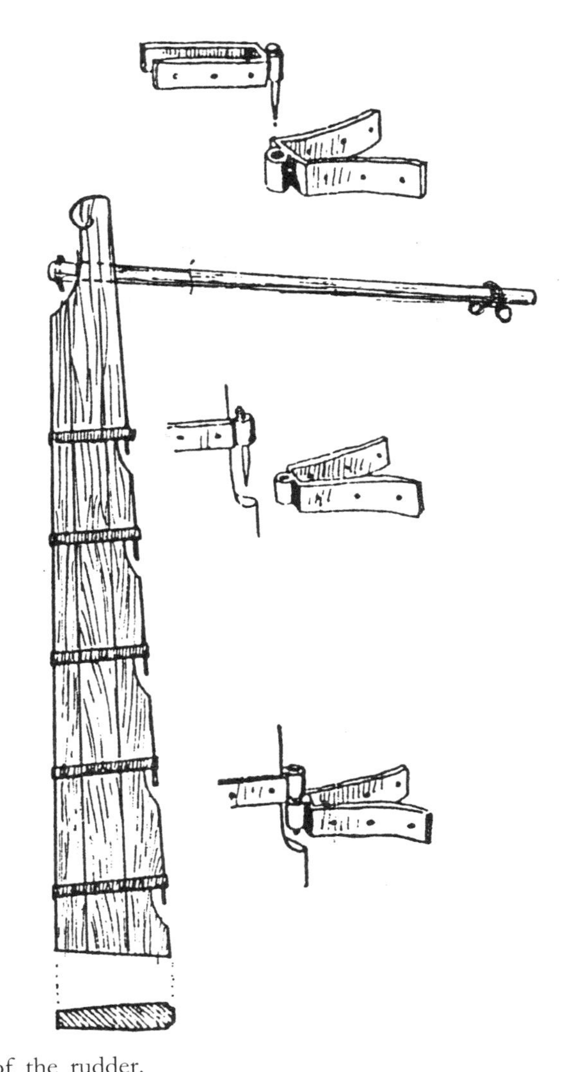

Pintles and gudgeons of the rudder.
In ancient times the lateral rudder was called *governaglio or goverale* ([that is, stabilizer], from the Latin *gubernaculum* [via Old Provençal *governal*]). The Latin term *temonem*, for 'rudder', is preserved in the Italian *timone*, deriving — as explained by G. Santi Mazzini — from the wooden yoke of an ox-drawn cart which controls the direction of movement of oxen. Thus the helm or tiller bar used to maneuver gradually came to signify the entire "directional" mechanism as well as its tiller or bar which lay next to it (thus Italian *agghiaccio*). In English and German instead the "oar" concept prevailed, as evidenced in their respective terms 'rudder' and 'ruder'. The ancient Italian term *governaglio* still survives in the French *gouvernail.*

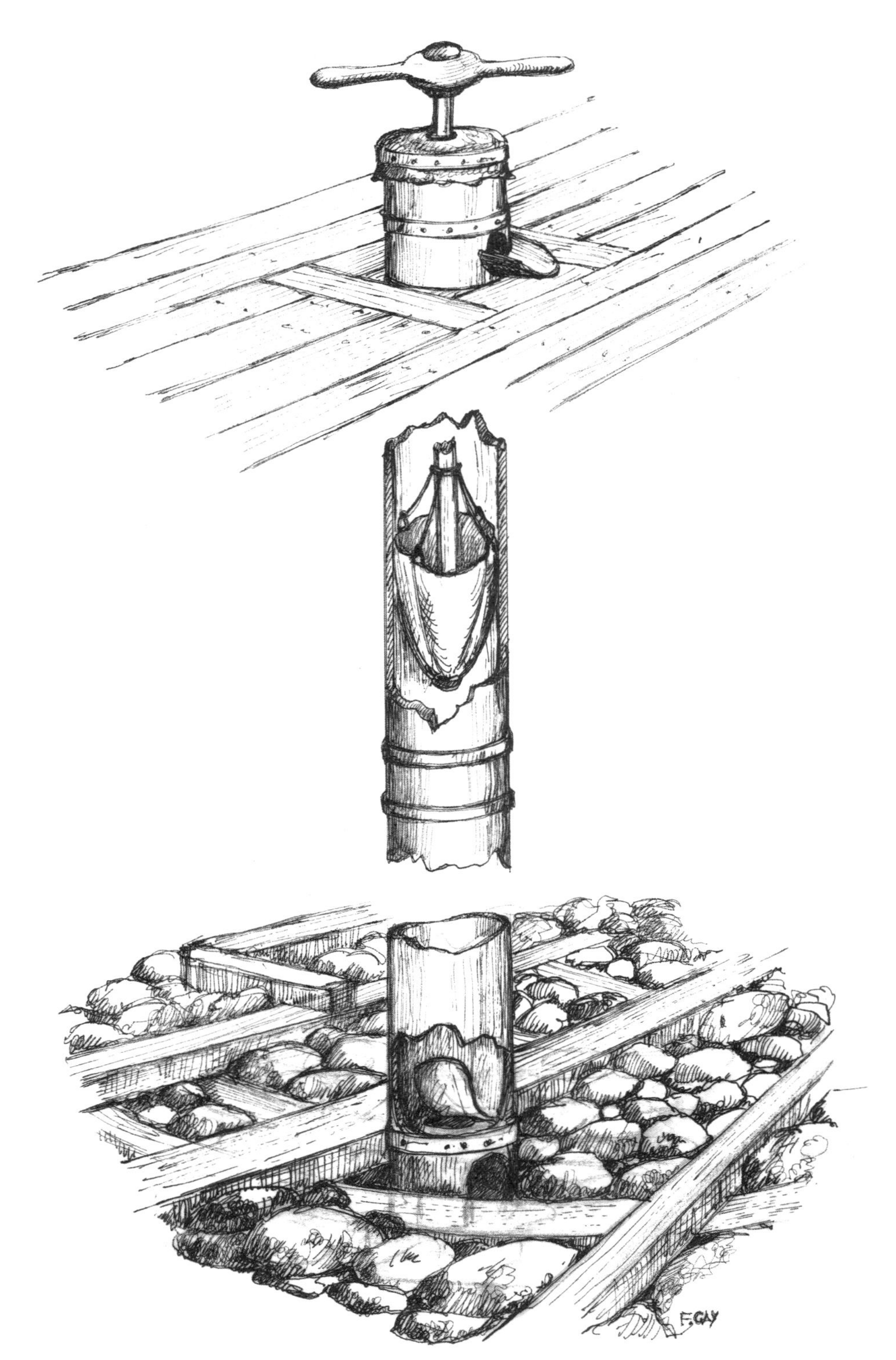

Schematic design of a bilge pump showing the riverbed stones arranged to serve as ballast.

The opening through which the mast passed, or mast-partner, which had a considerable diameter, was reinforced with suitable stiffeners between the beams an d closed, all around the mast, with wooden wedges that controlled the correct positioning of the mast itself. To render it water-tight, the hole was then covered with wax-impregnated canvas.

Between the quarterdeck and the castle, the left-over space, long approximately one half the ship, hosted a large hatchway used to load or unload goods into and from the hold. For these heavy operations, permanent tackles were used. Since such tackles were hinged on the mainmast, the ladder had a twofold function as it served also as the gaff hoisting mechanism.

Ballast. – In the depths of the vessel, under the bottom boards separating the hold from the bilge, there lay the permanent ballast, consisting of round riverbed stones — sometimes gathered in canvas bags — carefully arranged so that they would not shift with the leaning of the vessel, and with channels provided to guide away the water collecting in the bilge near the pumps.

These pumps were enclosed in a square box that extended from the bottom of the bilge up to their outlet on deck. The box was called pumpcasing or well, i.e., bugle well.

The temporary ballast, which was loaded on board when the vessel sailed without a cargo ('in ballast'), varied with what could be found on location wherever the ship had unloaded. It could be sand ('bad' ballast) or crushed stone ('good' ballast) or other heavy material ('good' or 'bad', depending upon the ease of handling and its tendency to produce mud in the well), but appropriately distributed to ensure the vessel's balance. A badly stored ballast, aside from the danger it would pose in case of displacement-induced canting of the ship, could affect the behavior of the ship. A defective distribution, either toward prow or toward the stern, caused a ship to tilt on her beam ends, rendering the vessel either too luff [gripping, i.e., tending to bear up into the wind] or too steery [falling off, i.e., bearing away right before the wind][21]. These inconveniences could however be obviated by shifting the ballast in a convenient way. Stowing the ballast was still a very delicate operation, to be performed only by skilled people.

[21] A luff ship is one that, unresponsive to rudder correction, tends to head into the wind. Another way to describe this is to say that the craft is "ardent," or eager. A steery vessel is one that, again without rudder action, tends to deviate or keep away from the direction of the wind.

Pumps. – The pumps, or bugles, just mentioned were two, and their good operation was vital for the safety of the ship. Each pump consisted of an elm-wood pipe, keckled to prevent cracking under the internal pressure, running vertically from the deck to the bilge, plunging to its lowest bottom. At the low end of the pipe there was the so-called lower pump-box or goblet, a small metal cylinder, fitting snugly within the pipe and equipped with a valve that opened only upwards. Inside the pipe ran a rod or shaft made to go up and down and operated by hand from the deck. The lower end of the rod was shaped as a valve consisting of a small upturned leather bag resembling a reversed umbrella; this, too, opened only from the bottom up. By pulling the rod upward, water would replace the air in the pipe, as it rose from the bottom; then the downward push caused the water collected in the pipe to go still upward, since it could not pass through the closed cup, and forced it to go through the valve at the top end of the rod, which would open under the pressure all the way up to the deck, exiting through a lateral opening in the pump's pipe, called cast-partner aperture or 'bugle light'. The water thus spilled on the deck was discharged outboard through the scuppers — those holes in the sides of the ship, just above the waterway, provided to let the water flow off the deck into the sea. Normally there were a good number of such holes to ensure a fast clearing of the deck in every situation, and they were lined with lead in order to prevent water infiltrations in the frame.

Only much later bronze pump assemblies were introduced because of their better sealing quality, which ensured much higher efficiency in disposing of the seawater which managed to infiltrate the hull and collect in the bilge. This water, in contact with the oak timber of the planking and the framing, caulking hemp and whatever else could gather in that basest of places, rotted immediately, turned black and putrid, and emanated pestilential fumes, causing at times the sailors who had to work below the deck to become ill; yet, the stenching water was also a good sign for seamen, to whom it meant that the hull took in little or no water.

It would not have been good practice, anyway, to let the nauseating stench of wellwater persist just as a form of reassurance for the crew, so from time to time the bilge water would be cleaned out by mixing it with some vinegar into the bottom of the hull, then pumping the dreg out to sea as well as washing the ballast stones.

Boats. – To the sides or on top of the hatchway — when this was closed with wooden boards and wax-impregnated canvas — found their place the two auxiliary crafts of the ship, the large boat, or *batel*, and the small tender, or *chalupa*.

The boat, on account of her weight and dimensions, was hard to haul onboard, and was thus frequently towed, as we already said. The capacity of this launch, a little less than 25 feet long, almost nine wide and with a three-foot tip, was such that, as supplies needed to be replenished it was used as a tender that did the job in about fifty trips. Besides being used for heavy cargo operations, the fact that it had a mast and lateen sail turned her into a most convenient vessel of exploration, since these voyages in unknown lands required multiple landfalls either for need of provisions, especially fresh water, or for surveying expeditions.

The small tender was employed for routine chores, especially to ferry men between ships; her length was about two thirds that of the launch and therefore about 15 feet. Retrieving her onboard, always on deck, meant departure time and an unequivocal signal to leave the vessel for whoever happened to be onboard but was not going to sail. A popular saying put it succinctly: "*batél dentro, amigos fuera*" [boat in, friends out].

In his Journal, Columbus mentions the ship's boats frequently; on October 14: "outfitted the launch of the *nao* and the boats of the caravels...;" and on November 16: "sent the boats of the ship and of the caravel...." Other such references pertain to the stranding of the *Santa Maria* on December 25 and 26.

Upright windlass. – Next in our imaginary onboard walk, one would find a capstan or upright windlass before the mainmast, unless otherwise located astern below the castle.

The location of this device requires a commentary to point out that, astern, it would serve well to lift anchors, to haul in cables and hawsers — operations that could not be performed without a capstan — including lifting the heavy yard of the lower-square sail, and loading or unloading heavy cargo, perhaps utilizing one or both yards of the square sails as hoisting arms. When instead the capstan is located fore, there would be less room to lay out the anchor cables making it equally hard to fit the sennits or braids to the cable and to handle the turning gear (wormshaft and turning wheel).

The old technique used to weigh an anchor before the chains and the slotted discs of the modern windlasses came into being is known to few so a brief explanation is not out of place here. The big anchor rope, soaked and hardened with water, could not be wound two or three times around the revolving inner shafting or spool-shaped cylinder capstan, as typically needed. It was then customary to pass a sturdy cable with several loops around the capstan, and tie together the two ends of that cable by means of a strong binding. This created a turning-gear — that is, a continuous cable ring extending from the capstan to a large block with one or more pulleys clasped to the inner face of the prow wheel, to which the rotating capstan impressed an endless circular motion. The braids or gaskets of the turning-gear were of strong hemp and such as to clasp the anchor cable onto the turning-gear with knots on-the-fly as soon as the cable came onboard through the hawse hole. Such knots were quickly made as the gear turned, then just as quickly loosened as the braids approached the capstan. While at one end the braids were progressively undone, others were clasped to the rope that kept coming from the sea, and so on until the entire rope was onboard and the anchor in its place on the ship's internal side.

With the windlass at prow, further utilization of the capstan would be cumbersome. As for the reconstructions so far realized, the windlass is usually found either aft or fore. The latter solution was adopted also by the Spaniards, and this means that the idea could be made to work unless — perhaps hidden in one of the mysterious large boxes spread here and there — they also featured a functional electric capstan, just as hidden in the hold was a diesel engine, destined to be employed as auxiliary propulsion.

Heinrich Winter, who wrote on this subject in 1968, actually questioned even the very existence of the capstan onboard ships of Columbus's times, maintaining that the technical realization of this machine would have occurred a century after the Admiral's voyage[22]. It is not known exactly on which authority he based his peremptory statement; perhaps he was referring to a more advanced mechanism, but it is indeed inconceivable that no mechanical apparatus was employed onboard these ships, for without such a thing no tasks requiring significant strength, superior to what is humanly possible, could not have been performed.

In support of our view is the episode of the stranded *Santa Maria* on Christmas Eve 1492, reported by Las Casas. He tells us that the Admiral intended to have an anchor carried offshore on the large tender, sink it and then haul the rope with the *cabestante*, i.e., with the vertical capstan, for the purpose of trying to pry the ship free from the shallows. A correct maneuver that any good seaman would have attempted — but which was not executed because the frightened men charged with carrying it out fled instead toward the *Niña*.

[22] Winter's long discussion on the origin of the words *capistano*, *cabestante*, *capstan*, intended to demonstrate that it was not a windlass, is unconvincing. We remain of the opinion that a windlass, capstan, winch, or some other sort of crankshaft were indispensable onboard to lift heavy weights.

On a thirteenth-century Winchester seal visible aft of the ship are two men working the bars of a horizontal capstan ot windlass, while two more at fore are guiding the anchor cable.

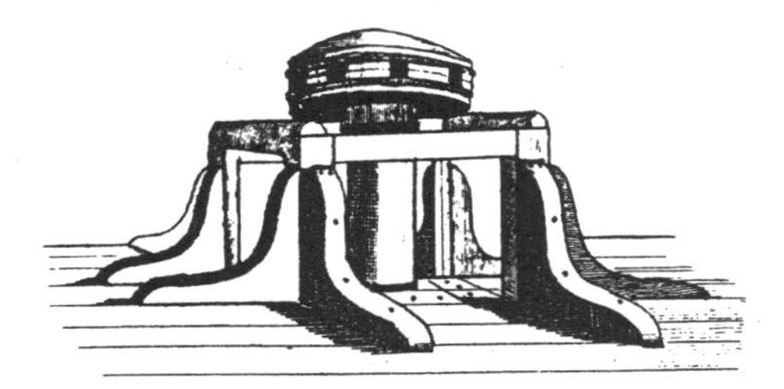

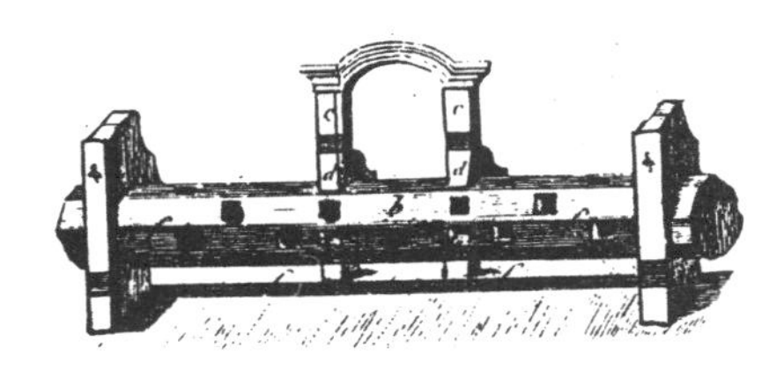

A fifteenth- or sixteenth-century capstan (similar to the device installed on recent Spanish reconstructions) next to a sixteenth-century horizontal winch.

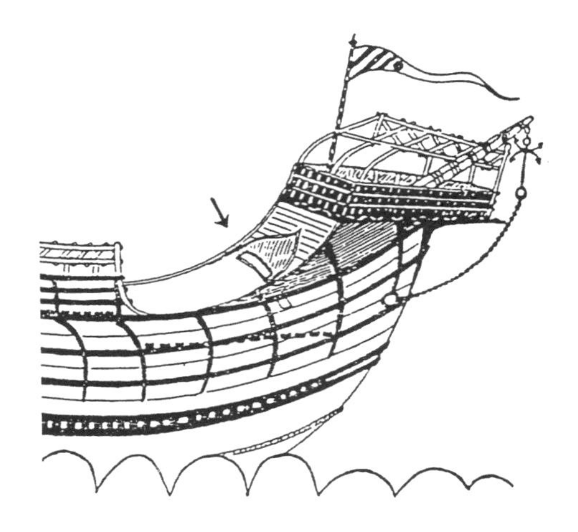

Two documentary drawings, among many, establishing the presence of transversal bitts at stern below the castle.

Above: From the Shipbuilding Treatise of 1445, an Italian work preserved at the British Museum.

Below: A well-known reproduction from the *Libre de Consolato [**] des fetes maritimes*, exhibiting the cable wound-up around the bitt, which has led many to think of a capstan.

Columbus, too, in his *Journal* recounts this episode but he does not elaborate on the actual details of the maneuver he wanted to perform to save the *Santa Maria*, nor does he mention the capstan. This lack of a direct mention, however, should not be misconstrued to deny its existence because, had the Admiral not had available a device capable of supplying the necessary power, he would not have been able to even think of sinking the anchor offshore, let alone ordering it.

One should concede that representations of windlasses onboard ships are not numerous. Yet, it should also be taken into account that artistic reproductions of the vessels are from the outside, with little focus on what was actually on the deck. If, moreover, the capstan was underneath the quarterdeck — as it is more likely — its invisibility would be doubly explained. In fact, some evidence of the existence of winches on ships has surfaced recently: in 1933-1934, the medieval port of Kalmar, in Sweden, was dredged to free it from centuries-old mud. It was during this operation that many wrecks were discovered, and among them was a small thirteenth-century merchant ship denominated Kalmar I, complete with a horizontal capstan. On the deck behind the mast of the 1380 Hanseatic cog recovered at Bremen, were found, in excellent state of preservation, a windlass and a vertical capstan. Their location high on a platform, as if constituting the quarterdeck, raised doubts — being in such a high position — about their utilization, at first sight, which would appear somewhat problematic. However, at the time of her sinking, probably as a result of a river flood, the Bremen cog was still unfinished. This fact allowed specialists to assume that a separate structure connecting the high platform to the hull, creating a veritable quarterdeck, was missing.

Careful inspection of a Winchester seal (see p. 143), reproducing a ship of the Five Harbors, clearly shows two men at stern intent on pushing on the bars of a winch, while two others at prow are pulling on the anchor cable.

Finally, the highly refined representation of a ship seen from above, in a detail of Sandro Botticelli's (or his school's) work "The judgement of Paris" (in the Cini Collection), shows in full evidence a capstan situated on deck between the mainmast and the mizzen mast. The painting was done between 1481 and 1482. These extant documentations sufficiently demonstrate that both capstan types, vertical and horizontal, were featured aboard medieval vessels.

Under-castle quarters. – Past the arch supporting the castle, one finds a narrow triangular space cluttered with cables and other riggings and crossed vertically by the foremast, obliquely by the bowsprit and transversally by a horizontal beam used as a bitt for docking and anchor cables. Farther up, at the extreme bow end, are two hawse-holes for the anchor cables, which are closed with leather caps during the long voyages and, right against the ship's sides, various other items of some use onboard but which do not have assigned space.

What we have called 'bitt' for docking cables, an indispensable element on every ship, is documented in a slightly mysterious way in some representations of historic vessels, among which we reproduce (see p. 144) illustrations from the 1445 Italian Shipbuilding Treatise (at the British Museum, London) and from the *Libre de Consolato des fetes maritimes* printed in Barcelona in 1502. The 'bitt' reproduction is the same included in the Mataró model. The illustration from the *Libre de Consolato* even shows the rope wrapped around the bitt, and right in front there is an upright element resembling a small column, but which in our opinion has nothing to do with the bitt; it could be a deck stanchion or pillar, or even the lower part of the foremast.

A last possible remark concerning the horizontal beam that sometimes, as in the Mataró model, is curved as a deck beam: from the way it is set it would be impossible to wrap a cable around it. Either some clasp is missing, or the cable was secured onto it by means of a binding.

The fire box. – Arranged somewhere on the deck in open air, perhaps a bit sheltered by the castle or the quarterdeck, there was this other important implement, the fire place where, weather permitting, food could be cooked (during Columbus's first voyage, steady fair weather did allow it, except for a few days during the return trip). To identify its precise location is not so important also due to the fact that it could be moved from one site to another, considering that it was a removable low, large iron box lined with refraction bricks or fire clay, resting on feet or broad ties to keep it raised from the deck and away from open wind. On this simple fire platform lighting was done with utmost caution — fire is the most feared enemy on board, especially for wooden ships. On the lit fire, securely fixed with hooks to prevent its overturning, was a cauldron or a large kettle for the daily menu, usually a soup of legumes and salted meat. Lighted at dawn it was kept burning until sundown. A goodly amount of firewood was stored onboard. Yet Columbus repeatedly cites in his *Journal* the need to land in order to restock the provisions of wood and water.

Water. – A freshwater barrel was kept on deck, this too where it was more convenient. Next to it there was a small container with a long handle scoop for drinking. It was not fresh spring water but, for non-extensive voyages such as those made by Columbus it kept reasonably well. Not even a drop of it got wasted,, and if any was left in the container, it would be conscientiously poured back into the big barrel. The water reserve was kept in oak, turkey oak or holm oak casks, jealously guarded and upkept in the hold by the master cooper. Despite every possible attention, as a consequence of the chemical reaction of sulfides and the decomposition of organic matter as well as of the heat-enhanced proliferation of bacteria, the water would turn yellowish in color after a short time, taking on a disgusting odor and taste, before finally becoming filled with micro-organisms. Still later, all these impurities would precipitate to the bottom, making the water potable again, except for the fact that the relentless motion of the ship kept the precipitate constantly stirred up. The preserved water could anyway be strained through cloth or charcoal, or purified with some other empirical means.

The water provision on Columbus's ships probably never reached such deplorable conditions, owing to the relative brevity of the crossings. And besides, regardless of its condition, the water reserve was replenished at every opportunity. For this operation[23], boats were sent ashore with empty barrels, which were cleaned and filled at the "well" or wherever there might be natural springs, either known or discovered by the sailors along the unknown coast, where the presence of water could be inferred from reliable clues. For Columbus, this task did not constitute a problem during his first voyage, because he always landed in places with abundant water.

The anchors. – Onboard all medieval ships, anchors were numerous -- a characteristic indeed not limited to vessels of that time period. A contemporary ship, too, typically carries at least two bower anchors, a stern anchor and a couple of spares. A vessel like the *Santa Maria*, featured two bower anchors (on each side of the prow), the one astern, most likely a four-fluke iron piece, kept under the castle for emergencies[24], and one or two replacement anchors like those afore, perhaps a bit smaller, kept in

[23] The Italian expressions *fare l'acquata* e *acquata* indicated aswell the source of water i.c. spring, well, river etc. these Italian ways of saying lasted through the middle of the XVIIIth century.

[24] The stern anchor, which certainly existed since it is an indispensable safety feature for any vessel, does not appear on any known old reproduction, except for that of a German carack of 1490, though this was not a very convincing picture. It is therefore legitimate to presume that it used to be placed in the interior of a ship, under the quarterdeck, and therefore not in sight.

the hold just in case the original ones were to be lost. The loss of an anchor was not a rare occurrence, since either the hemp cable broke as it rubbed against submerged rocks, or the heaving crew could not pry it free from the hold, and it remained caught in an irregular bottom. If irretrievably lost, it was necessary to abandon it, at the further loss of many yards of cable. On February 17 the *Niña*, with Columbus onboard, lost two anchors after trying to moor close to St. Maria island in the Azores, because of "a furious sea and the many rocks there existing," writes Las Casas. A number of kedge anchors or grapnels were carried for the tenders, but could be very useful as well for maneuvering the ship.

The number of the anchors described is of course only a hypothesis, but, quite realistically, good sailors like Columbus or the Pinzón brothers would not have sailed off without a sufficient supply of implements so indispensable to a vessel, particularly in far-away lands where they knew they might not be able to replace them.

The shape of medieval anchors has more or less remained unchanged until the end of the nineteenth century: a long iron shaft from which two flukes or claws branch out, each ending in a triangular palm, designed to take hold on the bottom. Assembled from separate iron bars, heated to incandescence and sledgehammer-struck to weld them together. The fact that the various parts of the anchors were rather thin and that the iron used was not always of good quality occasionally caused the flukes to break off under high stress, right where they were welded to the shank. At the opposite end the shaft was forced into a wooden stock set crosswise with respect to the flukes and was intentionally longer, so as to cause the anchor to flip over at sea bottom, with one of the flukes facing downward and dragging into the bottom.

The gripping action of an anchor is guaranteed not only by the flukes' catching the bottom, but also by its weight, which helps them to retain their grip. Not surprisingly, there is no specific information about the weigth of the anchors of Columbian ships; one possible estimate, considering the size of the *Santa Maria*, would be half a ton for both fore anchors which lay during the navigation behind the castle, their flukes set horizontally on the bulwark, while the more cumbersome shank was set standing straight up. Latching the anchors in this position to prevent them from shift and damaging the hull because of the random shaking of the ship, they were set onto robust wooden blocks and fastened to the sides with strong bindings, tunneling through special holes under the bulwark, or secured to suitable rings fixed at shipside. The end of the rope was fastened with a specific anchor knot to the anchor ring atop the shank;

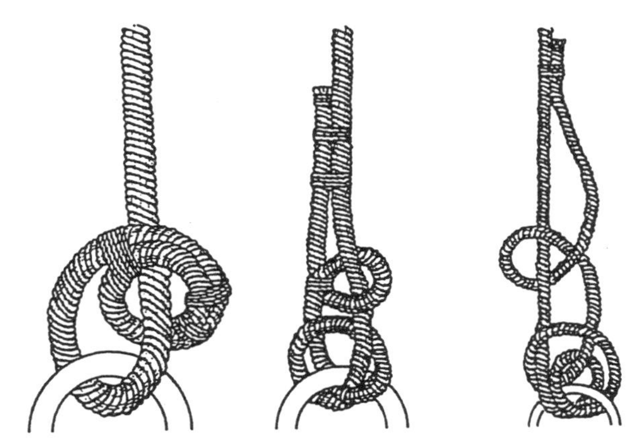

Three types of anchor knots.

Nomenclature of an anchor:

1 shank
2 square
3 nuts
4 crown or crown neck (cross piece, diamond)
5 arms
6 flukes (bridles)
7 ears (wings)
8 ears' bills
9 anchor-ring
10 eye
11 stock
12 stock bindings
13 ferrule (bushing)

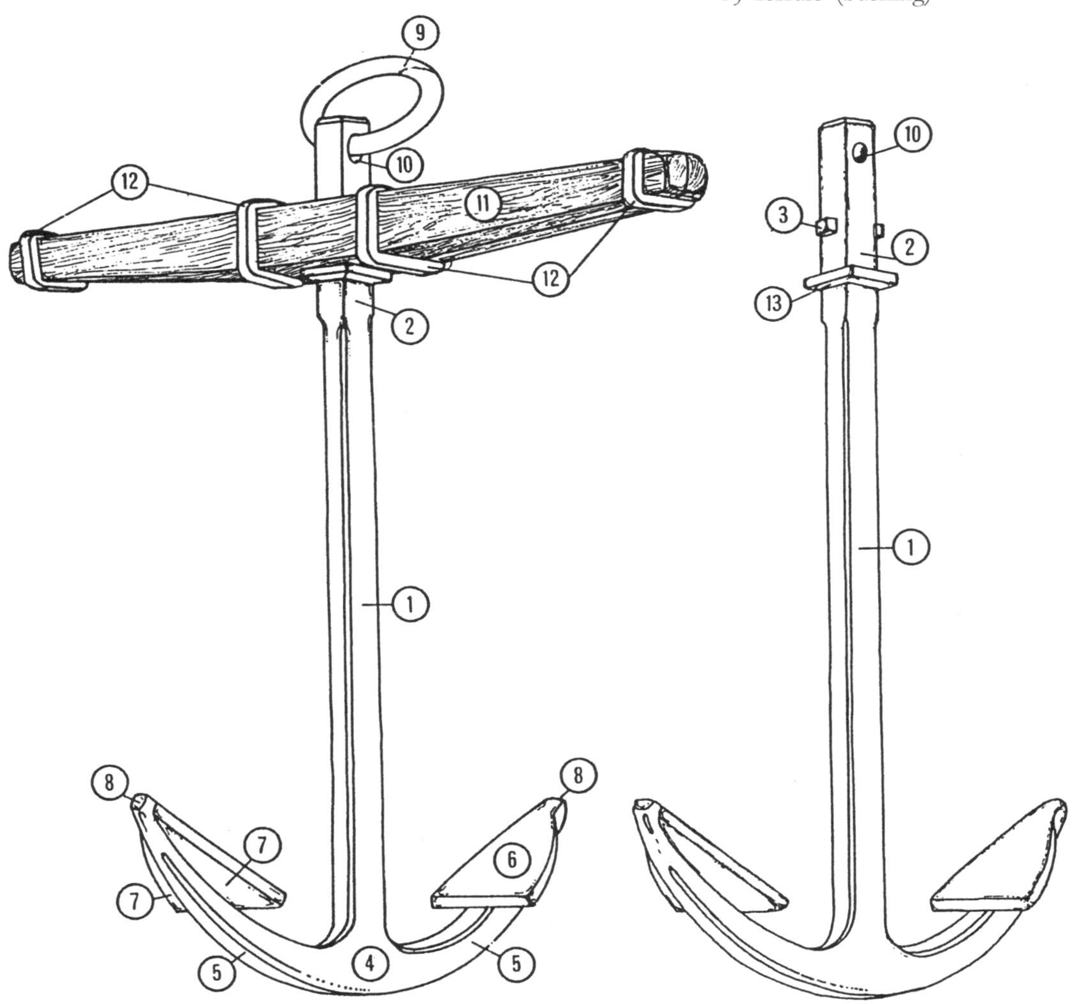

Sketch of a carack drawn by B. Bonfigli in 1486.
Visible (shown by the arrow) is the head of the transversal beam used as a bitt, jutting outside the bulwark. This element could have been used also as a capon crane, although its position does not seem suited for it. Well in view is also the horizontal bitt under the castle. Also noticeable is the direction of the planking that connects the hull to the castle structure, overlapping from aft to fore — against logic it would seem — to help the water flow during pitching.
Astern, the dredger is quite evident: on it butt-end the strong external bands reinforcing the planking. The entire drawing is well-detailed and documents many characteristics of a large carack of the time, including the typical droproof framing at bow and stern which, fitted with awnings, were probably meant to offer passengers an additional shelter area, cool and well-ventilated. The foremast is not shown here.

it then passed through the hawse hole, came on board under the castle and was coiled up on deck, if it was not feasible to put it into the hold.

Sometimes on its crown or diamond, i.e., the point where the shank connects to the flukes, the anchor had a ring both to hoist the anchor on board or tie to it a cable with a floater to indicate, in shallow waters, where the anchor had been sunk. In the museum of Port au Prince, Haiti, an anchor is preserved that was found about two centuries ago in a field one and a half chilometers from shore. It is claimed to have belonged to the *Santa Maria*, but it could just as well be the anchor of any coeval ship.

When it came time to cast anchor, a ship would line up dead on the wind until she stopped, at which point the anchor, freed from its halyards, was let fall down to seek bottom. In the meantime, with sails taken in, the ship would slowly move backward, pushed by the wind, and cause the anchor cable to become taut as the anchor itself turned and gripped the bottom; just the right length of cable was let go, before wounding or blocking it onto the bitt under the castle, as previously described.

Inversely, at the time of sailing, the ship had to haul low on the anchor cable — hence the necessity of having a capstan on board — drawing to the point of floating vertically over the anchor's position. This was the moment calling for maximum effort to trip the anchor from the bottom, and, once freed, a ship had to veer to sail until the anchor surfaced below board. Next a sailor had to hook a tackle to the anchor ring, hoisting it to the bulwark and fastening it in place. One century after Columbus's time, the tackle became part of a suitable small crane (the capon crane) jutting outside the parapet wall, an idea that at the end of the fifteenth century apparently had not yet struck anyone's fancy.

To be sure, there can be seen occasional drawings reminiscent of the capon crane earlier than the sixteenth century. Some of the cogs painted by Carpaccio exhibit a beam head projecting from shipside afore. This detail is more evident on a carack drawn by Bonfigli in 1486 (see p. 150), where it can clearly be seen that such a beam end is just the outer part of the mooring. The same thing can be seen in the already mentioned dry-docked ship painted by Sandro Botticelli (The Judgement of Paris). Its location, however, looks too low and exceedingly far out to operate effectively as a capon crane. Considering that — as stated earlier — since the anchor had to be brought on board and its weight easily reached several quintals, it could not be hoisted by hand without a leverage point for the tackle, it was a matter of necessity to devise a system enabling this operation. As information on this point is lacking, we imagine that it should have been possible to hook [with one or more pulleys] the upper block of the tackle to the foremast yard and thus use the latter as a mobile and orientable crane.

Additional deck items that readers might find interesting include: on the inside wall, at the water-way[25] level, we have already mentioned the scuppers or drainage holes, and, along the parapet, numerous elements serving the purpose of fastening the riggings and cables indispensable for all kinds of operations. We will thus point out belaying cleats, saddles or latches, fairleaders, bitts, eye-bolts, treenails or locking pins, etc., of various sizes, depending on the dimension of the ropes.

he Reserve ["woods"]. - Certainly, another prominent concern on a vessel that was set about to accomplish a long and unforeseeable voyage such as a discovery expedition, was to keep an adequate stock of timber: logs to build spare masts — the smaller ones — and yards, perhaps ready to be installed, as substitutes for those that might accidentally break; squared beams to use as props in case of leaks, or boards to replace planking sections, in short a small stock of materials for emergency maintenance and repair with in-house resources. All this timber, stored on deck, well-stacked close to the main hatchway, was under the direct responsibility and competence of the master carpenter. In the last century all this material had the half-jesting denomination of *woods*. Similarly, this was also the fifteenth-century nickname used, with a little irony and a bit of nostalgia for the green forests of the terra firma, just as the potable water cask available to the crew was called *fountain*.

The Artillery[26]. - Weapons were not an unusual presence on medieval crafts, since the seas at that time were plied by a lot of good people as well as many wicked rabblerousers practicing piracy as a life style. Therefore, as a good cautionary measure, it was unavoidable to have military hardware onboard, and the *Santa Maria* and the other two ships were no exceptions in this regard.

In several passages of his *Journal*, Columbus mentions the actual firearms featured on his ships. On October 7, 1492, he writes: "The *Niña* signaled land sighting with a warning bombard shot and raised their flag atop the mast"; and again, on January 2, 1493, to show cacique Guacanagarí — who had gone to much trouble as a friend to help him — the power of

[25] Water-way is that strake which, at deck level, runs all around its rim internally to the framing to which it is fixed. By extension the name applies also to the deck rim on which the scuppers or water holes are opened.

[26] The word *artillery*, in ancient times, denoted bows and arrows. As late as 1511 one finds comments such as this: "nowadays artillery includes two things: guns and bows." The first illustration of a cannon appears on an English manuscript of 1326 and the first written reference can be found in a decree of the municipality of Florence dated that same year.

Spanish weapons: "He proved to him the power of his weapons and the consequences of bombards like the one he had set up and ordered a shot into the side of the *nao* that was beached. It was a timing demonstration, very useful against the Caribs, that allowed him to see how far the bombard shot went as it perforated the size of the *nao*, landing way out into the sea."

At the end of the fifteenth century, the melting of cannons was still in a rudimentary stage, although the art of melting and molding metals was quite advanced for other items such as, e.g., church bells. Generally, small artillery pieces were manufactured using forged iron rods, circularly set like staves of a cask and welded together by hammering. Around this barrel, which would not withstand the internal pressure originating from the powder blast, hot iron rings were force-fitted, much like the stave-holding hoops. The bottom end was molded by turning rods inwards (in a Bolognese document of 1397, a 'pail-shaped bombard' is mentioned). Other smaller artillery pieces could be manufactured from a single metal sheet, rolled up like a cylinder and hot-welded. Still in the fourteenth century, even larger artillery pieces were built by assembling several elements. For a bombard manufactured in Caen at the end of that century, 2100 pounds of forged iron and 200 pounds of steel are reported to have been employed. Its internal barrel was made of longitudinally-set iron strips, carefully forming a continuous surface and held together on the outside by a number of binding rings. Once the metal work was completed, artisans wrapped 90 pounds of rope around the bombard. A full leather liner was then sewn over this wrapping, to prevent the rope from rottening and the iron from rusting.

In the breech of the barrel, still open at both ends, a detonation chamber was inserted. It was a gunpowder cartridge-case, that is, a container shaped approximately like a beer mug, sometimes fitted with a handle for easier handling. Filled with gunpowder and locked shut with wedges at the end of its tube, it was loaded with a round stone or iron shell, held in by a retaining wad. Afterwards, following an approximate calculation against the target, a red-hot iron tip was laid next to the touch-hole of the firing case to lit the powder which set the shell off into its short journey toward the target.

These light-weight, breech-loading bombards[27] (the small-caliber cannons installed on Columbus's ships, weighted approximately 250 pounds)

[27] The very first cannons, whether of the long or short pipe type, whether vase or bucket shaped (bombard) or *ad modum tubae* (pipelike), were all made of a single piece and muzzle loaded. Soon, breech-loading guns and their casing mechanism were introduced, but not for long, since the muzzle-loading system was preferable both in terms of reliability and less likely to harm the gunners in case of malfunctioning. The word bombard (lombard in Spain), replaced the primitive term 'catapult' their very first denomination. (D. Pope, *Le macchine infernali*. Mondadori, 1965).

rested on an elm cradle from a single log, carved to house the gun barrel just like the lower section of a mold and fitted underneath with two crosspieces ending in the trunnions. The cradle-mounting of the cannon was secured to the pedestal by robust bindings. The aiming was done both by shifting the barrel from side to side either manually or with levers, since the barrel was provided with handle rings that also served to secure it to the shipwall; the up and down shifting instead was done by inserting wedges under the support beam, front or back. This kind of adjustment did not matter much, anyway, because the target was always near, since it did not exceed one or two hundred yards, making for accurate firing.

The performance limitations of these weapons did not so much depend on their primitive conception or manufacturing imperfections (at the very end of the fifteenth century wrought iron works documented the skill and the precision of armours acclaimed as masterpieces of forged steel). Rather, their effectiveness was conditioned by awkward gun-carriages and unreliable ammunition. The latter in particular, as cast iron balls or roughly hewn stones, were not as round as they should have been. Generally, bombard balls were of stone, so much so that old time military writers called 'stones' also the metal balls, on account of their common projectile nature. The wad-wrapped balls were then loaded into the barrel, to offset the loose spots between the rough surface of the ball and the smoother lining of the barrel. Such loose fittings allowed most of the gas produced by detonating the powder to escape, lessening the shots' effectiveness and wearing out the inner chamber of the cannon even faster.

Admittedly, the stone balls could damage the side of a ship (as can be seen from Columbus's pride in the fact that the ball shot from the *Niña* had pierced right through the wall of the wreckage of the *Santa Maria*) much more than armed men, since they would harm only the ill-fated souls who happened to be directly on their trajectory. The few, light metal cartridges already in use, filled with pebbles or lead pellets, proved to be much more deadly against groups of people much in the same way as a hunting shell spreads its pellets against a flight of sparrows.

On board the *Santa Maria* the bombards (or lombards, as they were called in Spain) were probably four, because that was the number typically found on Catalonian and Aragonese trade ships to Italian or Berber lands, rather unsafe places. Certainly unknown lands beyond uncharted seas must have been regarded as potentially dangerous. The remaking of these

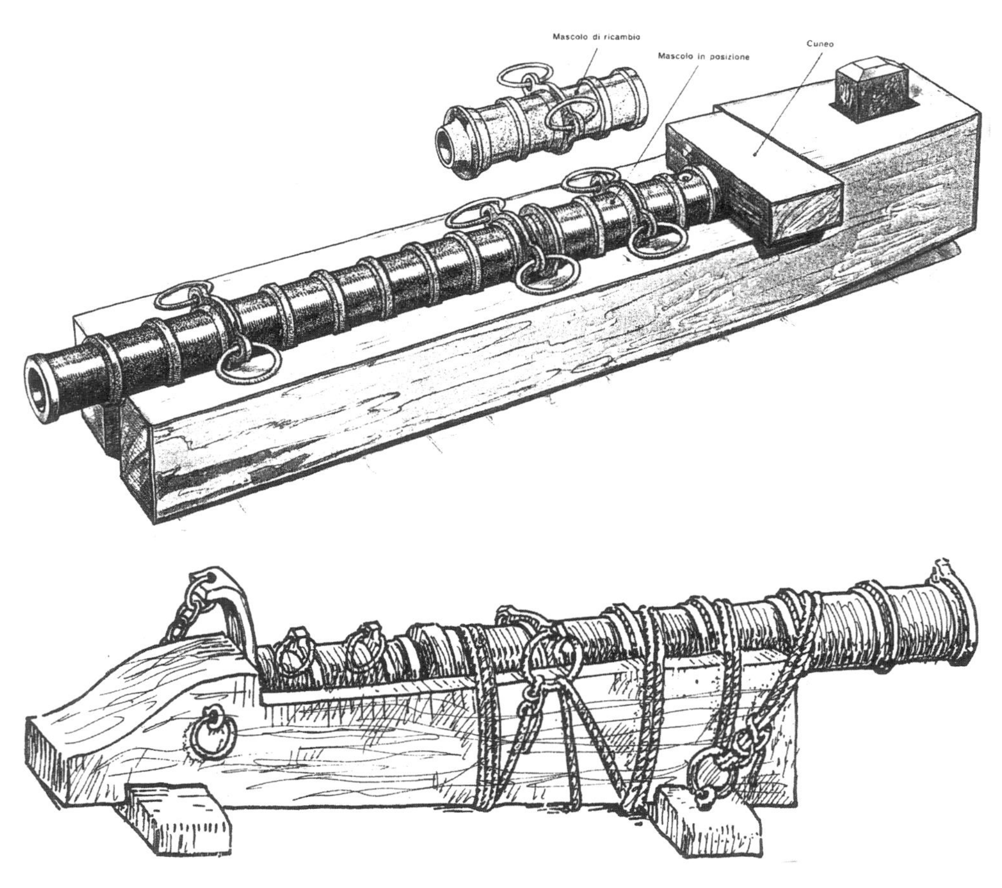

The cannons onboard the large English carack *Mary Rose* were not much different — aside from their dimensions — from the bombards of Columbus's ships (from a drawing by Max Miller). The lower sketch, drawn by Martínez Hidalgo, shows a bombard cradled and tied down with cable loops.

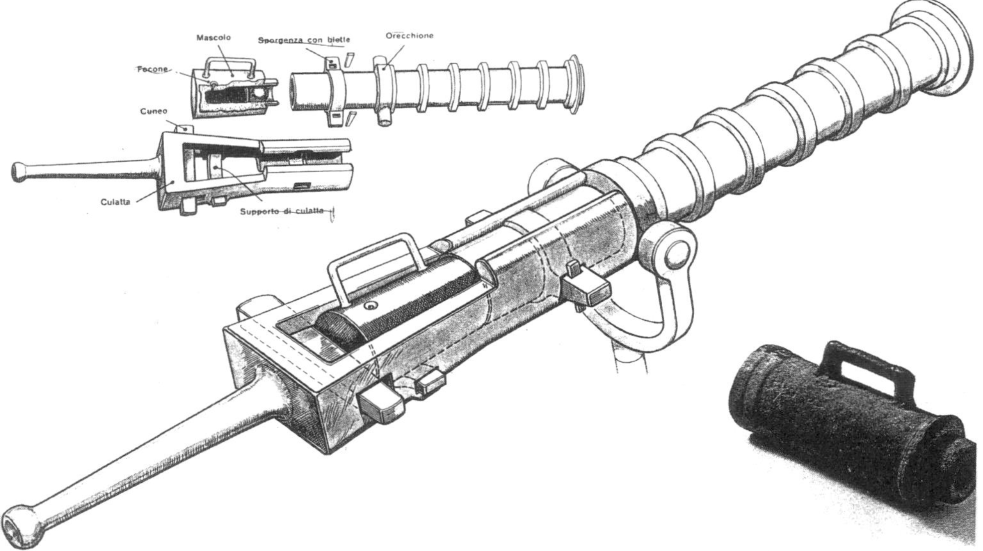

A falconet [a kind of light field-gun] or small cannon of around 1470. The weapon, which shot stone balls, here shows its cartridge-case [for the old breech-loading mortars] (drawing by Max Miller). In the detail, a bronze cartridge-case explosion chamber.

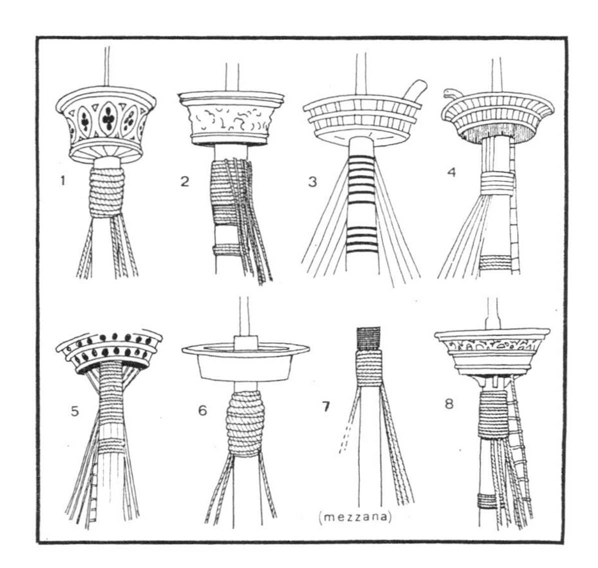

A selection of shroud-fitted masts: 1) from Gentile da Fabriano, c. 1425 (Vatican Gallery); 2) from a silver *Nef*, c. 1465 (St. Anthony Basilica, Padua); 3) carack, from G. Benincasa's *Atlas* (University Library, Bologna), c. 1465; 4) *idem*, from B. Ghirlandaio (Decorative Arts Museum, Paris), c. 1485; 5) *idem*, from a woodcut (National Library, Paris), c. 1485; 6), 7) idem, from Carpaccio (cycle of St. Ursula, Venice), c. 1490; 8) from a silver *Nef* (Nuremberg Nat. Museum), c. 1500 (The fourth type is uncommon: see the ends of the shrouds reaching the crowsnest).

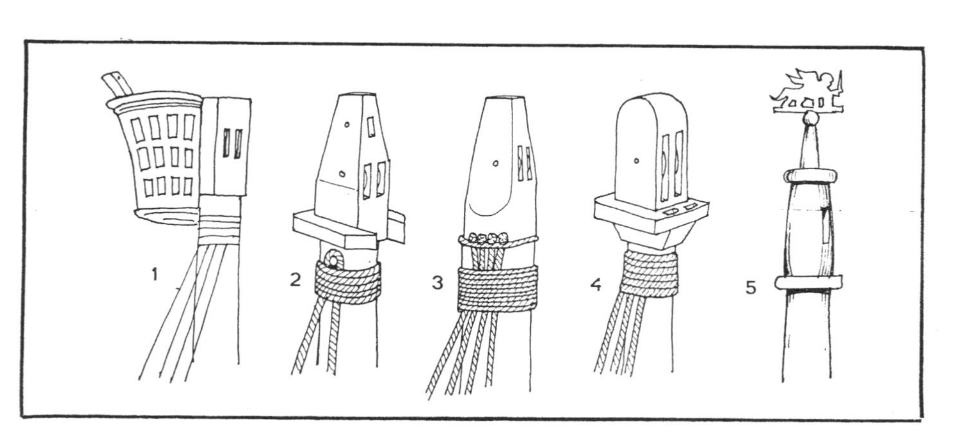

Mastheads and shrouds of lateen-sail ships: 1) from Reewich's woodcut of a commercial galley, c. 1483; 2) from an eighteenth-century *xebee* [a small Turkish three-masted vessel], Science Museum, London; 3) from a model of a Maltese galley, 1760, Science Museum, London; 4) from a model of a nineteenth-century pink, Adge-Herault Museum, France; 5) banner mast, St. Mark's square, Venice, (actual detail).
(From *Navi e modelli di navi*, 1976).

weapons, based on the numerous specimens arrived to us, have resulted in reproductions about five-feet long and with a muzzle width of three to four inches. Located on the weather deck, below the castle, they protruded outboard through round port-holes, usually capped by a wooden plug. Each caravel, being smaller than the *nao*, probably carried only two cannons.

Another commonly seen firearm certainly existing onboard the Columbian ships was the falconet, a breech-loading swivel gun, smaller than a bombard, with a bore of one and a half to two and a half inches. The falconet did not have a gun-carriage, as it simply straddled with its two lateral trunnions a swiveling and pivoting fork hinged to the flag boards of the quarterdeck. Its explosion chamber was set in a sort of receptacle, forming a single piece with the barrel and held steady with the usual wooden or iron wedges. It was a very manageable weapon that could be aimed in all direction and, loaded like a gatling gun, could truly prove lethal against an attacking crew.

And finally, Columbus himself mentions in his *Journal* the harquebus, an old type of musket, that is, a portable firearm consisting of a simple iron barrel attached to a wooden box. It was muzzle-loaded, pressing down powder, wads and projectiles with a wooden rod; its large type was hand-held stock under the arm, while its heavy barrel rested on a forked staff; the ignition of the powder was attained by match or wick, held in one hand over the explosion chamber hole.

Furthermore, there must have been other single-man weapons onboard, such as crossbows (which Columbus mentions), bows, pikes and spears, as well as armors, helms amd shields, to complete an arsenal hardly needed in the mostly peaceful Caribbean world.

Shiplights and lanterns. - The most recent reconstructions take exception to the existence of an offrail light as an authority symbol on the stern crowning ornament of the *Santa Maria*. Only the Spanish replicas, among the most recent ones, display a poop decorated with a showy beam light.

Common acknowledgment has it that the stern light only later became a sign of distinction reserved to vessels carrying leading naval officers. The number of lights was in correlation to the officers' rank. We point out, for instance, that on the Venetian ships such a light (called *fanò*) was the exclusive prerogative reserved to captains of the *Galleas* (large galleys), to the Harbor Chief, to the Governor of Prisons and to the Fleet Commander-in-chief. Specifically, the group of three lights decorated only the most prestigious ships, the flagship of the Admiralty General in wartime, and that of the General Commander-in-chief.

However, at the end of the fifteenth century these distinctive insignia had not been implemented yet, or so at least it appears from observing the copious still extant iconography, which would have undoubtedly highlighted such a prestigious and decorative element.

Wolfram zu Monfeld cites, in support of this thesis, a very well-known tapestry representing the Spanish-Portoguese fleet which in 1535 moved to attack Tunis, including, he points out, the great *Santa Anna*[28] carack of the Maltese Knights and several of the most important vessels of that time. None, however, is featured with lights.

It is consequently important to interpret correctly the only passage of Columbus's *Journal* where lights are mentioned, that of Thursday, November 22, 1492, the day after Martín Alonso Pinzón's [unauthorized] departure with his *Pinta*: "the Admiral proceeded all night toward land and had some sails taken in and showed a light all night long because it seemed that he [Pinzón] was coming toward him; and the night was very clear and the light wind favorable for coming [back] to him had he so wished." The *farol* should not be regarded as a stern light, but as the fire or lantern kept lit purposely to signal one's position way up on a mast or a yard so as to be easily spotted. Had the *Santa Maria* been equipped with an ornamental light, it would have been burning every night for the purpose of keeping the small fleet together; thus it would make little sense to call attention to this light as a distinctive occasion when it was on every night.

Throughout the night, barely a few indispensable lights were kept lit, for fear of possible fires. The compass lantern dimly illuminated the deck below the quarterdeck, with another, perhaps, above the quarterdeck as a rare privilege for the Admiral's small cabin. José Martínez Hidalgo recalls that in 1517, on the first voyage of Charles V to Flanders, as part of a fifty-two ships fleet, an iron lamp was usually handed every night to the ladies when they took leave, but shortly thereafter the captain would inspect the cabins to ensure that they were turned off, making exception only for those of the King and the Infanta, that of the pilot

[28] On this huge ship, a true mastodon fitted with 130 cannons (large and small), sailed — it is claimed — 1500 individuals: sailors, soldiers, 40 musicians, and 32 chaplains; there were four kitchens, a windmill and small wooden boxes with flowers and shrugs to adorn the stern.

and the one under the quarter deck below which the sailors rested until the whistle would call them.

Oars. - Some have hypothesized with Monleón the presence of some oars to be employed in particular circumstances such as, for example, in case of calm winds. Considering the dimensions of the ship, very long oars would be needed, that is, cumbersome to store when not in use. Rowlocks should then have been available, but certainly not mounted above the parapet because in that case the oar blade could never reach the water. Perhaps the scuppers might have served as oarlocks (with the risk of damaging their lead liners), or some other suitable holes, allowing to row from a standing position, and facing the bow. This kind of complication, the dimensions of the ship and the modest effective service oars could provide are convincing reasons why Monleón's line of thinking is rightly to be discarded.

In case a becalmed ship needed to reach a zone where a light breeze was blowing, it was much simpler to resort to doing what even larger vessels would later do, i.e., to tow the ship using her tenders.

The rigging of the Santa Maria

In the preface to his *Decades de Orbe Novo*, Peter Martyr of Anghiera writes: "owing to his [Columbus's] insistence, he was granted three ships by the King's treasury: a freight vessel with topsail and two other ones, for the Spaniards, caravels." This is the reputed passage (previously cited in its full original version) that deceptively led some scholars to misintepret the meaning of the terms *caveatum* and *sine caveis* used by Peter Martyr, taken to mean, respectively, "with and without hold" and, therefore, "with or without deck." We have already pointed out that attentive scholars, who generally reject for technical reasons the idea that the two caravels lacked a deck, suggest that the words should be understood as with and without top, i.e., crow's-nest. Admittedly, it may not be denied that Peter Martyr, a few lines further down, is unreliable when he states that Columbus sailed with two hundred and twenty men of Spanish nationality, a figure, as we shall see, at least twice as large as actual fact.

The general rigging of a top-fitted ship is documented in dozens of representations and texts. In addition, all doubts are removed on the basis of Columbus's declaration about the rigging of the *Santa Maria*. He listed the sails his ship could hoist, in a passage that we have reported beforehand but do repeat here for clarity's sake: *maestra [o papahigo] dos bonetas y trinquete y cabadera y mezana y vela de gavia...* [mainsail, two bonnets and fore sail and spritsail and mizzen sail and topsail]. A three-mast ship, then, such as she appears on any *nao* illustration of the time, and in every later reconstruction. The Matarò model, according to Pino dell'Orco's reconstruction, has only two masts, but it cannot be ruled out that it were fitted with a low foremast, too, given the large space remaining between the main mast and the prow.

The main mast, much bigger than the others both height- and diameter-wise, rose almost at midship, before the quarterdeck. Its oversize dimensions were justified by the fact that it had to support the larger and more critical sail, but also a sign of compliance with a medieval tradition that called for a main mast of gigantic proportions. Martínez Hidalgo figures for the main mast a 26 inch diameter at the mast-partner (i.e., at the point where the mast passes through its opening on the deck) and 16 inches in correspondence of the mast-heads. The full height from the deck box to its top of the mast is reconstructed to reach 65 feet. Adding a small topmast, its respectable total height is approximately 88 feet.

Some authors believe that the mast was a single piece all the way to its tip, reaching scarcely plausible heights of over 100 feet, as in D'Albertis's reconstruction. To push the mast past its top would have meant a needless waste of material; and since the topmast had to support a very small sail, we think that it may have been a simple, thin yard, similar to a flag staff of enhanced functionality and attributes.

It could also be, however, that the mast, of considerable diameter, rather than a single log, was actually the composite of several mortised beams fitted together or around a thinner post. Proof of this way of thinking is in the numerous bindings which, at regularly spaced intervals, wound around the mast, a common detail that, at least for the mainmast, appears on all the pictures of ships of the time.

Going through a mastway, the mast reached deep into the hold, fitting into a stronghold box fastened to the keelson. In all of the most recent reconstructions, at its cross point the mast exhibits a belt of wooden wedges intended to keep it in position correctly, achieving a particular slant regarded as the most useful for balancing the sails system.

The mast was secured laterally by six or more robust shrouds (up to eight in older reconstructions), capped beneath the masttop and stretched underneath either by upper and lower eyebolts fastened to inside-wall rings or, better, to iron futtock plates, hooked on the wall, i.e., planks along the outer timber, or on outside staves.

Any of these arrangements can be regarded as valid, since contemporary iconography documents all of them, just as it sometimes depicts shroud fenders vis-a-vis iron plates attached to the rail. Prior to the adoption of ratlines[29] on Mediterranean ships, the rigging up and stretching of the shrouds was done in an entirely different way from the one necessitated in more recent times, that is, ever since masts started getting taller and taller making it necessary to develop different sections, connected together by a system reliable enough to safely support the ropes against the trestle-trees. Anyone with a modicum of knowledge of sailing rigs is aware of the fact that on vessels with sectional rigs the top of each mast ends in a square section. At the base of the square-section portion, the actual *trestle tree*, two transverse beams can be fixed one on each side (in a bow-to-stern direction), serving as a support for the base of the upper mast. These transverse beams are the *cross trees* onto which each shroud could conveniently and securely rest after rounding the mast on the opposite side.

From an interesting article by Pino dell'Orco, printed in 1979 in the Florentine magazine *Navi...* [*Ships and Shipmodels*], we reproduce a drawing (p. 156) which shows eight different types of shrouds tensing, dating back to iconographies between 1425 and 1500 c. As it may be observed, in the totality of cases the shrouds fan out not from the mast top but from a heavy cable wrapping set well below the top itself. What was hidden by this encumbrance would not be clear, without consulting much later models of lateen sails and solid-masts ships (i.e., having single-piece masts, without any upper spars), at the top end of which one or two slots-holding pulleys were located, through which passed the halyards. These typically Mediterranean masts, lacking cross trees, had the shrouds tensed the same way as on the *Santa Maria* and other coeval ships, whose main mast was almost certainly of a single-piece (a fact that, however, cannot be ascertained beyond any doubt, as the top of the mast remains hidden by the crow's-nest).

It is immediately evident that the shrouds were not capped, in other words they did not wind around the mast, but came straight down the side of the mast itself. At least two ways, of many, the shrouds engaged the mast can be identified: knotting or pinning.

In the first case the shrouds, each being a single cable with a knot at its extreme upper end, were laid against the mast at the desired height and strongly tied by frapping all around it, either leaving the knot exposed or, more likely, binding over it, too. The ensuing binding fastened the shroud

[29] The ratlines are those tar-coated thin hemp-ropes transversally tied onto the shrouds so as to form the steps for climbing upward.

to the mast with the knot preventing it from sliding down. Even more reliable appears to be the second method; with it, a double-length shroud was folded and hung from a peg inserted in the mast at the desired height, thus forming a pair of shrouds. A series of such pairs yielded the desired number of shrouds; finally a solid frapping, like that described for the knot system, secured the shrouds to the mast.

For the low-end tensing of the shrouds, we have various and conflicting testimony — a further indication, according to Dell'Orco, of the diverse traditions in ancient seamanships. Dell'Orco identifies three main tensing systems:

- tackle with blocks;
- tackle with dead-eyes;
- tackle with hearts and scores;

"As it happens in many aspects of the naval architecture," writes Dell'Orco, "these three systems appear to have been adopted in a reciprocally exclusive or conflicting manner, with no identifiable rule. Thus contemporary iconography (which we must trust when details are represented with such precision as to leave no doubt that they have been lifted from real life) shows that some ships have Nordic-type shrouds, i.e., fitted with ratlines, but very simply tensed, whereas others have Mediterranean-style shrouds but tensed the Nordic way.

– Tackle tensing is done with single or double blocks with a variable number of runners or hauling ropes (called single, triple, quadruple, quintuple and sextuple) and pulleys fitted to them.

– Channeled blocks tensing is similar, except the tackle is not made up of pulley blocks, but with a single-hole block with three channels or slots. The tackle, once the runner is tensed, remains fixed (one of these was found on the bottom of the harbor in Palos).

– Heart with score blocks tensing differs only for the shape of the block: instead of a single hole it has three of them through which the runners pass. This system was developed later and not in use before the mid-fourteenth century.

All three methods may be viewed as realistically feasible for the shrouds of the mainmast of reconstructed *Santa Maria* models.

A still lingering doubt is whether the main mast shrouds of the Columbian flagship were fitted with ratlines, or not. Right at that time this minor but very useful invention began to spread from Northern Europe to the Mediterranean area. The oldest reconstructions (Spanish Government 1892, D'Albertis, Monleón) featured the ratlines: Guillén Tato limited himself to one row of ratlines between two shrouds, others — and we endorse this latter solution more — would rather be satisfied with a simple

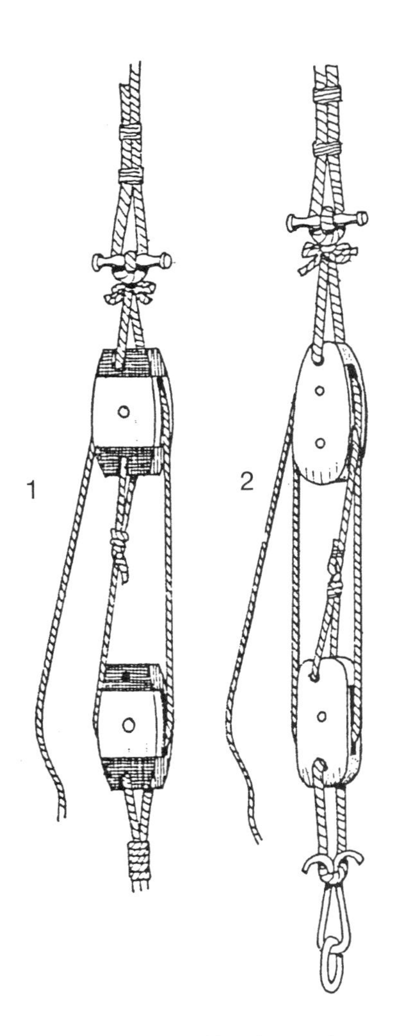

1) shrouds tackle from the model of a Catalonian ship (the Mataró *Nao*), c. 1450, Prince Hendrik Museum, Rotterdam;
2) shrouds tackle from the model of a large galleass called *La Royale*, c. 1690, Naval Museum, Paris.

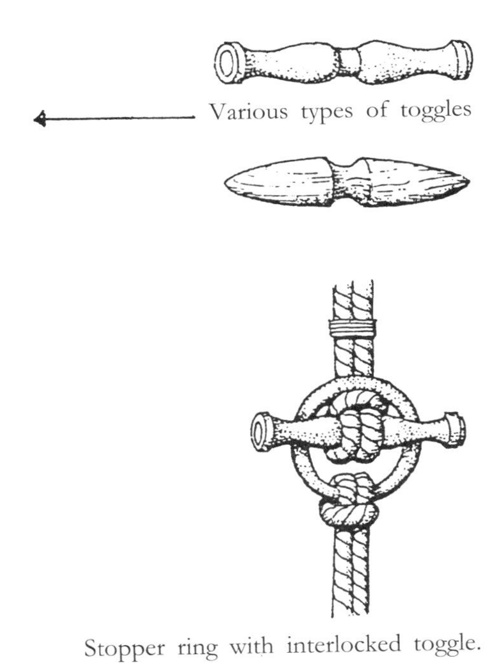

Various types of toggles

Stopper ring with interlocked toggle.

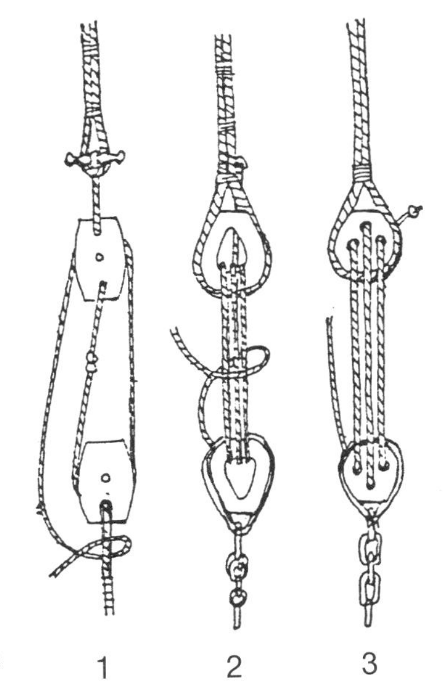

1) Tackle with blocks
2) Tackle with dead-eyes
3) Tackle with hearts and scores

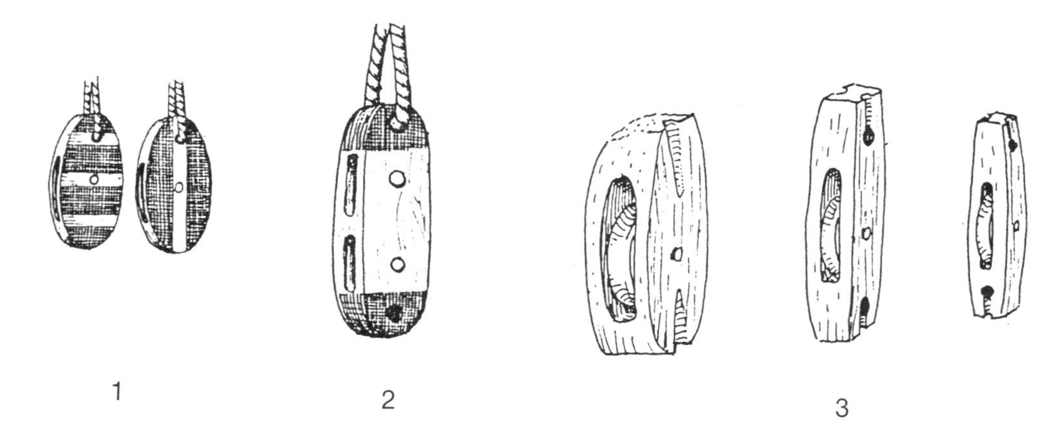

Some medieval blocks. 1) Painted block of a triangular-sail ship frescoed in the Chapel of the Spaniards in Santa Maria Novella, Florence (c. 1340); 2) double block, from Carpaccio's St. Ursula cycle, c.1495; 3) three blocks salvaged during works on the Riddencholler canal in 1930, from a small ship wreck, dated between 1450 and 1523.
(From Dell'Orco, *Navi e modelli di navi.* Florence: Lusci, 1979.)

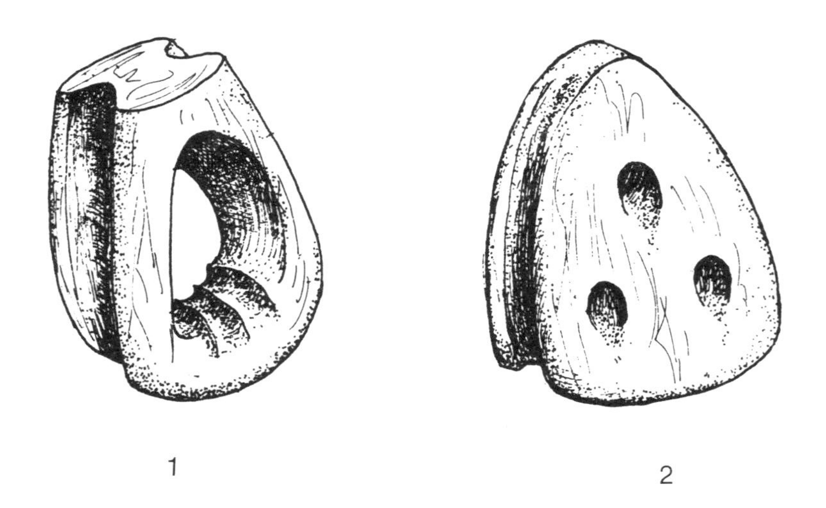

Main types of dead-eye blocks: 1) Slotted or channelled block. A block of this kind has been found at Palos on the bottom of the harbor. 2) Heart-with-scores block.

rope-ladder [the *biscayn*] standing against the mast, sufficient to climb to the crow's-nest. The *biscayn* is a ladder formed by two ropes holding, at regular intervals, wooden rungs. The latest Spanish reconstruction, too, has the ratlines.

As far as the much shorter and lighter fore and mizzen masts (Martínez Hidalgo gives a figure of about 14 inches in diameter for the foremast), i.e., the shrouds were certainly rigged with either simple or double tackles, working as standing elements[30] on hearts bolted into position on the foremast. This kind of rigging of the smaller masts is the one featured in almost all reconstructions, including the recent one by the Spanish Commission. Consequently, there could not be ratlines on this two masts, and besides, they would be useless since there was no need to climb them.

Both masts were slightly tilted, the foremast fore, and the mizzen aft. Not everyone, however, shared this view: D'Albertis, both in his project and in the models created for the city of Genoa, set the three masts of both the *Santa Maria* and of the two caravels rigorously vertical.

The main mast was secured afore by a big stay, that starting from the fastening point of the shrouds, wrapped around the mast and pulled downward with channeled blocks, forming standing on the sternhead, or possibly embracing the cut-water as it can be seen on the "drawing" of the Spanish reconstruction (but not on the actual replica) or in Zu Monfeld's reconstruction.

Of the two minor masts, only the foremast had a stay leading through a block to the bowsprit's tip and ending on the forecastle, where it was secured to a bitt or a belaying cleat. The mizzen mast, being lateen-rigged, did not have a stay.

The bowsprit, too, as it had to support only the small spritsail, was not subject to particular stresses and did not have either bobstays or guy-ropes (bobstays are those standing rigging that hold the bowsprit down [preventing any bobbing], the guy-ropes are those holding it laterally, like shrouds).

[30] This is a typical sailing term which, when used (as it is proper) in reference to equipment, requires a word of explanation. It refers to some elements of the rigging whose function depends upon their fixed, unmovable position. Such is the *standing* rigging, including those parts that once installed remain in place (e.g, the shrouds), as opposed to the *running* rigging (e.g., sheets, halyards, yards, etc.). Standing is also the point to which one end of a piece of running rigging may be tied, so as to remain fixed, while the opposite end, passing through a block or a tackle, is called the runner. Standing elements are also those construction units in the hull that support other elements laid onto them (e.g., the ones standing under the deck beams).

The crow's-nest, or 'cage', placed on top of the main mast, consisted of a wooden frame covered with boards forming the floor and, on the sides, had uprights joined high up by a rim and covered with painted leather or light wooden staves.

On the cage floor a hole (the lubber's hole), in correspondence of the anchoring point of the *biscayn*, allowed access to it from underneath. Proiecting from the cage rim there were one or two poles, to which a hoisting block was attached, most useful for delivering arrows or stones in case of combat. That particularly elevated point provided in fact the best vantage point for hitting the decks of hostile ships during enemy confrontation; on merchant ships, however, it was above all a look-out point and a location from which to maneuver the topsail.

All reconstructions show agreement as far as the larger yards (main yard, fore yard, lateen-sail yard) that are presented as being formed by two pieces overlapping for about half their length, in a 'Southern' fashion[31], making for a longer and more resistant yard than those made from single logs. The two pieces forming the yard had circular sections, except in the overlapping portion, which was so worked as to leave the two adjoining surfaces rather than totally flat, one slightly concave and the other a bit convex, for better coupling. The smaller yards of the topsail and spritsail, owing to their short length, were made of a single piece.

Every yard had, obviously, halyards that, when the mast was made in one piece, ran through suitable pulleyed blocks, placed at the upper end of the mast. Otherwise the mainmast and foremast halyards, which were certainly double, ran through two blocks suspended below the cage, or through two pulleys inserted in two cheeks or parrels fixed near the top of the mast. The halyards then turned downwards, terminating with a tackle tied to a large bitt, fitted with blockes and multiple pulleys, located behind the mast. This large bitt, because of the strain to which it was subject, had to be very robust; it penetrated the hull and was anchored above to a transverse beam and below to a floor timber [the central piece of each rib] of the frame.

For the halyard of the fore yard, much lighter than that of the main mast, a large bitt was probably superfluous; a tackle fixed to a standing heart on the castle deck was sufficient.

Beside the halyard — and perhaps a downhauler to force-drive the descent of the yard if its own weight would not pull it down — the yards

[31] In the Northern regions of Europe yards had long been built in one piece, perhaps because of local abundance of tall, straight trees, suitable as yards.

had braces that kept them suspended in a oblique position. The braces are running riggings that hold the yard at its ends and keep it horizontal, that is, at right angles. It is an ancient habit, on Good Friday, to "uncross" the yards so that they would not retain, on this day, the position of the Holy Cross. Naturally, this was done in port and not during sailing.

Generally the main yard had four braces, two at the its tips (the yard-arms, where some riggings are fixed) and two toward the middle, consisting of simple tackles whose pull line reached a block fixed to a heart on the main deck, next to the mast. In the harbor, the yard was lowered to rest on the bulwarks. Almost similar were also the braces of the foreyard, which however were only one pair. This yard, too, when the sail was not utilized, was lowered onto the forecastle deck.

The custom of lowering the yard to work on the sails, for example bending them to or unbending [i.e., removing] them from a yard or furling them, eliminated the need for ratlines — that enabled sailors to climb the mast rapidly — or catwalks — foot-ropes stretched under a yard, to which they hung at several points forming a sort of festoon, to stand on and move along the yard. (Catwalks will be introduced on ships around 1600.) But if needed, the sailors could straddle the yard or even walk-balance along it, if we are to trust what can be seen in many epochal images. The same was true of the mizzen mast. The small spritsail yard had its halyard and downhauler, too, to lower it onto the castle when it was not needed, and was supported by two simple braces.

Every yard was connected to the masts by means of parrels or trusses constituting a collar of two or three rows of superimposed parrel-trucks — thimbles or small hardwood balls, with through holes and a holding cable, the parrel rope. To keep the rows of trucks clustered together some dead-eye blocks acting as ribs were inserted between each vertical series, blocks that had as many holes as there were rows of trucks. This simple device, which will look more evident by looking at its picture (p. 169), linked the yard to the mast without causing excessive friction, and facilitated its sliding when the yard was hoisted or lowered, on the same principle as that of a rudimentary but efficient ball bearing.

To allow their trimming, yards were fitted with double braces, passing through a block strop-clasped to the yard's end or hanging from it with a short pendant. The braces of the mainmast yard, which had to be the strongest, reached with one end a standing heart located externally to the bulwark of the quarterdeck while the other end, after going through the block at yard tip, was routed back below and secured to cleats located on the deck or on the bulwark. The braces of the foremast made a similar run ending at midship, those of the spritsail terminated on the forecastle. Separate mention should be made for the small topsail yard and we shall do so when discussing the sail system.

All running rigging was made of hemp. Likewise the standing riggings were of hemp, but tar-coated. More economical weed [espartograss, also known as cord-grass] ropes were used as well, though for jobs requiring less endurance and for river moorings, where the hemp ropes did not guarantee good results.

Blocks and dead-eye ribs were all made of wood. Pulleys, too, were made with very hard woods, such as, e.g., the sorb [apple] tree, cut along the run of its fibers to prevent splitting under strain.

The hole through which the iron pin passed had a thin collar clasp, also made of iron. As for the blocks and dead-eyes, they came in numerous shapes and dimensions, depending on the demands of their function: heel- and violin-shaped blocks, multiple upper and lower dead-eyes, blind hearts, channel hearts, single and double blocks, sheet bending blocks with single and double cable tackles, with clasp or tail or toggle, etc.

Seafarers have always been clever and full of ingenuity in making their rope and pulley devices. Knowing nothing of formal mechanics, they managed to conceive cable systems suitable for any type of usage, and thanks to which the strength of a few men could suffice to move great weights. Skilfullness in the use of cables and the ways of joining and fastening them with the innumerable marine knots, each of them suited to a specific function, the cable-splicing art and that of performing the many onboard jobs, even if just for embellishment, using the cordage, was part then as much as not long ago, of the personal background of every sailor, unskilled in any other trade except his own, because upon its good application his very life depended.

The sails

In all epochs sails have been manufactured in similar ways, sewing together fabric strips of relatively modest size. Sail canvas — though perhaps later than the end of the fifteenth century — was generically called *olona* from the name of the French Brittany village of Olonne in the Aunis (Vandée), where the better-known weaving mills were located. There was also the *Melisia* canvas, manufactured at Beaufort in the Maine and Anger in the Loire districts. Various types of canvas differed for their warp and weft characteristics, as well as for heft and related strength.

A sketch illustrating a medieval crow's-nest (there were several different types, many of which well-represented in paintings of the time). The bucket beside the top served as a dummy-waiter to supply the men on top with weapons and sundry things.

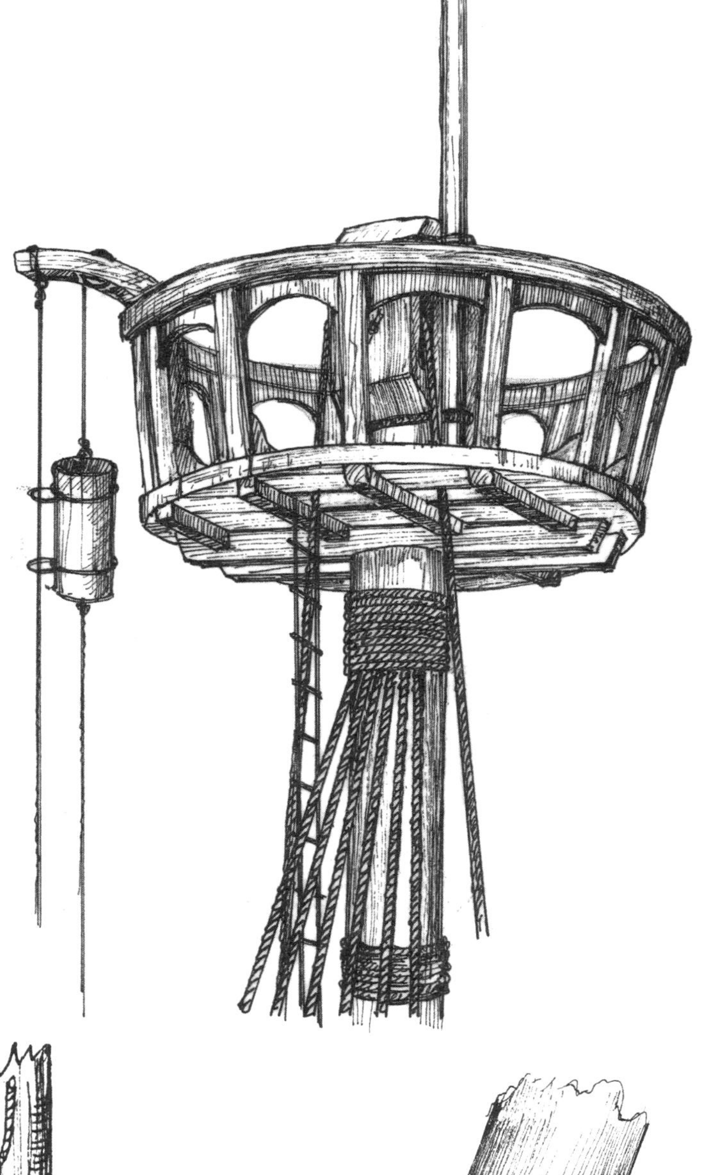

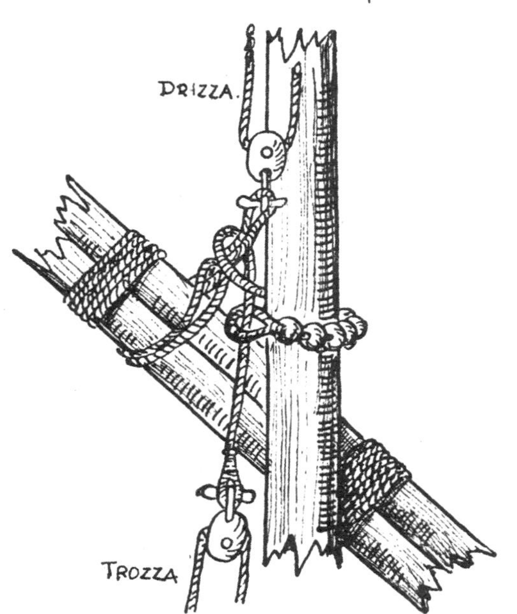

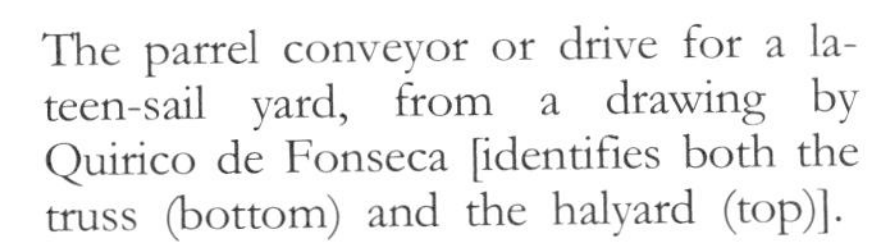

The parrel conveyor or drive for a lateen-sail yard, from a drawing by Quirico de Fonseca [identifies both the truss (bottom) and the halyard (top)].

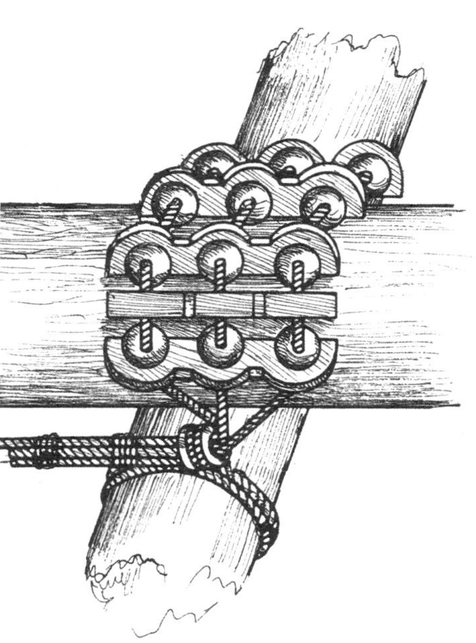

The parrel or truss of the main yard with its parrel-truck [small wooden balls] ensemble.

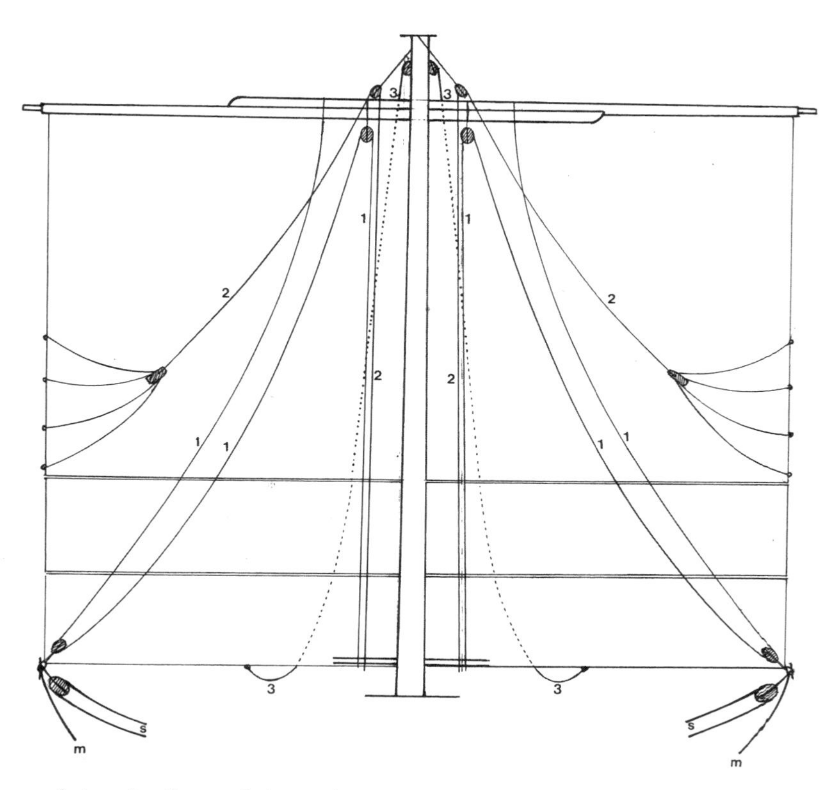

Diagram of the clewlines of the main mast.
Legenda: 1 clew-line lift or brail loader - 2 bowline loader - 3 buntline loader - s: sheets - m: tacks or rails.

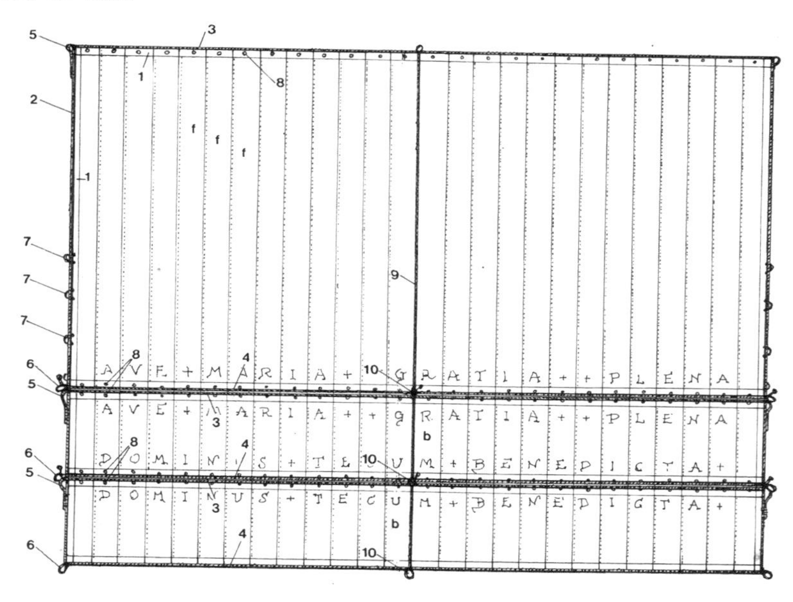

Sketch of a fifteenth-century sail (fore side).
Legenda: f sail-cloth strips - b bonnets or spars - 1. Tabling or edging - 2. Leech-rope or edging cord - 3. Earing rope or top head-rope - 4. Foot border or bottom head-rope - 5. Earing eyes - 6. Clew eyes - 7. Bowline eyes or bull's eye cringles - 8. Earing eyelets - 9. Ridge rope - 10. Clew-cringle holes of the ridge rope.

Thus, there were light-sail canvasses, and those for moderate winds or strong winds. Lower-quality, tar- or lint oil-impregnated cloth had a purpose as waterproof coverings.

A hemp breadth or bonnet used in the fifteenth century was approximately two feet wide. Once a sufficient number of breadths were overlapped and sewn together, they were suitably cut to obtain a sail of the desired shape; its hems were then reinforced by edging or *tabling*, which prevented fraying with marline, a thin but strong cord used for winding the ends of ropes. It also served as the edging to sew onto the canvas's edge a thin rope, called *bolt-rope*, which had different names depending on which side of the sail it was located: earing or head-rope at the top tabling where the sail was joined to the yard, edging cord or leech-rope on the vertical sides, foot or bottom head rope, at bottom tabling. At each corner, the boltropes were folded to form eyelets and reinforced with a marline forming the roband cringles on top and the clew cringles at bottom. On the sail's tabling, strenghtened eyelets were provided to attach the ends of the bowlines and, above the foot tabling, a series of eyelets for tying the second bonnet sail (the first or lower one was fastened onto the second). The large mainsail's, fore side, was vertically divided into two, or, sometimes, four parts by boltropes sewn onto the sail itself. These bolt-ropes had a foot eyelet, to be pulled with a sort of cable fastened to the mast or behind it. This arrangement, which caused a sail to bulge making it quite inefficient, served to reinforce an oversized sail preventing it from getting worn by rubbing against the robust forestay when swelling under the wind's thrust[32]. An expedient that would soon disappear when sail planes started to be fractioned in several elements.

As we already know the sails of the *Santa Maria*, let us look at their specific functions: the large mainsail supplied most of the forward thrust; the foresail, at slightly more than a quarter of the mainsail's size, contributed to the propulsion, but served especially to ensure the fore balance of the sail system, making the vessel to fall off to leeward [i.e., making the ship

[32] A sail is most efficient when it is taut. The concavity that the sail takes on under the force of the wind decreases its efficacy, since the section around its perimeter does not meet the wind perpendicularly, but obliquely, and the more obliquely the more concave is the sail. The airmass impacting the sail at the boltropes is deflected toward the bottom where it adds to the thrust by the air flowing directly to that area. Hence the fuller the sail, the smaller becomes the surface it opposes to the air stream, consequently decreasing the thrust imparted to the ship. A further consideration is that the higher the sails, the lesser the thrust for the boat: the riggings' high-level thrust cause the prow to down-pitch, wasting at least part of the propulsion.

steery]; the mizzen lateen sail had the opposite function of keeping the ship luff, that is, leading it windward; the spritsail, on the bowsprit, it too useful when running free, served especially for jibing. The small topsail we shall discuss shortly.

The sheets of mainsail and foresail were double-whip, standing at a heart bolted astern externally to the bulwark; the pull line, through the block fixed to the clew's eye ran fully outboard, through a groove made in the bulwark itself, before coming onboard and ending at winged bollards, fastened to the bulwark.

The single-line sheets of the spritsail ran to bollards on the forecastle. The tacks or clewlines — that is, the ropes by which the windward clews of lower sails are pulled afore to keep the sails as full as possible when heading into the wind — were simple, without tackle. The tacks of the mainsail reached inside the hull through a grooved hole ending at a bollard. The clewline of the foresail, so that it could be kept as far forward as possible, went through a grooved cable hole at the cut-water level running all the way to the opposite side of the hull. The spritsail had no pull-lines.

The sheets — for clarity's sake, it is better to call the leeward section 'sheet' and the windward section 'clewline' — of the mizzen lateen sail were double, with each hawser passing through a block set on the castle deck, and ending at a bollard. In some reconstructions, for example in the 1892 Spanish one, the mizzen mast is shifted so far aft that the sheet point is fixed at an outrigger, jutting forward from the stern rail.

A very important feature of a lateen sail is its flexibility to move from one to the other side of the mast, depending on whether one is sailing on port or starboard side[33]. We have already commented on this earlier(see also pp. 43-44). To be able to do so it is necessary that the car (i.e., the lower and thicker spar of the yard, the peak being the upper part) be switched from side to side of the mast thus freeing the sail to catch the wind on either side without encroaching on the mast, which would compromise its integrity and negatively affect its efficiency.

In few replicas, but especially in several model reconstructions (likely on account of the fact that they would never really sail), this feature has not been taken into account: the car is too long and the space insufficient

[33] On a given course, the engagement position of the hawsers (engaged means trimmed up) applies to the entire sail plane, except when the ship is running in favorable winds (in which case, the lines on either side are not engaged). So, when the port (left-side) lines are operating we say that the ship is sailing on port side, that is, it receives the wind from port side and the sails fill up toward the right; in the opposite case, we say the ship is sailing starboard side (hence receiving the wind from that side).

for its complex maneuver referred to as *making the car.* Also, both the halyard and the parrel of the yard must be handled in such a way as to facilitate rather than obstruct this operation, as it would happen with a short parrel which embraces only half the mast and is insufficient to form a complete ring around it (see p. 169 for an instance of a correctly applied parrel, studied by Quirico de Fonseca) or in the case as well of a halyard runner or tye if carried too far astern. In all fairness, however, it should be pointed out that such mistakes are excusable on a drawing or in a model, as they would be corrected, in actual replicas, by the person actually responsible for operating the riggings.

To gather the sails onto the yard prior to hauling it down (not to reef the sails as it would be done nowadays, but actually to haul down the yard), some specific rigging existed which, by analogy with systems later developed, could also be referred to as clewlines (see p. 170).

The clewline or clewgarnet loaders[34] of the main sail and foresail had their standing points on the yard, tunneled through a block fixed to the clew of the first or of the second bonnet if these were bent, or through the sail itself when there were no bonnets (as it was the case for the foresail), before returning to the yard tunneling through a block near the standing point and ending up on the main deck, where they were fastened near the shrouds. They were used to gather the top of the sail around the center of the yard, sternwards.

The bowline loaders or furlers had, on the other hand, the task of gathering onto the yard the two sides of the sail (which had bowline eyelets). All reconstructions describe them as a double trap, fixed to the eyelets of each leech line. The trap cable departs from a block under the yard, and descends to the main deck. Since the loaders were double, one on each side of the sail, the latter could easily be gathered and tucked under the yard. This operation will result more evident by consulting the already cited p. 170. Some reconstructions do not have bowline loaders for the foresail: perhaps it was assumed that they were unnecessary, considering the small size of the sail.

The spritsail did not have cables because, owing to its reduced dimensions, it could be easily gathered by pulling its yard toward the forecastle. As this was a sail used only at certain speeds we frequently see, on reproductions of ships of this time, a spritsail yard, with its sail furled, lying on the forecastle.

[34] These are the rigs, in the clewlines group, which are used to raise the yard toward the sheet point of the sail.

The lateen sail had, generally, just one clewline, a mainsheet loader that brought the clew of the mainsail toward the yard; if the sail was large it could have additional rigs to reef even the boltrope onto the yard (an arrangement frequently documented for the large sails of lateen caravels). This sail, too, was gathered by lowering it to quarterdeck level.

We have earlier explained the bowlines or edge ropes of a sail. Their existence is known for certain on fifteenth-century ships from numerous sources that show them starting from the leech lines of mainsails and foresails, in appropriate eyelets and going to a block at the end of the bowsprit before descending on the forecastle, where they are tensed. This arrangement was reported also in the latest Spanish reconstruction, while on the one proposed by W. zu Mondfeld the mainsail loaders go to blocks placed on the shrouds of the foremast.

Minor issues related to rigging certainly cannot be resolved with absolure certainty. Although a ship's rigging may be generally codified, its real features could later be modified by the boatswain responsible for its good performance. He could introduce any suitable modifications designed to improve it or make it easier to handle and more efficient. In the end, whether a bowline cable goes through the bowsprit or a shroud ensemble is a matter of relative unimportance, what matters is that it functions properly and does not obstruct other operations.

Topsail. - Above the mast top — or 'cage' for Spaniards and Italians, since it actually had the look of a basket or a cage — on ships coeval to the *Santa Maria* rose a small spar, according to someone an extension of the main mast, very thin, almost a flagstaff (on reproductions of ships from that epoch, often a flag can be seen waving on it). On this small mast, with a simple halyard, a yardlet could be hoisted, provided with two light braces and two pendants. On this yard, which even on the oldest reconstructions (such as D'Albertis') is very short, a small topsail was attached. Let us recall that the Romans, too, had introduced a second level of sails above the mainsail, with two sails placed on each side of the mast, forming a triangle whose two acute angles reached the mast's end and the yard's tip. The system devised by the Romans had a much greater efficiency than the small medieval topsail.

Earlier reconstructions conceived of this sail as trapezoidal, with a very short base to fit the yardlet and a very wide top so that the sheets departing from its lower clews could easily reach the ends of the main yard. This interpretation was later much criticized as it was not in accordance with the uses of the time during which the *Santa Maria* sailed. Indeed, a similarly shaped sail appears only in images of vessels of the first half of the following century (see Diego Ribero's chart of 1529), while on those regarded as coeval[35] to the *Santa Maria* the topsail, when spread[36], looks like a small square cloth of mimimal impact for the ship's speed. Other images — like the one showing a fifteenth-century large cog preserved at the Greenwich National Maritime Museum (see p. 177), or the one drawn on a chart By Jacopo Gastaldi in 1548 — the shape of this small sail is actually triangular with its tip at the bottom, thus requiring a single main rope fixed to the mast top.

In just about every modern reconstruction the topsail, assumed by now to be small and square[37], is shown with its sheets secured to the sides of the cage, while the braces of the yard reach the rear of the cage itself. Now, frankly, a sail like that would serve no purpose, except perhaps for improving the esthetics of a ship. The almost vertical braces of the yardlet could have a very limited effect on its trimming and the sheets of the small sail, being perhaps maybe one and a half yard apart, could only have allowed it to gather itself as a graceful windcatching bag. This, of course, on running courses; when heading into the wind, it was almost impossible to keep the sail spread out without its flapping independently, thus slowing down rather than assisting the forward motion of the ship.

[35] We mention here a few instances: the ships depicted in the nautical charts by Grazioso Benincasa (1482) and Juan de la Cosa (1500 or 1501); in the *Peregrinatio in Terram Sanctam* by von Breidenbach (1486); in the Neapolitan landscape preserved at the Museum of St. Martino (between 1464 and 1479); and especially in that inexhaustible source of information about medieval ships which is the St. Ursula cycle, painted by Vittore Carpaccio between 1493 and 1495.

[36] A sail is "spread" when, once the sheets have been hauled in, is completely distended.

[37] Not by everyone, though. Sergio Bellabarba, in a 1979 article in the journal *Navi e Modelli di Navi*, shows that he is not convinced: "Yet the length of the top yards of Carpaccio's vessels is not in harmony with the hypothesis of a very small sail, which moreover would not have required two or three top shrouds. The trapezoidal sail," he adds, "was in my opinion already in use beside the small triangular one, whose sheets, in the early sixteenth century, terminated on the cage. This is demonstrated first by a landscape view of Genoa of 1507, exhibiting a trapezoidal topsail; then, indirectly, by the fact that already in 1507 a third-order sail, the top gallant, is reported in use on the English ship *Regent*, followed in 1509 by a French ship and in 1514 by the famous *Henry Grace a Dieu*, rigged with upper and lower top gallants. It is clear that a third order of sails can hardly be reconciled with a topsail of the kind we are considering (square)." (From "La vela quadra," by S. Bellabarba and G. Osculati in *Navi e Modelli di Navi*, January 1979.) The topsail on the foremast appeared for the first time during the voyage of Vasco da Gama (1498). By 1520 it can be considered a commonly adopted feature.

A sail to be effective, had to have at least its sheet points set apart. Guillén Tato, in his widely criticized reconstruction of the *Santa Maria* as a caravel (1929), solved this problem by giving the sail, kept very small in size, a trapezoidal shape, with long sheets running toward the tips of the mainyard.

The recent Spanish reconstruction, originally made with the topsail sheets on top of the cage, showed the incongruity of such an arrangement, at least as claimed by the boatswain of its crew. The matter was solved by drawing the sheets to two blocks, sewn midway the mainyard braces. Again, minor adjustments, as we said earlier, of the type every seaman expects to face on his craft until a satisfactory solution is found. They are the kind of changes that deflate any doctrinary approach or codification of how properly a ship should be outfitted.

This explains why this ongoing problem is nothing new. Although many images of that time show sails with their sheets gathered on the mast top, others point to different solutions. At the Alte Pinakothek in Munich, for instance, there is a painting by the Meister der Heilige Sippe, titled "The legend of St. Anthony the Hermit," on some small ships noticeable in the background the sheet point of the topsail is on the lower yard while the sheets follow a path more evident on the sketch at p. 181 than from any description.

The caravel Pinta

In comparison to the notoriety of the *Santa Maria* the two Columbian caravels, *Pinta* and *Niña* take backstage. Yet without them the expedition would have been ill-fated, because, after the wreck of the *Santa Maria*, there would have been no means to return to Spain and bring news of the discovery.

We have already discussed in general terms a caravel's hull and the essential characteristics of this type of ship. We shall now, on the basis of the many executed replicas, analyze what a Columbian caravel might be like, beginning with the *Pinta*.

The term "pinta" may have meant painted, multi-colored, or colored. It may have been a nickname, as it was commonplace, later adopted as a proper name. Back then not much importance was attached to a ship's name, other than as an implied recommendation to good fortune or divine protection, especially so when giving the vessel a saint's name; hardly ever would one have found the ship's name nicely framed or posted astern.

A large cog in a woodcut preserved at the Greenwich National Maritime Museum. It is possible to see the triangular shaped topsail, with a single sheet secured to the cage. The mainsail and foresail have the central boltrope fastened with a sort of sheet around the mast. The bowlines of the mainsail are also well visible, and should not be hauled taut since the ship is running free. The topsail does not have cables.

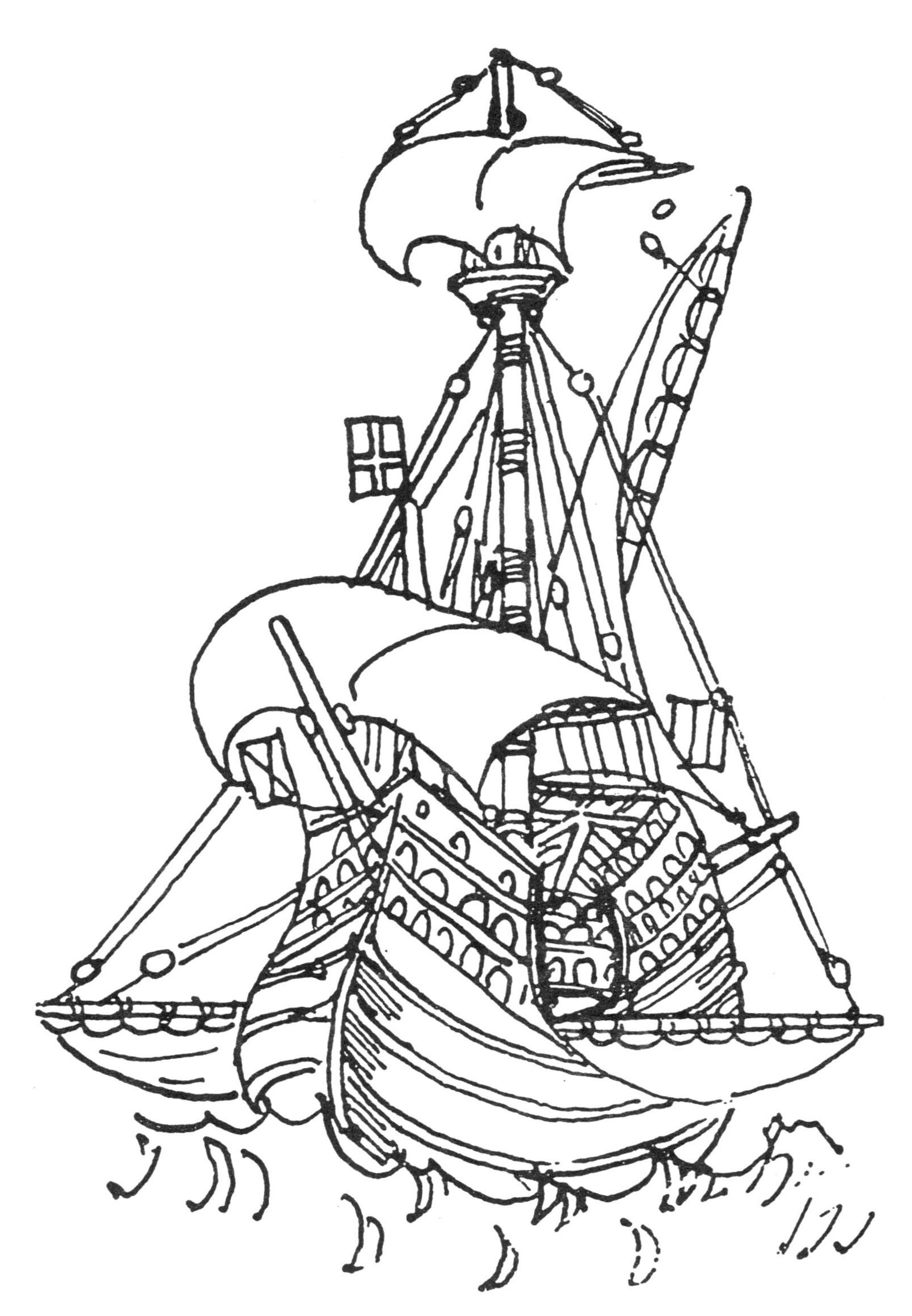

A large carack in a 1510 Portuguese chart of the Indian Ocean. Notice the square topsail, with three sheet points (one is in the middle); this drawing, unfortunately, does not indicate where the sheets may end up. Worthy of notice as well is the mainsail yard with furled sail, lying on the bulwarks, with braces stretched out far, owing to the uncommon position of the yard.

Building on its name's indication, one could with some realism imagine the hull of the *Pinta* painted brightly, at least along the rails and the flag boards, as indeed is still done for fishing boats, the only surviving instances of small naval ownership (albeit with the exclusion of all private yachts), where the owner is also the "master" (a master being, for coastal trade vessels, what the captain is for merchant vessels).

If we observe the beautiful Portuguese fishing boats, with their high and fluid prows so similar to the caravels, one finds that they too are painted in showy colors. Only one objection may be raised against the hypothesis of a "multicolored" *Pinta*: the related cost of paint.

As for the dimensions of the *Pinta* most reconstructions produced a model slightly larger than the *Niña*. A consequence deriving, perhaps, from the fact that the very name by which this ship is known as well as that of her owner, Juan Niño, both possibly mean "little one" or "young girl." Or else, from the fact even that she is always mentioned last and was captained by the younger of the Pinzón brothers.

The various reconstructions of the *Pinta*, attempted during the last one hundred years, have attained quite different results, as it might be expected.

The first full-size reconstruction of the *Pinta* and the *Niña*, if it could be called a reconstruction, was the one realized in 1892 by the Cardona shipyards at Barcelona, on commission by the United States' Government. The American Navy lieutenant C. McCarty Little was sent to Spain to close a deal with the shipyard, but the financial means at his disposal were too limited to cover the full construction costs of the two ships. A compromise decision was reached to purchase two active sailships with adequate hulls that had plied the North American routes, and to transform them into caravels — a feat in itself jeopardizing its success, given such premise. In order to modify as desired the look of the two hulls, which already had little in common with the lines of a caravels, each hull was cut off at the stern, but that considerably worsened their nautical qualities, to the point of making the vessels almost ungovernable under sail. The *Niña*, whose finished hull did not resemble in the least that of a caravel, had the following principal dimensions: main deck length, 62.3 feet; waterline length, 52.4 feet; keel length, 52.5 feet; maximum beam, 20.8 feet; depth of hold, 12.6 feet. She was outfitted with three lateen-sail masts (as the original ship would have been at the sailing from Palos, but not at her arrival in the New World) and with a long bowsprit fitted with jibs, probably with the intent of balancing her ill-fated sail system.

The *Pinta* took on truly the aspect of a small galleon rather than that of a caravel, with a high forecastle and just as high a quarterdeck aft, and a square stern.

A rigging with three masts and bowsprit was typical of a *nao* with topsail. All told, she was a graceful small ship, even though she had nothing in common with the way the real *Pinta* is now believed to have been. Her main dimensions were as follows: weather deck length, 78.7 feet; waterline length, 65.6 feet; keel length, 61.2 feet; beam, 27.3 feet; depth of hold, 14.5 feet.

Because of their inadequate seaworthiness, the two ships were transferred from Barcelona to Huelva for the celebrations of the fourth centennial under tow of the American gunboat *Bennington*. From Huelva, either towed by the gunboat or by the cruiser *Newark*, the two ships reached Havana, on April 9, 1893. Afterwards, with Spanish crews (Cuba was at that time under Spanish sovereignty) but always on tow, they called on at Quebec and Montreal, and finally made it to Chicago, to be shown at the World Exposition. One of the two ships caught fire at the end of the Exposition, the other sunk in 1915.

Monleon also ventured into reconstructing the two caravels, incurring in many mistakes and approximations typical of the time. His *Pinta* was a lateen caravel as it likely was before, but not at, her sailing from Palos; the mainmast had shrouds with ribs, improper on a caravel and the mizzen mast was at the extreme stern, a feature that would make it difficult maneuvering its yard when changing sides. This Monleonian *Pinta* had an overall length of 75.4 feet and 61.5 feet at the waterline.

In his study on Columbian ships D'Albertis, considering that the *Pinta* must have been of markedly smaller size than the *Santa Maria*, followed the same reasoning based upon cargo capacity in terms of barrels that he had fashioned for the Columbian flagship.
Assuming that her hold had room for at least three rows of casks, which, in his words, "required a 4.25 *codos* pillar, i.e., a 10.4 feet depth," to which we must add half a *codo*, or 0.92 feet, for the thickness of the boards of the bottom panel as well as for that of the deck beams; and, finally, approximately one *codo*, equal to 1.84 feet, "to account, below deck, for some space available above the barrels and also because required by the waterlines, thinner than those of a *nao*."

> D'Albertis reasoned:
> I shall follow these general rules, modifying only slightly the length-to-width ratio for the two caravels, especially of the *Pinta*

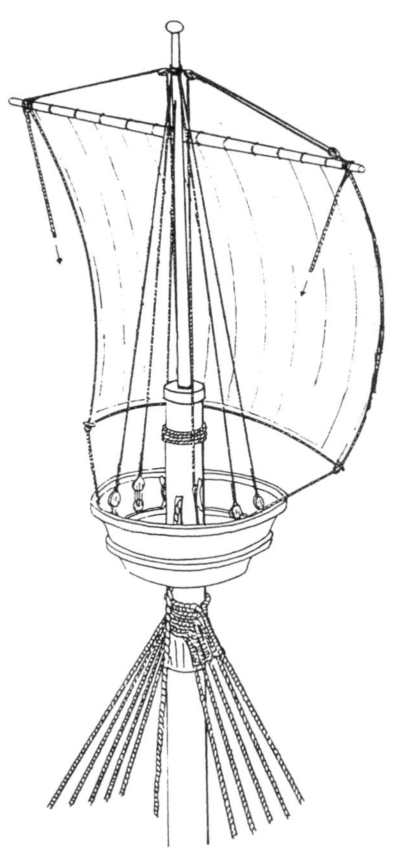

Hypothetical reconstruction of "original" topmast and sail as they first appeared (*circa* 1460). In the sketch, the cage appears set above the capping of the lower shrouds. The system for tensing the small top shrouds is purely speculative. The asymmetrical braces (a single and a double) are reported in many fifteenth-century iconographic documents. The running path of the clewlines is uncertain. (Drawing by Giorgio Osculati from *Navi e Modelli di Navi* - 1979).

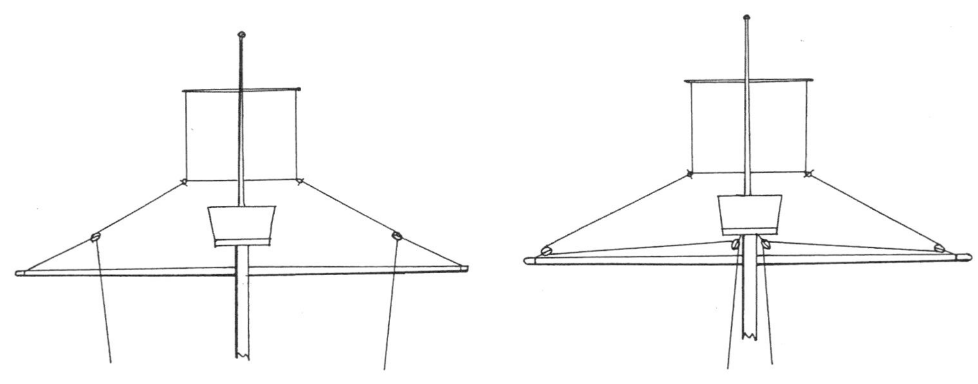

Two different routing systems for the topsail sheets, as can be seen on some of the ships in the background of the painting "The legend of St. Anthony the Hermit" by the Meister der Heilige Sippe - Alte Pinakothek, Munich.

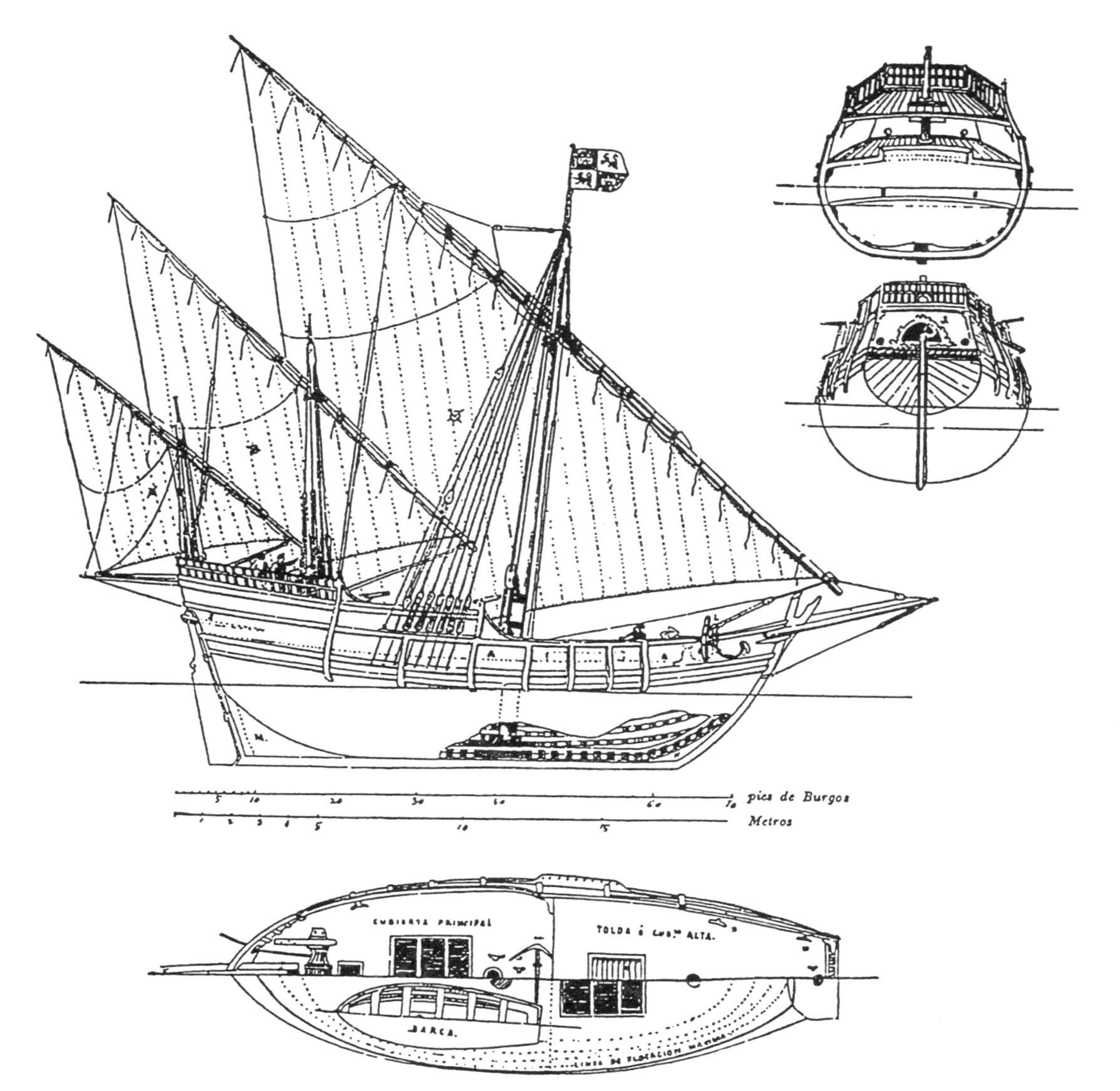

The caravel *Pinta*, as a lateen caravel, in Monleon's 1892 conjecture.

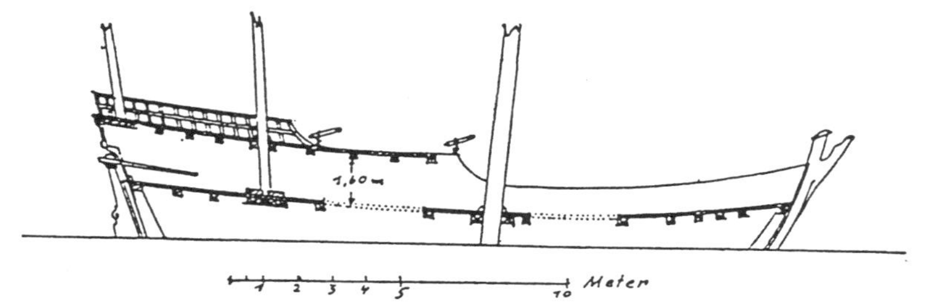

Monleon's longitudinal section of the *Pinta*, according to Heinrich Winter.

about which Columbus in his diary writes to be the *mas velera*, or the fastest. I take the liberty to incorporate this modification in the ancient shipbuilding formula, since from all the definitions there follows that the caravel a rather long and thin hull, when compared to that one of the ships. I shall therefore make the *Pinta* somewhat longer than the *Niña*, as the greater length permits thinner waterlines, and consequently higher speed.
With this in mind, the likely dimensions of the *Pinta* could be the following:

- *Puntal*, or depth of hold, *codos* 6 equal to 12.3 feet;
- *Manga*, or max. beam, *codos* 13 equal to 23.9 feet;
- *Eslora*, or max. length, *codos* 45 equal to 82.7 feet.

As in the case of the *Santa Maria*, if the modern tonnage formula is applied to these dimensions, there results a 154 tons caravel, corresponding to 110 *toneladas* of the time.

As can be seen the *dos, tre y as* formula is no longer observed on caravels and the length, for D'Albertis' *Pinta*, comes out to be about thirteen feet, higher than a *nao* would have been.

D'Albertis concludes that "perhaps experience was already convincing shipbuilders that it might pay to increase the length-to-width ratio of the hull; and exactly to this modification, suggested by experience, the caravels owed their higher speeds."

In his model of the *Pinta* realized by commission of the City of Genoa D'Albertis added to the ship, in contrast to Peter Martyr's *sine caveis* [without mast tops], a sighting place[38] rather than a true top, surmounted by a topsail (which, considering the absence of a cage, would have been difficult to spread or gather) and fitted the mainmast with shrouds and ratlines in the fashion of square sails. For the *Pinta* to be transformed from lateen into a square rig, it was not necessarily required that the shrouds to be replaced, for the old rigging could be updated, if nothing else, for reasons of economics, by simply adding a couple of elements to her tackle-driven system of pulleys and ropes, thus improving it. D'Albertis also shifted the mizzenmast way back onto the poop, following Monleon's idea, an arrangement remarkably negative, for the mast has less room for

[38] The use of the top cage as sighting spot was apparently not congenial to Columbus's crew, and such a function of the top is never mentioned in the *Journal*; instead, when the men are ordered on watch in anticipation of a land sighting, it is stated that they were to take position on the castle, the "highest spot" on the ship.

the shrouds, and maneuvering the yard becomes more difficult when changing sides.

In justification of his adoption of a topsail on his model of the *Pinta* D'Albertis claimed that no document conflicted with his hypothesis: "if the *Niña* with just the means available onboard could be transformed from a lateen into a square caravel, and her mainmast possibly fitted with a small spar (for the flag), it is all the more reasonable to suppose that the *Pinta* had one such spar having been a square-sail caravel from the start.

Independently from such considerations, the modified arrangement also seems to fit both the existing mast assembly and the sailors' tendency to take advantage of any little wind by deploying the largest possible sail surface, without ever forgetting that the *Pinta* actually was the fastest of the three crafts. Finally this caravel, having square sails, necessarily had the 'figure head' needed for trimming foresail and spritsail." But it would seem here that D'Albertis uses the word 'figure head' improperly, as this is, as is well known, the ornamental figure frequently decorating the bow of a ship, which was not yet common in Columbus's time.

Martínez Hidalgo, in his project excuted in 1963, produced a *Pinta* with the following dimensions:

- overall length of 74 feet, and deck beam of 22.1 feet;
- depth of hold of 11.1 feet,

with a 60.91 *toneladas* displacement, i.e., 85.4 current tons, a figure that looks quite plausible. He also fitted the mainmast with shrouds provided with ratlines.

In 1955 Wilfried Dunn presented his own *Pinta* model, which did not deviate much from the almost one-hundred years older and highly criticized project of Monleon. The two most recent *Pinta* reconstructions to our knowledge are the actual one, built by the Spanish Commission for the fifth centennial celebrations, at the Cartagena arsenal in 1991, and the on-paper reconstruction drawn by Wolfram zu Monfeld and associates.

The former amounts to a classic caravel with a slightly raised bow, foresail, square main sail and lateen mizzensail. The shrouds for the mainsail are tensed with dead-eye blocks but unconvincingly provided with ratlines, which were, as we have repeatedly said, unnecessary to climb a mast that had no top and whose sails could be spread and furled by hoisting or lowering the yard.

Zu Monfeld's reconstruction makes the *Pinta* out to be the smaller caravel, accepting a theory that we have already disputed, according to which this vessel was changed from lateen into square during a stop at the Canary Islands. Monfeld's vessel, shown in its two versions, lateen and

The caravel

PINTA

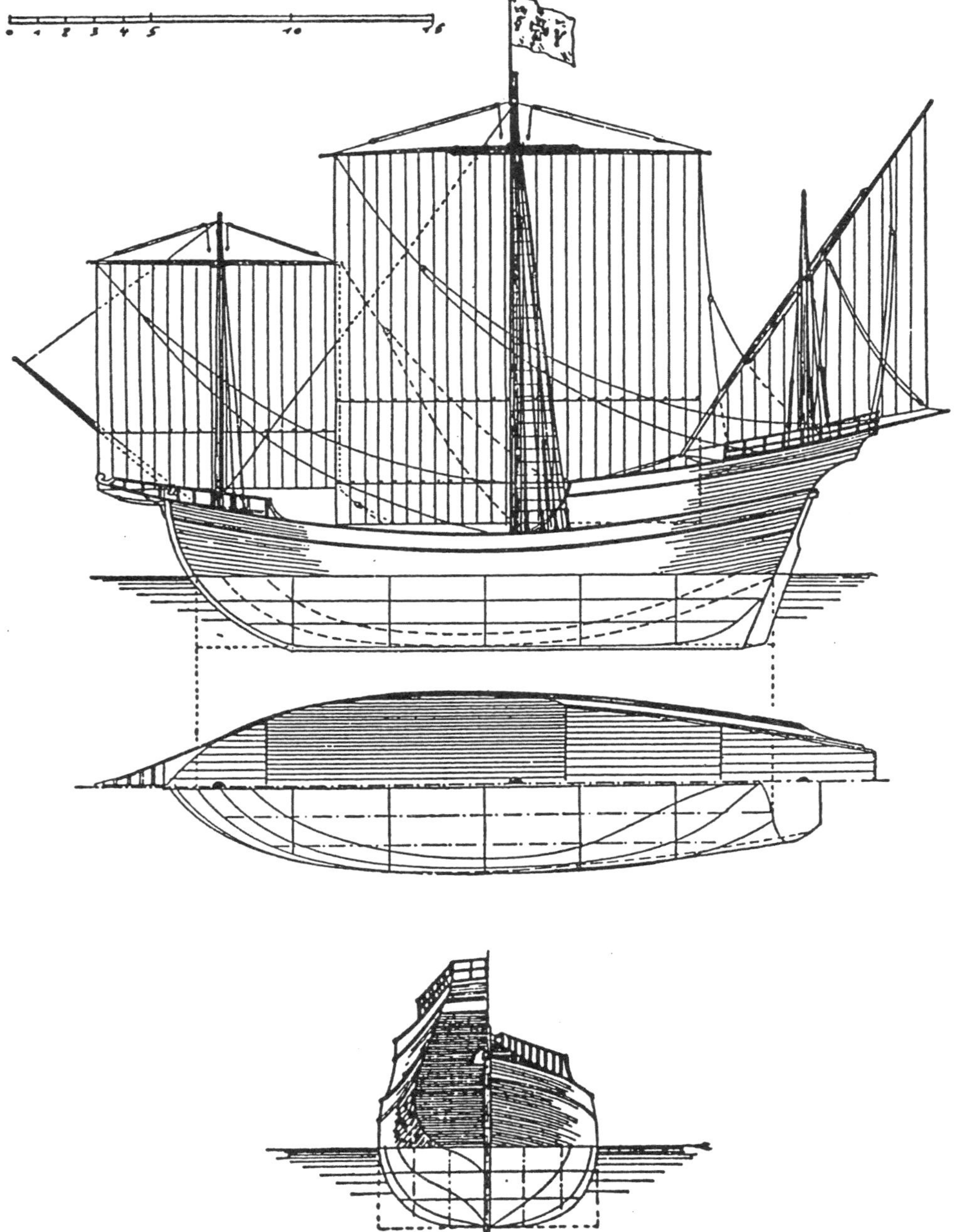

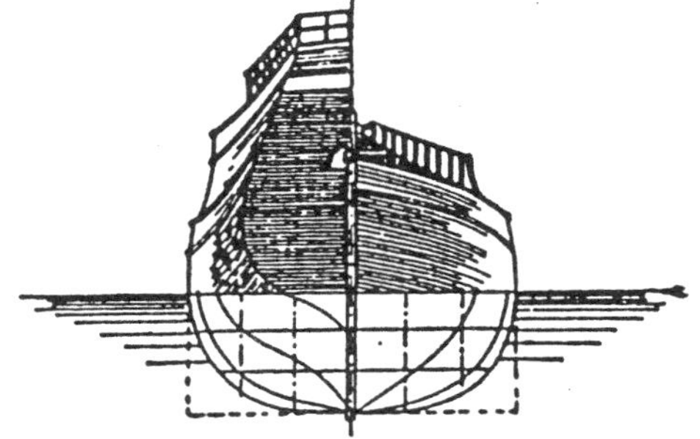

The caravel *Pinta* in D'Albertis' first reconstruction of 1892. In this model he modified to a good degree the original vessel adding a cage and a topsail to a mainmast fitted in the style of a *nao*, and moving the mizzensail way back astern.

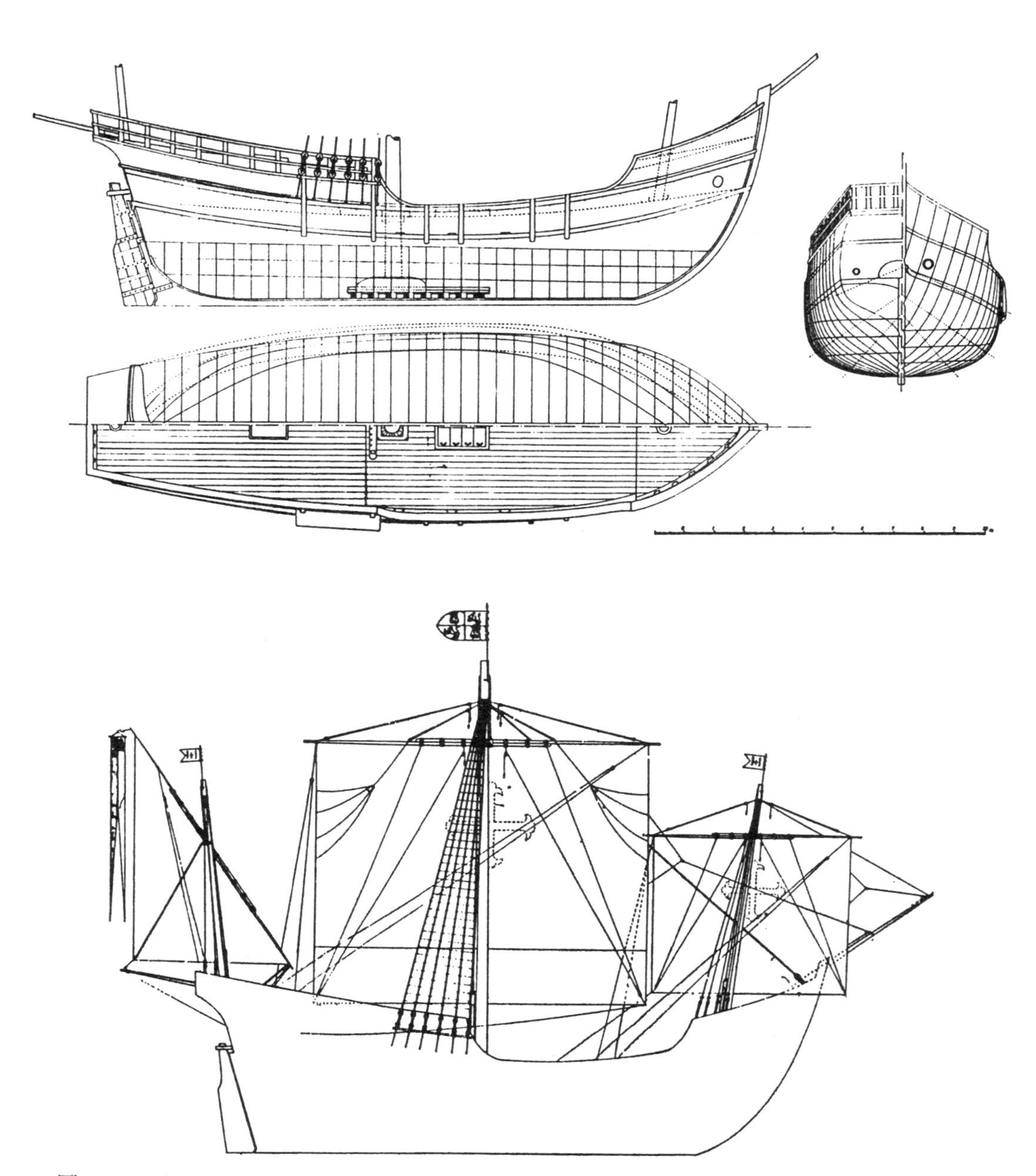

The caravel *Pinta* according to a study by José Maria Martínez Hidalgo y Terón, director of the Barcelona Naval Museum. This study, dating back to 1963, remains one ot the most plausible reconstructions of the ship.

square, actually brings about the change from the former to the latter by merely shifting the second mast afore, without modifying anything in the arrangement of the other two masts.

A list of all features from the various reconstructions, after rejecting the more improbable solutions, would yield a *Pinta* with the following characteristics.

A fully decked hull had two hatch-ways leading to the hold, a large one for the cargo and a smaller one for regular access. In almost all the reconstructions the *Pinta* is privileged, with respect to the *Niña*, with a raised bulwark at prow, like a fake forecastle fitted with a small bridge, under which the anchor cables and other encumbrances could be stored. This "gift" to the *Pinta* is not really justified except for the well-meaning intention of giving the larger of the two caravels a more imposing aspect, even if, undoubtedly, raising her bow improved her seaworthy qualities. At stern, there was no quarterdeck with the ship sides raised to support a half-deck, under which the most remarkable thing was the long tiller. This elevated platform above the deck certainly did exist, and is confirmed by a *Journal* entry for September 25, when it is written that Martín Alonso Pinzón "climbed" the stern to signal to Columbus a presumed land sighting. At prow, behind the foremast, there was a capstan or a windlass to hoist the anchors. We would rather imagine this machine behind the main mast, to be used, in addition, to lift the yard of a lateen-fitted mast, which the *Pinta* had before being transformed into a round caravel, or to hoist the large yard of the main mast following the modification. Furthermore, we envision on deck the lifeboat, the fire box, the large bitt for the main yard, spare timber and, perhaps, even four or six oars, on account of the low freeboard of a caravel, which could realistically allow this auxiliary propulsion system in case of lack of wind (we are not, however, fully convinced of this and, if so, oar propulsion might have served for short hauls, certainly not in ocean sailing). Like the other ships, the *Pinta*, too, was equipped with a number of bombards, muskets, etc.

The rigging of the *Pinta*, when the caravel sailed from Palos, had been transformed from lateen such as it was, into square (round caravel). A changeover that must have originated from Columbus's careful reflection on the kind of winds' regimen he might expect. There was no previous experience of Atlantic crossing, only from sailing routes to the Azores and the Canaries, which did not need trade winds, and voyages along the African coast performed by the Portuguese, for which lateen sails were better suited. Columbus was certainly in possession of some data on oceanic streams and winds, and indeed he was aware that constant winds blew westwards from the islands. He was an expert seaman who, for sure, knew how to take advantage not only of his own, but of others' experience as well, so with variously gathered information, he had an elaborate if not very precise idea about what he should expect.

Columbus himself in his letter "Art of sailing" states: "I have dealt and conversed with wise men, both clerics and laymen, Latin, Greek, Jews, Moors and many more of other religions and Our Lord has assisted me in this inclination, since from Him I have received the faculty of comprehending." We believe that — as Taviani has demonstrated — it was in fact his "faculty of comprehending," of being able to synthesize all the information received that made him choose the westward course from the parallel of the Canaries, avoiding the belt of calms and shifty winds between the Azores and the Canaries, thus without overshooting the northern limit of the north-easterly trade winds in that season, and with full awareness that on the return crossing he should — as indeed he did without hesitation — exploit by reaching the latitude of the Azores the westerly winds, dominant during the winter.

The reasons for changing the sails system were mentioned earlier. When running with favorable wind careening or lurching, that is, leaning sideways, is frequent, because the center of propulsion of the ship shifts closer to the stern, the prow rises, and the helmsman is forced to perform a tiresome task of constant compensation. The large lateen sails, slackened to the maximum extent to catch the wind, dip their sheet points into the water during a lunge, and their height puts stress on the ship, with the prow tending to sink deeper (a high sail, as it has already been pointed out, is the least efficient one). Finally, a change of tacks implies the exhausting work of shifting the yard ("making the car"), whereas with a square sail one needs only to brace the yards in a different way.

On this basis, probably, Columbus convinced Martín Alonso Pinzón of the need to change his rigging before starting the voyage. For Vincente Yáñez's *Niña* either there was no time, or more direct hard evidence was needed to convince her master, which explains why it was later done at the Canaries.

It was, in any case, a radical makeover for both caravels, not a simple addition to the foremast of a square sail, as sometimes the Portuguese did. The operation itself, however, did not present excessive difficulties. If the caravel was three-masted, as apparently the *Pinta* was, the biggest mast was at midship, and had a yard longer than the ship's length, with a shorter mast fore and an even shorter one at extreme aft. To repeat, in order to turn the sail system into a square one, the larger mast was left at midship,

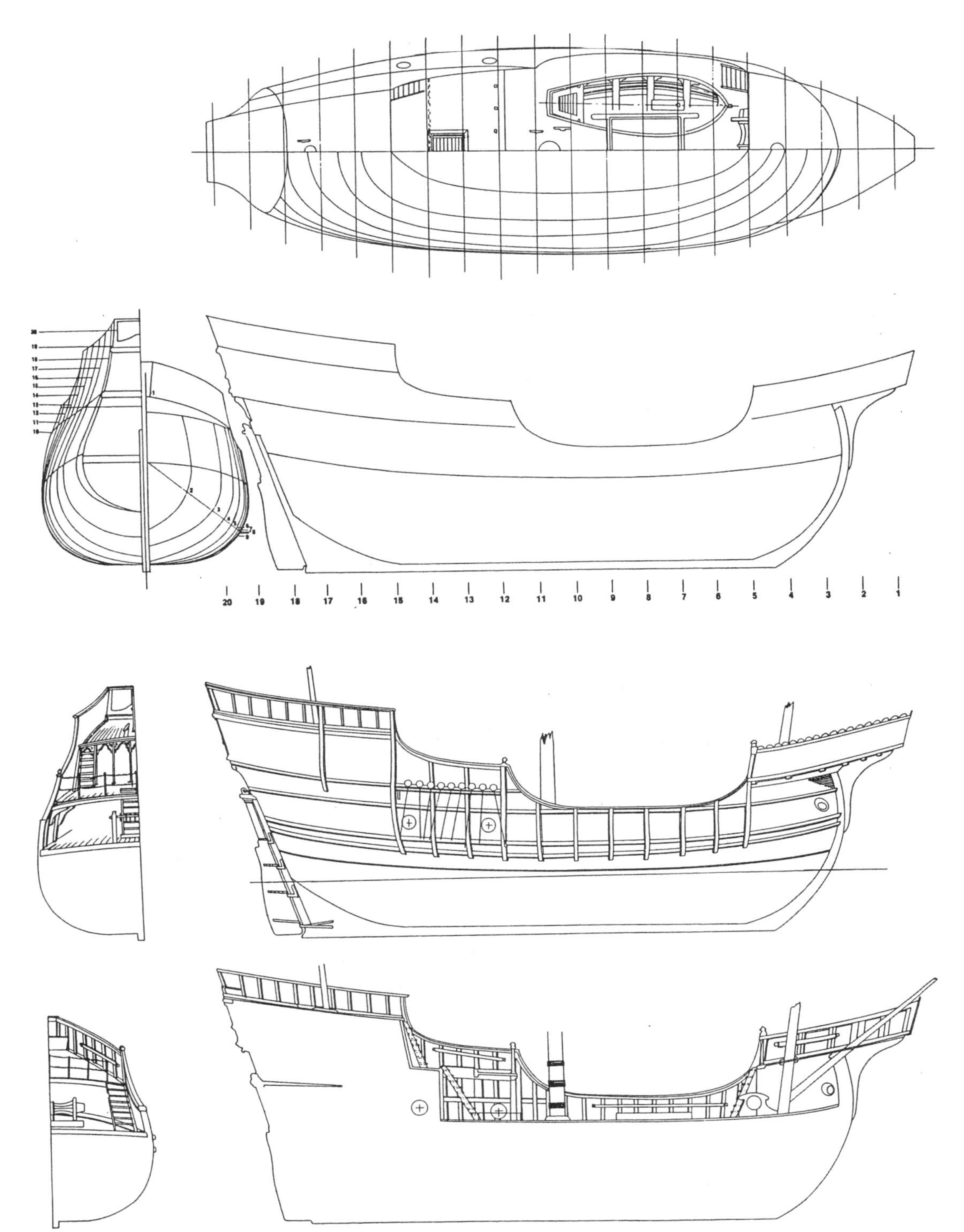

Reconstruction of the *Pinta* according to Wilfred Dunn (1985). The ship looks like a *nao*, which makes the reconstruction seem implausible.

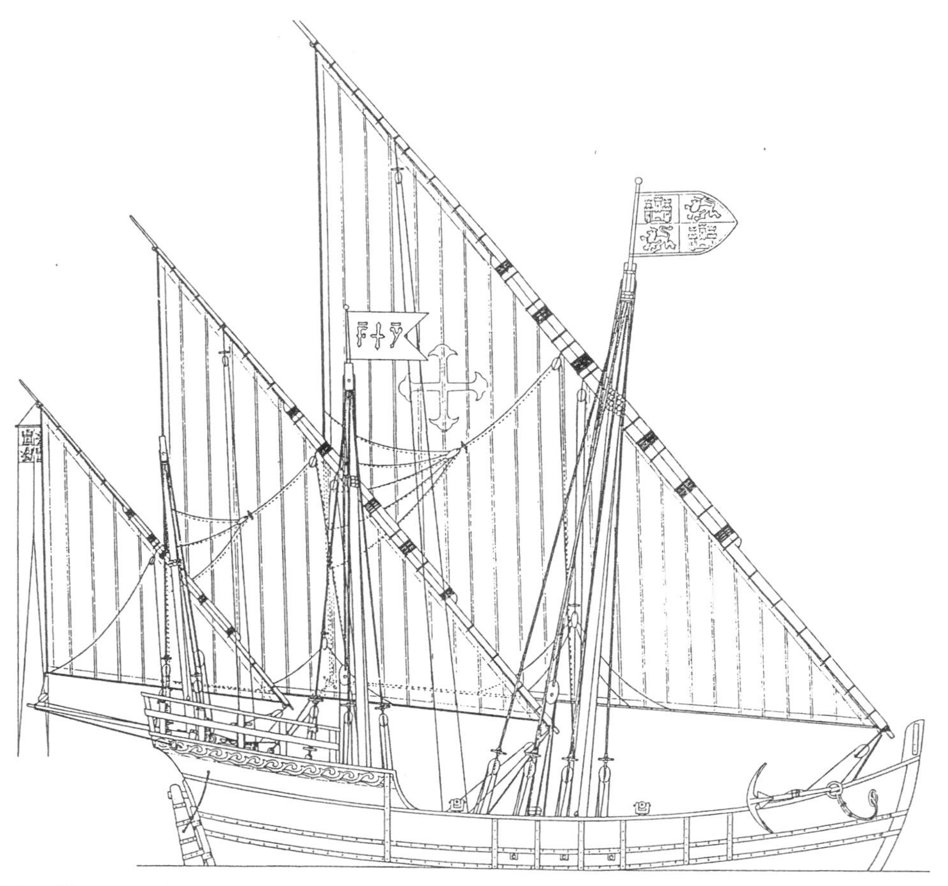

The *Pinta* as a lateen caravel, in the 1991 project studied by Wolfram zu Mondfeld, Peter Holz and Johannes Soyener.

The same *Pinta* modified as a square caravel simply by shifting the second mast foreward. Notice the solution adopted for the central sheet of the mainsail (shown by the arrow).

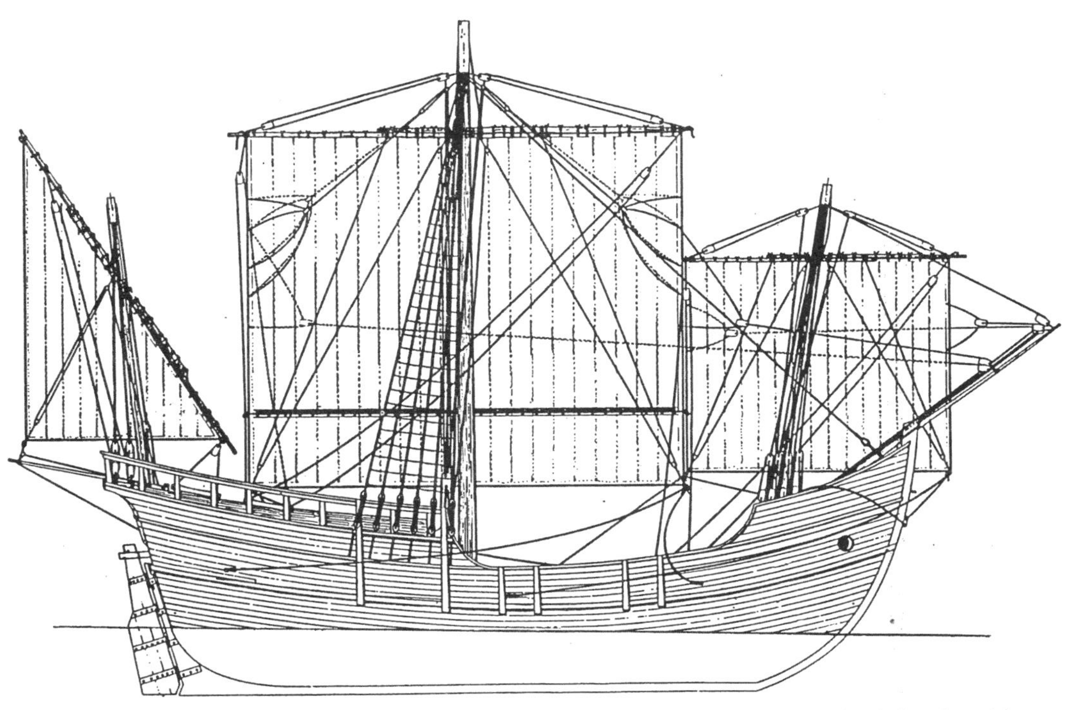

The *Pinta* reconstructed in 1982 in the arsenal of Cartagena on behalf of the Spanish Commission for the celebrations of the fifth centennial of the "discovery."

The *Pinta* reconstructed following D'Albertis' indications. Model preserved in the Maritime Museum at Genoa-Pegli.

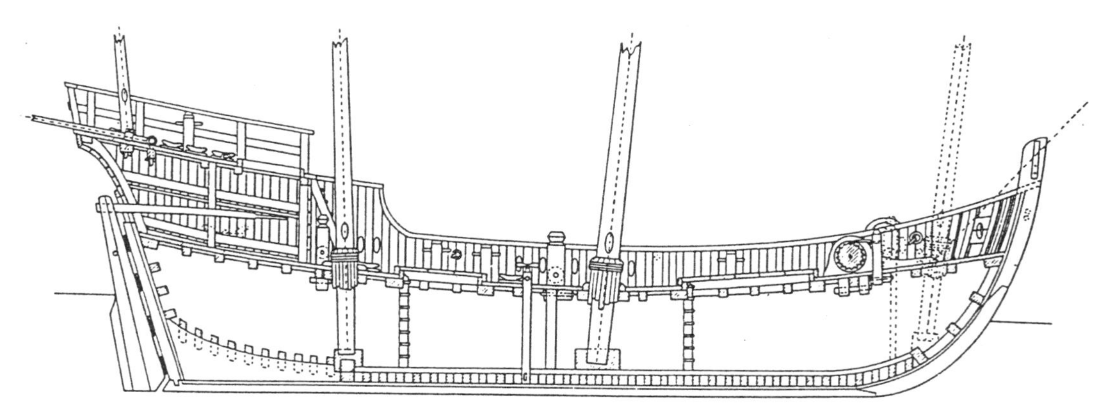

Sectional and side view of the *Pinta* by zu Mondfeld, Peter Holz and Johannes Soyener. In the sectional view, the mast's shifting is highlighted in fully dotted lines.
Although we do not concur with the hypothesis that the *Pinta* was the smallest of the Columbian ships, we believe that these authors' proposal regarding the transformation of a lateen caravel into a square one (as was the case for the *Niña*) illustrates such possibility perfectly.
The PINTA - A caravel of the first Columbian flotilla -1492
The *Pinta* according to a reconstruction by Franco Gay, with a sail plane as a square caravel (round caravel) at the departure from Palos.
Hypothetical longitudinal section, cross sections and views from prow and stern of the caravel *Pinta*.

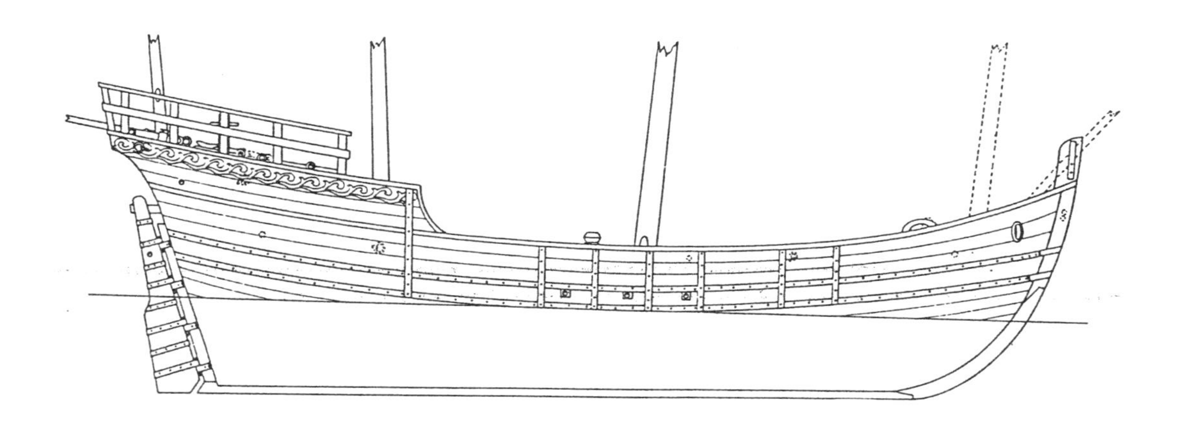

slightly slanting it foreward perhaps to adjust the sails center as needed, and the second mast was shifted to prow, making a foremast out of it and, finally, the third mast was either left in its place, or moved a bit forward if doing so seemed an advantage.

Each adjustment depended on the behavior of the ship under sail, which could be verified only while sailing. At prow an outrigger had to be installed, whose function was to give support to the foremast stay and to the bowlines blocks.

The yards could be made out of the old spars; there was enough material to do so and for the sails, if it was inconvenient to purchase some new ones, they could be partially cut out from the old lateen sails manufacturing them into two square ones. All reconstructions assign the *Pinta* a mainsail with only one bonnet.

The standing riggings did not require any change; the shrouds kept their tackles, but new stays had to be fitted. The running riggings were just as we previously described them for the square sails of the *Santa Maria*. The *Pinta's* transformation in the project by Zu Mondfeld and others as they had imagined it (reported here on p. 190) shows the procedure very clearly. "The modification of lateen vessels into square ones," wrote Martínez Hidalgo "following the Spanish example, was adopted also by the Portuguese once they appreciated its advantages, at the beginning of the sixteenth century." The Portuguese fitted the square sail on the foremast, leaving the others lateen. "Occasionally, they hoisted on the foremast a second square sail of smaller surface. The results were good, but scarcely significant and for that, Fonseca called it *Mestizia* rig." That much was done with the large sixteenth- and seventeenth-century caravels, about which we have commented previously.

The *Pinta*, transformed into a *redonda*, was a good ship. All the problems lamented in the first days after sailing were resolved during the voyage. It was a vessel not in perfect conditions at departure time, combining aging structures with poor maintenance. After all, the citizens of Palos possibly tried to repay their debt toward the Crown by complying with the order at the least expense.

The caulkers of Palos, charged with putting the ships back in working conditions, did a poor job and when Columbus reprimanded them, instead of showing more conscientiousness, they simply deserted him. Columbus, after the known incident of the rudder, says that the ship was leaking and "wished to get another vessel right there, if one could be found." He could replace neither the ship nor the sailors, however, since it would have been a particularly difficult task to find among the Spaniards in the Canaries people ready to jump at such an adventure without reservations. Therefore he had the *Pinta* repaired, and in a short time — the damage probably was not too serious — and thereafter the vessel performed well.

Running free, the *Pinta* proved to be the fastest ship of the flotilla, but when heading into the wind the *Niña* overtook her because, so Las Casas reports, the *Pinta* had her mizzenmast damaged. This problem with the *Pinta*'s masts, however, turned out only in the return voyage and it seems strange that it could not be fixed with onboard means, considering that the mizzen mast was very small. It may have been the case that the sail system was not balanced, and this defect became more evident when sailing close-hauled.

And in regard to the speed of Columbus's ships, we want to mention a learned and interesting study by Admiral Mario Ingravalle, published in *Rivista Marittima* in the January and February 1989 issues.

The data recorded by Columbus in his *Journal* can tell us only what his estimation was and refer to the nautical mile length used by the navigator, and about which many doubts persist (1,234 meter according to D'Albertis; 1,587 in Navarrete's opinion; 1,306.92 according to the American researchers Junge and Marden's most recent statements; and 1,480 on the authority of Morison, Taviani, Charcot and others, this last value having been assumed by Ingravalle for his calculations), and on the basis of an approximate estimation of the time employed, as well as keeping in mind the primitive if not outright measuring instruments and the unknown rates of the ocean currents.

The highest speeds recorded by Columbus, who sailed almost all the time with a constant northeasterly trade wind blowing at starboard quarter and a calm sea, were, by his own estimate, of 7 knots with peaks of 9.6 knots (excluding the unbelievable registration of 12 knots on October 8). These values refer to the *Santa Maria*; the caravels would have attained higher rates, with top speeds close to 11 knots.

These figures are considered too high by almost all Columbian scholars. J.B. Charcot, on the basis of his own nautical and sailing experience, concludes that the ships could reach but not surpass the eight-knots mark. Morison maintains that the top speed held by the *Santa Maria* was the one recorded on the evening of October 11, when the wind freshened considerably, and estimated to have reached 9 knots (9.6 according to the value recorded by Columbus), but other scholars do not require values above 7.5 knots for the *Santa Maria* and 9 knots for the caravels.

From the replicas that have actually navigated, we know that the 1892 Duro and Monleon's *Santa Maria*, with a favorable stiff breeze attained an average speed of 5.8 knots — perhaps not at the top of her performance — while Guillen Tato's model reached 8 knots. The values recorded by the latest Spanish reconstructions were not made public, as an unexplicable secrecy is still kept about these reconstructed ships.

So far, we have focussed on maximum speeds, although a more important value in judging the efficiency of a ship is average speed. Considering all the pertaining factors, over a total distance of 3,117 nautical miles Ingravalle figures the average to have been 3.81 knots, "a somewhat approximate value, but one that can be regarded as very close to reality, in view of the many secondary uncertainties (approximate departure and arrival time, small deviations from the set course, etc.)." It should also be remembered that, between September 20 and 25 the ships endured about forty hours of calm wind. Over the entire crossing, however, the ships took advantage of 300 miles of favorable current drift that Columbus, although sensing their existence, could not quantify. Therefore, Ingravalle's calculation rests on the estimation that

> the 'net' distance on which to figure the actual (average) speed of the ships, i.e., the distance covered with favorable winds only, figured to be about 2,817 miles. Admittedly, to the extent that this figure is uncertain as the value of the currents Columbus encountered is also uncertain, the mean speed would amount to 3.45 knots....

Not satisfied with the figures he obtained reasoning on the reported data, Admiral Ingravalle decided to delve into a theoretical study based on the design features (geometrical elements of the hulls, dimensions and properties of the submerged sections, estimated propulsion force, keel conditions, etc.) — of the modern replicas, of course, since none of the original construction data are recorded.

After examining all the possibilities, Ingravalle was able to conclude that the *Santa Maria* could have reached a maximum speed of about 8 knots. The two caravels, in his estimation, would not have exceeded 8.5 knots.

Admiral Francesco Quieto, reviewing Ingravalle's study, held the above estimate to be "still optimistic," and scaled it back to 7 knots reasoning that, in order to increase speed by even a half knot, a thrust under sail equal to 3,300 pounds would be needed, which would in turn entail a 28.5-knot wind and waves as high as 15 feet, that is, simply prohibitive conditions for keeping the canvas fully hoisted.

From all of the reported studies one realizes that the question of maximum speed, most accurate and conscientious calculations notwithstanding, is still far from having been solved. In the end, the only acceptable figure of reliable approximation is the one regarding the average speed value, which after all is also the most useful.

As a final observation concerning the *Pinta*, let us recall that it was from this vessel that on the dawn of October 12, 1492, a sailor named Rodrigo de Triana (Juan Rodríguez Bermejo) sighted in the waning glimmer of moonlight a land on the horizon; a moment later, Martín Alonso Pinzón ordered a bombard fired, thereby signaling to the flagship that the long voyage had attained its goal.

At the end of the tempestuous return from the discovery voyage, the *Pinta* landed at Bayonne in Galicia. There Martín Alonso Pinzón received the Crown's order to join the Admiral at Palos. So he did, but just before his vessel entered the harbor Martín Alonso deserted her perhaps because, as seriously ill as he was, he did not feel like listening to eventual reproaches related to his numerous acts of disobedience from the Admiral. Fifteen days later the man who had played an important role in the discovery died, without enjoying his part of the triumph.

After her return to Spain, at Palos, on March 15, 1493, no further news was recorded of the *Pinta*.

The caravel Niña

Traditionally considered the smaller of the two caravels, the *Niña* was built at Moguer on the bank of the Rio Tinto, and originally named *Santa Clara*, after the city's patron Saint. Her owner was Juan Niño and from him comes the nickname by which the ship is universally known.

Christopher Columbus always showed a great predilection for this small caravel that, after the *Santa Maria*'s wreckage, brought him back to Spain overcoming the storms which caught him from February 12 to the 15, 1493 and on March 3 and 4, before he called at Lisbon. *Si no fuera la carabela diz que muy buena y bien aderecada, temiera perderse*, wrote the Admiral in his *Journal*. In addition, during the return voyage, the *Niña* had little ballast and Columbus, after the mid February storm, hurried to weight her down at the Azores with timber and stones found on the beach and also by filling the empty casks with sea water.

The *Niña* accompanied Columbus, who by then had become one-half owner of the ship, in his second voyage; he chose her as his flagship during the exploration of Cuba. With her, Columbus returned to Spain in 1496 with about a hundred people on board. Back to Cadiz, the caravel then made a voyage to Italy with a cargo of wine; off the coast of Sardinia she was captured by certain pirates but her crew, with the help of some inhabitants of Palos who were themselves among the pirates, managed to win her back. She again sailed on the 3rd February 1498, bound for the West Indies on occasion of the third voyage of Columbus who, in 1499, finding himself in serious financial troubles because of the rebellion in the colony, sold her to Diego Ortiz. The last news regarding this adventurous caravel mentions her en route to the Coast of Pearls in 1501. These episodes, if reported truthfully, cast some doubts on the traditional opinion that the *Niña* was in fact the smaller of the caravels.

About the *Niña* there is a relatively exceptional amount of information, when considering the overall scarcity of news surrounding the Columbian ships. Michele da Cuneo, who traveled on the *Niña* as far as Cuba and on it returned to Spain in 1498, wrote that the caravel "held approximately 60 *toneladas*," and we also know that on the Italian voyage she took onboard 51 *toneladas* of cargo. We are more inclined to believe these data, which corroborate each other and would reflect a vessel with a carrying capacity of about eighty modern tons (indeed common for a caravel of the epoch), rather than to D'Albertis's conclusions and the dimensions he estimated:

- maximum length, 79 feet
- beam, 23.9 feet
- depth of hold, 11 feet

which would imply a ship of 105 modern tons.

To these data D'Albertis had arrived conjecturing that the *Niña*, a little smaller than the *Pinta*, would actually be wider than the latter "because, beside being less speedy, it is proven from Columbus's *Journal* that although with insufficient ballast [...], she was still able to withstand the gale that caught her near the Azores, a feat impossible to achieve had the *Niña* not possessed excellent shape stability." A further proof, perhaps, that baseless conclusions may be evinced in support of a prejudicial thesis.

In 1962 then lieutenant Carlos Etayo ordered built at Pasajes (Guipuzcoa) a caravel-shaped vessel that he named *Niña II*, with which he retraced Columbus's voyage from Palos to San Salvador, meeting very inclement weather and requiring, to complete it, seventy-six days, a commendable feat from the standpoint of seamanship because carried out with a really small craft. To his *Niña II*, in fact, Etayo had applied the following dimensions: length 42.6 feet, beam 11 feet, depth of hold 6.4 feet. The boat was fitted with two lateen-sail masts, with the possibility of hoisting a square sail in place of the larger lateen sail.

Björn Landström drew in those years a *Niña* with a length of 100.1 feet, a beam of 28.5 feet and depth of hold at midship, of 7.5 feet. Heinz

Gronen, in 1986, published in *Das Logbuch* the drawings of a Portuguese caravel with two masts and lateen sails, having the following dimensions: length 79.7 feet, beam 23.3 feet, depth of hold 5.9 feet. Martínez Hidalgo's reconstruction, instead, had the following size values:

- length, 70.4 feet;
- beam, 23.3 feet;
- depth of hold, 9.2 feet
- draft, 5.8 feet
- cargo capacity, 52.7 tons.

For Martínez Hidalgo as well the *Niña* had two masts, increased to three after the transformation into a *carabela redonda*, a modification performed at the Canaries.

Furthermore, among the reconstructions of caravels that can be regarded similar to the *Niña*, one might include two ships, the *Boa Esperança* and the *Bartolomeu Dias*, built at Vila de Conde in Portugal, between 1987 and 1990. These two caravels have similar dimensions. Those pertaining to the *Boa Esperança* are as follows: length 78.1 feet, beam 21.6 feet, depth of hold 10.7 feet, total sail surface 235 square yards, and a cargo capacity of 123 tons. For safety reasons the two ships are also equipped with a small auxiliary diesel engine.

In 1988, the *Bartolomeu Diaz* retraced the voyage of the great navigator whose name it bears, as far as Mossel Bay, where the fifth centennial of the voyage was celebrated. Now the ship is preserved in a dedicated museum at Mossel Bay, which opened in 1989.

The *Boa Esperança* (see p. 85), completed in 1989, called at Bruges for the commemoration of the founding of that city, made a voyage to Madeira and Morocco, will participate to the World Exposition at Seville and later on, in 1993, will visit the Western African countries "discovered" by the Portuguese; then in 1995, she will sail to Brazil, for the celebrations of the fifth centennial of the discovery.

The recent Spanish reconstruction of the *Niña*, outfitted as *carabela redonda*, executed at Huelva in 1992, exhibited the following measures:

- overall length 70.2 feet;
- beam 20.6 feet;
- depth of hold 6.6 feet;
- total sail surface (as a square caravel) 179 square yards;
- displacement 100 tons.

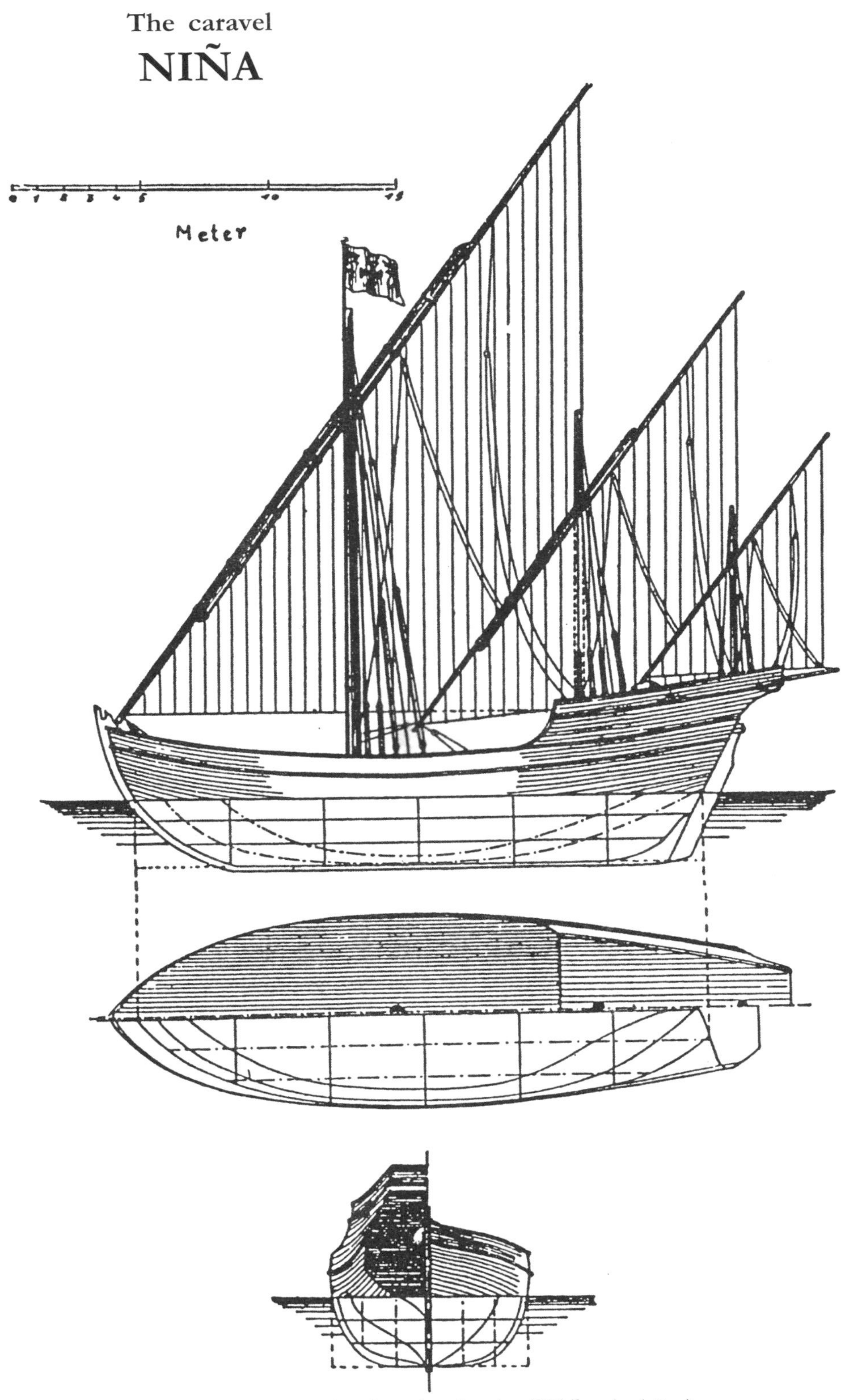

The *Niña* in the first drawing by D'Albertis (1892)

Above - Model of the caravel *Niña* according to D'Albertis's reconstruction, preserved at the Genoa-Pegli Maritime Museum.

Below - Detail of the same model.

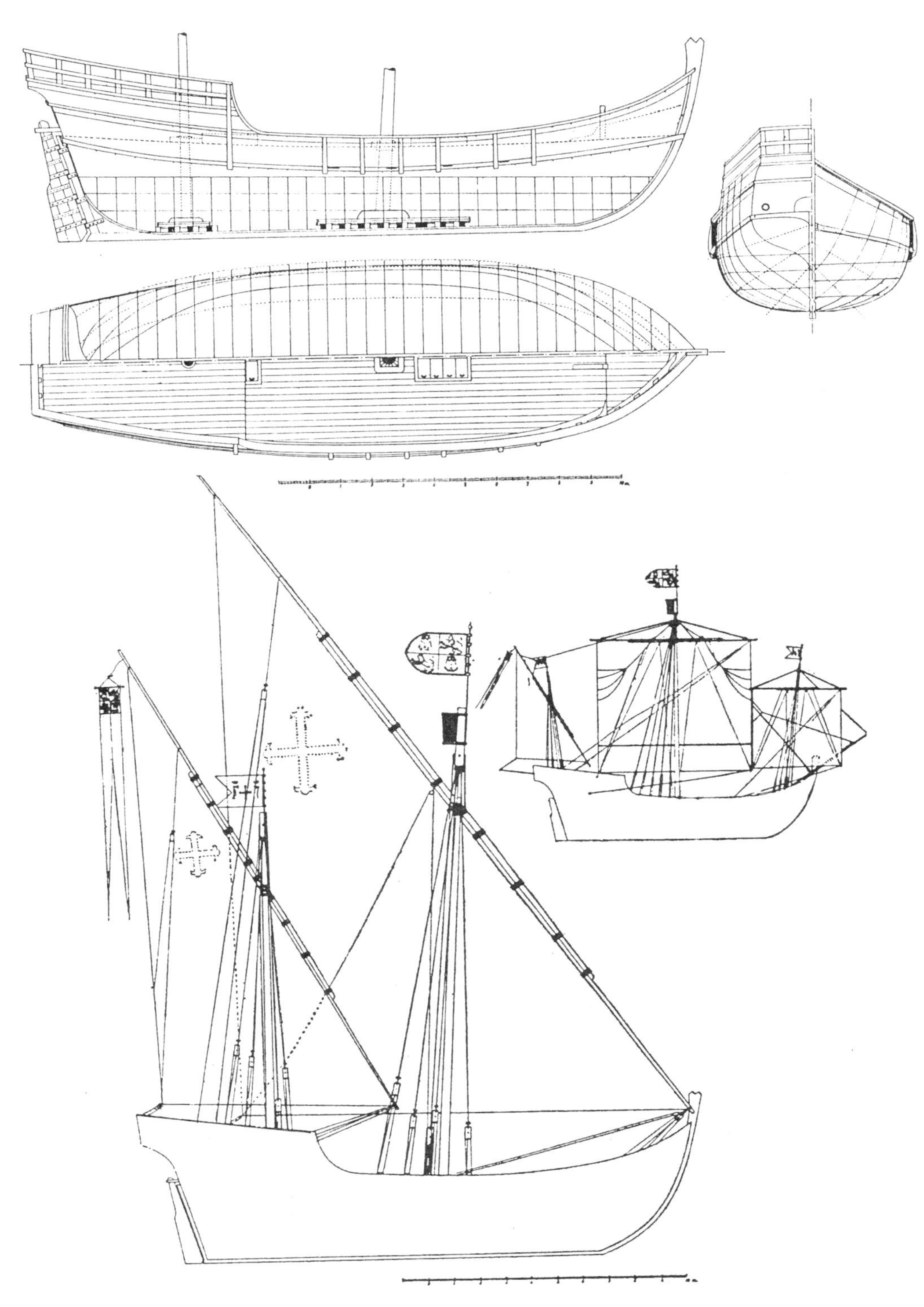

The caravel *Niña* according to the 1963 reconstruction by José Maria Martínez Hidalgo y Terán, director of the Barcelona Naval Museum. Martínez imagined the *Niña* as a two-mast caravel with sails much developed heigthwise. In the small sketch, the ship after her transformation into a square caravel.

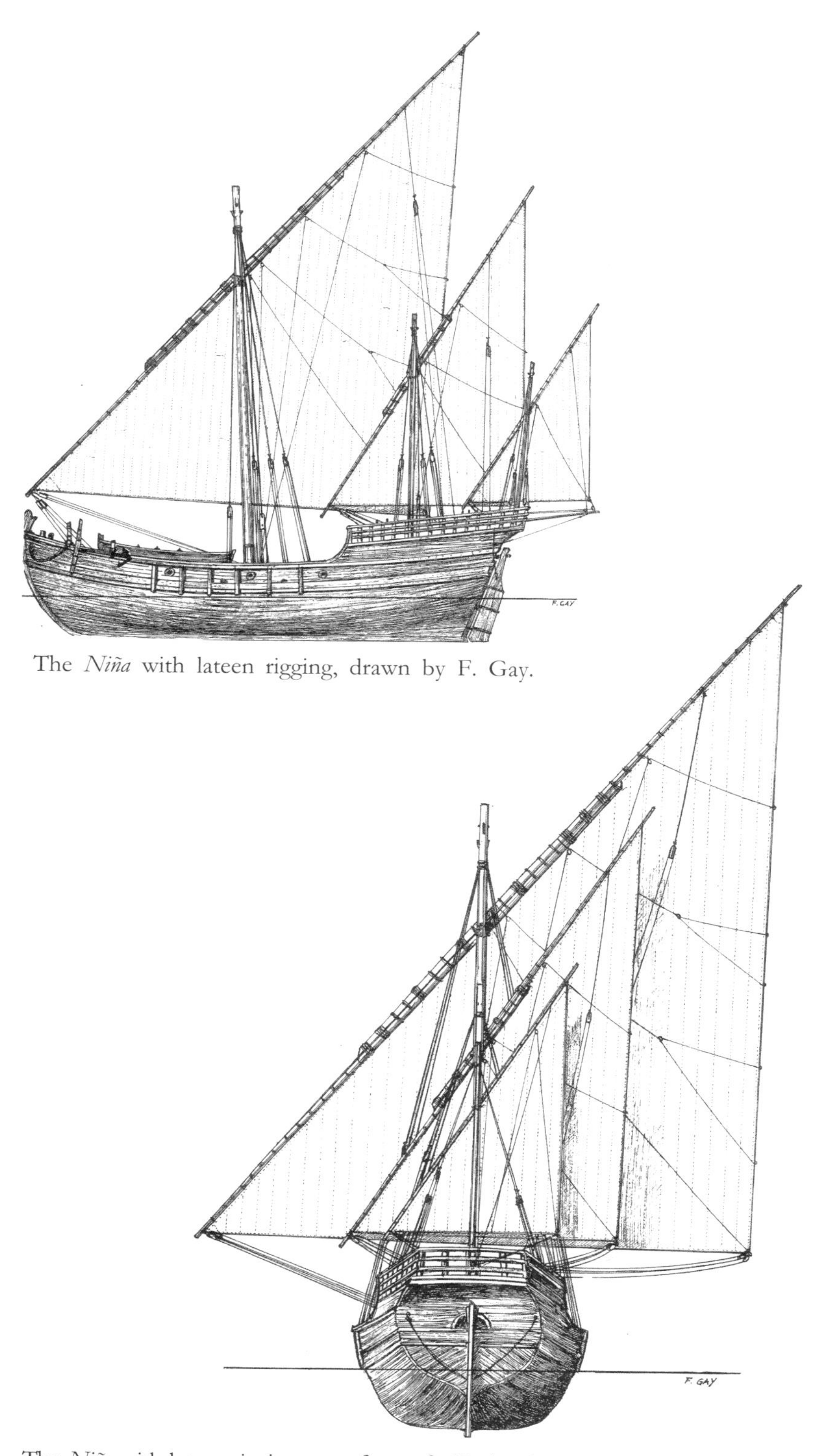

The *Niña* with lateen rigging, drawn by F. Gay.

The *Niña* with lateen rigging, seen from aft. Notice the great extension of the main lateen sail.

The reconstruction of the *Niña* executed at Huelva in 1981, on behalf of the Spanish Commission for the Fifth Centennial celebrations.

The *Niña* with square rigging. The second mast has been moved fore and fitted with a square sail; the central mast featured a square sail and an outrigger — a novelty added to the bow.

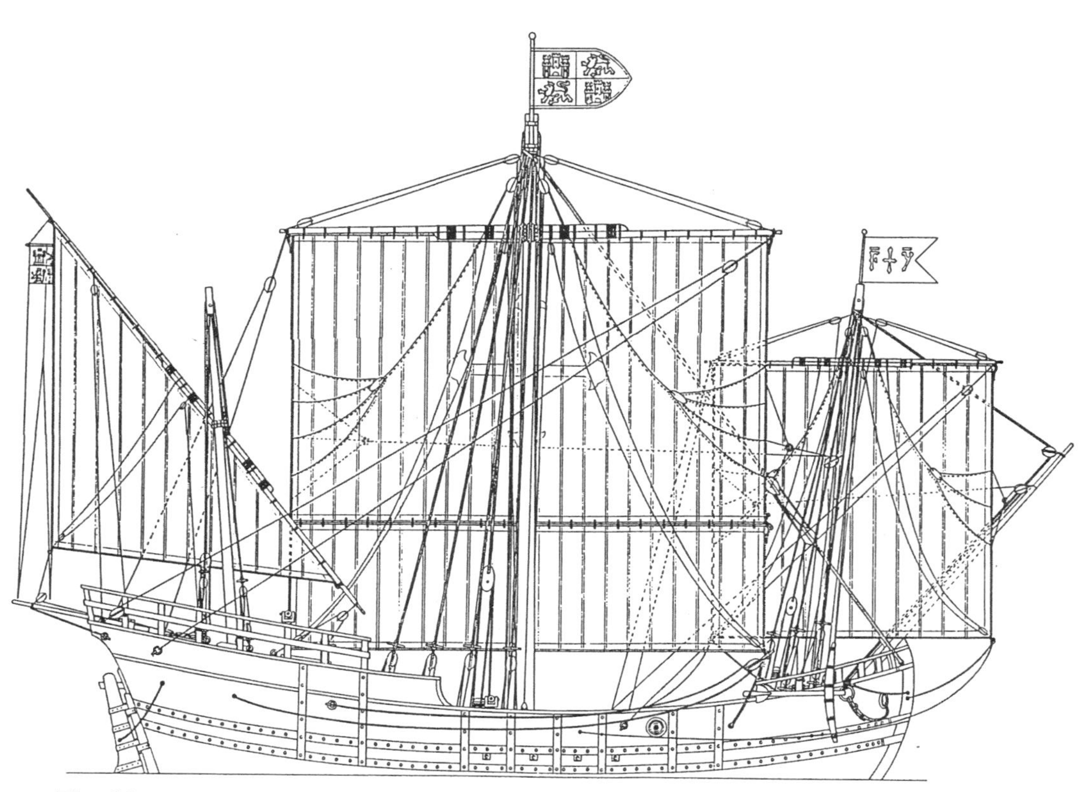

The *Niña* as a square caravel in the drawings by Wolfram zu Mondfeld, Peter Hoz and Johannes Soyener. The three authors held the *Niña* to be the larger of the two caravels.

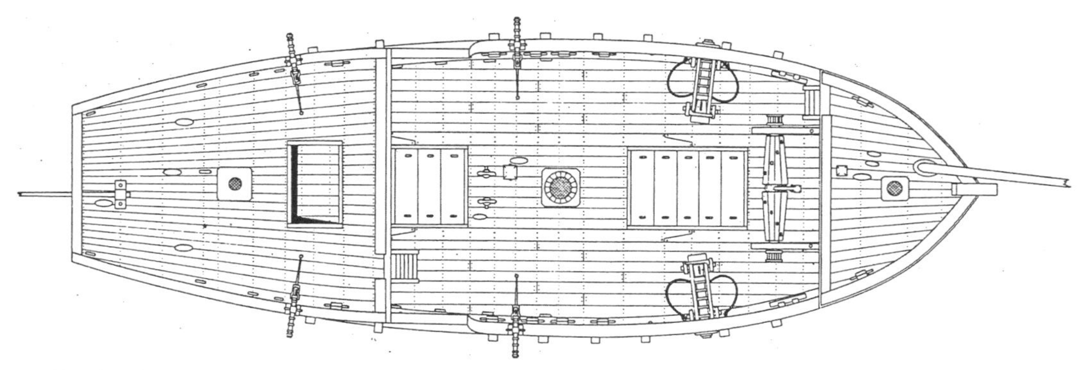

Deck of the *Niña* in the project of the Zu Mondfeld group. The ordinance consists of two bombards and four breech-loading falconets. The capstan is installed at bow.

And finally the reconstruction of the *Niña* presented by the group led by Zu Mondfeld has the following dimensions:

- length 72.2 feet;
- beam 21.2 feet;
- depth of hold 6.6 feet,

values that are virtually identical to those of the Spanish reconstruction.

Summarizing — as already done for the *Pinta* — it appears that what can be evinced from the various reconstructions is that the *Niña* was very similar to her sister ship. She was fitted with a continuous weather deck with two hatchways, of which the central access was larger. Martínez Hidalgo figured it to be a 5.1 feet wide square, a rather small opening for the passage of a 4.9 feet long barrel. The ship certainly lacked a castle or a prowside elevation, since she was still lateen-rigged when sailing from Palos (and probably at the Canaries there was neither the time nor the opportunity to perform other major modifications). She had a gallery at stern — like the *Pinta* and, so it looks, all caravels — to protect the helmsman, shelter crew members and others and, from that superelevated point, afford a wider view of the horizon as well as of the ship and sails.

What else has been said with regard to the *Santa Maria* and the *Pinta* could also be repeated here for the *Niña*. This small vessel probably had its capstan on board — its location still undetermined — a good supply of anchors (considering that, after loosing two of them at the Azores, it could still anchor), a launch on deck (it certainly had six oars), weapons similar to the *Pinta*'s, including bombards, breech-loading falconets and swivel guns.

From the *Libro de Armadas*, it would seem that the *Niña* was outfitted with three anchors, with one a good 200 pounds heavy. However, it looks like both the reported number and weight of the anchors, are a bit on the lighter side. The bombards of the *Niña* are cited by Columbus in his *Journal* when, on October 7 he writes that the ship fired one shot to signal land sighting, and again when she made a show of it before cacique Guacanagarí.

At her departure from Palos, the *Niña* had a lateen rigging. The uncertainty, among the various scholars who took an interest about her, concerns rather whether she had two or three or even four masts, as hypothesized in a recent graphical reconstruction by the National Geographic Society, based on information that Eugene Lyon allegedly found in the *Libro de Armadas* preserved in the archives at Seville and containing news items related to the expeditions in the New World starting from 1495. Among those, there is a signed receipt from a Pedro Frances regarding a vessel bound for *Hispaniola* in 1498, named *Niña* but also known as *Santa Clara* (which would prove the identity of the *Niña* with sufficient precision), and filled with details about sails, rigging and various onboard items.

Even if the *Niña* in 1498 had a fourth mast (it would have been a bonaventure mizzensail with lateen sail, located at extreme stern [hence its "back-sail" denomination]), things would not be much different. The rigging is not something immutable and during the service life of a ship there could be many reasons to either change it or improve on it. A bonaventure mizzen yardlet is a small thing and can be set up in short order using supplies ordinarily available onboard.

Regardless of whether she were two- or three-masted, upon reaching the Canary Islands, the *Niña* changed her rigging. The works were probably executed at Las Palmas by the crew, with the assistance perhaps of a small local shipyard.

The *Journal* does not spend too much time on this subject, nor does it provide precise indications as to places or dates. What happened is more than summarized by Las Casas in a single notation for events occurred from August 9 through September 5, in which, as far as the *Niña* is concerned, he makes quick work of it, a single sentence actually: "They switched the *Pinta* into a round [caravel] because it was lateen rigged," even citing the wrong name, because the modified ship was not the *Pinta*, but the *Niña*. A mistake that can be easily explained since in preceding sentences Las Casas was writing about the *Pinta* and her name "stuck in his pen," as one used to say.

In any case, we know that Columbus called at the Canary Islands on August 9 but, because of bad weather, he could not reach Gran Canary any earlier than the 11th; he sent there Martín Alonso Pinzón with the *Pinta* (and the *Niña*?), to try and find a better ship; he himself continued on to Gomera where he remained until the 23rd, waiting for news from Pinzón while contracting for the charter of another ship that had been proposed to him. Having not reached an agreement, he returned to Gran Canary on the 25th and there found Pinzón, just back after his fruitless search of a suitable substitute for the *Pinta*. And it is probably after this date that the decision was made to refit the *Pinta*, upon realizing the impossibility of replacing her. If so, the actual operation would have been performed from August 25 or 26 to September 3 or 4, not enough time, in our opinion, to careen the entire ship. Perhaps Pinzón sailed around in the area, leaving the *Pinta* to be worked on, but in that case there would not have been enough days to change the rigging of the *Niña*.

One could keep advancing diverse hypotheses, for none of which, however, there would be much corroboration. Beyond all speculations, the fact remains that in that period of time, the *Niña* changed her rigging; if she was three-masted, she underwent the modifications already described many times; if she had only two masts, an additional small mizzen mast had to be provided; if instead, according to the latest supposition, she was four-masted, the required work was essentially the same, and the two stern masts were left in place.

All considered, we believe that the shrouds and tackles were left just as they were with the lateen rigging without featuring outboard ribbed tensors, as implied by some reconstructions. At prow it had been probably necessary to install an outboard pole to support the bowlines' return cables and the foremast stay. An additional spritsail is excluded by all replica models, as it is also the case for mast top, topsail and related yardlet: all models rule these out. Similarly, all replicas show a mainsail with a single bonnet.

Chapter V

THE CREWS

The names of almost all the men who boarded the Columbian ships are known; only three names remain uncertain out of the ninety individuals who followed Christopher Columbus in his daring enterprise. The credit for this discovery, which Taviani regards as "definitive", belongs to an American scholar, Alicia Bache Gould, author of a series of essays on the subject, following her uncovering of the rolls of the registered men. Last-minute changes might account for the still extant uncertainties concerning the three individuals in doubt.

It should be added that the crews' components, to a great extent, did not embark with enthusiasm, not because of cowardice as they were all experienced seamen, but because the upcoming feat was generally thought of as bordering on insanity. What convinced them, more than the Sovereigns' orders compelling the city of Palos to furnish ships and crews, more than the presence of soldiers under Juan de Peñalosa's command, was the example of Martín Alonso Pinzón, an influential and bold Palos shipowner who decided, along with his brother Vincente Yáñes and many members of his family, to participate in the discovery voyage.

Following is the list of the crew members. An asterisk next to a name signals those people cited in the *Journal* whose presence, therefore, on board the ships cannot be questioned.

Santa Maria

– Cristopher Columbus - general captain

– * Juan de la Cosa, from Santona, owner of the ship and master captain (*maestre*)

– Peralonso (or Pero or Pedro) Niño, pilot

– * Diego de Arana, from Cordoba - adjutant major (*alguacil mayor*) [39]

[39] We adopt this definition taken from the Navy's terminology, to underscore the role of this officer, who oversaw administrative and judicial functions aboard.

– * Rodrigo de Escobedo, from Segovia - fleet recorder (*escribano*)
– * Pedro Gutiérrez - Court's stewart (*scalco - repostero de estrados del Rey*)
– * Pedro (or Rodrigo) Sánchez, from Segovia - royal inspector (*veedor real*)
– * Luis de Torres - interpreter (a converted Jew who knew Caldeian and Arabic)
– Juan Sanchez - surgeon (*cirujano*)
– Chacu, Basc - boatswain (*contremaestre*)
– Domingo de Lequeito - second boatswain (*segundo contremaestre*)
– Antonio de Cuéllar - carpenter (*carpentero*)
– Domingo, from Biscayne - sailor and cooper (*marinero y tonelero*)
– Lope (Lopez) - caulker (*calafate*)
– Juan de Medina - sailor and tailor (*marinero y sastre*)
– Diego Pérez - sailor and painter (*marinero y pintor*)
– Bartolomé Bibes, from Palos - sailor (*marinero*)
– Alonso Clavijo, from Vejez - sailor (*marinero*)
– Gonzalo Franco - sailor (*marinero*)
– Juan Martínez de Açoque, from Denia - sailor (*marinero*)
– Juan de Moguer, from Palos - sailor (*marinero*)
– Juan de la Plaça (Plaza) - sailor (*marinero*)
– Juan Ruiz de la Peña, from Biscayne - sailor (*marinero*)
– Bartolomé Torres (or de Torres), from Palos - sailor (*marinero*)
– Juan de Xeres, from Palos - sailor (*marinero*)
– * Rodrigo de Xeres, from Aiamonte - sailor (*marinero*)
– Pedro Yzquierdo, from Lepe - sailor (*marinero*)
– Cristóbal Caro - silversmith, precious metals assayer and cabin boy (*platero y grumete*)
– Diego Bermùdez, from Palos - cabin boy (*grumete*)
– Alonso Chocero - cabin boy (*grumete*)
– Rodrigo Gallego - cabin boy (*grumete*)
– Diego Leal - cabin boy (*grumete*)
– Pedro de Lepe - cabin boy (*grumete*)
– Jacome (or Jacomel) el Rico, from Genoa - cabin boy (*grumete*)
– Martin de Urtubia - cabin boy (*grumete*)
– Andres de Yébenes - cabin boy (*grumete*)
– Juan Portugués, Negro from the Canaries - cabin boy (*grumete*)
– Pedro de Terreros - Admiral's attendant, later butler (*camarero*)
– * Pedro (or Diego) de Salcedo - Admiral's attendant (*paje*),
for a total of 39 people.

Gould adds to this list a Bartolomé Garcia, a not better specified *Maestre* Juan (could he be Juan Sanchez?), and a Sancho Ruiz de Gama, helmsman, whose name is, by the way, mentioned in the *Journal*, bringing the real total to 42.

Pinta

– * Martin Alonso Pinzón - captain (*capitan*)

– * Cristóbal Quintero, from Palos - owner of the ship, hired as a sailor

– * Francisco Martín Pinzón, from Palos - actual master captain (*maestre*)

– * Cristóbal García Sarmiento - pilot (*piloto*)

– Juan Reyal - adjutant (*alguacil*)

– Master Diego - surgeon and pharmacist (*cirujano y botecario*)

– * García Fernández (or Hernández) - provisioner (*despensero*)

– * Juan Quintero de Algruta, from Palos - boatswain (*contremaestre*)

– Anton Calabrés, Calabrian - sailor (*marinero*)

– * Francisco García Vallejo, from Moguer - sailor (*marinero*)

– Alvaro Perez - sailor (*marinero*)

– Gil (or Gutierre) Perez - sailor (*marinero*)

– Diego Martín Pinzón, nicknamed el Viejo, from Palos - sailor (*marinero*)

– Sancho de Rama - sailor (*marinero*)

– * Gómez Rascón, from Palos - sailor (*marinero*)

– * Juan Rodríguez Bermejo, known as Rodrigo de Triana - sailor (*marinero*)

– Juan Veçano, from Venice - sailor (*marinero*)

– Juan Verde de Triana - sailor (*marinero*)

– * Pedro de Arcos, from Palos - cabin boy (*grumete*)

– Juan Arias - cabin boy (*grumete*)

– Hernando Medel (or Mendez), from Huelva - cabin boy (*grumete*)

– Francisco Medel (or Mendez), from Huelva - cabin boy (*grumete*)

– Alonso de Palos - cabin boy (*grumete*)

– Juan Quadrado - cabin boy (*grumete*)

– Pedro Tegero (or Tejero or Terreros) - cabin boy (*grumete*)

– Bernal - the captain's cabin boy and personal help (*grumete y criado del capitano*)

for a total of 26 people, to whom Gould adds a Juan Bermùdez, from Palos (cited in the *Journal*) and a Rodrigo de Triana, from Lepe, a different person than Juan Rodríguez Bermejo (a native of Molinas, instead), for a full crew of 29 people.

Niña

– * Vicente Yáñez Pinzón - captain (*capitan*)

– * Juan Niño, from Moguer - owner of the ship and her actual master captain (*maestre y proprietario*)

– Sancho Ruiz de Gama - pilota (*piloto*)

– Alonso Maestre, from Moguer - surgeon (*cirujano*)

– Diego Lorenzo - provider (*despensero*)

– Bartolomé García, from Palos - boatswain (*contremaestre*)

– Alonso de Morales - caulker (*carpentero*)

– Juan de Arráez - sailor (*marinero*)

– Ruy García - sailor (*marinero*)

– Rodrigo Monge - sailor (*marinero*)

– * Bartolomé Roldán - sailor and apprentice helmsman

– Juan Romero - sailor (*marinero*)

– Pedro Sánchez, from Montilla - sailor (*marinero*)

– Pedro de Villa - sailor (*marinero*)

– García Alonso, from Palos - cabin boy (*grumete*)

– Andrés, from Huelva - cabin boy (*grumete*)

– Francisco, from Huelva - cabin boy (*grumete*)

– * Francisco Niño, from Moguer - cabin boy (*grumete*)

– Pedro de Soria - cabin boy (*grumete*)

– Hernando de Triana - cabin boy (*grumete*)

– Miguel de Soria - cabin boy and the captain's attendant (*grumete y criado del capitan*)

for a total of 21 people. In Gould's list Ruy García, Francisco from Huelva and Pedro de Villa do not appear, whereas are registered the names of Pedro Alonso Niño as the pilot[40] and of Juan Arrias from Tavida (a Portuguese) as a cabin boy and of Pedro de Arraes as a sailor. The total number of people on board does not change.

From these rosters of names, bits of information emerge about some of the men making up the crews. First of all about their origin: they are almost all Spaniards, with the exception of the Genoese Jacome el Rico, the Portoguese Juan Arias, the Calabrese Antonio Calabres, the Venetian Juan Veçano and the Canarian Negro Juan Portugués, besides, of course, Christopher Columbus. Among the Spaniards prevailed those from Palos, Moguer and Huelva, towns of a single, homogeneous territorial area. As for all the other crewmen, a few were from inland cities such as, e.g.,

[40] Pedro Alonso Niño of the *Niña* is a different person than the Pero (or Pedro) Niño embarked on the *Santa Maria*.

Andrés from Yébenes and Antonio from Quéllar (province of Segovia); from the Seville region was Juan Verde; from Santander came Juan de la Cosa, Ruy García and others; from Biscayne Chachu, Domingo de Lequitio, Juan Martínez de Acoque, Juan Ruiz de la Pena, Martín de Urtubia; all these areas were obviously capable of supplying excellent seamen. Still, Columbus chose Palos, which, apart from being designated as the ships' provider — albeit not spontaneously — was near the La Rabida convent, where he had lived for a long time and could rely on the help of friends who could also be heard in high places, such as friar Antonio Marchena and friar Pérez.

Another distinctive factor was that many people from Palos, Huelva and Moguer, were bound by family ties, which made for a greater feeling of unity and promoted a certain harmony among the crews.

Some historians have maintained that Columbus was accompanied by individuals of the worst reputation, that is, by many gallows birds, pardoned on account of their acceptance to partake in an adventure full of risks and unknowns. However, in this regard, too, Alice Gould has scaled down this thinking, as she found only four such rogues: Alonso Clavijo, Juan de Moguer, Bartolomé Torres and Pedro Yzquierdo. Torres had killed Juan Martín, a town crier or tax collector in Palos. Once taken into custody, he would have certainly ended up hanging from the gallows, had his three companions not helped him to escape. All four men had vanished, but the justice of the time, which did not waste time in trifles, had branded all four with a death sentence *in absentia*. As they learned they could be graced by partaking in the expedition, they enlisted and embarked on the *Santa Maria*. Being probably among those left behind at *La Navidad*, the reprieve that was granted to them may have extended their lives only a short while.

About this episode, P.E. Taviani concludes in the first volume of the *Nuova Raccolta*:

> Columbus then went to the near city of Moguer to make public another royal ordinance of 30 April, addressed to all the authorities of the cities and villages along the Andalusian coast. It announced Columbus's voyage and ordered that the outfitting and manning of the ships be aided in every way. Columbus had received another royal ordinance, this one practically granting a pardon — or, rather, suspension of proceedings and sentence — to those charged with crimes who should enlist for the expedition overseas. Columbus, then, can ship criminals, condemned either to prison or to death,

> and he does so. But how many are there? Contrary to tradition and legend, research of documents of the period reveals that there are only four...[41]

Elsewhere Taviani claims that, if they were not exactly four, they were nevertheless very few, indeed a negligible percentage compared to the total number of the participants.

Some clarification may be in order concerning the specific tasks of crew members. Beside the pilots, boatswains, carpenters, coopers etc. who were prescribed part of the crew for all ships and whose functions are self-explanatory, one may note the presence on every vessel of a surgeon (not a modern-day physician, but someone indeed capable of intervening to set bones, to practice blood-letting, treat wounds, perform amputations etc.) and also — albeit on the flagship only — of a tailor, a silversmith (so convinced was everyone that they would find a bounty of precious metals), an interpreter with a rather useless knowledge of Caldeian and Arabic, a couple of court officers acting as inspectors and royal notaries and finally the *alguaciles*, in charged of the water supply and police and surveillance functions, to maintain law and order on board.

There were, at least for the first voyage, no ecclesiastics or missionaries. According to a singular theory proposed by Simon Wiesenthal, the reason was to be found in Columbus's Jewish origin (which was indeed never proved). A much simpler assumption could logically be that seldom church people took part in discovery voyages before then. Only later their presence became customary, as the need to evangelize pagan souls after the conquest grew in importance. Otherwise, all religious services on board were in the care of the captain, who presided over the recitation of daily prayers.

[41] Cfr. *The Journal*, II, 16, p. 91. In: Nuova Raccolta Colombiana, English transl. by Farina and Beckwith.

Chapter VI

LIFE AND COMMON LAW ABOARD THE MEDIEVAL SHIPS

To complete an overview of the typical environment of medieval seafaring, something should be said about life aboard ship and the then traditional customs of the merchant marine. We refer to customs of the 'merchant' marine because the discovery voyages, though sponsored by governments, were the sole responsibility of privately owned ships and crews extraneous to the military or national "navies," no matter how embryonal as they might have been at the time.

Sailing vessels were immune to the travail of rowing or the plight of slavery, which had plagued the Mediterranean fleets. Their small crews, instead, were composed of free people, who received regular pay for their work and — a point worth noticing — were protected, as much as possible, by a set of common laws in all seafaring countries, as well as by customary rules that recognized duties and rights.

Many collections of such laws are known, for virtually every maritime city issued her own book of rules, without however conflicting with those of other cities, since the problems addressed were essentially identical everywhere.

We wish to recall here, among such texts, the *Roles d'Oleron*, in force on the French Atlantic coasts; the *Damm Judgments or Westcapelle Laws*, applied in the Flanders; the *Maritime Rights of the Hanseatic League*; the *Customs of Amsterdam*; the *Sea Consulate* of Catalonia and that of Provence; the *Amalfi Tables*; the *Maritime Right* of Ragusa, etc. These consuetudinary laws, put in writing so that they could become common knowledge and be used in seamen's hiring contracts, were observed throughout the entire Middle Ages, with several of them remaining in force for a much longer time.

Without really delving into this subject and straying too far from our purpose, the general principles that governed the relationships between seamen and maritime entrepreneurs can be recalled. Such knowledge should help to understand better the attitudes of captains toward their crews and, in particular, to explain the reasons for the apparent lack of toughness or ability to impose their own authority, so frequently found not only in Columbus's case, but for many other navigators of the time as well. To be sure, the maritime customs mentioned here applied directly to the merchant marines and their commercial operations, involving the transport of goods. Yet, allowing for some indispensable adjustments, even for the discovery voyages and their different purposes and varying circumstances, the people involved had a set of expectations and were not inclined to see their particular interests disregarded.

Seamen came generally from the people inhabiting the harbors and small coastal villages, who, consequently, had lived of seafaring activities for generations. Their actual civic status was admittedly minimal: often indeed they did not even bother with their fathers' names, sometimes actually not remembering it. If born elsewhere, they often did not even know where they had come into this world. This explains why ships' rosters frequently carry, next to a name or nickname, the phrase "he himself does not know whence he came."

A sailor would normally sign on for a voyage or for a certain period of time, freely choosing the ship and the shipowner with greater guarantees of trust and convenience. Owners, conversely, did likewise, hire trustworthy or skilled people preferably from those they already knew.

We have previously mentioned what happened when Columbus was searching for crews for his first voyage. The municipality of Palos was bound to supply the ships and that it did, but as far as providing people ready to enlist and follow a visionary, a virtual unknown and a foreigner to boot, in his enterprise, there were no volunteers. Actually, several people, as they realized the risk, in order to avoid being caught up with the King's orders, chose to leave town and disappear (an easy thing to do at that time).

The situation took a radical turn when Martín Alonso Pinzón, a well-known man and a shipowner whom the folks of Palos had followed in many profitable undertakings, possibly not all legal, decided to back Columbus and to join him together with several members of his own family. Only then, thanks to this reliance on the Pinzóns, arguments about the riches that could be found in the newly discovered lands started to take hold and to permeate the minds of seamen.

In an ordinary merchant voyage a sailor would receive one third of his pay at the time of enlistment, one third once the freight was unloaded, and the final third at the voyage end. There was however the risk that a sailor, once arrived at the port of call, having already been paid two thirds of the salary, would disappear, judging it worthwhile to lose the final third still coming to him, against the chance of making two more thirds with a new enlisting. This was not the case, quite obviously, for those taking part in a discovery voyage, as one could not realistically expect to make calls in commercial ports where such option could be exercised To commit someone more strongly to a favorable outcome of a discovery undertaking, they would be allowed to carry a small amount of goods of their own, miscellaneous items they could sell wherever they made landfall, or they could acquire partial ownership of the freight, paying for the quota with their work. The sailors departing from Palos may also have been allowed to bring along a small quantity of those glass beads, bells and mirrors that the natives apparently liked so much, and the Spaniards used to profitably barter.

In merchant voyages, sometimes the contract allowed the sailor, if he had not found miscellaneous items to carry, to take onboard some water kegs (always useful aboard) which, in case the cargo were to be thrown overboard to salvage the ship, would have been refunded at the rate of wine casks.

All this could of course be accomplished more easily when merchants and seamen were of the same country, had long known each other and enjoyed reciprocal trust. Several were the methods to bond a sailor to the ship and her cargo, and all achieved the favorable effect of securing a labor force that would be dependable, adverse to turmoil and interested, in case of danger, to save both the ship and her load, rather than just their own lives.

Moreover, at a time when capitals were scarce, such systems enabled one to put together a commercial enterprise — meaning even a single trip — with very modest means, and in case of success, start a new one and so forth. Small-time capitalism, but profitable for everyone involved. The economic benefits, in case of a successful navigation, could be great, considering that trade was still based at that point in time on low volumes of goods. Sometimes one or two trips were sufficient to repay the value of the ship. On the other hand, the high-end risk was the possibility of losing everything in a storm or because of a treacherous rock.

A ship could also engage in what later will be termed "freight solicitation," i.e., unload a cargo at the port of call and load another headed to some other place and so on, possibly coming back to the port of departure after several years. In this case the contract could be based on miles traveled and sailors required to bind themselves to the ship, regardless of destinations. A similar contract may well have been adapted to a discovery voyage.

Desertion was always a captain's nightmare owing to the risk of remaining without help to bring the ship back home, or having to hire a mustered-up and possibly untrustworthy crew. The wandering people found in foreign ports seeking to be enlisted frequently belonged to a scarcely reliable class of seamen. In this respect all maritime laws sought to discourage the habit of abandoning ship without reason, hitting the sailor especially in his pocket, and sentencing him to return the entire amount of the pay received, plus an equal amount in fines, or to bear the expenses for hiring a substitute. Sailors who fled with the money risked, if caught, a lashing, a prison term, and could even face death if repeat offenders. The worst punishment, however, was the loss of his trade, as they became banned and no one wished any longer to hire them or, if anyone did, they would do so in scoundrel-conditions. Usually, to discourage ill intentions, sailors were forbidden to go ashore at ports-of-call, a precaution that was still in use, at times, on military vessels as recently as the last century. Sailors were even responsible for the safety of their ship at anchor and especially so in very busy harbors, where accidents could easily involve more than one vessel.

During discovery voyages desertions were very rare, because very few sailors would prefer the natives' lifestyle to that, hard as it might be, of their own country and environment. Some would chance it anyway, noticeably in places where the mirage of gold overtook many people's minds and their sense of reality. In several cases natives had to be enlisted, whether willing or unwilling, to make up for crew defections, deaths or other circumstances.

Sailors were fully covered in cases of accident or disease contracted during service: their care was at the shipowner's expense; the owner was also bound to furnish them free board and to assign someone to assist them. If a sailor had not recovered before the ship's departure, he could be left behind, but was still entitled to what was due him in its entirety. In case of death, payments would be made to his widow and children.

In a nutshell, maritime laws protected shipowners and the workforce in equal measure; all considered, any modern-day union official would have deemed their arrangements satisfactory. The sailor was bound to his ship only to ensure the good outcome of the enterprise and for common safety in case of danger, while preserving rights that guaranteed him his free-man status — a dignity that included, among others, the right not to be beaten.

He had his "territory," the fore part of the ship, just as the captain's was at the stern; even a captain could not encroach beyond midship with threatening intentions. Trani's Codex spelled this out, establishing for instance that: "The above cited Sea Consuls proffer and establish that no captain may hit any sailor; the latter must, however, escape toward the bow and standing before the windlass chain utter three times the words: on the side of my sovereignty, do not touch me. Were the captain go beyond the chain to beat him, the sailor had the duty to defend himself and if he in so doing killed the captain, he should not be banned."

This "territorial" subdivision on a vessel is documented also in the finale of a lullaby type of song that a cabin boy was to recite after the morning prayers of the *Pater Noster* and Hail Mary:

Diosnos dé buenos dias,
buen viaje,
buen pasaje haga la nao,
senor capitan y maestre y buena compañia, amen,
Asi faza buen viaje, faza muy buenos dias
dé Dios a vustras mercedes, senores de popa y prora.

Scuffles onboard had to be actively avoided. A captain's duty was to "reconcile all conflicts" like a good father. And for the guilty party who offended or lied there were pecuniary compensations to be paid to the injured side. The most serious crimes, those which entitled the captain to put the offender ashore at once, were swearing, "messing things up," stealing and lust.

A sailor could refuse to carry weights, even items of his ship, which meant that all loading and unloading operations had to be effected by port laborers and not by the crew. Moreover, the sailor could not be sent to dangerous places except, quite obviously, on the vessel on which he was embarked and only for the sake of common safety, just as he was bound to participate fully in efforts to save "his" ship or assist other ships in trouble, receiving, in this latter case, compensations or indemnifications paid by those rescued as a result.

What sailors could not have was comfortable beds and savory food, given the material impossibility to supply either one. In the evening, those sailors who were not on watch looked for a suitable corner on deck or a place under the castle where to lie down, wrapped in their gray cloth overcoat. Some lucky ones owned a light mattress, a comfort generally reserved on board to ranking officers and senior sailors. On the *Santa Maria* only Columbus, as far as it is known, could board in a cabin above the castle, with a bed, a writing desk to consult his charts and some chests where nautical instruments and few other valuable things on the ship were stored. The other officers probably had a curtain to separate a section of the quarterdeck. It does not look like there would be enough room to create other reserved lodging spaces.

The discovery of the New World brought to European sailors a precious gift: the swinging cot, a naval version of the hammock (*Kamaki*) that the Caribbean natives used to hung between two trees to swing in the fresh breeze during their lazy days, unaware that their pleasant habit would make a not altogether insignificant contribution to the advancement of sailing conditions.

Sailors, just like everyone else onboard, had to sleep fully dressed in order to be always ready to be called on in case of necessity — a habit, if not an obligation, still partially preserved in the navigation trade.

As for the food, it must be acknowledged that the diet of seamen was certainly spartan, but no worse than that of poor people ashore, except for the lack of fresh provisions. The daily ration included salted meat or fish, lentils, peas, lard, hardtacks and honey. It was up to the sailors themselves to complement this fare with fresh catch, fishing with lines or nets in areas that, according to reports, were very rich in fish, which could be caught without much difficulty. So much so, in fact, that in the ocean flying fish would even jump onboard on their own, a thing never experienced before.

As much as possible, live animals brought on the ship were kept in special coops or pens, so as to ensure fresh meat for at least some time. The few pieces of information on hand are not sufficient, however, to know with certainty the nature and quantity of the provisions carried onboard by the Columbian ships. These must be inferred from contemporary customs and the scanty news accounts that can be gleaned from archival documents.

The "Sea Consulate" saw fit to prescribe that sailors should be given hardtacks daily, meat on Sundays, Tuesdays and Thursdays, and for the remainder of the week a soup of fava beans, chickpeas or lentils, and dried fish. Columbus, in a letter addressed to King Ferdinand, listed, in addition to the aforementioned products, also figs, almonds, raisins and rice. He moreover maintained that wheat and flour were vital, that hardtacks should be well-seasoned but not old, and the flour pre-salted at the time of milling.

Columbus moreover considered olive oil and wine indispensable as well, instructing that oil, used to cook meat and fish, had to be preserved in earthenware jugs, whereas wine in large wooden barrels, should be sealed and fastened to avoid shifting by effect of the ship rolling. Wine was even used to rinse meat and legumes, and would in the end become the most common drink onboard, since water tended to spoil very fast. Beer was drunk only by North Sea sailors.

When Columbus called at Gomera in the Canaries, before starting his crossing into the unknown, he took on board large amounts of salt-cured beef and pork, live animals and firewood for the kitchen.

The Natives' hammocks (*kamaki*), which Spanish sailors discovered in the Antilles, were quickly adopted onboard ships to help crews rest more comfortably.

A careened caravel in a tranquil and isolated cove, lying ready for hull repair and cleaning operations. (Drawn by D. Pansolin from a tempera by B. Landström.)

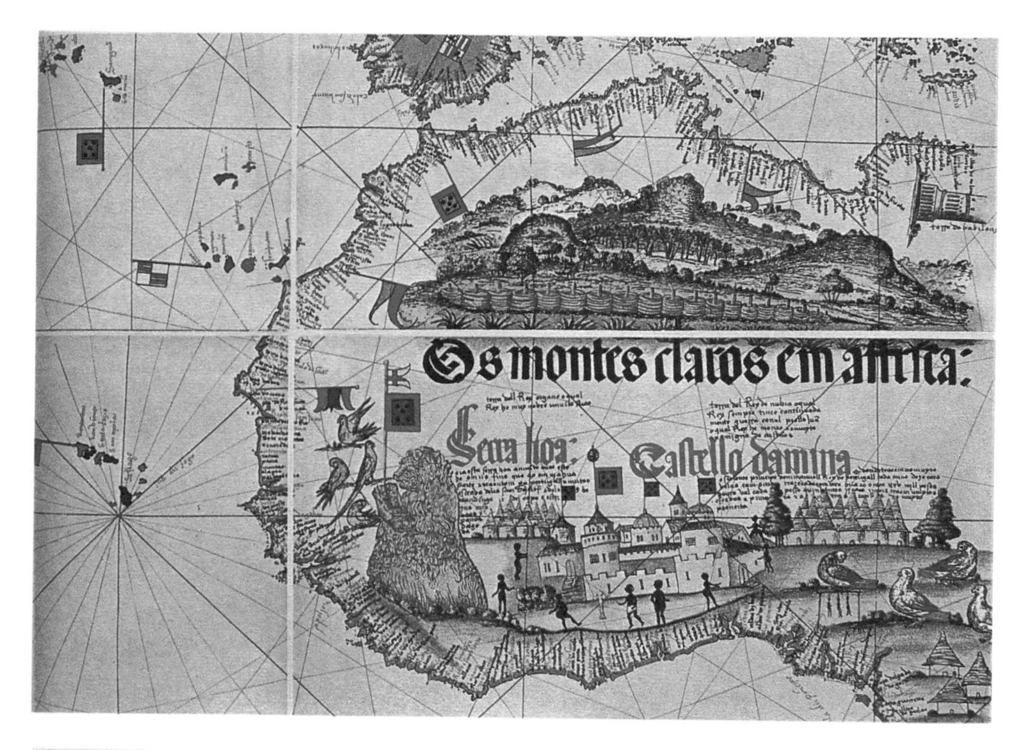

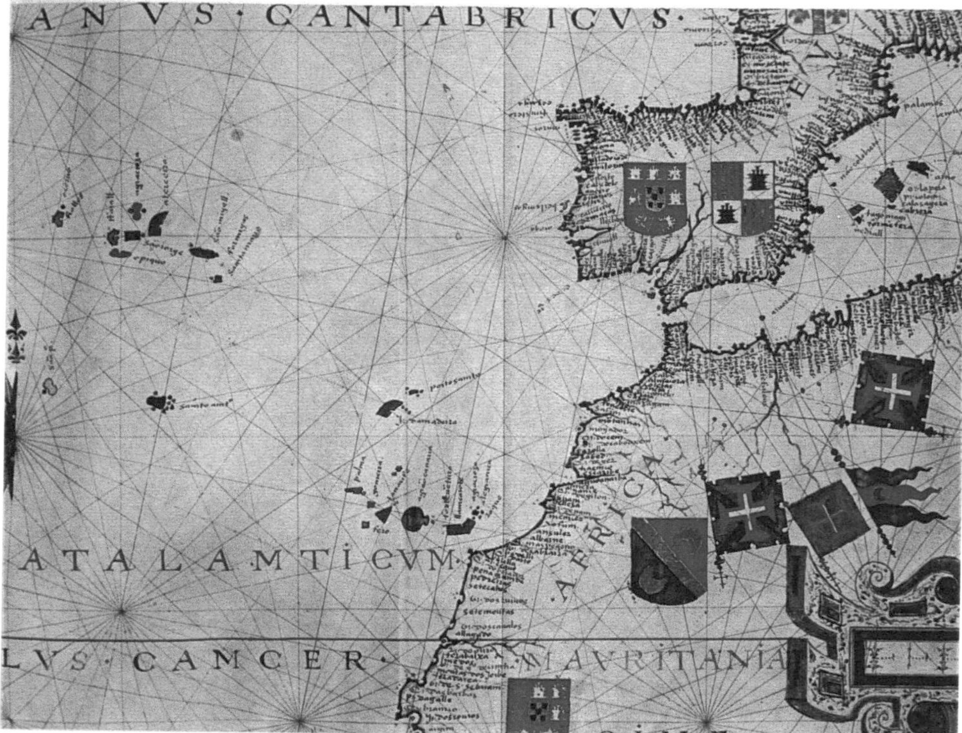

Examples of sixteenth-century nautical charts (details); luxury editions, certainly not of the type used by ship pilots. Charted are the placenames or coastal toponyms densely drawn and with the rhumblines networked marking the intersecting courses.

Detail of a well-known woodcut in which the pilot of a sixteenth-century ship can be seen, comfortably sitting at a desk while checking the compass' declination relative to the North Star, his right hand lowered on the instrument in the direction of the star. The drawing is full of inconsistencies. Aside from the two land-type cannons on each side of the quarterdeck, the pilot is armed (on the wrong side, incidentally) with a showy as well as useless sword, which would certainly make the compass needle go haywire.

Techniques of observing the sun's height with the cross-bow [a quadrant-like instrument]: 1) by direct observation; 2) indirectly, to avoid blinding.

It is presumed that the food was prepared by cabin boys, since there was no cook onboard. The captain's attendant might have prepared some special dish for his master and the officers but, generally speaking, everyone was served from the same cauldron: one warm meal daily, at eleven a.m., before the change of the guard. The captain, the master, the pilot and other persons of rank traveling on the ship ate at a table, the others where they could find room. When the meal was ready, a cabin boy would signal the crew with one of the traditional, lullaby-like songs that marked daily routines, a custom, indeed, more than a real necessity, because in less than one hundred feet of space no one could miss what was happening on a ship at any moment:

Tabla, tabla señor capitan y maestre y buena compañia,
tabla presta, vianda presta,
agua usada para el señor capitan y maestre y buena compañia
Viva el Rey de Castilla por mar y por tierra,
quien le diere guerra,
que le corten la cabeza,
quien no dijeren amen,
que no le den de beber,
tabla en buena hora,
quien non vinieré que no coma[42].

The sailors would line up at the firebox, their bowl extended toward the kitchen attendant while saying *por la mesana* and received their abundant, if not refined meal.

A major problem in long sailings was that of fresh water. To preserve drinkable water was a problem that found a solution only at the beginning of the nineteenth century with the adoption of iron boxes, which allowed for the loading of greater quantities of the liquid as well as its good preservation. At the time to which we are referring, however, water was kept in wooden barrels and, as mentioned, remained good only for a limited period of time. The purification methods were not particularly effective, and people had to resign themselves to drink yellowish and foul-tasting water. To be out at sea, surrounded by so much water, and suffer of thirst, had sharpened sailors' ingenuity since ancient times. They had noticed

[42] "Table, table sir captain and master and all good company / the table is set, the food is ready / water as usual for sir captain and master and good company / long live the King of Castile by land and sea / Who made war on him / will lose his head / Who won't say amen / will get nothing to drink / Table is ready, in good time / Who doesn't come, doesn't eat." (Cfr. P.E. Taviani. *The Voyages of Columbus. The Great Discovery.* Transl. by M. Beckwith and L. Farina. Vol. 2, p. 32.)

that steam and humidity had no salt contents, and that therefore it was-possible to obtain small quantities of fresh water through evaporation of seawater. In 1520 John Anglicus suggested two ways of making seawater potable, by boiling and filtering it. But the quantities thus obtained were modest and could help only a few people to survive. Water distillation would be perfected only in the nineteenth century.

As long as transoceanic navigations were not exceedingly long and it was possible to call at islands or lands where vegetable and fruit would be plentiful ensuring therefore that the supply of vitamins could be replenished through the intake of such foods, scurvy — the scourge of seamen — did not make its appearance. Fifteenth-century navigators remained immune from it. The first cases of this illness, caused exclusively by a lack of vitamin, occurred on Portuguese ships bound for India, as these vessels had to ply much longer courses than it took to reach the Americas. The disease was thought to be contagious, and was attributed in turn to poor personal hygiene, cold weather, humidity, "miasmas" or noxious vapors coming from shore. Several centuries would have to go by before suitable measures were introduced to stamp it out, until it was discovered that the disease was caused by lack of vitamins and could therefore be countered by eating fresh fruit and vegetables.

As the primary needs of eating and drinking were satisfied, there remained concern for clothing and cramped living that, likewise, could not be underestimated.

When the sea was calm and the weather clear, the men would take advantage of it to wash themselves and their own clothes. An opportunity very much appreciated, considering that clothing was limited to the few items that a seaman could take along in his small chest, which served both as a closet and a stool. Normal clothing consisted of canvas pants and shirts and a hooded wool overcoat; wool socks, wood and leather clogs and a cone-shaped red wool cap called *gorro* (well-known were those manufactured in Toledo). On cold nights, an additional gray or brown cape that doubled as a blanket when sleeping provided more comfort. Canvas apparel, waterproofed with linen oil, helped sailors on watch duty, protecting from the rain or the spray of the waves. People of rank, when and if any were onboard, wore their own clothes, perhaps better looking but not much more comfortable than the sailors'.

Personal hygiene was certainly not a high priority, as they washed in sea water. Yet sailors managed to keep rather clean with more than occasional help from rain or rough seas.

The captain or master. The captain of a ship had no special titles, but enjoyed recognition as an honest, clever and lucky man of repute (luck was highly prized among people who widely relied on superstition). These qualities helped him to establish a career step by step besides saving money for later.

The captain (or master, which was the same) was responsible for the ship and the cargo entrusted to him as well as for most decisions, but typically he was only partially in charge of the navigation, whose responsibility fell to the pilot except in specific cases.

The democratic principles regulating sailing vessels were perhaps derived both from Viking or Norman traditions, and from the intrinsic necessities of seafaring: it behooves everyone sailing to follow common agreements, albeit under a sole deciding authority. The accepted norms generally recognized by all seafaring entities, considerably restricted the powers of the man in command of a ship. Thus, for instance, the master had to consult with the crew before sailing and obtain a majority consent; the responsibility of sailing with bad or worsening weather had to be shared by everyone. The owner was responsible to the merchants for the goods loaded on the ship and, when any merchant wished to accompany his merchandise, the master was obliged to provide for him; in a situation of danger, in which it might become necessary to throw the cargo overboard in order to save the ship, he had to obtain the merchant's approval. One can well imagine the kind of conflicts that would then arise in such emergencies between captains, who cared for the ship, and merchants, who did not want to lose their cargo. But in all instances, too, it was the majority of the sailors that decided and, in order for a captain to be cleared of any wrongdoing, it sufficed that at least three of the crew members, upon their return, would swear on the Gospels that the dumping at sea had been necessary.

The captain could fire a sailor only after five serious infractions (involving theft, fighting, refusing to obey and, as mentioned, blasphemy; on this latter point, however, enforcement may have been lax or less than scrupulous because, as easily as sailors cursed, they just as frequently in a most natural way prayed and took vows). Traditionally, as reported in the *Roles d'Oleron*, the captain had to exclude a sailor from eating three consecutive times ("pull off the tablecloth"), in other words, he had to take at least three days to calm down and think about the case. Such small-scale democracy enforced on medieval ships may help us to understand some of the constraints bearing on the behavior of great seamen, who had to bow to decisions imposed by crews certainly less dedicated than they were.

One may recall, to quote a single example, Bartolomeu Diaz's arrival into the bay of Algoa, after doubling the Cape of Good Hope; he had then the certainty to be already in the Indian Ocean. Ahead of him lay open the so longingly sought course for the Indies, as well as the shores of East Africa, inhabited by civilized peoples. Also not far away there might be the kingdom of Prester John. These considerations certainly enhanced his desire to sail on and conquer entirely for himself the glory that would later be bestowed upon Vasco da Gama. That was not, however, the way his crews saw it: tired after a long voyage and convinced they had already done enough, they opted to head back home. All that Diaz was able to obtain was a few days' respite, sufficient to let him push a little farther up to the Fish River, where the coastline turned north-east, a confirmation that the southern tip of the African continent had been overtaken. But it was not a mutiny: it was merely the crews' right to express, by majority rule, that they felt the voyage had attained its goal right there and then.

In the history of Columbus's voyages there is a series of probatory facts showing how little power the individual formally in command actually held. In ignorance of the rules common among seafaring peoples at that time, one could justifiably conclude that the Admiral had no aptitude for command. Luckily, he was gifted in both the art of persuasion as well as of deception. By resorting to either in turn, he managed to lead his men as far as he wanted to go.

To the point is the episode of when the rudder of the *Pinta* slipped off its hinges, twice in a row. Columbus had some suspicions as he wrote in the *Journal*, but did not take any action or start an inquiry: he was content to get the damage repaired and be able to proceed.

Closer to landfall, he had to go to great pains to convince his men not to give up. Then came the wrecking of the *Santa Maria*, when

> As it was calm, the sailor in charge of the ship decided to go to rest, leaving a shipboy at the rudder, a move expressly prohibited by the Admiral — regardless of bad or good weather — known to all so that they might not let shipboys in charge.

Yet, once they saw that the Admiral had retired to sleep, they all followed his example and left the rudder in the hands of a cabin boy who steered the ship onto the shallows. Material for a Court Martial — but Columbus did nothing more than report that "Our Lord so wished." And the master in charge of the watch (Juan de la Cosa, also the owner of the ship), thus principally liable for the mishap, after being ordered to lower the launch at stern end, haul an anchor and cast it in the open sea to try and save the ship, did nothing but get on the lifeboat with other men and flee toward the *Niña.* Such reproachable episodes might have been equally deserving of a harsh punishment which, however, the Admiral had no power to impose.

Another episode Columbus could only complain about was the defection of the *Pinta*, which Martín Alonso Pinzón masterminded without ever informing the Admiral. He set out in search of gold mines, from November 22, 1492 until January 6, 1493. The relationship between Columbus and the older Pinzón had become tensed, owing to incompatibility of character and to both men's pride, but nothing would seem to justify this grave infraction, which could have endangered the outcome of the entire expedition. Columbus went no farther than to condemn the fact, accusing the Pinzóns of "arrogance and greed" because "they had not heeded or obeyed his commands and, on the contrary, they kept on doing and saying many untrue things" against him. This time perhaps it was expedient for Columbus (who had a bit of a tendency to feel persecuted) to dissemble rather than making a bad situation worse.

Such were then the reduced powers of a commander at sea, and Columbus, his pompous title of Admiral notwithstanding (a title, it should be recalled, that designated an administrative office and juridical, rather than military, implications), who had practiced professionally in the merchant marine, naturally complied with its rules. Quite different a conduct would he instead exhibit as Viceroy when, in spite of his good disposition and religious nature which counseled him against extreme decisions, he felt compelled to intervene harshly against whomever rebelled against his ruling (and therefore, as he reasoned, against the Sovereigns' authority), and to order the hanging for some wretched people.

But returning to the figure of the master or captain, as one tries to define his privileges — indeed very few — what stands out is a captain's right to take a servant with him and, whenever possible, to have a small room of his own, in which he would sleep fully dressed, like everyone else. He ate at the table with other persons of rank on the ship and the stern was his territory, but these were minor distinctions that, if observed, granted him some dignity which would differentiate him from the mass[43]. If he wanted different food, he had to stock his pantry at his own expenses.

[43] Even today a ship's captain, especially in the navy, lives on board in relative seclusion. The reason for this isolation resides in the fact that an order, to be executed, must be issued by a superior authority, almost surrounded by a sort of sacral aura, which would be diminished through daily and intimate contact with subordinates. On small medieval ships, for lack of space, this could not happen, and it was one of several reasons compounding the limited authority of the person in charge.

The pilot. – Just below the rank of the captain was the pilot. He, too, was trained from the ranks. He had learned his trade from other pilots and had to demonstrate that he could do it well. In reality, he was the navigation officer; he calculated the ship's position, so that he would know at all times where it was, and advised the master about the course to take. In difficult waters, close to shorelines, near the entrance of a bay, a river-mouth or a strait dotted with dangers, he would receive help from a local expert when available, who, just as modern pilots do, would come on board from shore on his little boat and assume control for navigating the local waters.

Henry the Navigator, as pointed out earlier, had instituted a sailing school at Sagres, where everything that had been hitherto learned about the science of navigation was taught. But that was the exception. In all of Europe every art or trade was learned only through apprenticeship, by imitating a master. Such a method had the additional advantage that professional mistakes judged serious by a mentor would brand the individual who had committed them, thus removing the chance that a clever but unskilled person could manage to captain a vessel.

The boatswain. – The boatswain was, as he would remain even later on during the height of the sailing era, the crew's boss and the person responsible for dealing with merchants concerning the stowing and conservation of their cargo. He superintended all marine operations, including the tough emergency decisions needed to save a ship in danger such as, e.g., getting rid of her masts by cutting them off. Being overall responsible for the ship also from this standpoint, it was his concern that everything onboard be in order. He supervised the work of carpenters, sailmakers, coopers, riggers, when any of them were present onboard, or the work of anyone else he trusted to do those jobs required for the maintenance of the ship, including careening, if needed. He might have enlisted the help of a petty officer.

And since we have mentioned this important operation — careening — it will be advisable to spend a few words about it for the benefit of those who may be somewhat unfamiliar with this subject.

The good performance of a hull depends in large measure on the cleanliness of its keel. The term 'careening,' or 'fairing,' encompasses all the operations that are required to clean, repair, and caulk the submerged part of the hull (the quickwork), a job that must be done periodically and is of basic importance.

When ships started crisscrossing into tropical waters, the need for careening became more urgent, because the underwater vegetation in those areas was more vigorous and the quickwork got covered with seaweeds and shellfish in just a few months span. The shellfish to be feared most was the [winter] borer or boring worm (identified by Linnaeus as *teredo navalis*), a shipworm that can reach a length of about two feet, whose larva sticks to any wooden receptacle, digging a recess channel that will be its lifelong abode. In a short time, thanks to the speed with which the worm reproduces (a single female can lay up to a million eggs), the wood, which externally presents only some tiny entrance holes, is consumed. Columbus made their acquaintance in the Caribbean and simply called this pest 'worms': they would destroy his ships in the fourth voyage.

To contrast against vegetation and incrustations, it was customary to spread onto the careen a mixture such as the one previously described (see p. 30), or other potions considered poisonous for underwater organisms. Cleaning the hull was an at least yearly task, with removal of the old layer and of all incrustations, melting the pitch of the planking with reed or stubble torches. As damage was repaired, a new caulking would be applied, if necessary, and a fresh coat of the mixture was spread, possibly blending it with the undamaged sections of the old. In order to perform these operations, the keel had to be dry docked, and if there was no appropriate equipment to do so, as it happened in faraway seas, it was necessary to find a tranquil bay with an unencumbered beach area where to bring the ship, and unload everything that could be removed so that the ship would stay afloat in shallow water. The next procedure involved leaning the vessel on its side with tackles pulling the masts, shifting weights onboard, propping up the structures by means of land-based winches. Once a side of the quickwork was in the open air, with the keel fully exposed, the careening took place before repeating the same operation for the other side.

The recorder (notary). – Another key figure aboard was the one in charge of recording, a learned man in an environment where it is doubtful that many would know how to read or write. As a man of unimpeachable honesty, absolutely trusted by both merchants and master, he checked each item of the cargo in full detail, requested warranties, bought the provisions, supervised their daily use, kept account of every expenditure and held the keys of the treasure chest. These were his administrative tasks, for which he received paper and ink (some statutory rules also prescribed that he be given a pair of shoes, to make him look more distinguished), and he had no share in any fatiguing work on the ship.

The alguacil (water officer). – This distinctive office befell an administrative clerk exclusively responsible for managing the extremely important duty of supplying and regulating water consumption onboard, but also in charge of judiciary police tasks. We believe that he could be compared to the adjutant of modern vessels, a petty officer entrusted with guaranteeing the internal security and the good order onboard and compliance with regulations as well as with the authority, should the need arise, to mete out the punishment.

Little more can be added about the working crew. Columbus barely mentions crew members in his succint reports, although its presence is necessarily implied, because without a crew a ship does not set sail. The main task for sailors, along with the captain, the pilot and the boatswain, was the watch shift that, according to Columbus's *Journal*, took place on a revolving basis every four hours, at 3, 7, 11 o'clock and so on. During the day, they enjoyed little rest because there was always a plethora of work needed to keep the ship in working order, from repairing sails and implements, to executing rigging jobs, maneuvers, etc. The warm meal served only at eleven force the watch guard just finishing his duty to put off his rest after the meal.

There are several studies about the salaries paid to the crews during the first voyage, especially by English authors, all of whom in the end refer back to Thatcher's well-known conclusions. The Admiral allegedly received 30,000 *maravedis* a year, compared to the 12,000 he received before his appointment. A *maravedi* was an old coin already struck by the Almoravides, after which it was named. It was originally a gold coin, struck also by the Portuguese; if referred to the 1958 values, according to Morison's calculations, the 12,000 *maravedis* salary would equal 83 U.S. gold dollars, or 16.5 English guineas [last minted in 1813 and worth 21 shillings]. Afterwards, silver *maravedis* were coined, equal to one third royal, followed by copper coins.

The same amount of 30,000 was paid to the captain, 20,000 to the master, 24,000 to pilots, 20,250 to boatswains, 12,000 to sailors, 8,000 to the apprentices, for an overall estimated expenditure of 520,000 *maravedis*, with an additional cost of 319,000 *maravedis* for provisions, 172,000 for the ships' charter, 155,062 for the various affairs, weaponry, etc., yielding a grand total of 1,166,862 *maravedis*.

CHAPTER VII

NAVIGATIONAL INSTRUMENTS

During the fifteenth century the art of sailing recorded an unexpected evolution. Throughout earlier centuries, European sailors had accumulated a wealth of experience which allowed them to navigate with confidence inside the Mediterranean basin and the Northern seas, without scientific knowledge or special instruments. All sea voyages took place along established routes that every sailor learned since his initiation to the trade, just as one does for the way home that one can walk in the dark, recognizing the right way from small but familiar signs.

The sense that seamen had to develop to the highest level was orientation, i.e., the ability to sense one's own position with respect to the cardinal points, a sensation that could be verified continuously with what nature offered, even when land was no longer visible on the horizon. The sun in its daily course, the moon, the horizon, the stars, the winds, recognized through the skin thanks to their characteristics of humidity, temperature and intensity, the clouds with their ever-changing shapes, height and colors, and the luminosity of the atmosphere, were all elements providing sensations imperceptible to land-based people, who in turn, by living in close contact with nature, such as farmers, lumberjacks or mountaineers, let other sensations regulate the rhythm of their lives. Sailing trips were, in any case, short, customary, never too far from the shore, whose conspicuous points of reference were all well-known. A trained seaman, without using any other instrument but his senses, knew how to recognize currents and their intensity, how to evaluate a ship's speed and therefore the distance traveled with sufficient approximation, and how to anticipate, from a number of signs, metereological changes with an intuitive accuracy that today, aware as we are of the highly technical means at our disposal, looks prodigious, while it was merely the fruit of centuries-old experience.

During the 1400s, navigators began to reach farther and farther into unknown seas. It was, however, a gradual exploration, which time after time permitted to acquire new elaborate experiences. Simultaneously, the progress of scientific speculation in general and about phenomena related to sailing, led to the elaboration of new instruments. The full impulse given to science by geographical discoveries and from geography to navigation marked, for this field as well, the end of the Middle Ages.

Nautical cartography. – Nautical cartography, a product of the late Middle Ages, must have been a widespread and highly prized activity, if we are to judge from its highly technical content, compared of course to the times, of the extant specimens; about 180 medieval charts have been preserved, between "real" maps and maritime atlases prepared between the fourteenth and the fifteenth century. The production was certainly much larger, but the major part of this material went lost for a variety reasons, not excluding their constant use aboard ships, under precarious conditions to say the least, which could not ensure their preservation.

The "real" charts, those actually used, were certainly less precious than the richly decorated ones, prepared for bibliophiles and private collections, or to be presented as homage to influential people; nevertheless they must not have been held as objects of little value, for they were recorded in inventories and notary acts relative to the ship that employed them. Of the known Medieval charts, only about thirty date back to the fourteenth century.

The earliest sailing charts did not show meridians or parallels, but only reticulated wind rhumblines, useful both to the cartographer, to draw the contours of shorelines, and to the seamen to follow their orientation. It has been in fact ascertained that such a network of lines was actually traced onto the parchment sheet before drawing the chart. The cartographers' *modus operandi* was, in a few words, the following: in the middle of the chart a rose was drawn, with its thirty-two wind directions depicted as straight lines running the whole length of the parchment. From the rose's center a large circle was then drawn and, next, at the points where this circle intersected the main winds, smaller roses were traced, from each of which departed their thirty-two rhumblines, these too extending over the entire map surface. The resulting network therefore provided documentation of the orientation of the shoreline with respect to the compass, and the specific rhumbs to follow to go from one point to another. It was not necessary to draw on the charts all thirty-two peripheral roses (one for each radius of the main rose). It sufficed to draw one half as many, or even fewer (depending on a map's dimension), avoiding thus to clog a map with too thick a grid, which would have made it more difficult to read, rather than improve its precision. The oldest charts show in fact only sixteen roses. Only after the second half of the fifteenth century did all thirty-two of them start to be depicted as a rule.

These old maps, drawn on the basis of compass values as well as the personal experience of the cartographers or from reports they collected — when not actually copied from previous charts — were not free of even blatant mistakes owing to the scarcity of informations, to errors made by the person who had made the observations, or even to the imagination of the cartographer himself who filled as he could those spaces about which he could not manage to gather any information. The coastlines were all in the same scale, without keeping into account the earth's roundness; for example, one mile of African shore had the same length as one mile in the North Sea. Thus, although distances were respected, their angles were fully deformed at the high latitudes, giving the coasts an unusual aspect (at least, to our eyes).

Using the chart it was possible to sail from a place, e.g., on the coast of Sicily, travel the number of miles shown on the map following the indicated rhumb line, and reach one's destination in the Gulf of Genoa. The scale in miles (1481 meters to the mile then, or a different length depending upon the system or the unit of measurement adopted by the cartograph) was drawn on the chart as a short bar, divided by vertical lines into so many small rectangles, each one divided, in turn, into four parts. Since charts were almost always of large size, each small rectangle represented 50 miles, while the distance between small dots was 10 miles. Every four rectangles the small vertical lines had a special mark to indicate a 50 league distance, each league being 4 miles. By using a double compass it was easy to carry over the scale in miles or in leagues onto the course to follow and thus come to know the distance in miles.

The very first attempts to produce greater-scale maps were made at the beginning of the 1500s (Portuguese charts by Nicolas de Cabreiro, in 1502, and by Lopo Homen in 1519). It was only in 1537 that Pedro Nuñes would prove that loxodromics[44], which should be straight lines, are curved lines spiraling up toward the Pole when represented on a flat surface.

The oldest known nautical chart is the one called 'Pisana,' preserved in National Library in Paris. This map, drawn on *velino*, a very thin parchment or vellum, represents Europe from the Atlantic coast as far as Bruges to the north and Trebizond [Black Sea] to the South. The chart was drawn at the end of the thirteenth century by an anonymous Genoese, probably on the model of an earlier chart. There is proof that even earlier nautical maps were in circulation at that time.

[44] The line joining two points on the earth's surface cutting through all meridians at a constant angle.

Though lacking in cartographic precision, the charts had an abundance of artistic embellishments, especially those destined not to the seamen's daily use, but to library collections or high-ranking noble estates. The cartographer would then display his ability in drawing and coloring the wind roses, decorating the maps' margins, providing fill-in figures in the lands' center, small ships and sea animals floating on waves, and coloring the names in different hues to visualize toponymic importance. Especially decorated were the Catalonian charts. To this matter we relate what Paola Presciuttini wrote in an article published in the 1992 *Agenda Nautica* of the Hydrographic Institute of the Italian Navy:

> Particularly showy and attractive are the flags in correspondence of cities, sometimes coated with sequin gold, which however are not a good chronological reflection because frequently they are not correlated to the actual political situation at the time of drawing; this anachronism is even more evident where, for instance, Christian standards flutter in correspondence of places subjugated by the Turks, perhaps to express the (psychologic) rejection of such an event on the part of the Western world. Mountain ranges with bizarre profiles are in green, tortuous rivers, typically with a screw-like course, appear in black, and the seas are represented by thick rippling blue lines, simulating the waves... The chart is enriched with information not only geographical but also political and economical, integrated with dense explicative annotations right inside or in the margins. Crowned heads or figures seated on a throne are intended to represent local dynasties' hunting scenes, tents and camels illustrate exotic places, while miniature castles mark important cities. At the end of the fourteenth century silhouettes of landmark monuments start to appear in correspondence of the toponyms. For instance, on a nautical atlas of 1373, the work of Francesco Pizigano, the cities are identified through distinctive, albeit partial, views.

These works of art were certainly not destined to be abused on board, where all that was needed to navigate were maps routinely made, actually often simply retraced from other maps by the pilot himself.

The charts cartographers compiled on the basis of compass indications were not devoid of gross errors. Correspondence to the truth depended upon the more or less veridical pieces of information one could gather. If some cartographers achieved higher reputation than others, they owed it to the greater truthfulness of their charts and to the amount of information they were able to supply to the navigators. Cartography flourished especially hand in hand with navigation-oriented countries such as Portugal, Catalonia, Genoa, Venice, and the Netherlands. After the discovery, the Casa de Contratación dominated the cartography sector, under the management first by Juan de la Cosa, then by Amerigo Vespucci and later by Sebastian Cabot; it produced updated nautical charts of the New World as the discoveries progressed, but with a restricted circulation policy so as not to help eventual competitors.

On a map, the pilot traced a ship's course, just as it is done today, marking the point he estimated to be and identifying the route stages -- an easy task presently thanks to perfected instruments, but much more difficult then, when the pilot had at his disposal only a compass, the stars in the sky and his own judgement with which to calculate the speed of his vessel.

The compass. – Mention of magnetized needles capable of showing the North appears in Europe after the eleventh century. Who should take credit for having discovered the property of magnetized iron to turn in a certain direction, if not the Chinese, who seemingly fathered all inventions? In effect, several Chinese references can be found concerning the use of magnetized needles also for terrestrial applications, but let us focus on documentation of its nautical uses. A treatise written around 1115 describes a needle inside a small cane floating in a container full of water, which does not point toward the true South, but shifts toward the *ping* point, that is, five sixths to the South. This would demonstrate that the Chinese used the needle aboard their ships for orientation and that they were aware of the existence of magnetic declination. How such practice later reached and spread in the West remains a mystery. Perhaps through the Arabs, or some intelligent merchant who had come in contact with the Eastern world, and let the West in on the use of the needle; in any case, it is proven that the application of a piece of magnetized iron floated in a wooden container (a non-magnetic receptacle was required) — the sailing *bossolo* from which derived the name "bussola" (compass) in Italian and the like names in other Mediterranean languages — was widespread, well before the legendary Flavio Gioia in 1300 (or 1302 or 1306) reinvented it or, more likely, perfected it.

Probably, it was just a matter of finding a way to change the precarious and occasional use of such instrument — subject as the water-filled box was to every motion of the ship — to a more stable and reliable unit in which the needle was suspended inside the box. The very existence of Flavio Gioia is now questioned by more radical scholars rejecting what is only probable evidence, yet, regardless, it was not until later on in the century that the adoption of the needle became widespread and the instrument subsequently perfected. Above the needle, now pivoted on a tip in the center of the container, was placed a light rotating compass card below the needle, and divided in 32 points of 11° 15' each, corresponding to the directions of the main winds. This division in points or marks, rather than in degrees, lasted as long as the age of sail vessels, since the degree of precision obtained dividing the points in half-points was sufficient for this kind of navigation.

As long as navigation was essentially close to the shore and determined by recognition of land spots and their coordinates to the cardinal points, figuring on sky observation as well as the seaman's individual instincts as contributing factors, it was possible to sail either without a compass (our fishermen worked without it until the beginning of the twentieth century, and in place of the chronometer they had a common, cheap alarm clock) or use it occasionally, but as vessels began to engage increasingly longer routes in unknown seas the compass became indispensable. The instrument, although treated with great care aboard, produced readings that did not always correspond with mental calculations; such whims ot the magnetic needle were blamed on a supposed "needle's idiosyncrasy." It was Columbus, during his extended navigations along the meridians, who discovered that magnetic declination, i.e., the difference between the North indicated by the instrument and the true geographic North, varied depending upon the position[45].

As knowledge of magnetic declination values was reported in reference tables ready for use, sailors were able to transfer from a *magnetic* course to the *true* one and to trace the latter on a chart. But all this took place after Columbus's voyages. It just so happened that it was he who first identified and interpreted this phenomenon, and modified his set course based on this evaluation.

Columbus thus was the first to ascertain the westward declination of the needle, whereas eastward declination had long since been documented in the Mediterranean.

In view of the critical impact this discovery had in accurately determining a vessel's course, we believe it useful to report what P.E. Taviani wrote about it, including Columbus's interpretation of it:

> In the entry for 13 September Columbus notes that at sunset the needles deviate to the west of the polestar, while in the morning

[45] For instance, Cape Aguglias, the southernmost point in the African continent, owes its name (meaning "Cape of the Needles") to the fact that Portuguese sailors had found out that there the declination was null and the needle's orientation coincided with the direction of the meridian.

they deviate to the east. We must also remember that in its apparent diurnal motion the polestar seems to describe a circle around the celestial pole. In 1492 the radius of that circle appeared to the observer to be the base of an angle of 3° 27' (it is smaller today). On 13 September Columbus's ships were probably crossing an area of zero magnetic declination. The compass needles, without deviating, were fixed on the celestial pole. The polestar, through its diurnal motion, seemed first to the right then to the left of the point indicated by the needles.

On 17 September, the fleet having entered the zone of western declination, the needles deviated at sunset sharply to teh left owing to western magnetic declination and the movement to the right of the polestar. Before sunrise, the polestar having moved to the left, the angle of deviation of the needles naturally was diminished.

Every day the deviation of the needles to the left grew. On the thirtieth, the fleet having probably reached the area of 7° declination to the west, Columbus observed that at nightfall the needles deviated a point to the west. At that moment the polestar was about 3° 20' east of the celestial pole. This angle, added to the 7° of magnetic declination, gave a total of a litlle less than a point (11 1/4°). At dawn, continues Columbus, the needles pointed "straight to the polestar," which in the meantime had shifted to the west of the celestial pole, reducing (though not eliminating) the initial angle of 11 1/4°. However, on this occasion the difference was not reported. Probably Columbus did not wish to point it out, for terror had overcome the pilots, and the crews were disturbed. The strange, disquieting phenomenon frightened them, and the word "return" began to pass among them.

Columbus was not the last to marvel and be impressed, but with his optimism he realized that it was a natural phenomenon, and since his pilots urgently needed reassuring, he did so with rare ingenuity. Most of the pilots did not know that the polestar described a small circle around the pole, but Columbus knew it and pointed out this star at dawn, when it was farthest to the west. The deviation, while still there, was thus insignificant. Columbus said that the compass needles were simply following the polestar: it had moved, and the needles maintained their ability to give direction. (P.E. Taviani. *The Voyages of Columbus. The Great Discovery.* Transl. by M. Beckwith and L. Farina. Vol. 2, pp. 205-6).

There is no direct way of knowing whether Columbus in his first crossing fully believed such a simple explanation or had indeed realized the nexistence of westward declination. In the third voyage [1498], however, in his letter written to the Spanish Sovereigns from Santo Domingo, he revealed his awareness of the fact that western declination increases as one proceeds eastward, and that "above all, he no longer attributed it" continues Taviani, "to the movement of Polaris, but to the shape of the Earth, i.e., the bulge to the southwest that appears on the equatorial coasts of the mainland" (ibid., p. 206).

Charcot, on the other hand, maintains that during his first voyage Columbus clearly did not believe in the explanation he himself had given to his sailors. He continued to carefully record the deviation values indicated by the needle relative to Polaris, and took into account all his observations [i.e. recorded readings] so as to arrive at the formulation of a rule to be applied in correcting his course.

As for the depiction of compass points, often painted with great artistic care to the point of qualifying as small ornamental masterpieces — even to the detriment of accuracy — the north was generally indicated with a stylized lily in the heraldic fashion, prompting some to conclude that the French invented the compass points. These nationalistically colored claims are always rather pointless, as they certainly do not prove the inhabitants of a nation to be in any way "superior" to others. In any case such an irrelevant claim is refuted, if need be, by the existence of older point cards from Amalfi which had adopted as the main cardinal point the East, the point of origin of both the sun and Christian Redemption (represented by a cross). It could also be added that if the lily implied a reference to the French Kings' coat of arms (who had assumed it as their symbol since 1150 with Louis VII — *fleur de Lois, i.e., fleurdelis*), the house of Anjou, collateral to the Capetians, reigned at that time also in the region of Naples.

After the improvements described previously, the "wooden box" that constituted the external case of the compass no longer contained water; instead, the needle rested, perfectly balanced, on a copper-pointed tip, rising from the bottom of the container. To reduce friction as much as possible, the needle (or two needles set side by side, or a small rhomboid frame whose main axis was formed by the needle), had a small agate cylinder perforated so as to hold the tip.

The methods of magnetizing the needles were several, with the simple-st being to rub such needles onto a natural lodestone [a strong variety of magnetite], dragging the end that had to turn toward the north pole over the south pole of the lodestone and the opposite end over the north pole. The magnetite, or love stone, was therefore a basic tool of the pilot, which he carried with him laid in an often lavishly decorated case.

Only in the fifteenth century the wooden box was replaced by a brass container (the mortar or "bed"), featuring at a later time gimbals suspension due, perhaps, to the ingenuity of Janiello Torriani, who served in Charles V's navy.

Measuring the traveled distance. – The other element needed in estimating navigation, beside a selected course, is the distance traveled in a given time. It is therefore necessary to know at which speed the ship has advanced while sailing between two points (of course, if the velocity is not constant, it becomes necessary to add several time intervals each at a different speed). To estimate velocity, however, one needed an instrument that could measure time with accuracy; but such an instrument did not exist at the time. There were small sand ampullas, certainly featured onboard, which however measured time intervals as long as half or a quarter of an hour, even though it was possible to manufacture — some were actually used — tiny one-minute and half-minute sandless globes.

The human body has, within itself, a rather precise time-measuring device, its pulse rate. It is not to be ruled out that this method to measure short time spans could also have been applied in calculating speed, together with the oldest system used by sailors — casting a floater log[46] [originally a wood quadrant] into the water from the prow and clocking the time elapsed until it was athwart the stern. The ratio between time and ship's length yields a reasonably precise measure of a ship's speed.

Until not long ago, sailors knew how to execute this calculation even mentally, by simply counting seconds. Several such measurements or readings within a short time interval would yield an acceptable average[47].

In the calculation of the course traveled, one had also to take into account wind-related drift values. Weak when reaching or running, but rapidly increasing with the wind amidship or close to the bow; a crude estimate could be made by estimating the angle between the wake left by the ship and her axis. The leeway drift caused by currents, on the contrary, being invisible could be incorporated in estimates only after repeated runs on a given route, mostly on the basis of guess perception of regimen and velocity of the dominant currents.

[46] 'Floater', or log in Dutch and English, refers to a succession of speed-measuring implements, variously termed as *log, loche, loc, locco, lok.*

[47] Much later, in the sixteenth and seventeenth century there appeared the 'log timer,' a crude spring-loaded device to measure time elapsed manufactured in the Netherlands, and the 'knot log' (which gives the speed by counting the number of knots on a line referred to as log-line] eased off into the sea) with the relative conversion tables to transform time values in knots.

Time measurement. – One of the problems that ancient navigators had to solve involved time measurement. The sun passing across the zenith signalled high noon for each locality, with a certain approximation which varied depending upon accuracy of the instrument as well as the care of the observer. That was the only moment when a seaman could "reset" his clock, since the tables that furnished the sunrise and sunset hours were yet to come. Gnomons and sundials were not instruments that could be used aboard, on account of the constantly changing position of the ship (sundials can measure only the local time at the point of installation), and also because a vessel would rarely be sufficently stable to serve as mounting platform. Something was then needed that measured time from the observed noon on a given day to the next one.

Egyptians and Greeks had used, in their times, the clepsydra[48], a water clock that could not, however, be adopted onboard because it had to have an immobile base. But already in the third century the principle of the clepsydra had been perfected with the invention of the powder hourglass, constituted by two small conically shaped glass globes, communicating through a tiny hole that let a fixed quantity of sand pass in a given time span. As soon as all the sand had gone through, it required that someone promptly turn the instrument over to start a new cycle. The Spaniards called these instruments *ampolletas or relojes de arena.*

A similar device, placed beside the helmsman, was for centuries the only, and indispensable, clock aboard. Obviuosly, on board there would be more than one clepsydra: owing to the fragility of the instrument, it was mandatory to have some spare ones.

In the construction of such an instrument, the most difficult operation was its calibration, i.e., determining the amount of sand required to measure exactly one hour or half hour, on the basis of either a sample presumed to be exact, or an astronomy-based method of measuring time. The "sand" was of finely ground eggshells and pulverized black marble, a mixture that after being kiln-dried was sieved nine times over. The calibration of the small hole was also a very delicate operation; frequently, instead of making the two small globes with a single blowing, it was preferable to manufacture them separately, joining them together with the interposition of a small metal collar with an accurately calibrated hole; the whole gadget was finally sealed with wax and put in a metal, wood or leather case, often artistically decorated, which protected the highly fragile glass, without impeding the observation of the flow of sand.

[48] From the Greek *klept*, 'subtract,' and *ydro*, 'water.'

Powder clocks had to be frequently checked against a properly calibrated sample because, with use, the powder became finer therefore transferring through faster: in other words the clock would "eat sand."

The clepsydra next to the helmsman was carefully turned over, after each full sand transfer, by one of the "counsellors" or by a cabin boy who did so while singing one of those pious rigamaroles that paced life on a ship (there remains a lingering doubt whether these monotonous litanies were actually recited, as tradition would have us believe):

Buena es la que va
mejor es la que viene
una es pasada y en otra muele.
[Good is the one that goes/ better is the one coming/ one is past and another is coming]

And time after time the singer increased the count until he said:

siete es pasada y en ocho muele.
mas moliera si Dios quisiera,
cuenta y pasa, que buen viaje faza.
[Seven is past and eight running/ more will run God willing/ count and carry on, have a good voyage]

At the end of the eigth ampulla, he called the new watch, monotonously singing:

Al quarto, al quarto señores marineros de buena parte
al quarto, en buena hora, de la guardia del señor piloto
que ya es hora, leva, leva.
[To quarters, to quarters sir sailors of the right/ to quarters in good time, to the pilot's watch/ Up! Up! It's already time]

Before the first night watch started, when the fire in the firebox was estinguished, the cabin boy sang a sort of prayer:

Benedicta sea la hora
en que Dios nació
Santa Maria que lo parió
San Juan que lo bautizó,
La guardia es tomada
la ampoleta muele,

buen viaje aremos
si Dios quiere.
[Blessed the hour/ when God was born/ St. Mary who bore him/ St. John who baptized him/ the watch has taken over/ the glass is running/ will have a good voyage/ God willing]

And during the night, counting started again:

Una va pasada
y en dos muele,
mas muelerá si Dios querrá.
etc. etc.
[One is past/ and two is running/ more will run/ God willing...]

During his voyage Columbus does not indicate whether he also used the quadrant, a very simple instrument made of a small wooden board or metal plate shaped like a quarter disc, fitted with a plumb line attached to the right corner of the board and graduated to 90° on the curved side. Looking at the height of the sun through two sights placed on one of the straight sides of the quadrant, the plumb line (or a small stick freely pivoting around its attachment dowel) yielded a reading in degrees on the graduated sector. Knowing the height the sun thus observed, at a given hour of a given day, one can figure the time. One can also derive the latitude, knowing at what angle the sun would stand above the horizon at a known latitude. Such readings were accurate within a one degree range.

Like for the quadrant, it is doubtful that Columbus could have used the astrolabe, a simple instrument with which to figure the night time from the positions of the Big Dipper stars in their nocturnal course around Polaris, a motion that describes a complete circle in 24 hours, like a hand on a clock dial but of 24, rather than 12, hours. Every sailor knew how to read such a celestial clock even without instruments — naturally, without the precision of the astrolabe.

Ship's position. – The calculation of traveled distance by estimation (a system used as late as the modern times) needed corroboration that could be provided only by figuring the ship's position, i.e., determining the latitude and longitude at which the vessel was at that moment.

Measurements of latitude were possible then because ever since the most remote times it had been noticed that the height of the boreal Pole above the horizon (identified by Polaris) changed with latitude (with, theoretically, its highest value at the pole and its zero value at the equator).

With the knowledge of the angle formed by the North Star above the horizon, the first notion of latitude was born. Once proven that the Earth was spherical, it was possible to conclude that the latitude of a given place, in degrees, would equal the pole's height above the horizon, in degrees. A similar calculation could be performed by measuring the sun's height at the zenith and comparing it against the right table which reported its values for the different seasons.

These measurements could be effected with high precision by using the astrolabe, which seems to have been invented by the School of Alexandria in the sixth century, but became well-known only from the twelfth century on.

"Did Columbus have the astrolabe, or not?", Taviani has wondered, pointing out that "the tradition says he did with some historians going so far as even proclaiming that it was the invention of the astrolabe that enabled the Genoese to discover America." In any case, other simpler instruments could take the place of the astrolabe. According to Morison, it could be evinced from the *Journal* of the first voyage that Columbus did not use such an instrument, nor would there be proof that he had adopted it in the following voyages. Charcot, on the contrary, has no doubts that Columbus did use the astrolabe. What is certain is that such a device did not become a feature on ships before the sixteenth century. It could be, however, that the Admiral, as he embarked in a rather demanding journey, wished to acquire the very best instrumentation available. The nautical astrolabe consisted of a bronze or copper disc (the mother board), 20 to 30 centimeters in diameter, cut off on top, i.e., on the arc by the line of sight so as to lower its resistance to the wind, but having a solid base, i.e., heavy gravity that ensured its vertical position. Atop the disc a ring kept it suspended at his center with an alidade that had two pierced finlets (or pinnules), through which to sight the star. On the plane of the mother board was placed a perforated disc (the 'net') on which a map was etched — of the most important stars of the tropics, and of the orbits of the sun and planets. By sliding thin discs (the 'platelets') between mother board and net, each one etched with the coordinates of various latitudes the instrument's field was widened. As the astrolabe was kept suspended, as steady as possible, a seaman would adjust the alidade and read the corresponding values off the instrument. Its accuracy, under favorable conditions, could vary by one degree which, in reference to latitude, could mean a misreading of up to about sixty miles.

A simpler, and naturally less accurate, instrument was the small "crossbow" (so called, as its shape recalled that of the homonymous weapon), a quadrant-like implement also referred to as 'Jacob's staff,' made from pearwood and consisting of a ruler with square section (the arrow), more than one meter long, onto which a rod or hammer (so called because of its shape) was made to slide perpendicularly. During the observation, the hammer's lower part was lined up with the horizon and the top aligned with the sun; the degrees, shown on a graduated scale, were read on the section.

Whereas latitude could be calculated, there was no way to determine the just as indispensable longitude, notwithstanding some empirical, though unreliable, ways to figure it out had been attempted.

Amerigo Vespucci, for instance, wrote this in a letter to Lorenzo de' Medici:

> As for the longitude I say that, in order to figure it, I had such a difficulty that I labored greatly to be sure about the distance that we had traveled in terms of longitude; and so much I toiled that, finally, I could not think of anything better than observing at night the planets' oppositions and especially that between the moon and the other planets. . . and I compared those against the Almanac of Giovanni da Monteregio built around the meridian of Ferrara, and searching for an agreement with the calculations in the tables of King Don Alfonso. . . and I found myself to be 82 and a half degree longitude from the meridian of Cadiz, 1366 and two thirds leagues, corresponding to 5455 and two thirds miles. The reason I assume 16 and two thirds leagues per each degree is because, according to Ptolemy and Alfraganus, the Earth has a circumference of 240,000 miles, that is to say, 6,000 leagues that, apportioned to 360 degrees, equals 16 and two thirds leagues for each degree.

This whole argument is based on inaccurate data, and the method elaborated by the Florentine navigator found no followers. A good, practical solution of the longitude problem was not to be found until the end of the eighteenth century, when advancements in watchmaking produced the chronometers, capable of measuring time with extreme accuracy. Knowing the exact time of one's location, as calculated by means of astronomical observation, and comparing it to the actual time at a place situated on the first meridian (or any reference meridian) it is possible to determine the exact longitude, the latter being the measure in degrees of the angle formed at the Pole between the first meridian and the observer's meridian; that is to say, the arc or time differential, at the Equator, between the first meridian and the observer's. In 24 hours, in fact, the sun travels the entire circumference of the earth, which can be divided into 360° and is therefore like a celestial clock where time and degrees correspond. But chronometers did not exist in the fifteenth century, and therefore guess estimates were all that sailors could go by in navigation.

The sounding lead. – Another indispensable instrument for navigation, used since remote times thanks to its simplicity, was the sounding lead: a plummet tied to a fine line wrapped in a casket, with a marking knot for every arm's length. Cast into the sea with the ship at a standstill or moving slowly, it measured the depth of the bottom, providing also information about the type of bottom because there was, at the base of the plummet, a tallow-filled cavity to which bottom particles would stick. When the type of bottom matched the one reported by portolans, the lead became a confirmation that the ship was where it should be.

The length of the lead line on Columbus's vessels was greater than the one on contemporary ships, which typically had a line of 100 arms. In the Sargasso Sea, thinking that algae rose from a shallow bank, Columbus had the lead dropped as deep as 200 arms, to no avail of course, because the shallower ocean depth of the mid-Atlantic ridge varies from 8,000 to 10,000 feet.

Columbus set out on his voyage with some of the instruments we have listed and summarily described, but probably not all of them. He was a good cartographer, with a good grasp of scientific knowledge, and, above all, a seaman who indeed trusted, more than anything else, his own instincts. This characteristic he would demonstrate several times during the first crossing and in the following voyages, too, on occasions that show how he gleaned from very minute clues sufficient information on which to base his decisions, or how he was able to relate his knowledge to new experiences, anticipating events with enough time to prepare for them. A clear example of some such faculties he gave during his fourth voyage, as he exactly predicted the approach of a hurricane over *Hispaniola*, on the basis of a single previous experience, yet capable to rise to the occasion and identify the telling clues.

It is therefore likely that he put only moderate faith in the inaccurate instruments that he had on board or in the calculations reported in astronomy treatises, latitude and longitude tables or, still, in almanacs that dictated the rules with which to establish the latitude by means of observation of the sun and the stars.

To avoid errors, he followed a very elementary method, that of programming his course entirely on selected parallels. From his own experience and that gathered from others — it is easy to imagine how eagerly he sought, throughout his preparatory years, any piece of information about oceanic navigation — he knew that, in August, at the latitude of the Canaries he would find constant easterly winds thus avoiding the calm band between the Azores and the Canary Islands. He rigorously followed a route on the parallel, with but minimal and occasional deviations, convinced as he was that at some point he would have found land. Without relying on chance, he programmed the return voyage as well knowing that at the latitude of the Azores, a place he had previously visited, during January and February the winds blew from the west. Likewise, when he sailed from Haiti, he headed north, reached the Azores' latitude and from there, sailing along the parallel, reached them in no time. Consequently, sailing always at a chosen latitude, by observing the height of the stars, must not have been a difficult thing. His genius was in being able to complete, with such a remarkable economy of means, a voyage fraught with imponderables.

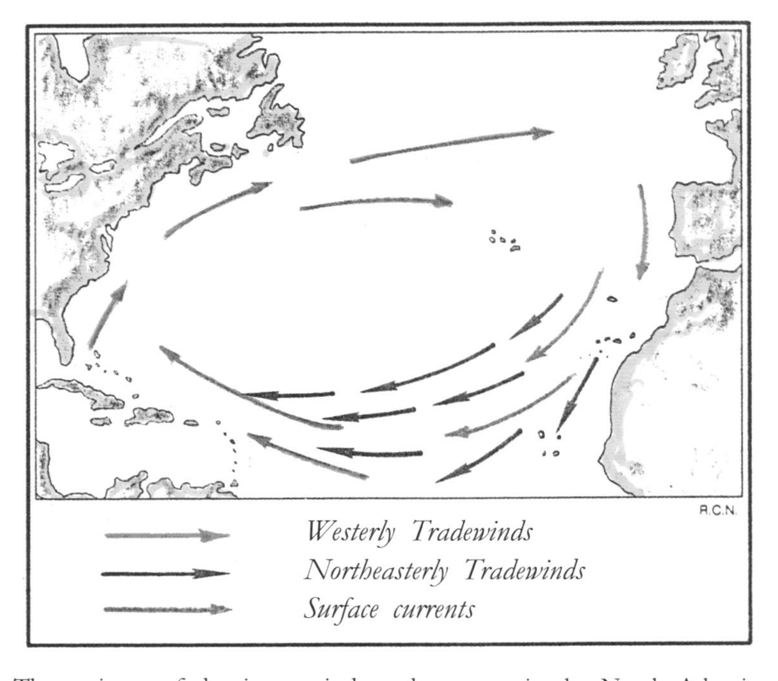

The regimen of dominant winds and currents in the North Atlantic.

Chapter VIII

THE OTHER SHIPS OF THE COLUMBIAN EXPEDITIONS

Barely six months after his happy return to Palos (March 15, 1493), Christopher Columbus, in command of a new and considerably larger fleet, sailed once again toward the West Indies, this time to consolidate the possession of the discovered lands, bring relief to the men left at La Navidad who — thanks to the extended contact with the natives — would certainly have gathered news about the course to follow to reach the mainland and about the location of gold mines, and finally to further the exploration and reach the "Indies," a goal barely sensed in the first voyage that now appeared in close reach.

The Sovereigns themselves had made clear the purpose of the new voyage: discover new lands, gather gold while finding its mines, and convert to the Christian faith the pagan natives, who appeared well disposed to receive it.

The departure of an imposing fleet of seventeen vessels, with approximately twelve-hundred men on board — counting sailors, soldiers to defend the occupied territories, several friars, one "physician," doctor Chanca, noblemen, the first conquistadors like Alonso de Ojeda, and explorers, such as Juan Ponce de Leon, who would garner the recognition of discovering Florida — took place from Cadiz on September 25, 1493. As anxious as Columbus and the Sovereigns were to pluck the fruits of the discovery, the sailing would have occurred even earlier, had it not been delayed by bureaucratic and administrative hurdles interposed by Juan Rodríguez de Fonseca, chairman of the special Royal Commission for Indian Affairs, earlier appointed by the King. Many complaints have been directed against this arid character and his close collaborators, treasurer Francisco Pinello and comptroller Juan de Soria, who, by their respective functions, were destined to attract the antipathy and dislike of which rigorous administrators are made objects on the part of enthusiastic squanderers.

But if the Admiral did not face too many special concerns in organizing in a short time such a large number of ships and men, and in gathering the supplies needed to found the new colony, it was likely the merit of the unhurried pace of the Commission.

It is not up to us to relate the vicissitudes of Columbus's second and later voyages. Our only concern is to mention the ships whose names have arrived to us. Their characteristics could not be markedly different from those of the vessels that had taken part to the first voyage, *naos* and caravels — the majority of the latter fitted as square, considering the good performance furnished by such rigging during the first journey.

Columbus's flagship was again a *nao*, with the same name as her predecessor, *Santa Maria*, and a burden of around 200 *toneladas*. Perhaps owing to her good nautical qualities — surprising for a ship of that type — she was nicknamed *Maria Galante*, the denomination most often used. We need not repeat here how the name of a ship was in those days somewhat fuzzily assigned, and how a nickname or a reference to her owner could often prevail on the original name.

Two other *naos*, the *Colina* and the *Gallega* (these, too, surnames) were part of the fleet and probably of smaller dimensions, for otherwise Columbus would have elected one of them as his flagship. As for the remaining crafts, very little is known, probably because, as previously remarked, the means used in carrying out very great enterprises had just modest relevance in the eyes of contemporaries, who focussed on the personalities responsible for the realization and on the marvels unearthed by the discoveries.

In reference to this, Taviani writes:

> That leaves 14 vessels of which twelve were square-rigged caravels, including the valiant *Niña*, renamed *Santa Clara*[49], commanded this time by Alonso Medel. On the first voyage Columbus had noticed that the excessive draft of the ships prevented or made extremely difficult movement up or into rivers, bays and shallows, between the coral reefs and the coast. Therefore he procured some smaller ships capable of crossing the ocean but also of sailing near the coast, in shallows and even large rivers.
>
> The two small caravels that Columbus took with him to explore Cuba in 1494 — the *San Juan*, under Alonso Pérez Roldán, and the *Cardera*, captained by Cristóbal Pérez Niño — were ships of this type. The others, like the *Niña*, were *carabelas redondas*, fitted with square sails on the foremast and the mainmast and a lateen sail on the mizzen mast. (*Voyages. The Great Discovery*, 2, 136-7)

[49] As previously said, *Santa Clara* was the *Niña*'s forgotten original name, after St. Clara, the patron saint of Mogher, the place where the ship had been built. It was later named *Niña*, after her owner's name, Juan Niño.

If we think of *Niña II*, the caravel reconstructed by Carlos Etayo in 1962, less than 45 feet long, which crossed the Atlantic without excessive difficulties in spite of bad weather conditions, one can imagine what the *San Juan* and the *Cardera* of the second Columbian fleet were like.

The voyage took place in ideal conditions and the fleet reached Dominica in twenty-five days or little more. Another demonstration that, with favorable weather, crossing the Atlantic did not present great problems, even for crafts of small dimensions.

Columbus's disappointments during the permanence in those places are known. The discovery of new and most beautiful islands, though lacking gold, the La Navidad fortress found destroyed, the dead companions, the return to Spain of twelve — out of seventeen — ships under Antonio de Torres's command, with many of the improvised colonists frustrated for not having found in the West Indies the much fancied treasures.

From April 24 to September 29, Columbus sailed with the *Niña*, the *San Juan* and the *Cardera*, meticulously inspecting the southern and eastern shores of Cuba, Jamaica and *Hispaniola* without finding trace of either gold or powerful rulers of wealthy nations. The failures of that first attempt at colonization should not take away from the advances the art of navigating had gained in that ocean that just a couple of years earlier was frightening to every sailor. As Columbus explored the new islands, three caravels arrived from Spain, led by Bartholomew Columbus; the same vessels made their way back to Spain carrying more of the unhappy and frustrated people. Then four more caravels followed, under the command of Antonio de Torres; these returned to Spain with five hundred natives instead of the promised gold — slaves, though not in chains, destined to receive religious instruction, the vanguard of those peoples of color which, reduced to actual slavery, would represent the grievous implication of the European colonization of the new lands.

Four more caravels, conducted by Juan Aguado, called at La Isabela, the colony's new town, in October 1495. As can be seen, the route was traveled quite frequently.

Another episode pertaining to navigation should be recalled, namely the first violent hurricane experienced in 1495 by Europeans, in the bay of Isabela, and which sank three ships at anchor there.

Peter Martyr of Anghiera reports that "when this cyclone reached the town's harbor, it sent to the bottom three anchored ships, breaking their moorings and this happened (causing even greater astonishment) without any sea storm or tempest, but twisting them around just two or three times."

Las Casas speaks of four vessels lost in a hurricane, so perhaps there had been more than one, with a second wreckage involving the fleet arrived in October 1495 under the command of Juan Aguado.

"It seems fair to conclude," writes Taviani, " that the ships destroyed were three: the caravels *San Juan* and *Cardera* and, probably, the *Gallega*".

This episode, or episodes if more than one, prompted the colonists to undertake a new, necessary activity: shipbuilding. The first fifty-tons caravel built in the New World was the *Santa Cruz*, nicknamed *India.* Let us for a moment consider that the construction of a ship of respectable size presupposes the presence of people capable of performing such task, of instruments for implementing it with a fully operational yard, from securing the acquisition of logs for masts to a steady supply of materials of various kind such as nails, hemp for the rigging, canvas for sailmaking, resins and other ingredients for the paints, pitch for caulking, etc. If one thinks that barely three years had elapsed since Columbus and his followers' landfall in the New World, one cannot but marvel in realizing how much the European settlement had progressed in such a short time.

With the *Niña* and the *India*, the Admiral sailed back to Spain on March 10, 1496, mooring at Cadiz the following June 11. On board the two ships there stood a crowd of two hundred and fifty-five people, including about thirty natives. The navigation was slow, owing to the absence of favorable winds, with these unlucky and numerous passengers forced to endure hunger and thirst, subjected as they were to a very strict rationing. As these people returned disillusioned from their adventure in the New World, after this additional suffering they undoubtedly swore never again in their lifetime to set foot on a ship's deck.

To set up a third voyage, the Sovereigns made available to Columbus eight vessels. Two of these, the indefatigable *Niña* and the *India*, sailed on February 23, 1498 from Sanlucar de Barrameda with a crew of ninety men under the command of Pedro Fernández Coronel, bound for *Hispaniola.* We know names and displacement of the other six ships, thanks to a document preserved in the *Libros de Armada* preserved at the National State Archives in Seville and transcribed by Angel Ortega in his work *La Rábida.*

In the contract laid down with Anton Marino from Seville for the ships' provisions, the following caravels are listed:

– The caravel of Alfon Gutierrez of Palos, named *La Castilla*, with a cargo of 70 toneladas, which had as master Andrés Garcia Galdin.

– The caravel of Andrés Martin de la Gorda, from Palos, which had as master Alfon Benítez and carried a cargo of 60 *toneladas*. It was named *La Gorda*.

– The caravel of Bartolomé de Leca, from Palos, called *La Rábida*, which had as master Garcia Alfon Causino.

– The caravel of Cristobal Quintero, from Palos, named *Santa Maria de la Guia*, with a cargo of 101 *toneladas*, sporting as master its owner.

– The caravel *Garza* of Francisco García, from Palos, with a cargo of 71 *toneladas*, having as master the owner himself.

There was a sixth caravel, not mentioned in the document.

Two of the ships of the third Columbian fleet are also known, according to Ferdinand Columbus, by the names of *Vaqueños* and *Correo*. Taviani explains the names' difference by supposing that *Vaqueños* was the nickname for *Castilla* and *Correo* that of the *Gorda*. In the first case the hypothesis can be accepted since *Castilla* is certainly a proper name and, as previously stated, nicknames were commonly preferred to an official name. In the second instance, it would seem that *Gorda* was the nickname rather than *Correo* because, aside from the fact that 'gorda' means big (and big the ship was not, with her 60-*toneladas* displacement), that was actually her owner's name.

With three of these vessels, then, the *Vaqueños* or *Castilla*, and the Correo (*Gorda*?), Columbus's flagship *Santa Maria de Guia* sailed as far south as the Cape Verde Islands and beyond to a point 9° and 5' north latitude and then headed due west, convinced as he was that at that latitude he would avoid the islands' vast archipelago, into which his previous expeditions had run, and find the Asiatic continent just ahead of him. He sent the other three ships, with his nephew Giannetto in command, directly to *Hispaniola*, to resupply Nueva Isabela (or Isabela la Nueva), or Santo Domingo as it had been rechristened by his brother Bartholomew out of respect for their father, Dominic Columbus.

With the three vessels under his command, Columbus arrived at an island characterized by a mountain with three summits. He called it Trinidad, one of the few names still current of the many assigned by Columbus, then explored the Gulf of Paria, entering it through a dangerous channel. He had reached the shores of modern Venezuela and we shall not dwell on whether he realized to have set foot on the continent rather than on another of the many islands. We shall also overlook his return to *Hispaniola*, the revolt of Francisco Roldán, the arrival of Francisco Bobadilla, commander of Calatrava, sent by the King to restore some order to the colony, the arrest of Diego, Christopher and Bartholomew Columbus and their being brought back to Spain to face the Court's judgement.

Columbus would make the sad return voyage on the caravel *La Gorda*, declining to be relieved of the chains Bobadilla had imposed on him.

Concerning the fourth and last of Columbus's voyages, we know with sufficient accuracy men, ships and vicissitudes [reported here below with some observations].

The Sovereigns, acceding to Columbus's insistence, granted him at their own expense four vessels, but under precise conditions: the Admiral should devote himself exclusively to discoveries, without interfering with the business of the new governor of *Hispaniola*, Nicolas de Ovando, and his two captains Alonso de Ojeda and Vincente Jáñez Pinzón. Further, to prevent conflicts, he was actually interdicted from calling at *Hispaniola*. "Only if the project were to fail, forcing him to return via the same route of the outgoing voyage, he was authorized to put into *Hispaniola*, but clearly only on the return leg, and only if and when this would look inevitable" (Taviani, ibid.).

The four ships given to Columbus were, according to the description by Ferdinand Columbus (who, however, wrote many years after the facts) "round top vessels," therefore crafts like the first *Santa Maria*, or else caravels rigged as *naos* with that round top that usually the square caravels did not have (and thus fitted also with a topsail). Columbus, however, in the report about this last voyage of his, complained about his ships, saying: "If the vessels of the Indies do not sail before the wind, it is not because they are heavy or have been built poorly; the strong currents existing in those seas, and the wind, make it impossible to sail close-hauled since they would lose in one day what they had gained in seven." It would seem so far that he was referring to square-sail crafts that only because of the currents do not perform well and handle themselves miserably when "luffing," i.e., they cannot progress if sailing close to the wind. And he goes on "for this reason, I shall never accept caravels again, were they even Portuguese lateen rigs, because they can merely navigate with a regular good wind, to wait for which it is sometimes necessary to remain in a port for six or eight months, and this fact should not cause any surprise because it is a very common occurrence in Spain." The complaint looks then to have been levelled against the caravels, which anyway are implied to be square and not "Portuguese lateen," known to be better suited to sail in waters characterized by fickle currents and variable winds.

At any rate, here are name and tonnage of the four ships:

– The first one, on which Columbus embarked, was the *Capitana* of 70 *toneladas*, under the command of Diego Tristano. It is known that Tristano received a monthly salary of 4,000 *maravedis*, with 2,000 earned by his assistant and by the pilot, a little more than 1,000 received by the cooper, the carpenter, the two trumpeters and the two bombardiers, 1,000 for the sailors and the cabin boys (of which there were fourteen and twenty, respectively). These figures do not agree in the least with those cited at the end of chapter six, from Thatcher's studies; they have probably been incorrectly interpreted.

It seems evident that the *Capitana* was not the ship's real name, but the indication that the Admiral was on board. In this case the name was preempted by the rank.

– The second ship was the *Santiago de Palos*, nicknamed *Bermuda*, from her owner's name, Francisco Bermúdez. She was under Francisco de Porras's command and carried Bartholomew Columbus. She was smaller than the flagship and carried a total of thirty-seven men.

– The third was *El Gallego* or *Gallega*; she could carry a load of approximately 60 *toneladas*, but she was fitted with four masts, having a countermizzen at the stern. Her captain was Pedro de Torres, who had taken part in all of Columbus's voyages. The crew numbered thirty-seven men.

– The last one was the *Vizcaina* or *El Vizcaino*, of only 50 *toneladas* — certainly a caravel — commanded by Bartolomeo Fieschi, a Genoese. Its owner sold her to the Admiral during the voyage. She carried twenty-three men, including a chaplain and a man of the Admiral's retinue.

Altogether, there were a hundred and thirty-five men and boys on the payroll, out of a total of a hundred and forty people on board, counting the Admiral, Ferdinand and Bartholomew Columbus and a couple of their suite's attendants.

Columbus's flotilla reached the Canaries on May 20, 1502 and, having completed the necessary resupplying, sailed from there on the 25; after a very fast ocean crossing, it called at the island of Martinica on June 15. During the navigation, despite its being performed in record time, it seems that the *Santiago* showed itself to be slow and not very seaworthy. Perhaps some such deficiencies compared to other ships were used by Columbus as an excuse for making sail to *Hispaniola* notwithstanding the Sovereigns' prohibition, with the declared purpose of exchanging his ship with a more efficient one. On June 29 the flotilla reached the mouth of the Ozama, in front of the harbor of Santo Domingo [*Hispaniola*]; Columbus did not go ashore but sent in his place the captain of the *Gallega*, Pedro de Torres, to ask for a replacement of the *Santiago*, even at the cost of buying or renting a vessel out of his own pocket. Governor Ovando replied harshly: no replacement and prohibition for Columbus to come ashore, in observance of the King's orders. As he was at anchor off Santo Domingo, Columbus sensed from certain clues — he who had had himself barely one or two direct experiences of the phenomenon — that a hurricane was approaching. That prompted him to send a messenger to Ovando, advising that the fleet of about thirty ships lying at anchor within the safe mouth of the Ozama river and ready to sail off to Spain with the riches amassed in the colony, should not leave its moorings because of the impending danger. The weather seemed calm, however, and nothing presaged that a tempest was moving in; so no one listened to the advice of a by now old and discredited Admiral, and the fleet was ordered to sail. While still in *Hispaniola* waters, the vessels were indeed caught by a violent hurricane and twenty of them either sunk or were thrown aground, including the ships that carried Columbus's nemesis, Francisco Bobadilla, and Francisco de Roldán, the rebel-rouser of the revolt at *Hispaniola*. All disappeared at sea together with the treasures and the papers of the prosecution against Columbus. The surviving vessels managed with great difficulty to take haven in the port or nearby bays; the only one to continue on the voyage and to reach Spain was, ironically, the *Guecha*, which carried the agent of the Columbus family, Alonso Sanchez, who had embarked with 4,000 gold pesos returned, as per the King's order, to their legitimate owner. The ships of Columbus's flotilla on the contrary had time to take refuge in a small bay, Puerto Escondido, which the Admiral had discovered during his previous explorations.

Having weathered the terrifying hurricane that destroyed Ovando's fleet, Columbus's vessels took off from *Hispaniola* for a very adventurous voyage along the coasts of Central America that ended with the loss of the last two ships of the flotilla on the shores of Jamaica.

For five long months Columbus explored in vain those coasts searching both for a westward passage leading to his eagerly coveted Asia, and for gold, coveted for by everyone, from the King to the sailors and Columbus himself, who wanted at least to prove to Spain that his voyages had not been worthless and yielded good returns to offset the expenses sustained. This voyage was a series of outright misfortunes and disasters: storms delayed progress; a boat sent ashore for watering was lost with all its crew; the search for a passage to the Indian Ocean in the maze of lagoons and channels brought only disappointment; the natives proved to be hostile; the *Gallega* had to be abandoned at Belén on April 16, because her hull, completely infested by *teredos*, was no longer seaworthy; and the same fate befell the *Vizcaina*, deserted at Portobello "because of the much water she was taking on." Neither the gold found in rather good quantities, nor the achievement of having reached the shores of a new continent could console Columbus, who felt weakened and ill, alternating moments of mystical exaltation to profound depression and regret for having failed in his lifelong dream.

With two surviving ships, Columbus left the South-American coastline, along which he had sailed, and headed back northwards. He discovered an island, which he called Tortuga for the many sea turtles that inhabited it and then, close to the Cuban shores, a tempest broke the mooring of the *Bermuda*, causing it to crash against the *Santiago*, seriously damaging both vessels.

The ships were in such conditions, as Ferdinand Columbus wrote, that it was necessary "to keep three pumps continuously bailing in each vessel and when a pump was being overhauled, the sailors had to make up for it with buckets." During the night between June 22 and 23, the water level in the *Bermuda* "rose so high that there was no hope to be able to salvage it, for the water almost overtook the weather deck."

The *Bermuda* and the *Santiago*, being no longer able to sail, were pushed aground in a bay Columbus had discovered in 1494 and called Santa Gloria. Side by side in the bay, propped with stanchions, and provisional superstructures arranged on the decks and on the castles for shelter and defense, the two vessels — their holds were now full of water, resembling ghost castles rising from the shallows — provided a stronghold to Columbus and his men (those still loyal to him, because part of them revolted and tried to reach *Hispaniola* on their own, without succeeding) for twelve months, as they waited for help to arrive. It did not happen until June 28, 1504.

Appendices

WHAT DID THE SHIPS OF COLUMBUS REALLY LOOK LIKE?

by FRANCESCO QUIETO

There is no naval archaeologist who has not tried his or her hand at reconstructing, at least on paper, the *nao Santa Maria* and the caravels *Niña* and *Pinta*; but, just as there is no agreement on what the great navigator really looked like, as his true appearance remains inaccessible, so various researchers propose, for the famous vessels, hulls and riggings so different that it becomes virtually impossible to underwrite one over the others. These reconstructions are actually numerous because, in the absence of dependable data or models, with only a few reliable pieces of information and a series of images and pictures of artistical rather than technical value, scholars took their privileged cues, fashioning replicas that featured the respective solutions they had chosen to emphasize. Some, for instance, started from estimated cargo tonnage; some were guided by the number of crew members assigned to the sailing operations, or by the most reliable of the coeval illustrations or narratives like Columbus's own in his *Journal*; others, more recently, derived inspiration from the famous Mataró model, certainly belonging to the second half of the fifteenth century but discovered in 1929 — and finally there are those who, like Guillén Tato, imagined the *Santa Maria* not as a *nao*, but as a square-sail caravel.

Actually, a focus on the technical characteristics of the ships is relatively recent; one could say that it started approximately one century ago, on the occasion of the fourth centennial of the European discovery of America. In fact still in 1870, in a fairly well-known booklet on Columbus's life, Arthur Helps dismissed this topic in a few words: "The vessels were all of small size, probably no more than one hundred tons displacement, and consequently no larger than the American yachts whose race across the Ocean from New York to Cowes was regarded as a proof of immense daring even in 1867. Yet Columbus judged them fit for the task." Not much to go on, although in describing the differences among the three ships, Helps adds: "The *Santa Maria*, under the command of Columbus himself, was the only one of the three vessels that had a full deck. The other two were caravels and had decks fore and aft, but none at midship, because they were built in such a way as to rise high above water level." The vagueness and inaccuracy of these remarks appear to us nowadays very evident; so much so that all the authors, on the basis of more dependable documentations, are presently inclined to consider the caravels, too, as fully decked ships; without a complete deck, it is highly unlikely after all that they would have been able to overcome the misfortunes that they had to face, especially in the difficult return voyage. Ironically, it was the larger ship, the *Santa Maria*, that was lost during Christmas night of 1492, after running aground offshore the island of *Hispaniola*.

The first full-size reconstruction of the *Santa Maria* took place in Spain in 1492, the fourth centennial of the discovery of America, thanks to Fernandez Duro and his collaborators. This ship proved able to cross the Atlantic under sail with no great difficulty. The ensuing reaction, on the basis of numerous other documents and of a more accurate examination of the ones already known, maintained with good reason that the aforementioned reconstruction displayed highly unlikely details for a ship of the end of the fifteenth century, such as, for instance, a square stern (which would become a common element on such vessels only a few decades later) as well as redundant sail surface and, more specifically, a trapezoidal topsail of remarkable dimensions, this, too, typical of a later epoch.

Still for the fourth centennial, the Genoese captain D'Albertis prepared an in-depth study of the Columbian ships, taking upon himself even the task of building some excellent models. Broad, containing a true wealth of information regarding the different units of measure of the time, his study focussed on cargo capacity and displacement (a subject of the utmost importance because it is from the exact determination of the load capacity that it is possible to reckon the real dimensions of a ship). In it, however, comparisons are established with the modern units of measure which occasionally turn out to be misleading, as shall be seen in detail a little later on.

Like Auguste Jal, a well-known French scholar who also delved into the theme of the Columbian ships, D'Albertis started, in order to establish *Santa Maria*'s size, from the number of crew members assigned to sailing the vessel and from an assumed cargo capacity of 170 *tonels*; to determine the dimensions, he adopted the formula *as*, *dos*, *tres* that, in its more common interpretation, took "*as*" as the pillar's height, "*dos*" as the beam equal to twice the pillar's figure and "*tres*" as the length of the ship, corresponding to three times the width. An undoubtedly empirical rule but based on centuries of experience and regularly adopted, with small variations, by all master carpenters.

Other interesting features about Columbus's ships (and especially his flagship), are the ones already mentioned by Guillén Tato who reconstructed the *Santa Maria* in full size, interpreting it as a large *redonda* caravel, i.e., fitted with square sails; that of Andersen who in 1930 suggested an interesting *Santa Maria* model, later followed and improved upon by a 1964 study by Landström; Martinez Hidalgo's fine reconstruction (illustrated by Adm. Ingravalle in his paper about the speed of Columbus's ships — *Rivista Marittima*, Jan.-Febr. 1989) which is possibly regarded as the most accurate; the original models by Mondfeld, of 1991, that uniquely incorporated features from the only extant contemporary model of a mid-fifteenth-century *nao*, the famous "Mataró ship"; Adametz' model, based on the Spanish Commission's studies of 1898; and finally the latest Spanish reconstruction of 1991 by José López Martínez realized, together with those of the other two caravels, for the quincentennial celebrations of the discovery.

Detailed examinations of these projects reveal noticeable differences among them in hull shapes, displacement and tonnage; they are similar only in the sail outfit, which is of the three-masted type that Columbus mentions in his *Journal* with reference to the *Santa Maria*: that is, spritsail under the bowsprit, a square sail on the foremast, a large square sail with bonnets on the mainmast, a topsail above the top, a lateen sail on the mizzenmast. The sizes of the respective sail surfaces are, however, remarkably different among them.

Table 1 illustrates configurations of sail surfaces as adopted in several reconstructions and models.

Some of the better known graphical representations, more or less contemporary with the discovery, collected in Table 2, may be compared with the aforementioned reconstructions. However, these generally are the work of engravers and cartographers and not of technical people, and therefore they can be considered interesting only from a general standpoint; it is virtually impossible to obtain from these drawings reliable suggestions about dimensions of any kind.

The main reason for the uncertainties on the dimensions of the ships depends above all upon the reality that in that period and for two centuries more, all vessels were the work of master carpenters, extremely jealous of their knowledge; they built a ship only on the basis of tradition, entrenched habits and direct experience. There were, therefore, no construction plans of any kind against which one could check the major dimensions of a ship and thus figure out a displacement value, the only sure clue to a vessel's size.

From existing documents, the only indicative data that indirectly relate to the dimensions of ships are cargo capacity values, at that time generally given as the number of wine caskets which could be transported. However, these were measured in different units of weight and volume, and, moreover, varied from city to city: a factor that makes it very hard to arrive at corresponding values expressed in present-day units. D'Albertis amply illustrates this topic in a learned study on the subject (mentioned earlier), providing specific references to various sources and data.

Displacement, capacity, hull weight, tonnage, weight and volume units

In order to examine Columbus's ships from a more technical standpoint, it is necessary to briefly remark about ways of assessing the size of a ship. Frequently, in talking about Columbian ships, confusion in regard to the various tonnages is generated even by esteemed authors, not least because of the inaccuracy of the sources. Let us then summarily see what is intended by the terms *displacement*, *capacity*, *hull weight* and *tonnage*.

The first three refer to weight measures; tonnage, on the other hand, is a measure of volume.

Displacement is the sum of the weight of the ship and the weight of the onboard cargo (the capacity).

Obviously the capacity is the difference between the net displacement of the (unloaded) ship and that of the fully loaded ship; it indicates therefore the total weight of whatever can be loaded onboard. An approximate determination of the size of a ship, starting from the loading capacity, can be obtained by establishing the principal characteristics of a hull capable of transporting such a load. The main difficulty in planning a replica of the Columbian ships rests in the fact that, unfortunately, only summary indications of their cargo capacity are available; they vary, depending upon the source, from 50 *tonels* (minimum) for a caravel to 200 *tonels* for a *nao*. First of all, it is necessary to correlate the ancient *tonel* to the current weight ton. Thus one must familiarize with the maze of fifteenth-century units of measure. Then in building the hull as realistically as possible, one should use wood cut in the robust and cumbersome sizes used in those days, as well as assemble them in accordance with the building techniques typical of that age.

In Seville and on the Atlantic coasts of Portugal and Spain, wine was typical merchandise and its unit of measure was generally the *tonel*, equal to two barrels with a gross weight of, so at least it seems, 2,000 pounds (pounds of the time were approximately 400 grams, or 0.88 present-day pound), or about 800 kilograms[1] in today's units. Each barrel occupied a space of 40 to 45 cubic feet (the cubic foot used in those regions equalled 0.280 cubic meter). 45 cubic feet then would correspond today to approximately one cubic meter.

The space taken up by the barrels in the hold, however, was much larger, owing to both their curved shape, and the unusable areas at each end of the hold itself.

After establishing, albeit approximately, the ratio between a *tonel* and a cubic meter, it is necessary to determine the number of *tonels* that could be carried by a ship. The most recent estimates indicate a cargo capacity between 50 and 70 *tonel* for a caravel and of 100 *tonel* for the *nao*. Following the estimate of Martinez, who attributes to the *Santa Maria* a loading capacity of just a little over 100 *tonel*, each one corresponding to a 1.38 cubic meters of volume (taking into account the excess of space they would require in the hold), through basic calculations one obtains a total tonnage of about 51 tons[2] (in units of 2.83 cubic meters); which would finally yield, after correlating volume and weight, a cargo capacity of 84 tons (in weight kilograms).[3] From the *Santa Maria*'s displacement of 203 tons as calculated by Martinez — certainly plausible, since his replica utilized timber following the original fifteenth-century techniques — one deduces that the weight of the cargo (84 tons) was only 42% of the displacement, versus values of about 60% for modern freight vessels and approximately 50% for the sailing ships of the past century. This is a direct consequence of heavy-weight hulls in ships of Columbus's times, which could reach 58% of the displacement, including however in such a percentage (implied by the definition of displacement) the weight of the ballast, provisions, spare parts, riggings and crew: certainly no less than 30 tons (in the case of the *Santa Maria*) that were not part of the paying load.

Had we accepted D'Albertis's estimates of a cargo capacity for the *Santa Maria* of 150-180 tonel, the resulting ship would be much larger, reaching almost 300 tons.

This whole way of reasoning, presented merely as an indicative calculation exercise, finds its shortcoming in the alleged conversion values

[1] According to Straticus, during the fifteenth and sixteenth centuries the *tonel* consisted of two pipes or casks; one cask weighted 27 *arrobas*; one *arroba*, 33 pounds. Then, 2 casks = 2 x 27 x 33 = 1,782 pounds.

[2] Starting from the consideration that 1,782 lbs (800 kg) need 1.38 m^3 of stowing space or, in tonnage tons, 2.83 m^3, one obtains 1.38/2.83 = 0.487 tonnage tons per each tonel. Taking into account a total cargo of 106 *tonel* (as Martinez assumed) the final result is 0.487 x 106 = 51.6 tons of tonnage.

[3] Resulting from multiplying 0.8 x 106 = 84 tons.

between fifteenth-century units of measure and modern ones. D'Albertis himself unwittingly experienced how treacherous such way of figuring can be. In his excellent book on the Columbian ships, as already mentioned, in calculating in modern units the tonnage of the *Santa Maria* he commits an obvious, incomprehensible oversight; in fact, in calculating the tonnage with the second commonly known formula of:

$$\frac{L.B.H}{4}$$ [4]

(where 1/4 is in place of 0,7/2.83, L = ship's length; B = width; H = pillar or depth of the hold, and 0.7 is the internal volume coefficient), he mistakes the tonnage ton of 2.83 m^3, which is derived from the aforementioned formula, with the other equal to 1 m^3, consequently misrepresenting the ensuing comparison instituted with the units of measure of Columbus's era.

Hull shapes. Construction plan.

Everyone knows that the performance qualities of a ship, with respect to flotation, stability, handling, velocity and seaworthiness depend, aside from the type of propulsion and the size of the vessel, upon the shape of the hull, that is, that part of the ship that generally cannot be seen, the least showy, but by far the most important, as implied by its name. Still today it is called the "live work," whereas anything above the waterline is part of the "dead work."
The shape of a hull can be gleaned from construction plans, but in Columbus's times, as already stated, no drawings existed, with ships being built directly by master carpenters acting as today's engineers, architects and builders, when, in reality, they were very highly skilled artisans whose craftmanship was passed on under the strictest secrecy, from father to son.

Since numerous illustrations in this book contain drawings — modern, obviously — of construction plans relative to the replicas of Columbian ships, I shall briefly say what such plans represent. Each plan typically shows on up to three normal planes — horizontal, longitudinal, and crosssectional or transversal — various perspectives as well as cross-sectional profiles of the hull.

[4] As it is known, the calculation of the tonnage, i.e., the volume of all enclosed spaces on the ship, follows different formulas, depending upon the vessel's type. D'Albertis has used for these ships the second or "simplified" formula, which is based on a volume coefficient of 0.7. Owing to the shape of these vessels, however, it seems better to assume a smaller volume coefficient, say 0.55, i.e., the one related to a ship's finesse ratio, using Martinez Hidalgo's characteristic data for the *Santa Maria*.

On the transversal plane, are reported the main section as well as other sections taken at regular intervals fore and aft; and, since the ship is symmetrical with respect to the diametrical longitudinal plane, the drawings reproduce the fore sections on the right and the aft sections on the left. The horizontal plane also shows the waterlines, i.e., the contour lines of the hull at differing immersion depths (these, too, taken at regular intervals) and parallel to the flotation line.

On the vertical or longitudinal plane, at least three longitudinal sections are depicted, in the direction of the ship's width.

The horizontal sections appear as curves on the waterlines plane and as straight lines parallel to the waterlines on the longitudinal and transversal planes. The transversal sections are curves on the transversal plane and straight lines, normal to the waterlines, on the horizontal and longitudinal planes. The longitudinal sections are curves in the longitudinal plane and straight lines, parallel to the plane of symmetry, on the other two planes. Since the three perspectives are always presented together, it is possible to form an idea of the general shape of the hull at a glance.

Longitudinal profile and main section are the two basic figures of a ship's building process. The longitudinal profile provides an idea of the overall size, type, immersion, free board, prow and stern shapes; the main section determines a boat's stability and displacement; the waterlines provide a reference of the warping fluidity or water-deviation angles for both the entry and exit angles of waterflow, critical in regard to vortex and wave formation. The longitudinal sections, finally, give information about fluidity behavior in the fore sections, and above all, on how the waterflow is funneled sternward. Special ratios between the principal dimensions L/B, B/T, B/H, inform the designer's work; these ratios vary depending upon the type of ship. For Columbus's vessels, which were no racing machines, but required solid stability and safety criteria, such values were governed by the well-known rule "*as, dos y tres*": L/B was equal to about three, B/T was larger than three and B/H larger than 1.5. The velocity index, or Taylor's quotient, equal to $V/\sqrt{L}$,[5] was not of great significance for the

[5] This is basically a velocity ratio, where V = ship's speed and $\sqrt{L}$ (with L = ship's length at the waterline) is a value proportional to the velocity of a wave having the same length as the ship's at her waterline. It derives from the theory of trochoidal waves, where the speed of a wave is equal to $\sqrt{\frac{g\lambda}{2M}}$ where g = gravitational acceleration, λ = wavelength. The higher the quotient $V/\sqrt{L}$, the greater will be, for displacement hulls, the specific wave resistance value.

ships of Columbus's times, since these vessels moved forward at low values of such velocity index, for which the wave resistance is almost absent; for those ships, the limiting factors were the immersed surface and the area of the main (beam) section.

From these basic indications about hull shapes, one can see why the caravels were chosen over *naos* and caracks in expeditions meant to explore and discover new lands. The caravels had less draft and therefore less immersed surface, thus potentially higher speeds; having as well a comparatively larger sail plane, they made it easier to get closer to shore and sail up rivers; lastly, they exhibited slightly finer waterlines, that is, greater fluidity given the reduced entry and exit angles fore and aft for the waterflow, thus offering less resistance to forward motion. Columbus himself, in his *Journal*, frequently praises the "mas velera" [having more sails] *Pinta* as well as the *Niña* ("our best sailing ship, she advanced swiftly"), whereas he points out, especially at the time of its loss, how the *Santa Maria* was not suitable for discovery expeditions (possibly contradicting what he had declared upon departure, as he claimed that "three ships very apt to such a feat were outfitted").

Upon examining the construction plans of some of the replicas of Columbian ships, it could be summarily stated that such projects belong to three basic types (see Table 7):

– U-shaped or lyre-shaped hulls, generally with low draft, sometimes sporting square stern and a large sail surface, including ample topsails reminiscent of the later galleons;

– V-shaped hulls but with maximum beam not at the waterline like the preceding group, but at deck level, high draft, round stern, smaller sail surface, smaller beam in correspondence of the waterline;

– roundish hulls with a nearly flat bottom, square stern, low draft, no forecastle, more refined waterlines and longitudinal lines more stretched sternward, with a good sail system, but without sprit- or topsail. Caravels generally belonged to this latter type.

The most recent critics, with regard especially to the Mataró model, consider the second hull type — the one with more draft and prevalently V-shaped sections that would, however, prove less stable without proper ballast — more realistic for the *Santa Maria*.

General considerations

It may be then concluded that, despite many studies, hundreds of models and the realization of several replicas, of the Columbian ships we do not know either the precise dimensions, or cargo capacity, or tonnage and displacement, or actual speed achieved. Even the type of vessels is they were is still debated: caracks, *naos*, or caravels with round transversal sections and a flat bottom, or more open and with deeper draft? Yet, it seems to me that these missing features were not determining factors in the success of the enterprise. What really mattered was the actual propulsion device, applied indifferently to caracks, *naos* and caravels: the three-masted rigging with square sails on the first two masts, and a lateen sail on the third one. The sail system is, as noted earlier, the single recorded technical characteristic of the *Santa Maria* reported by Columbus in his *Journal* (see Table 8). Square sails were particularly suited for navigation with steady wind blowing from the aft sectors, the predominant force both during the outgoing voyage with northeasterly trade winds, as well as in the return crossing, farther North, with the northwesterly trades. This was in essence the great intuition of Columbus, who, over the objections of some of his valiant captains, had the *Pinta* so rigged right at departure time, and the *Niña* modified later during the stop at the Canaries. Furthermore, the distributed arrangement of the sails over three masts along the ship allowed greater flexibility by suitably modifying the sail surfaces on the three masts depending upon the course and the conditions of weather and sea, thus correcting eventual pulls toward or away from the wind and, in other words, remarkably improving the overall stability. So much so in fact, that this kind of rigging, thanks to its multifaceted nature and undisputed ease of trimming and handling, would remain substantially unchanged throughout the following centuries of sailing on galleons, frigates, corvettes and war vessels, all the way to the magnificent narrow-beamed clippers of the nineteenth century.

Conclusion

Having examined the different aspects of Columbian ships as they have been envisioned in more or less recent conjectures and reconstructions, one cannot deny the absence of a definitive answer to the original question of what the vessels on which Columbus sailed for his first voyage really were like. This, however, is not so critical. What matters most about the Navigator is neither his portrait, nor his birth, previous adventures, ships, private life, etc., but rather his determined action and indomitable faith in the courageous pursuit of his goal. Like all seamen, I indeed like to remember him just as he presents himself in the *Book of Prophecies* (1501): “I have lived since my youngest days a sailor’s life and shall continue doing so. This is a driving trade that urges his followers on to try and unveil the world’s secrets.”

TABLE 1

Rigging Plans of replicas and models of Columbus's ships

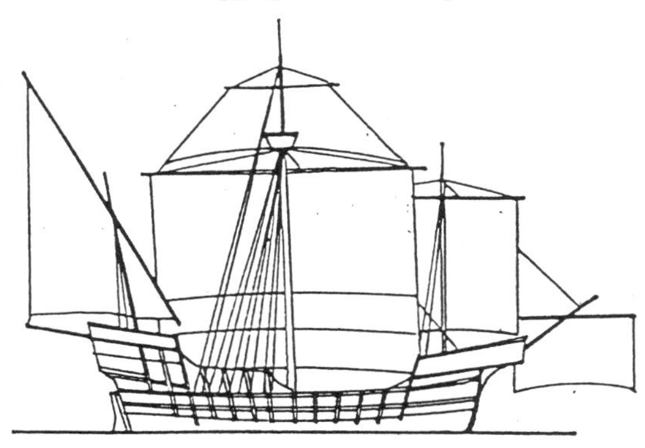

Santa Maria [from top to bottom] as reconstructed by the Spanish Commission for the Fourth Centennial (1892)

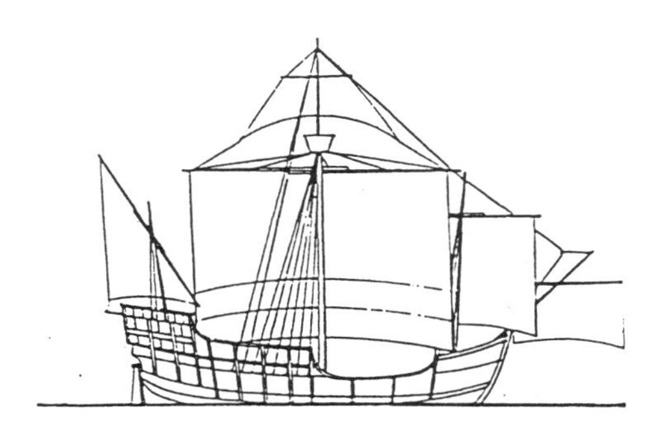

seen as a *redonda* caravel by Guillém Tato (1929)

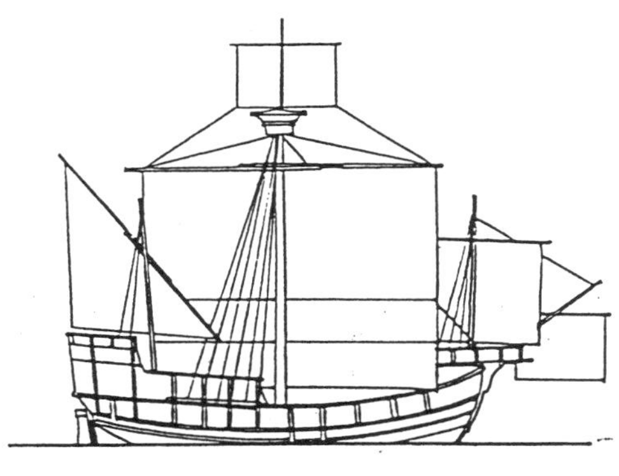

in Biörn Landström's model (1961)

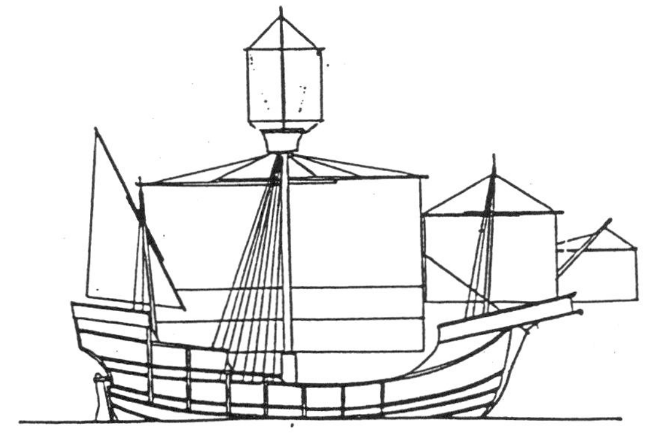

nin the reconstruction by the Spanish Commission for the Quincentennial (1992)

TABLE 2

Representations of ships of Christopher Columbus's era

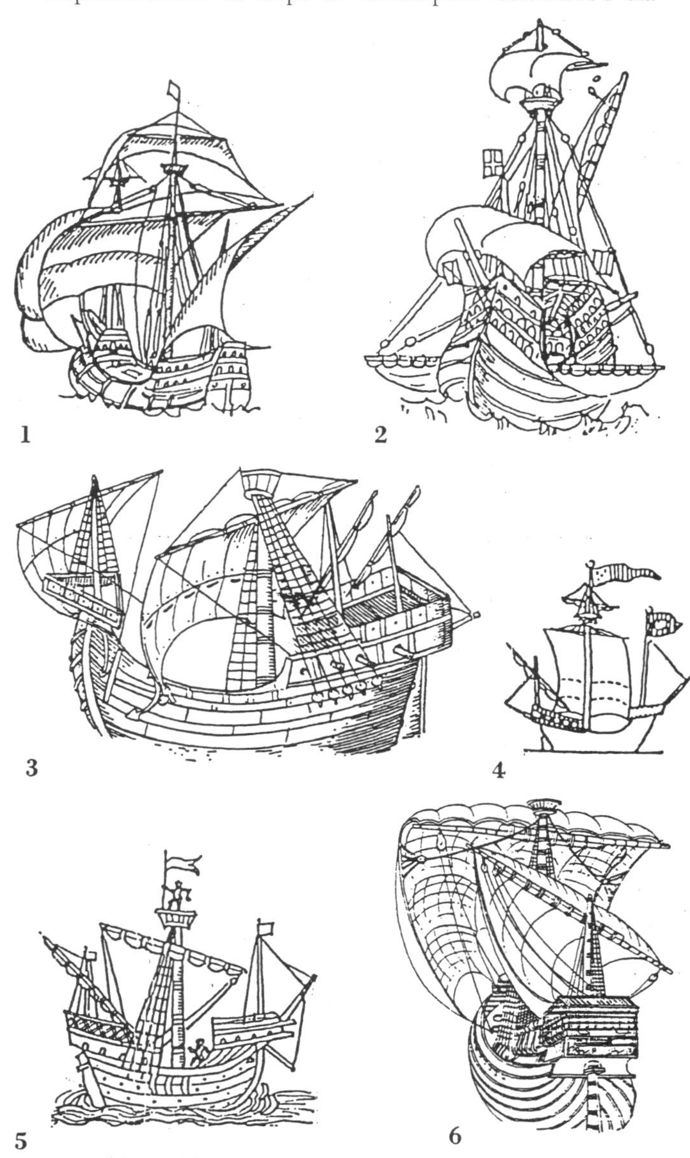

Fig. 1: Square-stern ship, with large sail surface and a wide topsail (from a nautical chart by Diego Ribero). Representations such as this influenced the basic choices of the Spanish government's project on the occasion of the Fourth Centennial of the Great Voyage (1892).

Fig. 2: Representation of the *Santa Maria* as a *nao* (from a Portuguese chart).

Fig. 3: A four-mast Portuguese ship, perhaps utilizing the mast of her launch (from a 1496 woodcut).

Fig. 4: A Portuguese ship drawn on the nautical chart by Juan de la Cosa, owner and master of the *Santa Maria* during the expedition.

Fig. 5: A *nao* (from a Portuguese nautical text).

Fig. 6: Modon's *Nao* from a 1486 codex. This right side image has been passed on with the title "OCEANICA CLASSIS."

TABLE 3

The *Santa Maria*, in Martinez Hidalgo's project (1964)

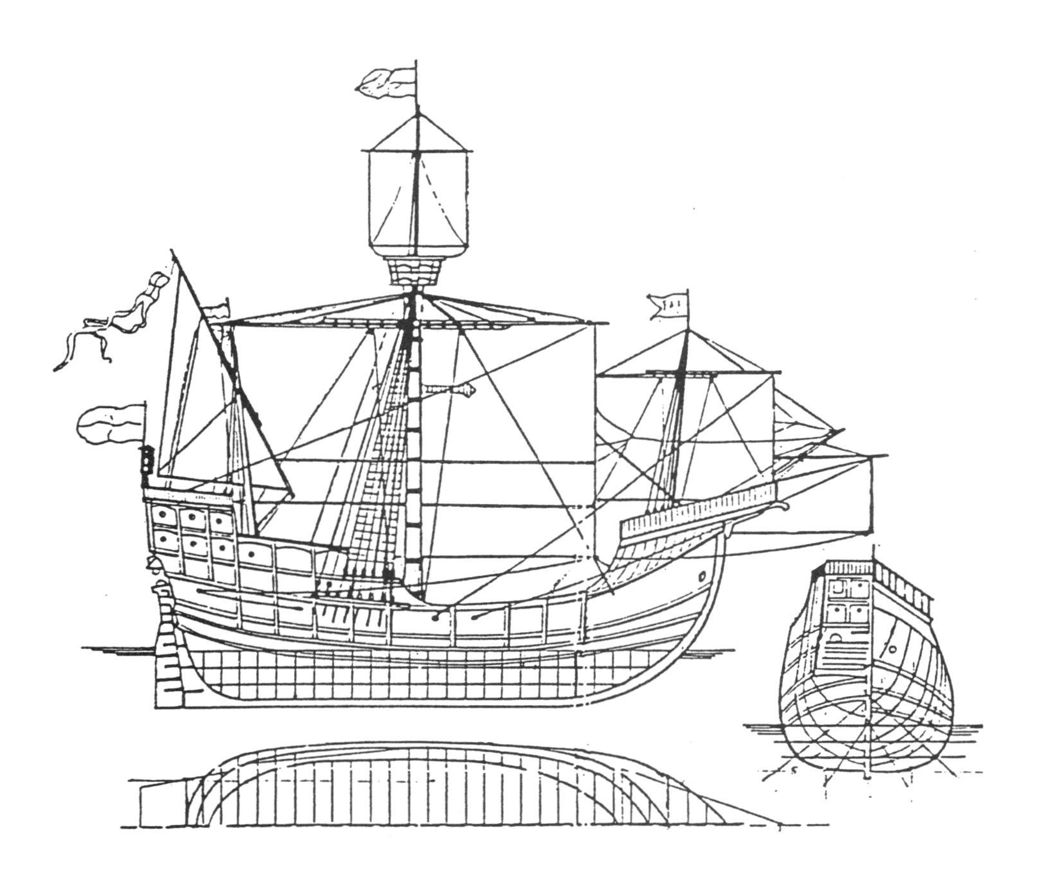

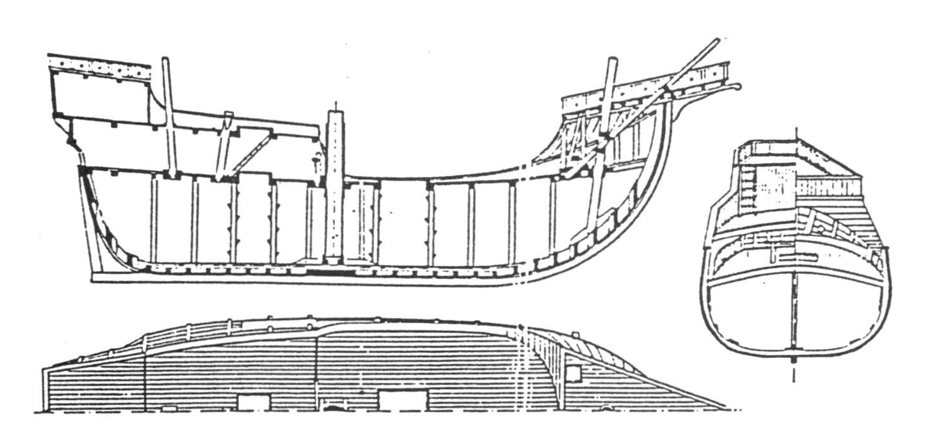

Main dimensions: L = 70.8 ft, B = 28 ft, T = 6.9 ft
D 6 283 tons, Sv 6 272 m^2

A well-balanced and certainly quite stable ship, with a round stern, rounded beam section and flat bottom. Reduced draft [live works], high free board.

TABLE 4

The *Santa Maria*, Mondfeld's project (1991)

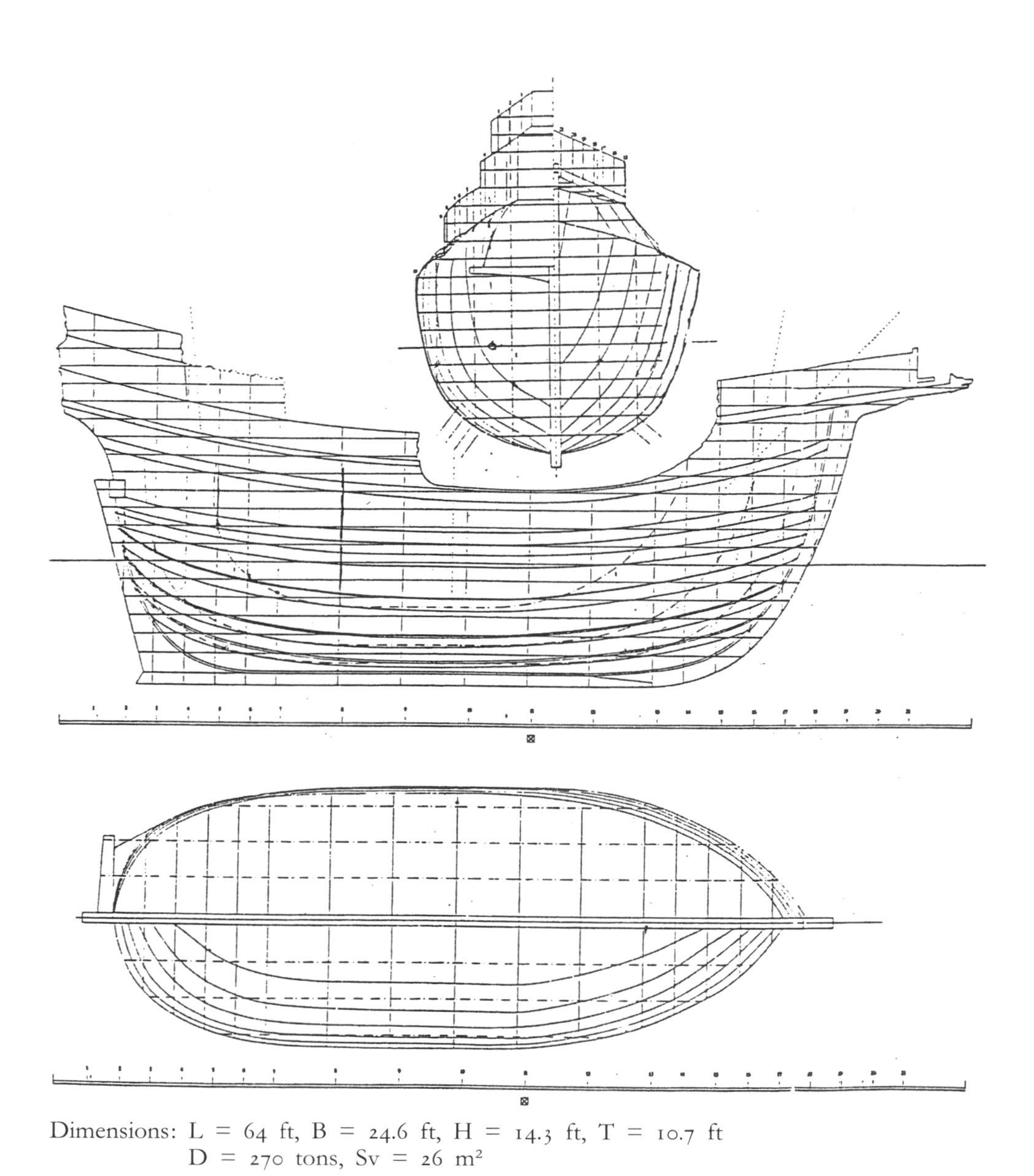

Dimensions: L = 64 ft, B = 24.6 ft, H = 14.3 ft, T = 10.7 ft
D = 270 tons, Sv = 26 m^2

Ship with V-shaped beam section, deep draft. The maximum width is measured at deck line, and not at the waterline. Exhibits a very high displacement relative to the length; she might have experienced stability problems, unless heavily ballasted.

TABLE 5

The *Niña*, project by Mondfeld, Holz and Seyoner (1991)

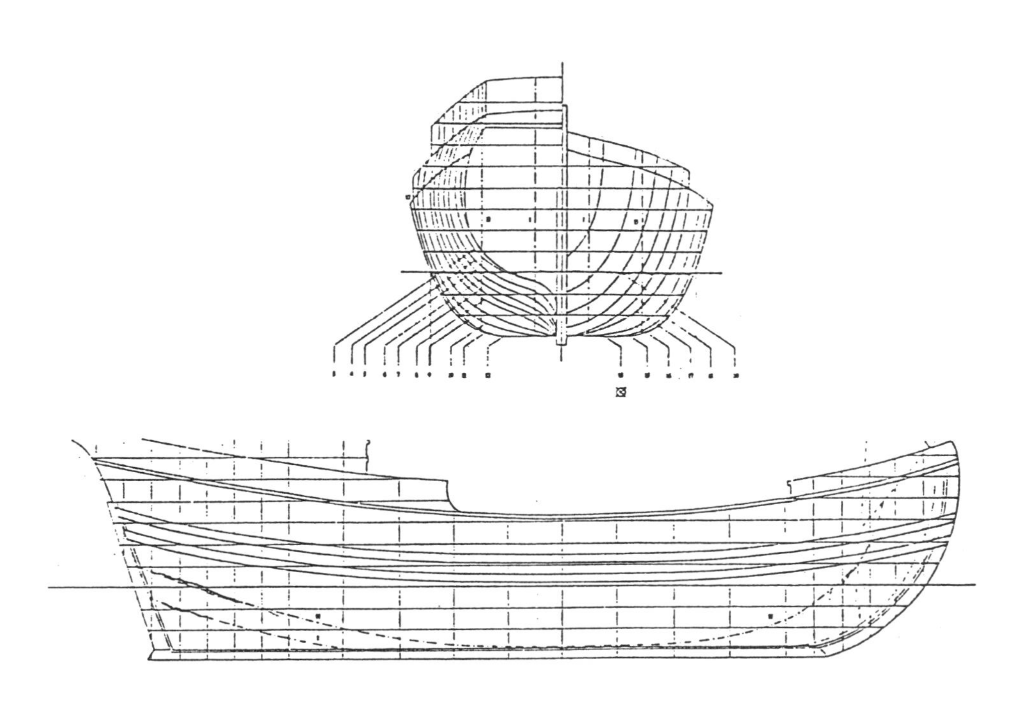

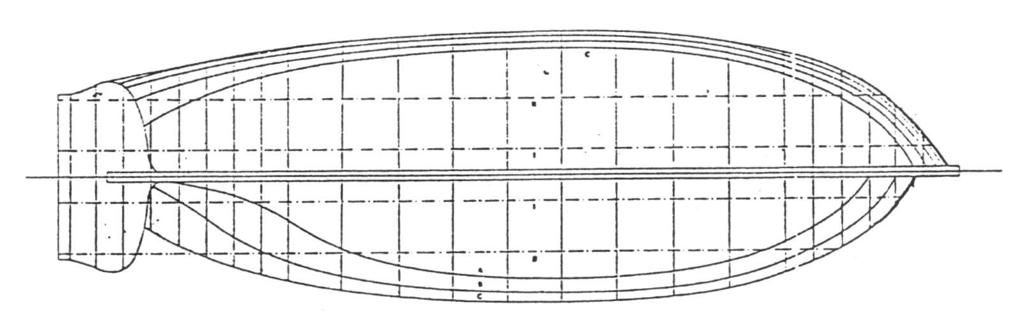

Main dimensions: L = 65.6 ft, B = 21.1 ft, T = 5.7 ft
D = 112 tons, Sv = 180 m^2

Mondfeld *et al.*, differently from other scholars, consider the *Niña* larger than the *Pinta*. Hull with a flat bottom main section, square stern, reduced incidence angle at waterline, that is, longitudinal sections cutting the waterline at a small angle, promoting good water flow.

TABLE 6

The *Pinta*, project by Mondfeld, Holz and Seyoner (1991)

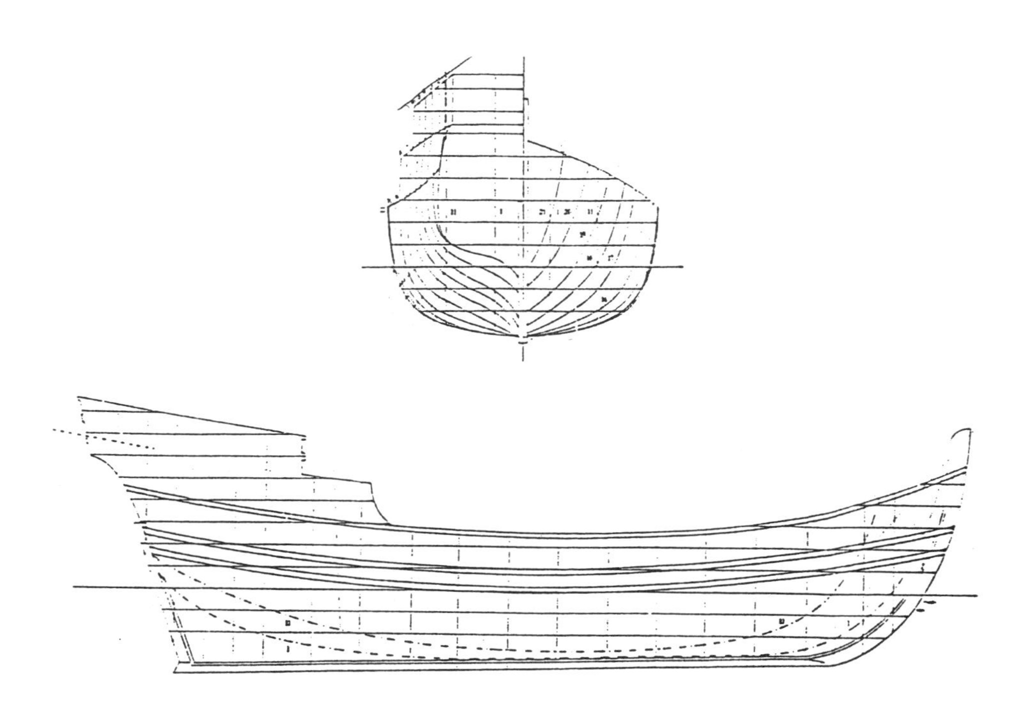

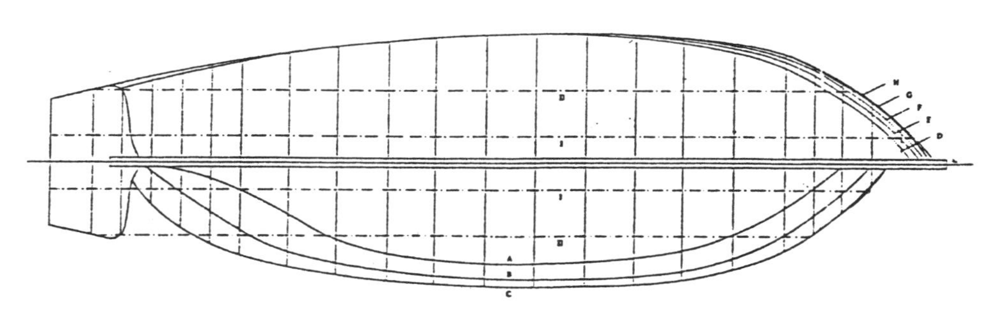

Main dimensions: L = 61.3 ft, B = 20.8 ft, T = 5.7 ft
D = 104 tons, Sv = 165 tons.

Mondfeld *et al.* consider the *Pinta* smaller than the *Niña*. The beam section is roundish and with a not completely flat bottom. The waterlines are thinned and the longitudinals cut the buoyancy line at a reduced angle, again, promoting good water flow.

TABLE 7

Types of main sections for *naos* and caravels

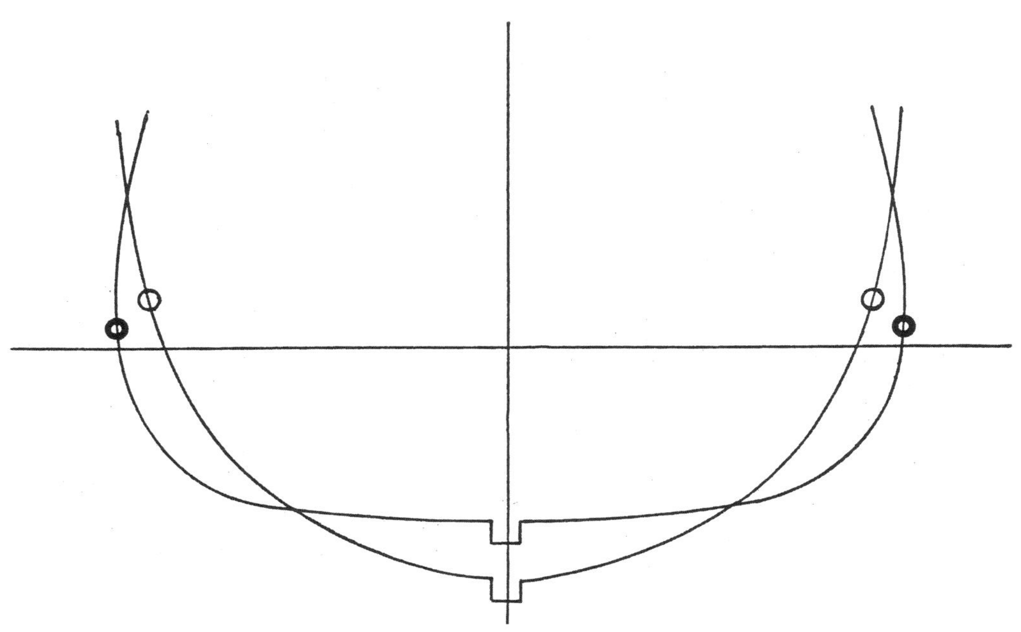

Nao: O V-section with a deeper draft and smaller width at the buoyancy line. Maximum width at deck.
O U-section with a light draft and greater width at the buoyancy line.

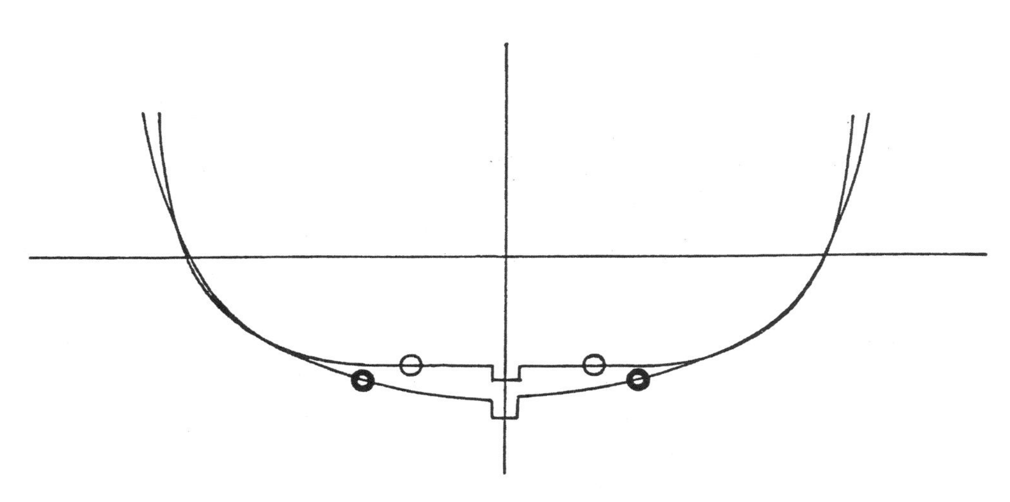

Caravels: O Flat bottom section, low draft and greater width at the buoyancy line.
O Round bottom section, deeper draft and a smaller width at the buoyancy line.

TABLE 8

SAIL RIGGING OF THE *SANTA MARIA*
as described in Christopher Columbus's *Journal*

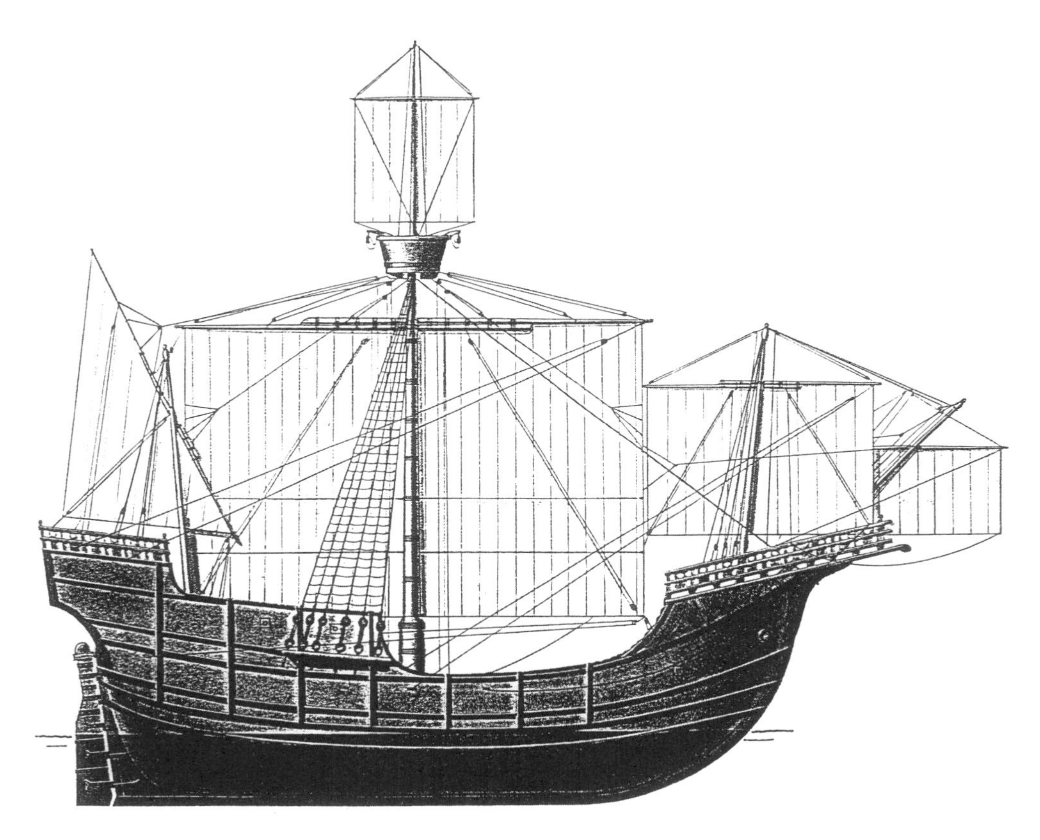

Sail rigging, following Columbus, in the most recent interpretation of the replica built in Spain on the occasion of the Quincentennial of the great voyage. Visible at fore are the spritsail under the bowsprit, and the square foresail near the foremast, and on the mainmast the large square mainsail with the bonnets (below) and the topsail (up above) and finally at the mizzenmast, aft, the lateen sail.

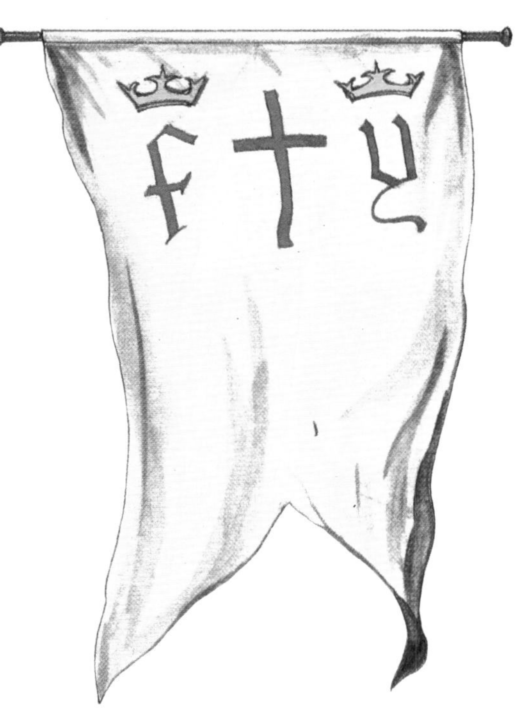

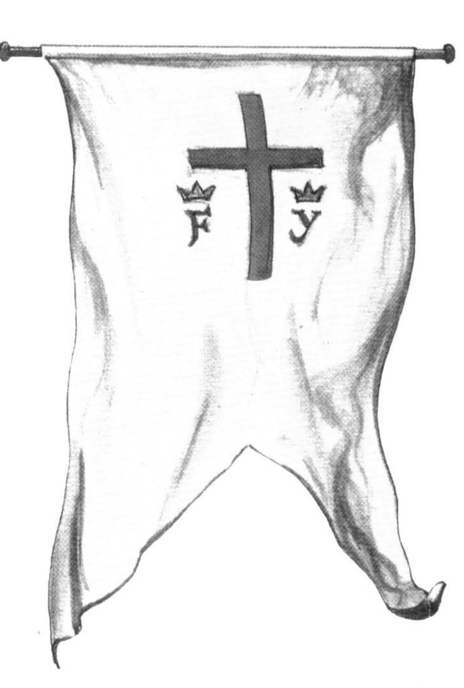

F. GAY

THE FLAGS OF THE COLUMBIAN SHIPS

by Aldo Ziggiotto

We know by the testimony of Christopher Columbus himself that the famous Genoese, while heading for the Indies, had flags and banners distinguishing his small ships. It would indeed be disappointing if in the pictorial representations of the three vessels we saw not even a hint of a standard or if Columbus, in those paintings or movies to him dedicated, were to go ashore on the new lands without holding a banner. This explains why we always find ensigns accompanying illustrations of the great feat, when in actuality they are simply artistic additions created to complete the scene, without any certainty that any of these flags may correspond to the originals, whatever they may have been.

It is hardly a mistery that such an important event has remained somewhat veiled and dotted with uncertainties, starting with Columbus himself whose physiognomy we do not know; what counts, in history, are indeed contemporary documents, not after-the-fact reports based on "hear-say" — and specifically in regard to flags, a most important expedition symbol, there is no contemporary record. Owing perhaps to negligence, or to hostility, or perhaps merely to wear and tear, whatever the reasons, the fact remains that not a single depiction has been handed down to us of the very flag that of such a memorable event was — one could say — the soul itself.

On his frequently inconsistent *Journal*, on October 12, 1492, in a confused prose possibly to be blamed on his limited literary knowledge of Castilian, the Admiral reports that — setting foot in the New World for the first time — he held a "royal flag" (the only one, probably, carried on the *Santa Maria*), while Martín Pinzón and Vincente Yáñez, who accompanied him, carried "two banners with a green cross," state banners that Columbus flew on all ships for identification (but, how many? two overall, or six, i.e., two for each ship?). Such insignia (for which nation? all with white background?) in addition to a green cross, carried also the royal initials "F" and "Y," both surmounted by crowns occupying each "one side of the cross," a description from which very little can be evinced.

Where, indeed, stood these royal initials of Ferdinand of Aragon and Isabela of Castile, precisely set under the horizontal crossbar or at each of its ends? And were they green as well or in gold? Which was their style? What did the crown look like? What shape did the Cross have, among the innumerable variations possible? Was it a Latin cross, or possibly similar to that of Alcantara, which would explain its green color? Furthermore: what did the cloth look like? Was it a gonfalon, a standard, a pennant, a banner? No definitive answer can be provided to all these questions, so that each reconstruction actually becomes a subjective interpretation of its proponents. Some of the most "fashionable" types are reported in the illustration [preceding the second appendix].

Even the only so-called contemporary illustration ever preserved raises doubts rather than shedding some light. I refer to a woodcut executed at Basel in 1493 in which can be seen, off the "Insula Hispanae" (i.e. *Hispaniola*), one of the Columbian ships (oar-propelled and therefore not corresponding to the truth at all) with two flags hoisted on two small masts aft. One of the banners is rather Swiss in appearance, for it displays the "Schwenkel," and this can be understood; less clear is why there is a lion on it, which could designate the León region (but alone? and why so?). The other ensign does not bear anything decipherable since it exhibits a mere diagonal design, whereas it should have displayed, if anything, the Castilian castle to complete the Spanish coat of arms.

Even so, however, doubts would still linger, because the arms of Castile and León had been put in each quarter of the coat of arms — and on his flag — by Ferdinand III, but two and a half centuries earlier, around 1030: the quadripartite standard was certainly in use aboard the royal fleet as early as the first half of the thirteenth century, carried during the conquest of Seville in 1248, was codified by Alfonso XIII and its adoption is documented as well in the merchant marine in 1284. A well-established traditional usage, then, without separation of the two figures. What is, therefore, the meaning of that flag? Could it be (less likely) a rough drawing of the ensign of the Aragonese navy, with seven horizontal stripes? Or is it just a fill-in substitution of the green symbolic flag, not clearly reproduced because hardly known?
Leaving aside this unclear and probably spurious representation, let us turn to more reliable testimony. The chart by Juan de la Cosa, Columbus's companion and owner of the *Santa Maria*. This chart, compiled around 1500, leaves in fact no doubt about the royal flag of that time: the drawing is sketchy but the flag clearly hoisted on a caravel's mast: it has the four quarters of Castile and León, it is rectangular and jagged at the free end (see p. 105). Surely this is the way the royal standard that Columbus carried must have looked, at least substantially. From Juan de la Cosa's map one should note the extreme simplicity of the Castilian castles (yellow on a red field) and of the lions of León (red on a white field), but still without the crown, which became customary in the sixteenth century.

In 1892, on the occasion of building a full-size reconstruction of the *Santa Maria* in Spain, the feeling was that this vessel, being the flagship, had to be richly endowed with the most pennants. Such a reconstruction was based on traditional sources (but not on actual evidence) and the fact that — comparatively speaking — Spanish ships of that time carried innumerable insignia by, making it, though, at best a conjecture. The *Santa Maria*, then, allegedly flew, besides the royal standard on the mainmast and that of the expedition (white with green markings, on the fore mast), a third one: namely, a white flag with the eagle of St. John bearing the arms of the Catholic Sovereigns clutched to her breast, on the mizzenmast. Furthermore, it was claimed that the ship carried three long forked pennants, a red one with imposing royal arms and a Crucifix on the foremast; the second, white with a green cross, on the mainmast and the third, on the yard of the mizzenmast, with the Castilian coat of arms. And, to top the decoration off, the ship was dressed fore and aft with shields along the bulwarks reproducing the suits of arms of Castile, León, Aragon and Sicily.

Lastly, still according to said "ideal" reconstruction, Columbus was thought, as an Admiral, to have a personal flag of crimson damask with gold embroidering representing the Crucifix on one side and the Virgin Mary on the other.

Built expressly on occasion of the fourth centennial of the discovery of America to be sent to Chicago for the 1893 World's Fair, the *Santa Maria* had to look at her best and had thus to be sumptuously adorned, flags and all, indeed a ship fit for the great adventure. Yet, as late as August 3, 1492, in reality, there was not even an inkling of this portentous enterprise: the modest support that Columbus could in fact garner (with the lure of profit rather than glory) was in sharp contrast with the outfitting of such a vessel, more appropriate for pageantry than for an insidious journey laden with the perils of the ocean.

Flags and insignia similar to those hoisted on the 1892 *Santa Maria* also appeared on the recent Quincentennial reconstructions and, generally speaking, on all — full-size, model-size and graphical representations — of the Columbian vessels. Although their appearance is not "authentic" from the perspective of the history of insignia, it cannot be denied that by now such decorations have generally become, we could say, a "contemporary tradition."

Bibliography

Among the innumerable works that deal with the life and navigations of Christopher Columbus, we mention only those containing relatively abundant news and considerations about the Columbian ships and seamanship during Columbus's times.

Bignardelli, I.O. *Con le caravelle di Cristoforo Colombo alla scoperta dell'America.* Turin: UTET, 1959.

Charcot, J.B. *Cristoforo Colombo Marinaio.* Florence: Giunti, 1973.

Columbus, C. *Relazioni di viaggio e lettere di Cristoforo Colombo, 1493-1506.* Edited by Rinaldo Caddeo. Milan: Bompiani, 1941.

Columbus, C. *Accounts and Letters of the Second, Third and Fourth Voyages. Nuova Raccolta Colombiana*, vol. II. Edited by P.E. Taviani, C. Varela, J. Gil, M. Conti. (English translation by M. Beckwith and L. Farina.) Rome: Istituto Poligrafico e Zecca dello Stato, 1997.

Columbus, F. *Le Historie della vita e dei fatti dell'Ammiraglio don Cristoforo Colombo. Nuova Raccolta Colombiana*, vol. VIII. Edited by P.E. Taviani and I. Luzzana Caraci. Rome: Istituto Poligrafico e Zecca dello Stato, 1990.

Ferro, G. *Le navigazioni lusitane nell'Atlantico e Cristoforo Colombo in Portogallo.* Milan: Mursia, 1984.

La Caravella, nei testi di Cristoforo Colombo, Fernando Colombo, Paolo del Pozzo Toscanelli e Bartolomé de Las Casas. Commentary by P. E. Taviani, P. Revelli, S. E. Morison, M. Quaini. Rome: Editalia, 1973.

La scoperta del Nuovo Mondo negli scritti di Pietro Martire d'Anghiera. Edited by E. Lunardi, E. Magioncalda, R. Mazzacane. *Nuova Raccolta Colombiana*, vol. VI. Rome: Istituto Poligrafico e Zecca dello Stato, 1990 (English translation by F. Azzola and L. Farina, 1992).

Le scoperte di Cristoforo Colombo nelle testimonianze di Diego Alvarez Chanca e di Andrés Bernáldez. Edited by Anna Uniali. *Nuova Raccolta Colombiana*, vol. VII. Rome: Istituto Poligrafico e Zecca dello Stato, 1990 (English translation by G. Triolo and L. F. Farina, 1992).

Manzano Manzano, J. *Cristoforo Colombo, sette anni decisivi della sua vita. Nuova Raccolta Colombiana*, vol. X. Rome: Istituto Poligrafico e Zecca dello Stato, 1990.

Martini, D.G. *Cristoforo Colombo fra ragione e fantasia.* Genoa: ECIG, 1987.

Morinson, S.E. *Storia della scoperta dell'America.* Milan: Rizzoli, 1978.

Taviani, P.E. *Cristoforo Colombo, la genesi della grande scoperta.* Novara: Istituto Geografico de Agostini, 1974 (revised third printing 1988).

Taviani, P.E. *I viaggi di Colombo, la grande scoperta.* Novara: Istituto Geografico de Agostini, 1984 (revised third printing 1992).

Taviani, P.E. *Cristoforo Colombo genio del mare.* Rome: Istituto Poligrafico e Zecca dello Stato, 1990.

In Christopher Columbus's *Journal* — that part of it which arrived to us thanks to Bartolomé de Las Casas' transcription — news about the ships is scanty, but fundamental because of its certain origin:

COLUMBUS, C. *Il Giornale di bordo.* With introduction, notes and cards by P.E. Taviani and C. Varela. *Nuova Raccolta Colombiana*, vol. I. Rome: Istituto Poligrafico e Zecca dello Stato, 1988 (English translation by M. Bekwith and L.F. Farina, 1990).

COLUMBUS, C. *Giornale di bordo, 1492-1493.* Edited by Rinaldo Caddeo. Milan: Bompiani, 1939.

FERRO, G. *Diario di bordo di Cristoforo Colombo.* Milan: Mursia, 1985.

History of the ship and of naval shipbuilding in general:

ANDERSON, R.C. "Italian Naval Architecture about 1445." *Marine Mirror*, 1925.

ANONYMOUS. *Fabrica di galere.* 16th-century manuscript. Biblioteca Nazionale di Firenze cl. XIX C 7.

ARTINANO, G. DE. *Architectura naval Española.* Madrid 1920.

BALDISSERA, B. *Visione del Brachio.* 16th-century manuscript. Archivio di Stato di Venezia, Archivio proprio Contarini 13,25.

BASS, G.F. et al. *Navi e città.* Milan: Fabbri, 1974.

BATHE, B.W. *La nave dalle crociate alle crociere.* Milan: Gorlich, 1972.

BATHE, B.W. et al. *The great Age of Sail.* Cambridge: Patrick Stephens, 1974.

CHIGGIATO, A. *Appunti su una nave da carico del XV secolo rappresentato in un quadro attribuito al Crivelli, conservato nel palazzo del Conte Cini a Venezia.* Typewritten, Museo Storico Navale di Venezia.

CRESCENZIO, B. *Nautica Mediterranea.* Rome: Bartolomeo Bonfadino, 1602.

FERNANDEZ D»URO, C. *Disquisiciones náuticas.* Madrid: Aribau y Comp., 1877.

BROGGER, A.W. and H. SHETELIG. *The Viking Ship.* Oslo: Dreyer, 1953.

FURTTENBACH, J. *Architectura Navalis.* Ulm, 1629; facsimile, Paris 1939.

HOWARD, F. *Sailing Ship of War, 1400-1860.* Greenwich: Conway Maritime Press, 1979.

JAL, A. *Archeologie Naval - Memoires 4, 5, 6.* Paris: Artus Bertrand, 1880.

LA ROERIE, G. And J. VIVIELLE. *Navires et Marins de la rame a l'hélice.* Paris: Duchartre et Buggenhoudt, 1930.

LACHER, P. *Die Schiffe der Wolker.* Olten und Freiburg in Brisgau: Walter Verlag, 1962.

LANDSTRÖM, B. *La Nave.* Milan: Martello, 1962.

LEVI, C.A. *Navi venete da codici, marmi, dipinti.* Venice, 1892. Reprint, Venice: Filippi, 1893.

LUSCI, E. *Modellismo navale statico antico.* Florence: Lusci, 1980.

LUSCI, E. *Enciclopedia di Navi e Modelli di Navi.* Florence: Lusci, 1977, 1978, 1979, 1980 (see especially the articles by Sergio Bellabarba and Giorgio Osculati under the title "La vela quadra").

NATKIEL, R. and A. PRESTON. *Atlas of Maritime History*. London: Weidenfeld and Nicolson, 1986.

ave. Entry of Enciclopedia Italiana, Rome 1935.

NEBBIA, U. *Arte navale italiana*. Bergamo: Istituto Italiano di Arti Grafiche, 1932.

NICOLÒ, T. DE. *Istrucion sul modo de fabricar galere*. Manuscript about 1550. Biblioteca Marciana, Venice.

PANTERA, P. *L'Armata Navale*. Rome: Egidio Spada printer, 1614.

PARIS, E. *Souvenirs de Marine conservés*. Paris: Gauthiers-Villars, 1886.

SJOVELD, T. *Gli scavi di Oseberg e le altre scoperte di navi vichinghe*. Oslo: Universitetes Oldsaksamling, 1962.

ROSSI, E., M. ALBERAI, A.M. FELLER. *Le costruzioni navali*. Progetto galeas per montes conducendo. Torbole 1989.

RANDACCIO, C. *Storia navale universale antica e moderna*. Rome: Tipografia del Senato, 1891.

VECCHI, A.V. *Storia generale della Marina Militare*. Florence: Tip. Cooperativa, 1892.

VINGIANO, G. *Storia della nave*. Rome: Convivium, 1955.

VOCINO, M. *La nave nel tempo*. Roma-Milano: Luigia Alfieri e C., 1942.

ZENI, C.G. *Con i remi e con le vele*. Milan: Gastaldi, 1958.

ZUANNE DE MICHIEL, S. DE. *L'Architettura Navale*. Manuscript, 1686. Copy at the Museo Storico Navale di Venezia.

Specific works about the Columbian ships or about ships of the same epoch:

AKERLUND, H. *Die Bremer Hanse Hogge*. Bremen 1969.

ALCALÀ GALIANO, J. *La Carabela Gallega o Santa Maria o la nao capitana de Colón*. Madrid: Estab. tip. de R.Alvarez, 1892.

BAYKOWSKI, V. *Hansekogge*. Kiel, 1991.

D'ALBERTIS, E. *Le costruzioni navali e l'arte della navigazione ai tempi di Colombo*. Racccolta di documenti e studi pubblicati dalla R. Commissione Colombiana pel Quarto Centenario della Scoperta dell'America. Rome: M.P.I., 1892. Part IV, vol. I.

ETAYO, C. *Naos y carabelas de los descubrimientos*. Pamplona: Industria Gráfica Azalar, 1971.

FONSECA, E.Q. DA. *La caravela portuguesa*. Coimbra: Imprensa da Universidada, 1934.

GUILLEN TATO, J. *La carabela Santa Maria; apuntes para su reconstrución*. Madrid: Imprenta de Ministerio de Marina, 1927.

KIEDEL, K.R. *Die Hanse Hogge von 1380*. Bremerhaven: Deutsches Schiffahrtmuseum, 1982.

LEITAO, M. *The Portuguese Caravel*. Lisbon: Comemoraçoes dos descobrimentos portugueses, 1989.

MONLEÒN, R. "Las carabelas de Colón." *El Centenario* (1892): vol. I, 51-61, 119-128.

MELEGARI, V. *Manuale delle tre caravelle*. Milan: Mondadori, 1992.

MONDFELD, W. zu, P. Holz, J. Sojener. *Die Schiffe des Cristoforo Colombo*. Herford: Koeler, 1991. [Plans in scale 1:50 of the three ships have been published in a separate folder, according to the three authors' reconstruction.]

WINTER, H. *Die Katalanische Nao von 1450*. Magdeburg: R. Loef, 1956.

WINTER, H. *Das Hanseschiff in ausgehenden 16. Jahrhundert*. Bielefeld und Berlin: Delius Klasing, 1968.

WINTER, H. *Le navi di Colombo*. Milan: Mursia, 1982.

Navigations and geographical discoveries:

APUZZO, A. *L'invenzione della bussola e Flavio Gioia*. Naples: Editrice Rinascita Artistica, 1964.

CALISI, M. *Il museo astronomico e copernicano*. Osservatorio Astronomico di Roma, 1982.

FONTOURA DA COSTA, A. *La marinharia dos descobrimentos*. Lisbon: Agência general das colonias, 1939.

LANDSTRÖM, B. *La via delle Indie*. Florence: Martello, 1964.

MARGUET, F. *Histoire Générale de la Navigation*. Paris: Editions geographiques, maritimes et coloniales, 1931.

MARTINEZ HIDALGO, J.M. *Historia y leyenda de la aguja magnética - Contribución de los españoles al progreso de la náutica*. Barcelona: Ed. Gustavo Gili, 1945.

NICE, B. *Grandi Navigatori*. Rome: ERI, 1946.

PARRY, J. *Le grandi esplorazioni che cambiarono il mondo*. Milan: Il Saggiatore, 1979.

PARRY, J. *Le grandi scoperte geografiche*. Milan: Il Saggiatore, 1982.

PUGLISI, G. *Navigatori senza bussola*. Supplement to *Rivista Marittima*, Rome 1971.

SECCHI, L. "Dell'astrolabio di Egnatio Danti e alcuni strumenti del XVI e XVII secolo esposti al Museo Navale di Genova Pegli." *Bollettino dei musei civici genovesi* (1979), I, 3.

TAYLOR, E.G.R. *The mathematical practitioners of Tudor and Stuart England*. Cambridge: Cambridge University Press for the Institute of Navigation, 1954.

See also the Columbian subject articles appeared recently on the *Rivista Marittima*:

FANTONI, G. "La scoperta dell'America: il primo avvistamento dell'isola di San Salvador." *Rivista Marittima* CXXI , 5 (1988).

FANTONI, G. and M. INGRAVALLE. "Alla ricerca della lega di Cristoforo Colombo." *Rivista Marittima* CXX, 10 (1987).

FANTONI, G. and M. INGRAVALLE. "Dove Colombo scoprí l'America?" *Rivista Marittima* CXX, 10 (1987).

FOSCHINI, I. "Il calendario Gregoriano." *Rivista Marittima*, CXV, 10 (1982).

INGRAVALLE, M. "Le fantasie geografiche di Cristoforo Colombo." *Rivista Marittima* CXIX, n.3 (1986).

QUIETO, F. "Un enigma lontano cinquecento anni: come erano veramente le navi di Colombo." *Rivista Marittima* CXXV (1992): 87-104.

Finally, on *Agenda Nautica 1992* of the Istituto Idrografico della Marina Militare, entirely devoted to the Columbian recurrence, there is an article by Paola Presciuttini, "Uno sguardo alla cartografia dalle origini all'era colombiana," ed uno di S. Rizza, "La meteorologia del Nord Atlantico e le condizioni del tempo durante i viaggi in America di Cristoforo Colombo."

Artillery and Weapons:

ARATEGUI Y SANZ, J. *Apuntes históricos de la artilleria española en los siglos XIV, XV, XVI.* Madrid: Rivadeneyra, 1891.

BIRINGUCCIO, V. *Pirotecnica, nella quale si tratta non solo della diversitá di miniere, ma dell'arte della fusione e getto dei metalli, far campane, artiglierie, fuochi artificiali ed altre diverse cose utilissime.* Ca. 1540.

BRAVETTA, V.E. *L'artiglieria e le sue meraviglie.* Milan: Fratelli Treves, 1919.

DROBNA, Z. and J. DURDICH. *Tracht, Wehr und Waffen des spaten Mittelhalters (1350-1450).* Prague: Artia, 1960.

MONDFELD, W. ZU, A. BAJERLEIN, M. KLINGENBRUNN. *Schiffs Geschutze 1350 bis 1870.* Herford: Koeler, 1988.

POPE, D. *Le macchine infernali.* Milan Mondadori, 1965.

TARTAGLIA, N. *Nuova scienza, cioé invenzione nuovamente trovata utile per ciascuno speculativo, matematico, bombardiero o altro.* 1587.

Marine usages, life onboard, miscellaneous:

CIANO, C. "Considerazioni sulla disciplina a bordo delle navi mediterranee nel XVII secolo." *Quaderni Stefaniani*, 1987.

FAY, G. "Far acqua e far l'acqua." *Rivista Marittima*, CXVIII (1985).

LIGABUE, G. *Storia delle forniture navali italiane nel medioevo.* Venice: Alfieri, 1968.

MANFROMI, C. "Cenni sugli ordinamenti delle marine italiane nel medioevo." *Rivista Marittima*, 1988.

MERRIEN, J. *La vita di bordo nel medioevo.* Milan Mursia, 1969.

QUATTROCCHI, G. *I prodotti del Nuovo Mondo.* Turin: ERI, 1985.

TAVIANI, P.E. "Il rancio di bordo delle caravelle colombiane." In: Ministero per i Beni Culturali e Ambientali, Biblioteca Casanatense. *Il rancio di bordo.* Catalog of the exhibition. Gaeta: Ed. Il Geroglifico, 1992. 367-378.

ZENI, C.G. *Con i remi e con le vele.* Milan: Gastaldi, 1953.

General history of the period. Naval history in general:

CARRETTO, G., C. LO JACONO, A. VENTURA. *Maometto in Europa.* Milan: Mondadori, 1982.

CIPOLLA, C.M. *Velieri e cannoni d'Europa sui mari del mondo.* Turin: UTET, 1969.

DAINELLI, G. *La conquista della Terra; storia generale delle esplorazioni.* Turin: UTET, 1964.

DAWSON, C. *La nascita dell'Europa.* Milan: Il Saggiatore, 1969.

DE BOSSCHERE, G. *Storia della colonizzazione.* Milan: Feltrinelli, 1972.

FRUGONI, A. *Le Repubbliche Marinare.* Turin: ERI, 1958.

LOPESZ, G. *La nascita dell'Europa; secoli V-XIV.* Turin: Einaudi, 1973.

LINDIGHER, H.C. *Gli imperi del commercio.* Milan: Rizzoli, 1981.

MOLLAT, M. et al. *Le navire et l'economie maritime du XV au XVIII siècles.* Conference on Maritime History, October 1956. Paris: Academie de Marine, 1957.

PIRENNE, H. *Storia economica e sociale del medioevo.* Milan: Garzanti, 1970.

RANDACCIO, C. *Storia universale antica e moderna.* Rome: Tipografia del Senato, 1891.

Storia del mondo medievale. Edited by Cambridge University. Milan: Garzanti, 1980.

VECCHI, A.V. *Storia generale della marina militare.* Florence: Tipografia Cooperativa, 1892.

Dictionaries of naval and marine terms:

AMORIN, J.P. DE. *Dictionario de Marinha.* Lisbon: Impresa National, 1941.

BARDESONO DE RIGRAS, C. *Vocabolario marinaresco.* Rome: Lega Navale Italiana, 1932.

BONNEFOUX, P.M. et E. Paris. *Dictionnaire de la marine a voile.* Anastatic reprint. Paris: Editions de la Fontaine au Roy, 1987.

CORAZZINI DI BULCIANO, F. *Vocabolario nautico italiano.* 3 tomes. Turin: Tipografia San Giuseppe degli Artigianelli, 1900.

Dizionario di marina medievale e moderna. Rome: Reale Accademia d'Italia, 1937.

GUGLIELMOTTI, A. *Vocabolario marino e militare.* Naples: Stab. Tipografico Androsso, 1866.

JAL, A. *Glossaire nautique.* Paris: F. Didot Frères, 1848.

LA GUARDIA, R. DE. *Dictionario Maritimo Español.* Madrid: Imp. del Ministerio de Marina, 1921.

LHUILLIER, C.M. et C.S. PETIT. *Dictionnaire des termes de marine, français-espagnols et espagnols-français.* Paris: Imprimerie de Delance et Bellin, 1810.

LORENZO, J. Y A. *Dictionario maritimo español.* Madrid: Fontanet, 1866.

MARQUES ESPARTEIRO, A. *Dictionnaire ilustrado de Marinharia.* Lisbon: Sociedad Astoria, 1841.

PARILLI, G. *Dizionario di marineria militare.* Naples: Stab. Tipografico Androsso, 1866.

PAASCH, H. *De la quille a la pomme du mat, dictionnaire de marine anglais, français, allemand, espagnol, italien.* Paris: Societé des éditions géographiques, maritimes et coloniales, 1924.

STRATICO, S. *Vocabolario di marina in tre lingue.* Milan: Stamperia Reale, 1913.

INDEXES

The Italian index system has been designed and realized by the Cultural Activity Service of the Enciclopedia Italiana Institute — founded by G. Treccani — Rome.

INDEX OF NAMES

(Note - The name of Christopher Columbus has not been included in this index)

INDEX OF PLACES

TABLE OF CONTENT

PRINTED IN THE SECURITY PRINTING PLANT
OF THE ISTITUTO POLIGRAFICO E ZECCA
DELLO STATO, IN ROME, 1997, ON
SPECIAL WATERMARKED PAPER
PRODUCED BY CARTIERE
MILIANI FABRIANO
PAPERMILLS

NORTE
NORTE 4 AL NORDEST
NOR NORDESTE
NORDESTE 4 AL NORTE
NORDESTE
NORDESTE 4 ALESTE
LES NORDESTE
LESTE 4 AL NORDEST
LESTE
LESTE 4 AL SVESTE
LE SVESTE
SVESTE 4 ALESTE
SVESTE
SVESTE 4 AL SVR
SVSVESTE
SVR 4 AL SVESTE
SVR
SVR 4 AL SVDVESTE
SVSVDVESTE
SVD VESTE 4 AL SVR
SVD VESTE
SVDVESTE 4 ALOEST
OESSVDVESTE
OESTE 4 AL SVDVEST
OESTE
OESTE 4 AL NORVESTE
OESNORVESTE
NORVESTE 4 ALOESTE
NORVESTE
NORVESTE 4 AL NORTE
NORNORVESTE
NORTE 4 AL NORVEST